ANCIENT FICTION AND
EARLY CHRISTIAN NARRATIVE

SOCIETY
OF BIBLICAL
LITERATURE

SBL
SYMPOSIUM SERIES

Gail R. O'Day, Editor

Number 6

**ANCIENT FICTION AND
EARLY CHRISTIAN NARRATIVE**

edited by
Ronald F. Hock
J. Bradley Chance
Judith Perkins

Ronald F. Hock
J. Bradley Chance
Judith Perkins,
editors

ANCIENT FICTION AND
EARLY CHRISTIAN NARRATIVE

Society of Biblical Literature
Symposium Series

Scholars Press
Atlanta, Georgia

ANCIENT FICTION AND EARLY CHRISTIAN NARRATIVE

edited by
Ronald F. Hock
J. Bradley Chance
Judith Perkins

Library of Congress Cataloging in Publication Data
Ancient fiction and early Christian narrative / Ronald F. Hock, J.
   Bradley Chance, Judith Perkins, editors.
         p.   cm. — (SBL symposium series ; no. 6)
   Includes bibliographical references.
   ISBN 0-7885-0431-2 (cloth : alk. paper)
   1. Bible. N.T.—Criticism, interpretation, etc. 2. Greek
literature—Relation to the New Testament. 3. Greek fiction.
4. Narration in the Bible. 5. Christian literature, Early—Greek
authors. I. Hock, Ronald F., 1944–   . II. Chance, J. Bradley.
III. Perkins, Judith, 1944–   . IV. Series: Symposium series
(Society of Biblical Literature) ; no. 6.
BS2361.2.A43   1998
225.6'6—dc21   97-49245
                                                   CIP

Printed in the United States of America
on acid-free paper

CONTENTS

ABBREVIATIONS

AA	*Archäologischer Anzeiger*
AB	Anchor Bible
AJA	*American Journal of Archaeology*
AJP	*American Journal of Philology*
Annals (ESC)	*Annals (Économie, Sociétés, Civilisations)*
ANRW	*Aufstieg und Niedergang der römishen Welt*
AS	*Anatolian Studies*
BAGB	*Bulletin de l'Association G. Budé*
BAR	*Biblical Archaeologist Reader*
BCH	*Bulletin de Correspondance Hellénique*
BETL	Bibliotheca ephemeridum theologicarum lovaniensium
BI	*Biblical Interpretation*
BJRL	*Bulletin of the John Rylands University Library of Manchester*
BritARSup	British Archaeological Reports Supplements
BTB	*Biblical Theology Bulletin*
BZ	*Byzantinische Zeitschrift*
CBQ	*Catholic Biblical Quarterly*
ClAnt	*Classical Antiquity*
C & M	*Classica et Mediaevalia*
CPh	*Classical Philology*
CQ	*Classical Quarterly*
CW	*Classical World*
CSEL	Corpus scriptorum ecclesiasticorum latinorum
DHA	*Dialogues d'histoire ancienne*
EPRO	Études préliminaires aux religions orientals dans l'empire Romain
EstClas	*Estudios Classicos*
FFNT	Foundations and Facets: New Testament
FRLANT	Forschungen zur Religion und Literatur des Alten und Neuen Testaments
G & R	*Greece & Rome*
GCN	*Groningen Colloquia on the Novel*
GRBS	*Greek, Roman and Byzantine Studies*
HSCP	*Harvard Studies in Classical Philology*

HTR	*Harvard Theological Review*
HUT	Hermeneutische Untersuchungen zur Theologie
ICC	International Critical Commentary
Int	*Interpretation*
JAAR	*Journal of the American Academy of Religion*
JFSR	*Journal of Feminist Studies of Religion*
JJS	*Journal of Jewish Studies*
JRASup	Journal of Roman Archaeology Supplements
JRS	*Journal of Roman Studies*
JRSMS	Journal of Roman Studies Monograph Series
JSNT	*Journal for the Study of the New Testament*
JSNTSup	Journal for the Study of the New Testament Supplements
JSOTSup	Journal for the Study of the Old Testament Supplements
JTS	*Journal of Theological Studies*
LCL	Loeb Classical Library
LIMC	Lexicon Iconographicum Mythologiae Classicae
LSJ	Liddell-Scott-Jones, *Greek-English Lexicon*
LXX	Septuagint
MSKP	Münchener Studien zur klassischen Philologie
NCB	New Century Bible
NovT	*Novum Testamentum*
NovTSup	Novum Testamentum Supplements
NRSV	New Revised Standard Version
NTS	*New Testament Studies*
Pap.Texte Abh.	Papyrologische Texte und Abhandlungen
PCPhS	*Proceedings of the Cambridge Philological Society*
PerRelSt	*Perspectives in Religious Studies*
PG	J. Migne, *Patrologia graeca*
PhW	*Philologische Wochenschrift*
PLMA	*Proceedings of the Modern Language Association*
P & P	*Past & Present*
PSN	*Petronian Society Newsletter*
PWSupp	Supplements to Pauly-Wissowa, *Real-Encyclopädie der classischen Altertumswissenschaft*
RE	*Paulys Real-Encyclopädie der classischen Altertumswissenschaft*
REG	*Revue des Études Grecques*
REH	*Revue des Études Homériques*
RHPh	*Revue d'Histoire de la Philosophie et d'Histoire Générale de la Civilisation*
RSV	Revised Standard Version

SBLDS	SBL Dissertation Series
SBLEJL	SBL Early Judaism and its Literature
SBLMS	SBL Monograph Series
SBLSBS	SBL Sources for Biblical Study
SBLSS	SBL Semeia Studies
SBLTT	SBL Texts and Translations
SNTSMS	Society for New Testament Studies Monograph Series
TAPA	*Transactions of the American Philological Association*
TDNT	*Theological Dictionary of the New Testament*
TLG	Thesaurus Linguae Graecae
TU	Texte und Untersuchungen
TWAS	Twayne World Authors Series
TZ	*Theologische Zeitschrift*
VC	*Vigiliae christianae*
WJA	*Würzburger Jahrbücher für die Altertumswisssenschaft*
WUNT	Wissenschaftliche Untersuchungen zum Neuen Testament
YCS	*Yale Classical Studies*
ZPE	*Zeitschrift für Papyrologie und Epigraphik*

INTRODUCTION

It is indeed a pleasure to make available to a wider audience this collection of essays which represents a sample of the papers that have been presented at the sessions of the SBL Ancient Fiction and Early Christian and Jewish Narrative Group. The Group, which was formally organized in 1992 through the efforts of Charles W. Hedrick, has attempted to stimulate interest in ancient fiction—the Greek novels in particular but the whole range of ancient fiction as well—among members of the SBL, and to promote scholarship on this body of literature and its relation to early Christian and Jewish narrative. In addition, since its inception the Group has deliberately sought interdisciplinary assistance, both on the Steering Committee and on the yearly programs. Consequently, classicists have been on the Steering Committee from the beginning and they have participated each year on the program. Their participation has proved most valuable not only in planning sessions and on the programs but also in breaking down disciplinary barriers, in introducing new perspectives and expertise, and in making new friendships.

For the selection of the papers in this volume I have had the generous and able assistance of my co-editors, J. Bradley Chance and Judith Perkins, and I speak for all of us in saying that the preparation of this volume has been made especially pleasant by the enthusiastic response of the authors to participate in this venture, in the prompt return of their revised papers, and in the high quality of the work they have submitted.

The organization of the volume reflects the two-fold nature of the Group's work. The first six papers deal with ancient fiction in and for itself, whereas the following nine papers relate early Christian literature in a variety of ways to ancient fiction. The volume also ably represents the interdisciplinary emphasis of the Group, as a number of the papers are by classicists (Konstan, Schmeling, Chew, and Shea), and the application of a variety of literary and narratological methods likewise gives a strong interdisplinary flavor to the volume (Chew, Shiner, Hedrick, Brant, Chance, and Aubin).

1

Viewed differently, the volume contains papers addressing both general issues and specific problems. Among the former are Konstan's reflections on the nature of fiction, Schmeling's typology of ancient narrative, and Thomas's consideration of the fluidity of texts in novelistic texts, both pagan and Christian. Among the latter are studies of individual novels, in particular Chariton (Edwards), Xenophon (Chew, Shea, and Chance), Achilles Tatius (Hedrick), and the *Life of Aesop* (Pervo and Shiner). Of particular note is the continuing fascination with a proposal of the 1890s, that Xenophon's *Ephesian Tale* is an epitome; several papers deal with the thesis, and come to terms with the peculiar features of this novel in a variety of ways (Chew, Shea, Thomas). Pervo's paper, the longest paper in the volume, is a learned, wide-ranging, and insightful study the *Life of Aesop*, including its relation to the gospels.

The relation of ancient fiction to the New Testament and other early Christian literature is also explored in a number of other papers, both in broad terms (Hock) and in relation to specific texts: Mark (MacDonald, Shiner, and Hedrick), John (Brant), Acts (Chance), Paul (Alexander), and the apocryphal Acts (Aubin, Thomas). These papers present a number of stimulating proposals: relating the secrecy motif in Mark to Homer's Odysseus (MacDonald), exploring the episodic quality of Mark's narrative (Shiner), placing Paul closer to the novelists than to the philosophers on the subject of marriage (Alexander), and reading the *Acts of Paul and Thecla* as an inversion of romance conventions (Aubin), to name just a few.

Finally, it remains to thank Gail O'Day, editor of The Symposium Series of Scholars Press, for her careful consideration of this volume and for her advice on preparing it for publication.

Ronald F. Hock
J. Bradley Chance
Judith Perkins

The Invention of Fiction

David Konstan
Brown University

The term "fiction" suggests falsehood, invention, pretense or make-believe, and in these senses it may be applied to a wide range of literary forms, including tragedy, lyric poetry, and even historiography, insofar as events described are taken to be untrue. In English, however, the term is especially associated with the novel. If I say that I am going to read a work of fiction this evening, it will not normally be supposed that I plan to curl up with Milton or Shakespeare. I wish to argue that the connection between fiction and the novel is not accidental; rather, there is a sense in which novels are fictional, whereas history, lyric poetry and tragedy are not. In addition, I claim that fiction in this sense pertains to the earliest surviving novels, which date to the first three centuries of the Roman Empire. Some scholars, who are inclined to locate the origins of the novel in 18th-century Britain, have relegated these ancient prose narratives to the lesser status of romances. But there is no sound basis for this distinction: leaving aside the Latin cases, that is, Petronius' *Satyrica*, the *Golden Ass* of Apuleius, and the anonymous *History of Apollonius King of Tyre*, there survive five ancient Greek narratives that meet any reasonable criterion for being characterized as novels. All five are long descriptive accounts of lovers separated and reunited in the end; they are carefully plotted, peopled with interesting characters, and related in artful prose without undue recourse to mythological or improbable events.[1] I shall be arguing, accordingly, that the rise of the ancient novel marks the moment of the invention of fiction.

If it is correct to associate fiction closely with the novel form, however, then its invention seems to have taken place unnoticed by contemporaries. For ancient critics did not hold the novel in high regard, and it never achieved the status of a canonical genre. This lack of recognition

---

[1] Cf. D. Konstan, *Sexual Symmetry: Love in the Ancient Novel and Related Genres* (Princeton: Princeton University Press, 1994) 205–6.

3

has led some scholars to suppose that nothing much happened when the ancient novel was born. Perhaps fiction in the modern sense was not, in fact, discovered in antiquity. Alternatively, fiction is as old as literature, and originates in Greece with the Homeric epics. Since an excellent miscellany of modern views on ancient fiction is now available, together with an extensive bibliography, there is no need to rehearse the question here.[2] In this paper, I develop the thesis that the ancient novel does represent the birth of fiction in an important sense of that term, though like all cultural phenomena it has precursors and antecedents. I attempt also to indicate the social circumstances that facilitated its conception.

If fiction is simply that which is not fact, then much of what is called history will come under the rubric of fiction. This is too broad: fiction is not the same as falsehood, which in turn may be subdivided into the two categories of lies and error, depending on whether the deception is intentional or not. Confusion on this question has bedevilled a number of investigations. Reardon, for example, rightly observes that "Fiction lies somewhere between the ideas of true and false, between fact and non-fact," and then in the next sentence confuses the matter by adding: "A work of fiction tells a story which is factually not true, but may in a sense be emotionally true." Thus, he continues, a child "will become aware that fiction, though it may not be reprehensible, is not fact."[3] So too, Louise Pratt remarks: "We may believe that these stories [in Homer] originated in real events, but the representation of those events has been so transformed by the artists' imaginations as to become fictional."[4] Later, Pratt observes (65) that "if archaic poetry is not unambiguously committed to aletheia [truth], the suggested affinity between the poet

---

[2] C. Gill and T. P. Wiseman, eds., *Lies and Fiction in the Ancient World* (Austin: University of Texas Press, 1993); cf. B. P. Reardon, *The Form of Greek Romance* (Princeton: Princeton University Press, 1991).

[3] Reardon, *Form*, 57; cf. 59–60: "Fiction cannot be recognized as fiction until fact is recognized as fact. But once fact is so recognized, once its importance as fact is understood, fiction is born, as a corollary and in the same movement"; also G. W. Bowersock, *Fiction as History: Nero to Julian* (Berkeley: University of California Press, 1994) 5–6: "Lucian [in *The True History*] tries to pull down the distinction between fiction that we accept as fiction and fiction that is presented as a record of real events."

[4] L. H. Pratt, *Lying and Poetry from Homer to Pindar: Falsehood and Deception in Archaic Greek Poetics* (Ann Arbor: University of Michigan Press, 1993) 23; cf. 24, 27–28.

and the lying Odysseus should not be dismissed so hastily."[5] Perhaps not, but the inventions of Odysseus are, in their context, lies, not fiction.

History differs from fiction in that it is *about* what really happens or has happened, even if at times, or perhaps in the main, it gets things wrong. Herodotus may of course have been mistaken about events in the Persian War; the point is that there is something for him to have been mistaken about. The property of "being about something" may be encapsulated thus: Herodotus' history, like all historical writing, has a referent.[6]

There is an analogous sense in which the Homeric epics have a referent. To be sure, the events and characters they describe are not necessarily regarded today as having historical veracity, although modern critics are in fact less skeptical on this matter than were scholars a century ago. The ancient Greeks, who by and large believed that there was at least a kernel of truth behind the *Iliad* and the *Odyssey*, were not appreciably more credulous than modern readers. The variability of opinion on the facticity of the Trojan War reveals the contingency of truth and falsehood in respect to historical events. Whether it did or did not occur, however, the status of the Trojan War as an event to be written about depends not on the current state of historical investigation but on the existence of a cultural record. The *Iliad* refers to the Trojan War as a culturally acknowledged phenomenon, just as Herodotus' history refers to the Persian War, whatever the degree of accuracy his account may have achieved. One indication that the narratives of Herodotus and Homer are alike in this respect is that it makes sense to say of both that they have embellished events or changed them or got them wrong—to say, for example, that Xerxes did not excavate a channel across the isthmus of Mount Athos, or that Achilles did not return the body of Hector for

---

[5] The implication is that Homer is not necessarily so different from Odysseus in his truth claims. It is worth noting that Odysseus never claims knowledge of what transpires among the gods, as Homer does; cf. J. S. Clay, *The Wrath of Athena: Gods and Men in the Odyssey* (Princeton: Princeton University Press, 1983) 21–22, citing O. Jørgensen, "Das Auftreten der Götter in den Büchern ι–μ der Odyssee," *Hermes* 39 (1904) 357–82. Pratt's idea (*Lying,* 37) of "commemorative fiction" is on my understanding of fiction a contradiction in terms.

[6] Contrast P. Lamarque and S. H. Olsen, *Truth, Fiction, and Literature: A Philosophical Perspective* (Oxford: Clarendon, 1994) 108: "To speak of what a work is *about* is not equivalent to speaking of its references"; they take "about" to indicate the theme or subject of a work of fiction (107–37).

ransom.[7] There are presumed to be sources of knowledge of the subject independent of the description proffered by the text itself. If the Trojan War is described as myth, then myth, like historical events, constitutes a ground of reference. Like history, mythical narratives depend upon a shared awareness of a tradition with a given cultural community.[8]

Fiction, by contrast, has no referent in this respect. It does not make sense to say that Longus, in his novel *Daphnis and Chloe*, was mistaken about the actions of the hero and heroine, or that he added or subtracted episodes. There is nothing in the cultural tradition for Longus to have been mistaken about. The only presumed witness to the actions of Daphnis and Chloe is the novel itself.

Daphnis and Chloe takes place on the island of Lesbos, which is a historical locale; the novel thus refers to some things.[9] I take it that it is a property of ordinary communication that descriptions are presumed to have a referent. One is inclined to believe of Troy or even of Oz that it is a place. The thing to be explained is rather the apparent suspension of referentiality in fiction. Ruth Ronen observes: "When truth is regarded as a relation between an extralinguistic state of affairs and a linguistic expression, it cannot be applied to fiction since fiction does not commit itself to extralinguistic states."[10] I should say rather that fiction does not commit itself to states, linguistic or not, outside the text. A reference in a text can be mapped onto a domain constituted in sensory experience or in another literary code. But the question I am posing is how fiction resists such a commitment. For alongside references to geography,

---

[7] Cf. T. G. Pavel, *Fictional Worlds* (Cambridge: Harvard University Press, 1986) 79: "the world of myths is not perceived by its users as fictional"; also 81: "the frontiers of fiction separate it off on one side from myth, on the other from actuality."

[8] Cf. R. Ronen, *Possible Worlds in Literary Theory* (Cambridge: Cambridge University Press, 1994) 39, citing R. Rorty, *Consequences of Pragmatism: Essays, 1972–1980* (Minneapolis: University of Minnesota Press, 1982) 132, as an example of extreme pragmatism that rejects the correspondence theory of truth: "Rorty proposes to see the relation of 'talking about' as 'one which may be *constituted* by discourse—since no more is required for talking about Sherlock Holmes . . . than that the words Sherlock Holmes . . . be systematically bandied about' (132). According to this view of truth in fiction, referring does not tie an expression to a physical object; the truth of a reference is determined by the very laws of discourse."

[9] R. I. Pervo, *Profit with Delight: The Literary Genre of the Acts of the Apostles* (Philadelphia: Fortress, 1987) 103, observes that the idea of "pure fiction" is "unrewarding," and notes: "Few ancient novelists pulled their plots and characters out of thin air." Plot is beside the point, but the characters in the ancient novels precisely are invented out of whole cloth.

[10] Ronen, *Possible Worlds*, 36.

psychological traits, moral truths, and other extratextual states, works of fiction also contain propositions concerning characters, events, and other matters that are understood not to refer in the ordinary way. Thomas G. Pavel remarks that to prove what is or is not the case concerning Mr. Pickwick, for example, we rely on a "simple reading of the text."[11] That is, there is no documentary or other evidence outside the text on which we can rely to settle the matter. But fiction is not just a matter of the absence of other evidence; it depends rather on the conviction, engendered by the genre, that certain propositions are meant not to refer. Fiction presupposes a contract or collective understanding according to which the habit of reference is curbed or inhibited.[12] It is this contract that discriminates fiction from falsity, which is a failed reference.

A fiction is different also from a supposition, which is a reflection on how things that are might be otherwise. In fictions, the impulse to refer is interrupted: *Daphnis and Chloe* is not an imaginary version of a life outside the text. The inhibition of referentiality may have literary advantages, for example that of concentrating attention on the text and its internal patterns. Thus summarizes the view of Michael Riffaterre: "In everyday language, words appear to refer vertically to the objects they represent, but in literature, in which the meaningful unit is the entire text and not the isolated word, lexical elements lose their vertical semantic force and act upon one another contextually, producing a new effect of meaning, *significance.*"[13] Such inner resonances are sometimes described as self-referentiality, but this usage ought not to be taken to imply a distinct "story world" to which the fictional text is understood to refer.[14] The fictional contract works rather to repress the habit of reference as such, or at all events the conviction that the status of the supposed referent is in any way independent of what is communicated in the text. The question under consideration is when, and under what cultural conditions, such a textual convention may have arisen.

---

[11] Pavel, *Fictional Worlds,* 28, citing G. Ryle, "Imaginary Objects," *Aristotelian Society, Supplementary Volume* 12 (1933) 18–43.

[12] On fiction as a "mode of utterance" and a "stance" that depend on practices of story-telling, see Lamarque and Olsen, *Truth, Fiction, and Literature,* 32–33.

[13] Pavel, *Fictional Worlds,* 118.

[14] On story worlds as the hallmark of fiction, see Andrew Laird, "Fiction, Bewitchment and Story Worlds: The Implications of Claims to Truth in Apuleius," in Gill and Wiseman, *Lies and Fiction,* 147–74, esp. 147; Ronen, *Possible Worlds,* 15; cf. W. C. Booth, *The Company We Keep: An Ethic of Fiction* (Berkeley: University of California Press, 1988) 17.

There was no space for fiction in those genres, such as epic and tragedy, which by convention had recourse to the repertoire of Greek myths in the selection of narrative material. For all that Homer, Pindar, and Euripides handled inherited stories in an imaginative and iconoclastic way, they could count on audiences to recognize departures from or corrections of the myth as it existed in other tellings. However daring the version, it nevertheless, as a version, referred to materials stored up in cultural memory.[15] Poetry and history are at one in this respect. So too, folklore constitutes a set of referents for literary narratives. Aesop's animal fables, for example, fail as fictions because they are understood to recount old tales. Perhaps Aesop's versions are especially clever or original, but they are nevertheless received as versions. Fictional narratives, on the contrary, are not versions of anything else, which is another way of saying that there is no body of traditional lore to which they refer.

Lyric and elegiac poetry are also referential in this sense. These expressive genres are normally first-person narratives, and the referent is the lives of the poets themselves. No doubt the love affairs described by Propertius or Ovid are largely fabrications, but that consideration underscores the point. To argue that Propertius did not do with Cynthia what he says he did is to acknowledge that the poem is *about* Propertius. This kind of response should not be dismissed as an example of the biographical fallacy in criticism. The poetry asks to be situated in a narrative outside the text. It presents itself as revealing, at least in part, an existing world; in reference to this world, lies and exaggeration, like those of Odysseus in the *Odyssey*, are perfectly natural.

So much for the absence of the fictional contract in historical narrative and epic, tragedy, fable, lyric, and elegy. The case of comedy, however, and of New Comedy in particular, is more difficult. The characters of New Comedy were not historical or mythological figures, nor were they people belonging to the immediate circle of the poet. They, and the stories they enacted, were made up by the playwright. The

---

[15] W. Rösler, "Die Entdeckung der Fiktionalität in der Antike," *Poetica* 12 (1980) 283–319, suggests that a sense of fictionality emerged in the centuries following Homer as a consequence of writing: first insofar as writing fixed a tradition that was previously generalized, and second insofar as it produced an audience that was alone with the written text as opposed to the more personal participation in oral performances (cf. summary on 285). Fiction in this sense indicates the consciousness that versions may depart from a canonical paradigm; it does not signify the inhibition of referentiality as such.

lack of external reference is suggestive of fiction. Indeed, certain ancient rhetorical critics discriminated narrative into three types, namely history, myth, and what they called *argumentum* or "plot," and they tended to cite New Comedy for examples of the last type. Thus, Quintilian writes (2.4.2): "we have three types of narrative: myth, which you get in tragedies and poems {i.e., epics}, and which is removed not only from truth but from the appearance of truth; fictitious story [*argumentum* = Greek *plasma*], which comedies invent, false but verisimilitudinous; and history, in which there is an exposition of something which actually happened."[16]

In Quintilian's account, both epic and comedy, as opposed to history, relate false events; they differ in that myths narrate impossible things, whereas comedies represent things that are plausible. Perhaps "fantasy" or "the marvellous" best renders Quintilian's use of the term "myth" here.[17] In any case, whether the action and characters derive from traditional tales or are freely invented is not at issue. Since Quintilian's division ignores the question of referentiality, one should hesitate to assign to *argumentum* the modern sense of "fiction." It evidently designates nothing more than a non-historical narrative that is credible as opposed to wildly exaggerated.[18] It is worth recalling that New Comedy did sometimes represent mythical stories; an example is Plautus' *Amphitryo.*

Nevertheless, many of the plots and characters in New Comedy are freely invented and do not refer to the mythical tradition. It may be that New Comedy is to be seen as a precursor of fiction; indeed, as I shall suggest shortly, the circumstances in which it arose bear some resemblance to those that generated the ancient novel. However, I should like to defend the intuition, represented in modern usage, that

---

[16] Quoted from D. C. Feeney, "Towards an Account of the Ancient World's Concepts of Fictive Belief," in Gill and Wiseman, *Lies and Fictions,* 230–44, esp. 232; my insertion in braces.

[17] I would suggest that marvellous narratives do not qualify as fiction just because they depend for their effect on the tension between the presumed referentiality of the narrative and its implausibility. Marvellous tales were a genre in antiquity; for mediaeval marvels, see D. Kelly, *The Art of Medieval French Romance* (Madison: University of Wisconsin Press, 1992) 146–204.

[18] Pavel, *Fictional Worlds,* 48, notes that writers *create* their characters, they do not *find* them; thus fictional worlds do not exist independently of the creation of the fiction. It may be worth remarking that classical philosophy did not in general concern itself with alternative or fictive worlds.

fiction has a particular affinity with the novel, and that dramatic comedy is in fact a different thing.

Classical New Comedy exploits stock plots and characters. Names are conventional: Demeas, for example, indicates an older man or father, Moschion an enamored youth. Indeed, the characters wore masks which indicated their general type, whether slave or parasite, cook or courtesan, or the romantic lead himself. There exists, as the context for New Comedy, a kind of archetypal or generic *senex* or *adulescens*, whose traits are partly given in the tradition. In this respect, the character Demeas resembles mythical figures: like them, his qualities and actions are particularized in a given version, but at the same time he incarnates a personality who is familiar from the cultural repertoire. There is more to be learned about Demeas than is available through Ryle's "simple reading of the text."

The referent for the events in New Comedy is, then, the stereotyped tradition, which the poet did more to vary than to invent. To be sure, the Greek novels too are fairly similar, if not exactly formulaic, in their general outlines. But the repertoire of comedy was reproduced in thousands of variations; Alexis alone is reported to have produced 245 plays (so the Byzantine dictionary called the Suda; cf. *PCG* Testimonium 1). There is no reason to suppose that the ancient Greek novels ever constituted so rich a tradition.

To illustrate the distinctive character of the Greek novel as a locus of invention rather than of reference to a cultural repository or *Gemeingut*, we may take two authorial interventions on the part of Chariton in his novel commonly called *Chaereas and Callirhoe*. Half-way through his tale, at the beginning of Book 5, Chariton explains:

> How Callirhoe, the most beautiful of women, married Chaereas, the handsomest of men, by Aphrodite's arrangement; how in a fit of lover's jealousy Chaereas struck her, and to all appearances she died; how she had a costly funeral and then, just as she came out of her coma in the funeral vault, tomb robbers carried her away from Sicily by night, sailed to Ionia, and sold her to Dionysius; Dionysius' love for her, her fidelity to Chaereas, the need to marry caused by her pregnancy; Theron's confession, Chaereas' journey across the sea in search of his wife; how he was captured, sold, and taken to Caria with his friend Polycharmus; how Mithridates discovered his identity as he was on the point of death and tried to restore the lovers to each other; how Dionysius found this out through a letter and complained to Pharnaces, who reported it to the King [of Persia], and the King

summoned both of them to judgment—this has all been set out in the story so far. Now I shall describe what happened next.[19]

Chariton begins the eighth and final book of his novel as follows:

> How Chaereas, suspecting that Callirhoe had been handed over to Dionysius, determined to avenge himself on the King and so went over to the Egyptian side; how he was appointed admiral and gained control of the sea; how after his victory he seized Aradus, where the King had placed his own wife for security, and along with her all his train and Callirhoe too—all of that has been described in the previous book. But Fortune was minded to do something as cruel as it was paradoxical: Chaereas was to have Callirhoe in his possession and fail to recognize her; while taking others' wives on board his ships to carry them off, he was to leave his own behind. . . . But Aphrodite thought this too harsh; she was growing less angry with him . . . ; having harassed by land and sea the handsome couple she had originally brought together, she decided now to reunite them. And I think that this last chapter will prove very agreeable to its readers: it cleanses away the grim events of the earlier ones. There will be no more pirates or slavery or lawsuits or fighting or suicide or wars or conquests; now there will be lawful love and sanctioned marriage. So I shall tell you how the goddess brought the truth to light and revealed the unrecognized pair to each other.[20]

The stereotyped plots and characters of New Comedy obviated the need for such reassurances to the audience. Plautus, in the prologue to an exceptionally serious play of his called *The Captives*, does indeed worry for a moment that his topic may sound too grim for comedy, but it is precisely the constraints of the genre to which he appeals in order to reassert the familiar pattern: "For it's pretty unfair for us to try, in our comic gear, to put on a tragedy all of a sudden" (61–62).

It is true that the authors of the Greek novels often allude to overtly referential genres in order to ground their narratives. Thus Chariton prefaces his story in a manner calculated to recall the histories of Herodotus and Thucydides: "I, Chariton of Aphrodisias, clerk to the rhetor Athenagoras, shall narrate a love affair that happened in Syracuse." Compare Thucydides: "Thucydides of Athens has compiled an account of the war fought between the Peloponnesians and the Athenians."[21] Chariton continues: "The Syracusan general Hermocrates, the man who defeated the Athenians, had a daughter called Callirhoe." Hermocrates was a Syracusan who lived toward the end of the fifth century BC, and he plays a substantial role in Thucydides' history. As John

---

[19] Trans. B. P. Reardon, in *Collected Ancient Greek Novels* (B. P. Reardon, ed.; Berkeley: University of California Press, 1989) 75.

[20] Trans. Reardon, *Greek Novels,* 110.

[21] Quoted from J. R. Morgan, "Make Believe and Make-believe: The Fictionality of the Greek Novels," in Gill and Wiseman, *Lies and Fiction,* 175–229, esp. 205.

Morgan writes: "Within the novels, the represented world is, without exception, explicitly identified with reality."[22]

In part, the incorporation of historical formulas may be understood as a symptom of the novel's catch-all quality. Mikhail Bakhtin identified the novel as the polyphonic genre par excellence, or rather quasi-genre, since it assimilates the voices of all other literary forms.[23] In this respect, the ancient novel is true to type. Thus, Chariton cites verses from Homer at critical moments in his text, suggesting perhaps that his work has the structure and dignity of epic. Elsewhere, he draws analogies between the scenes he describes and the stage effects of drama, and passages of the dialogue resemble the stichomythia or line for line exchanges typical of tragedy (5.8). Scholars since Erwin Rohde have sought in such passages evidence for the origin of the novel in one or another traditional Greek genre. Steve Nimis, however, suggests: "Prose can be thought of as the process of weaving together pieces of language that *do* have some native context into a heterogeneous text that does *not*."[24] Once relocated in the fabric of the novel, the snatches that recall referential genres are detached from their prior function.

The protagonists of Chariton's novel are in fact connected only in the loosest way to the historical context of classical Syracuse. Their story—the "love affair" or *erōtikon pathos* that Chariton mentions in his opening sentence—has no reference either to actual events or to a tradition of myth and commonplaces like those of epic, drama, and lyric poetry. The classical Greek novels differ in this respect from mediaeval romances. Douglas Kelly observes:

> First, virtually no romance fails to claim one or more sources, whether oral or written, in Latin or a vernacular; this conforms to expectations enunciated in the arts of poetry and prose and to medieval conceptions of invention as distinct from creation. Second, romance narrators tend to prefer written authority, especially when it is taken or construed to be that of an eyewitness. . . . Romance derives its emphasis on *matière* and topical truth from medieval historiography.[25]

The Greek novels do not seek in any serious way to locate their stories in a culturally acknowledged tradition. The romantic experiences they narrate are not presented as versions of tales authorized elsewhere.

---

22 Morgan, "Make Believe," in Gill and Wiseman, *Lies and Fiction*, 198.

23 M. M. Bakhtin, *Problems of Dostoeyevsky's Poetics* (C. Emerson, trans.; Minneapolis: University of Minnesota Press, 1984).

24 S. Nimis, "The Prosaics of the Ancient Novels," *Arethusa* 27 (1994) 387–411; quotation on 402.

25 Kelly, *French Romance*, 145.

Accordingly, they neither depart from nor conform to stories that are given independently in the tradition. The central love story of Chaereas and Callirhoe does not invite a judgment on its truth, falsity, or fidelity to what is known. It ventures to stand on its own.[26]

Chariton's may be the earliest of the surviving Greek novels, dating to the first century AD or perhaps as early as the first century BC (2nd-century AD papyrus fragments provide a terminus ante quem).[27] The author claims to be from the city of Aphrodisias in Asia Minor, but his book was read in Egypt, as the existence of bits on papyrus indicates, and doubtless in many other places in the Greek portions of the Roman Empire. The novel was a genre that traveled: indeed, it was the exemplary type of mobile literature, since it was not bound by any requirements of performance to a particular locale, the way epic recitations, dramatic productions, and lyric songs in principle were. The novelists identify no specific addressee, and there is no reason why the original or primary readers of the Greek novels should be imagined as residing in Aphrodisias rather than in Alexandria or Antioch. To cite Steven Nimis once more: "Prose is a more abstract discourse than its poetic predecessors because it is not tied (or imagined to be tied) to a specific locus of production and reception."[28] The novel lacks spatial roots.

Correspondingly, the characters within the novels are famously in motion over the entire Mediterranean world, from Sicily to Persia, Thrace to Ethiopia. The world within the novels is a cosmopolitan one, detached from local or parochial communities. People from all over the empire, coming from as far away as India and Italy, mingle and interact and fall in love with the hero or heroine. The world of the novels is too diverse, too polyglot, too diasporized to be represented as a culturally unified space. In this respect, too, the novels tend to go beyond a single determinate cultural referent, whether in historical memory, mythical

---

[26] Jan Scholtemeijer, "*Historia Augusta*, knolskrywer(s) . . . òf knollesers . . . òf knolle vir lesers," Universiteit van Pretoria nuwe reeks nr. 212 (1985), suggests that the *Historia Augusta* is best read not as history or as biography but as a historical novel. Today, with the genre of fiction in the dominant role, history may appear as a fictional world: "My father maintains that history and fiction are interchangeable," says a character in Walter Abish's novel, *Eclipse Fever* (New York: Knopf, 1993), cited from D. Johnson, "How Mexican Is It," *The New York Review of Books* 40.15 (23 September 1993: 39–40); quotation on 39.

[27] J. N. O'Sullivan, *Xenophon of Ephesus: His Compositional Technique and the Birth of the Novel* (Berlin: de Gruyter, 1995) 1–9, 145–70, makes a good case for the priority of Xenophon of Ephesus.

[28] Nimis, "Prosaics," 405.

tradition, or the local performance codes of personal poetry. There is no uniform tradition to serve as the primary reference for so dispersed a narrative.

Instead, the novels themselves appear to function as a common point of reference for their various readers and readerships. Ancient critics seem not to have contemplated the significance of the fact that the Greek novels, as fictions, inhibit reference to a tradition outside themselves. But at least one novel—Longus' *Daphnis and Chloe*—perhaps contains a hint that the author was conscious of the novel's referential autonomy. For Longus represents his tale as the interpretation of a picture that has been explained to the narrator by an expert exegete. Thus the reference for art is more art: in place of the cultural signified encoded in a narrative tradition lies another signifier, suggesting a hermeneutical mise-en-abyme. What is more, the picture itself may be—one cannot be absolutely sure—the one set up in a shrine by the protagonists themselves at the end of the story. John Morgan captures the quality of this aspect of the text neatly: "The prologue to Longus' novel," he writes, "is complexly self-referential" (p. 218), and he refers to Longus as "a second-order imitator" (p. 216). But, as Morgan also notes, the hero and heroine at the end of Xenophon's *Ephesian Tale* "dedicate an account of their experiences in the temple of Artemis at Ephesus" (p. 209), and in other instances too there are indications that "the novel is authorized from within."[29] Literature, now articulated as fiction, reverses the relationship between model and copy: the model is the work itself; rather than respond to a common cultural stock, it offers itself as an exemplum.

I suggest that this convention of internal valorization, which is central to the experience of fiction, was at least in part motivated or made possible by the internationalization of the early Roman Empire and the corresponding production of a universalizing narrative form designed for global dissemination. In this respect, the mobile, deracinated world described in the novels resembles the world itself at a moment when the

---

[29] Nimis, "Prosaics," 405; cf. D. Maeder, "Au seuil des roman grecs: Effets de réel et effets de création," *GCN* 4 (1991) 1–33, on the opening mise-en-scènes in Longus' *Daphnis and Chloe* and Achilles Tatius' novel, in which "the veracity of the narrative flirts with fictionality" (10). One may compare Achilles Tatius' description (*Leucippe and Clitopho* 5.3) of a painting of the rape of Philomela that reproduces as well the pictures embroidered on her robe. I am reminded also of a painting by René Magritte that hangs in the New Annex of the National Gallery in Washington D.C., entitled "La condition humaine," which represents a painting, on an easel, of a landscape seen through the window in front of which the painting is standing.

world might seem to transcend local particularisms. The Roman Empire had brought multiple cultures under its umbrella. The culture of the Roman Empire as a whole, however, was still relatively contentless, in the sense that there was no universal tradition constituted out of a generally accepted set of referents or paradigmatic narratives. The novel thus achieved a precarious autonomy from collective memory and heritage. Rather than addressing a defined and self-conscious cultural group, the novel constructed for itself a literary community of readers whose point of common reference was the novel itself. The implicit awareness on the part of writers and readers of the novel's referential independence is what constitutes the genre as fiction.

If New Comedy seems to be a precursor of fiction, the reason may be that the social conditions in which it was produced in some ways resembled those in which the novel flourished. It is impossible that all of the 245 plays produced by the comic playwright Alexis were staged at the official dramatic festivals in Athens. Almost certainly, Alexis and others wrote also for the traveling troupes of actors who put on entertainments in cities all around the Mediterranean, at a time when the Hellenistic kingdoms were contributing to a partial relaxation of city-state exclusivism. Correspondingly, as Niall Slater has observed, the comedies tended gradually to eliminate purely local allusions that might not be intelligible to audiences outside of Athens, such as mentions of obscure Attic demes.[30]

I have been arguing that the novel, as a genre particularly suited to global distribution, could fill a partial vacuum in the cultural milieu of the early Roman Empire, offering stories that were not necessarily valorized by reference to a specific repertoire of shared narrative materials. These circumstances enabled the emergence of a readerly agreement to withhold the referential response. It is just this convention or compact that constitutes fiction. The reasons for association between fiction and the novel as a form are thus apparent.

The cultural space of the Roman Empire, however, was not dormant. Traditions new and old were continually contending for position and hegemony. Douglas Edwards, indeed, interprets Chariton's novel as a part of a strategy on the part of his native city of Aphrodisias to enhance its power by projecting the "religious, political, and social dimensions" of

---

[30] N. Slater, "The Fabrication of Comic Illusion," in G. Dobrov, *Beyond Aristophanes: Transition and Diversity in Greek Comedy* (Atlanta: American Philological Association, 1995) 29–45.

its own deity, Aphrodite; Aphrodite's connection with Julio-Claudian dynasty, Edwards suggests, could win sympathy at Rome.[31] The fictional romance, on this view, is the vehicle of a rivaly among cult sites seeking to promote their local traditions and to connect them, where possible, with myths specific to the imperial center.

Another tradition making its bid for authority in these centuries was Christianity. In an extraordinary study, Glen Bowersock has suggested that tales of the marvelous (which he calls fiction), and a preoccupation with their veracity, were given a decisive impulse at the time of Nero by the circulation of New Testament texts, thanks to their strange intimations of cannibalism (i.e., the eucharist) and their concern with resurrection; the latter, he suggests, accounts for the popularity of the *Scheintod* in the Greek novels. Whatever the truth of this account, the Gospels do not constitute the referent for these episodes, for the Christian narrative had not yet gained universal authority. On the contrary, allusions to the Christian master plot are, if Bowersock is right, mixed in with pagan traditions, and are symptomatic of the multiplicity of cultural repertoires to which the novels may appeal but which do not provide them with a common myth. Hence the restraint on referentiality and the disposition to take the novels as fictions.

Bowersock notes further that

> as the popularity of the novelists grew—and the papyri increasingly suggest that it did—it was perhaps not surprising for the Christians to pick up in turn and to exploit the very genre that seemed to have come into being, to some degree, as a response to stories of theirs that were now enshrined in the canonical Gospels. By the early third century at the latest, the Christians, to our knowledge, had acquired at least one major novel of their own along the lines of the polytheist ones and in evident imitation of them.[32]

This Christian "novel" is the *Recognitions* attributed to Clement, recounting a meeting between Clement and Saint Peter. Bowersock adds:

> The emergence of martyrologies, beginning in the second century, soon made more novels like the *Clementine Recognitions* superfluous. The martyr narratives were to provide the basis for an abundant production of instructive fiction in the centuries ahead, although the earliest martyr acts, based as they were on carefully maintained protocols of interrogation, had rather more historical veracity than was to be characteristic of the genre later. (141)

---

[31] D. R. Edwards, "Defining the Web of Power in Asia Minor: The Novelist Chariton and his City Aphrodisias," *JAAR* 62 (1994) 699–718; quotation on 704.

[32] Bowersock, *Fiction as History,* 139.

That these narratives, including the *Recognitions,* present themselves as true accounts belies their status as fictions. All manifestly have as their point of reference the Christian paradigm or tradition. By its growing authority as a new universal myth, Christianity in fact disrupted the development of fiction as a literary practice and convention.[33]

The ecumenical scope of travel that marks the emergence of fiction in classical antiquity bears a resemblance to the journeys and adventures recorded in *The Acts of the Apostles* and the Pauline epistles. Where the novelists experimented with self-referential fictions, however, Christianity sought to fill the cultural void by providing a new referent commensurate with the global scale of the Roman Empire. In this respect, the stories in the Bible assumed the authority of the panhellenic traditions incorporated and canonized in the Homeric epics a millennium earlier. For this reason too, the ascendancy of Christianity signalled the end of fiction as a literary medium. Henceforward, there was a general disposition to understand narratives as referring to a culturally shared matrix of characters and narrative motifs. There was thus no longer a role for the referential autonomy of the Greek novels, and the rebirth of fiction had to await the second coming of the novel in modern Europe, when the extension of cultural horizons and the conflict of traditions were again favorable to the narrative sovereignty of the text.[34]

---

[33] Purely literary figures too may enter the cultural tradition and thus become a referent. This is why Pavel, *Fictional Worlds,* 34 can assert: "Had Hamlet married Ophelia, they would have lived happily ever after."

[34] It is not an accident, moreover, that in modern times the European literary form that has most penetrated the cultures of the colonial world has been the novel (along with the short story). I wish to thank Victor Caston for his penetrating comments on an earlier version of this paper.

The Spectrum of Narrative: Authority of the Author

Gareth Schmeling
University of Florida

I

Classicists and theologians look at the ancient world in different ways, probably because of their training or more likely because of the guardians of their training. As Socrates points out in *The Republic* (374E) about the original guardians, the disposition of a culture's *phylakes* (guardians) depends on the *paideia* or training of these guardians, who instinctively identify what is familiar and just as instinctively chase away what is not. To pay attention to texts, phrases, words is what the guardians of classicists train their students to do. This approach to close textual reading in education is a construction of *paideia* largely now peculiar to classics.

I would like to begin with a few remarks about the differences between classicists and theologians. To accuse classicists of being the quintessential secular humanists, while true, sheds little light on the debate. It is no more helpful than to say that a classicist is a biblical scholar gone bad. In the best tradition of Greece and Rome I have plagiarized the following remarks from so many authors, my literary and professional ancestors, that I can no longer attribute their sources. It is really plagiarism, but in today's tolerant classification, it is easily subsumed under the literary/critical term intertextuality.

A meeting of theologians and classicists to discuss the nature of narrative employed by ancient novelists and New Testament era writers seems to me to hold great possibilities. In normal academic life these two disciplines do not often mingle: this is strange but true. A shared interest in Greek and Latin has not always led to especially close ties. Perhaps theologians and classicists are somehow different.

The differences surely go back to the education of theologians and classicists. Theologians have constituencies in the field, they have a public, and a place to send students for jobs. Then too, religion plays an important role in everyday 20th century society. For their part, classicists study dead white European males—in all fairness we should note that classicists also study a few dead people from the Near East (e.g., Lucian, Heliodorus) and North Africa (Apuleius)—are politically incorrect, and are the butt of jokes by artists as varied as the novelist Amanda Cross and the cartoonist of "Doonesbury." Most theologians have actually gone out into the cruel world among working people: it seems almost a rite of passage for them to enter the alien culture outside the academy. The young theologian comes back from the field a wiser person.

The classicist submits to what appears a long course of study but is really an apprenticeship to a guardian. The would-be classicist prepares set passages for translation and explication before the guardian who year by year instills in the student less and less tolerance for error. The guardian passes on to his protégé a love for the text, such as its author probably had, and an abhorrence for textual error—even small ones.

Classics implies the study of the best literature, which implies a privileged status for one culture, the foundation of Western civilization. Where, however, does the word "classics" come from? It seems that Roman citizens were divided into five classes for tax-paying purposes based on property qualifications, and citizens in the first or highest tax class were called *classici*, classics. It was not until Aulus Gellius (fl. AD 150), however, that we find the word classics used to describe something great in literature. When literary problems arise, Gellius (*Noctes Atticae* 19.8.15) advises his readers to consult model authors of the past, the great writers of the past, the classics: *id est classicus adsiduusque aliquis scriptor, non proletarius* ("a first-class and tax-paying author, not one of the proletarians").

Classicists study texts which are long separated in time from us, which are recognized as serious staples of Western culture and which enjoy a privileged and authoritative position. Classicists search for meaning, unity of themes, or unity inspired by an author whose utterances helped to create the foundation of basic Western values. Veneration for texts which come to be held as classics or, if you will authoritative, has a concomitant consequence, a veneration for authors who become authoritative: Aristotle and Virgil are examples. As an authority the classical author interprets, makes sense of, and unifies his culture.[1]

---

[1] Author, authority, and power are words whose meanings easily overlap. The literate person, even if he possesses only shop literacy, was a person of power; the bibliography on this is enormous, but see W. Harris, *Ancient Literacy* (Cambridge:

II

The authority behind an oral or written work in antiquity is often said to be a Muse, who externally or internally works in a writer. Homer and Virgil, however, and for example, are not only inspired by the Muse, they become servants for the Muse, priests, the *vates*, the interpreters of the wishes of the gods. Virgil relates to his readers what the gods intend for the future of *The Empire,* i.e., the future of humanity. This *vates,* the one who understands how the future will develop, has god in him. Even a writer as secular as Ovid confesses that a god possesses him: *AA* 3.549 *est deus in nobis et sunt commercia caeli; Fasti* 6.5 *est deus in nobis, agitante calescimus illo; ex Ponto* 3.4.91–94 *nec mea verba legis . . . / ista dei vox est, deus est in pectore nostro, / haec duce praedico vaticinorque deo.* In Apuleius' *Metamorphoses* (8.27) we read that an inspired priest is *divino spiritu repletus.*

The author who is not an eyewitness seems to need some sort of connection to the event reported which would allow him to be included in the category of omniscient narrators. And how does one become omniscient? In the classical world one is omniscient if connected to a being who is omniscient, i.e., a god, a priestess, a seer.

In 2 Pet 1:21 we read: "but holy men of God spoke as they were moved by the Holy Ghost," and in 2 Tim 3:16: "All scripture is given by inspiration of God." The usual Greek word for narrative, omniscient or otherwise, in Greek novels and Lucian is διήγησις, which is the term Luke uses in his opening verse of chapter 1, and in 1:2 he also resorts to the authority of αὐτοψία, eyewitness. In her essay on mental maps in narrative Loveday Alexander notes that Luke adds support to his claim of *autopsia* by combining the use of we-narrator with the use of redundant place names.[2] Luke's narrative is thus based in some part on eyewitness

---

Harvard University Press, 1989), and a corrective work, *Literacy in the Roman World* (J. Humphrey, ed.; JRASup 3; Ann Arbor: University of Michigan Press, 1991). In the early centuries AD we see, for example, the appearance of saints' lives and acts of martyrs whose authors or subjects commanded enormous authority by virtue of the power of their persons and the power of the words written by/about them. Their story is told and circulated in words. See J. Perkins, *The Suffering Self: Pain and Narrative Representation in the Early Christian Era* (London: Routledge, 1995). Words have power and words in a network have even more power; see D. Edwards, *Religion and Power. Pagans, Jews, and Christians in the Greek East* (New York: Oxford University Press, 1996).

[2] L. Alexander, "Narrative Maps: Reflections on the Toponymy of Acts," in *The Bible in Human Society: Essays in Honour of John Rogerson* (M. D. Carroll *et al.,* eds., JSOTSup 20; Sheffield: Sheffield Academic Press, 1995) 17–48, plus 8 maps. This

support: he retreats from relying totally on omniscience.[3] But what actually happens in a Luke narrative? At 22:39ff. we read that Christ goes off some distance from his disciples and prays to his Father. When he returns to his disciples, he finds them asleep. From what authority does Luke learn the words in Christ's prayer? From the same authority Thucydides and Livy learn their speeches? No one, not Luke or any disciple, hears the prayer. There were no αὐτόπται, eyewitnesses. The modern reader, however, cannot by-pass Luke: if Luke narrates, we are informed; if Luke is silent, if he reports only what he has seen, we are blind.

Eyewitness account, αὐτοψία, is a form of authority of which Lucian is fond. In the opening paragraphs of *A True History* (1.2) he states: "I shall say one thing which is true, and that is, I am a liar."[4] And who could doubt the authority of his eyewitness account? Lucian is of course parodying the need writers seem to feel to cite some authority, even if what they are about to narrate is fiction—or perhaps he is parodying the need readers feel to be assured that there is some authority. In his *Toxaris* (12) Lucian comically exaggerates the reliability of the authority of his sources. He has Mnesippus say: "Well, then, as Zeus Philios is my witness, I solemnly swear that whatever I shall tell you, I will say either from my own knowledge or from information obtained of others with all the accuracy that was possible, without contributing any dramaturgy on my part."[5]

---

study replies to the work of P. Gould and R. White, *Mental Maps* (2d ed.; Boston: Allen & Unwin, 1986).

[3] On the literary and narrative qualities of Luke and other New Testament writers, see R. Pervo, *Profit with Delight: The Literary Genre of the Acts of the Apostles* (Philadelphia: Fortress, 1987); on the interplay between ancient novelists and early Christian writers see R. Pervo, "The Ancient Novel Becomes Christian," in *The Novel in the Ancient World* (G. Schmeling, ed.; Leiden: E. J. Brill, 1996) 685–711, and R. Hock, "The Greek Novel," in *Greco-Roman Literature and the New Testament: Selected Forms and Genres* (D. Aune, ed.; SBLSBS 21; Atlanta: Scholars Press, 1988) 127–146.

[4] Emphasis on truth might in fact be only a reaction. It seems to me that the natural human condition is to lie. Lying is also more entertaining, since the truth is often both dull and hurtful. Lucian pokes fun at Ctesias, historian of the 5th–4th century, who told lies as well as Lucian and is probably seen more as a rival in the art of lying than as an object of derision. A book on lying or lies as a literary genre in the ancient world is a real desideratum; in the meantime we do have *Lies and Fiction in the Ancient World* (C. Gill and T. P. Wiseman, eds.; Exeter: University of Exeter Press, 1993), and G. W. Bowersock, *Fiction as History, Nero to Julian* (Berkeley: University of California Press, 1994).

[5] Perhaps since the time of Ctesias, historiography has become more and more like stage drama, hence the description "tragic history"; cf. F. W. Walbank, "History and Tragedy," *Historia* 9 (1960) 216–234.

Both Dictys of Crete and Dares the Phrygian (pseudonyms) claim to have been eyewitnesses to the Trojan War and thereby claim exceptional authority. Dictys and Dares structure their narratives as though they were the unadorned records or diaries of individual soldiers, writings not unlike the Latin *commentarii*—"The title *commentarii* is a literary understatement."[6] On purpose such *commentarii* are rhetorically simple, stripped to the bone, as it were. In order to be members of this genre, the *commentarii* of Dictys and Dares are rhetorically unadorned and carefully without art, but since today's classicists' main interest is focused on rhetoric—and rhetoric can be defined simply as the necessary literariness to be worthy of study—these *commentarii* fall outside the interests of classicists. An attempt to report the facts and nothing but the facts with no attempt at persuasion cannot be taken as serious literature.

In the opening chapter of the *Apocolocyntosis* Seneca states emphatically that what he is about to say is true and that he has an eyewitness. All of his emphasis on truth is, however, to be understood as an emphasis on the false. Seneca pretends that his readers are questioning him about his sources: how could he know what had happened to Claudius? Seneca writes: "This is the authentic truth. If anyone inquires about the sources of my information, first—if I do not want to—I shall not reply. Who is going to compel me? . . . Who ever demanded sworn referees from an historian? But if it is obligatory to produce the authority (*auctorem*) behind my account . . . he is the superintendent of the Appian Way. . . ."

In the closing chapters of both Xenophon of Ephesus' novel and *Apollonius King of Tyre* the narrators state that the heroes of the narratives deposited a copy of their adventures in the temple of Diana at Ephesus. The implied or assumed source of the resulting novels is thus the narratives discovered in the temple by the men who became the author of the novels. The authority of the author is a written document which had been produced by eyewitnesses.

The eyewitness record need not be a written document of the action; it could be a pictorial representation of the adventures of hero and heroine. The implied source of the novels of Achilles Tatius and Longus is the paintings which stirred the imaginations of the narrators to comment on and to enlarge. Authority rests on ecphrasis, words written about something visual. We can see such a device at work in Apuleius

---

[6] M. von Albrecht, *The History of Roman Literature* (rev. G. Schmeling; 2 vols.; Leiden: E. J. Brill, 1997) 1.413.

(*Met.* 6.29). He implies that he could know the story which he is narrating because he had access both to the ass' memory and to an implied picture. Charite is speaking: "I shall perpetuate the memory of my present calamity and of divine providence by dedicating in the vestibule of my house a panel painted with the picture of our present escape. People will come to see this simple tale, and will hear about it when stories are told, and the pens of the learned will perpetuate it."

Authority of the author rests outside the ancient novel, however, if we follow Reinhold Merkelbach,[7] who contends that ancient novels are in fact religious works and that their classification as secular novels is owing to scholars' lack of understanding. For Merkelbach ancient novels are *Mysterientexte,* meant to be intelligible fully only to those properly initiated into the mysteries. The authority of the author is thus his privileged position as an initiate, an insider. Lucius in Apuleius' *Metamorphoses* 11 does not give the reader imaginative prose fiction but rather an expression of personal experience. Susan Suleiman[8] would term Apuleius' *Metamorphoses* an authoritarian fiction or a *roman à thèse*—if Merkelbach is correct. If the writer hopes to teach a lesson, the writer acquires a special kind of authority in which he not only knows more than others, he knows better than others, and what he knows is the truth. Such novels or works infantilize the reader: the writer knowing that what he writes is good and true encourages the reader to yield to his superior authority.

III

In the ancient world historians and novelists accept that which is handed down to them as true or traditional. The traditional story, the μῦθος, to some became an oppressive tradition and led writers like Xenophanes to reject the μῦθος in favor of a reliance on their own critical and rational skills in order to examine empirically the world around themselves. To this rationalism Herodotus adds ἱστορία, information gathered by inquiry. Thucydides relies on a superb memory and can recall verbatim numerous long speeches: he is in fact as omniscient as the novelist who reports speeches which he could not have heard.[9] I do not challenge the fictiveness of Chariton but rather the factuality of ancient

---

[7] R. Merkelbach, *Roman und Mysterium in der Antike* (Munich: C. H. Beck, 1962).

[8] S. Suleiman, *Authoritarian Fictions. The Ideological Novel as a Literary Genre* (New York: Columbia University Press, 1983).

[9] See note 4.

historians. To pour salt into the historical wound, Hayden White[10] reveals that historical writing is governed by modes of narrative and by tropes (rhetorical forms) which do not merely embellish but more profoundly constitute the structure of historical narrative.[11]

In his work *Did the Greeks Believe their Myths?* Paul Veyne[12] makes a strong case that ancient historians accepted even unlikely stories (if they were widely held) handed down by their ancestors, as having some historical basis; they rejected only the most unlikely elements of these stories but accepted the bulk of them. Sources of stories are not scrutinized carefully, and the authority of the author/source is not questioned diligently, for the tradition is taken to be true in its outline. Chariton accepts the story of the battle of Syracuse in 413 BC, selects or omits or adds events, and then passes the story down to his reader. For his part the reader leaves his own world, enters that of Chariton's narrative, and believes what he reads—believes it, that is, as long as he is living in it. Later, however, does he disbelieve Chariton's whole narrative, or does he amalgamate it or parts of it with Thucydides' story? Whether the events in Thucydides or Chariton are historically true is really of secondary concern. What matters is whether or not the reader (at best) believes them to be true (i.e., the author has been persuasive)—or the reader (at worst) does not question if they are true or false. Veyne concludes that "a world cannot be inherently fictional; it can be fictional only according to whether one believes it or not." Northrop Frye[13] phrases the same thing in this way: "The original criterion of truth is personal: a theory is true because a tradition of sufficient authority, or a person representing that tradition, says or endorses it."

---

[10] H. White, "The Historical Text as Literary Artifact," in *The Writing of History: Literary Form and Historical Understanding* (R. Canary, ed.; Madison: University of Wisconsin Press, 1978) 41–62.

[11] Cicero *Ad Fam.* 5.12 writes to the historian L. Lucceius, who has agreed to write a history and include Cicero's achievements: "Shame deterred me when I tried on several occasions to discuss this matter with you [so I am writing about it in a letter because a letter cannot blush]. . . . So I openly ask you again and again to eulogize my deeds with more vigor than you perhaps feel and in that same vein to disregard the guidelines of accuracy in writing history and to remind you of that partiality [which] if it will enhance my merits more clearly, please do not disdain it and in view of our friendship please bestow even a little more partiality than truth allows."

[12] P. Veyne, *Did the Greeks Believe Their Myths* (P. Wissing, trans.; Chicago: University of Chicago Press, 1988) 21.

[13] N. Frye, *The Secular Scripture: a Study of the Structure of Romance* (Cambridge: Harvard University Press, 1976) 17.

Historians and novelists try to tell an interesting story and to hold the reader. Through an array of rhetorical devices both try to convince the reader, and both carefully select a relatively few events out of the total for retelling, connect them in a series—to show cause and effect or to show the natural workings of Tyche—and give the reader a narrative with a beginning, middle, and end. A goal of ancient rhetorical education, the ancestor of education in classics, which suited both historian and novelist, was to train students who could then compose narratives, says T. P. Wiseman, ". . . for which it was of no significance whether the material used was true or merely plausible . . . provided that it was convincing."[14]

The novelist wants to offer something believable, and the historian wants to be believed: both record events, attribute motivation, and from a small sampling portray a universalized suffering which arises from the events. Not only in historiography but also in the novel we find evidence that the writer proposes to deal with reality and in fact aims at veracity. But truth is not necessarily a valid measure by which to judge the differences between history and the novel: assigning motivation to historical characters renders them similar to actors in novels and renders the historian (like external narrators of novels) omniscient.

The novelist uses a wide array of literary devices to persuade his readers to believe. If the historian is interested only in the truth, why not lay out the facts unadorned? Adornments are used to persuade, are in fact necessary for the novelist or the rhetorician to make the worse cause appear the better. Facts are supposed to speak for themselves; falsehoods and products of the imagination must be sold by literary devices. Any narrative employing literary devices must be held suspect.

In antiquity does it just seem that historians write literature first and history second? From the opening lines to the end, their language calls attention to itself as something strange, something set apart from its need to be employed to relate the facts. Words, phrasing, sentences, arrangements, rhythms all draw the reader's eyes and ears from the message to the medium: the rhetoric of such an historian turns out to be no less an artifice than that of the novelist. By dressing his history in all the trappings of literature, the historian confuses the critic: the historian wishes to compete for the hearts and minds of his reader with the same devices employed by the novelist. The weight of evidence is seen as worth less than that of art, and the critic consequently experiences difficulties in

---

[14] T. P. Wiseman, "Practice and Theory in Ancient Historiography," *History* 66 (1981) 375–93, esp. 389.

discernment, because the historian has disguised his work as something to be judged against works of literature. If the historian appeals to the authority of literature, i.e., to the criteria by which literature is judged, the critic perhaps should not be faulted for not evaluating his work as history. If the author bases his own authority on the evidence he has gathered, the critic should respond accordingly; if, however, the author's authority rests on the arrangement and style of presentation of the evidence, on the quality of the interpretation rather than on the evidence alone, the critic's judgment should not be deprecated for failing to recognize the author's intent to write history.

IV

When we look back at ancient classical narratives we must always bear in mind that the writer is more interested in the moral lessons to be learned from the example of an individual than in the scientific, sterile evidence of fact. The moral lesson is the point, the moral of the narrative. As M. J.Wheeldon says: ". . . the act of interpreting historical content was . . . an act of moral judgement."[15] Narratives are not explanations of mass movements or of structural changes but of the moral decisions of individuals, who much earlier in Homer's day were called heroes. We could thus define the narrative in classical history as "a chaotic conglomerate of countless individual stories of a more or less exemplary nature . . . and this narrative recording of events in historiography was based on the belief that history was made by individuals"[16]

An approach to some narratives from the ancient world in the period from the late first century BC to the early fifth century AD might be considered in a schematic form like the one below. This diagram, of course, has all the faults of attempts to impose a unifying scheme on a wide variety of historical and literary works. No one work is all fact or all fiction but rather a blending of the two, in which one or the other dominates. Thus each work appears between two extremes along the spectrum and is seen as more or less fictional. A second determinant for placing works along the spectrum in the diagram is the authority of the

---

[15] M. J. Wheeldon, "'True Stories': The Reception of Historiography in Antiquity," in *History as Text: the Writing of Ancient History* (A. Cameron, ed.; Chapel Hill: University of North Carolina Press, 1989) 33–63, esp. 59.

[16] P. Lützeler, "Fictionality in Historiography and the Novel," in *Neverending Stories: Toward a Critical Narratology* (A. Fehn, ed.; Princeton: Princeton University Press, 1992) 29–44, esp. 30. The reader interested in the various aspects of the ancient novel might wish to consult the essays in *Novel in the Ancient World* (see n. 3).

author: with some justification we can say that Tacitus (less fictional) at least attempts to provide a narrative with more basis in fact than the others in the chart; Longus at the other extreme creates a narrative whose only authority is aesthetic quality and intertextuality with pastoral works. A conclusion implied by the arrangement of the diagram is that ancient narrative is a medium which binds together history, biography, and the novel and determines the basic nature of certain literary forms.

For the literary critic . . . everything in words is plasmatic, and truth and falsehood represent directions, or tendencies in which verbal structures go.

Frye

Authority of the Author in Narrative

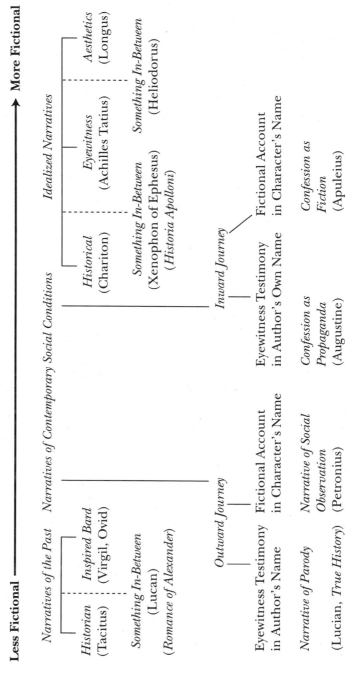

Less Fictional ⟶   **More Fictional**

Narratives of the Past   *Narratives of Contemporary Social Conditions*   *Idealized Narratives*

Historian
(Tacitus)

Inspired Bard
(Virgil, Ovid)

Something In-Between
(Lucan)
(*Romance of Alexander*)

Outward Journey

Eyewitness Testimony
in Author's Name

Fictional Account
in Character's Name

Narrative of Parody

*Narrative of Social
Observation* (Petronius)

(Lucian, *True History*)

Historical
(Chariton)

Something In-Between
(Xenophon of Ephesus)
(*Historia Apolloni*)

Eyewitness
(Achilles Tatius)

Something In-Between
(Heliodorus)

Aesthetics
(Longus)

Inward Journey

Eyewitness Testimony
in Author's Own Name

Fictional Account
in Character's Name

*Confession as
Propaganda*
(Augustine)

*Confession as
Fiction*
(Apuleius)

Pleasurable Reading or Symbols of Power?
Religious Themes and Social Context in Chariton

Douglas R. Edwards
University of Puget Sound

Henry J. Cadbury, eminent Luke-Acts scholar, once remarked that he knew of no other text that exhibited more examples of the "idiom and ideas" in Acts than Chariton's *Chaereas and Callirhoe*.[1] Richard Pervo,[2] myself,[3] and a few others[4] have written extensively on the relation between Acts and Chariton's text. The surprise is that more have not done so. One reason may be that many have taken uncritically the position that the romances, especially the so-called erotic or romantic variety (Chariton's work is often mentioned as one of the best examples), were written to entertain. For New Testament scholars this may make the ancient romances immediately suspect. Certainly Acts is not erotic nor simply written to entertain goes the reasoning. Typical is a recent work on Acts that ends a brief encounter with the ancient romances with the rhetorical caveat, "was Acts intended to entertain or to inform in an entertaining way?"[5] Clearly, this writer assumes that the romances were written for entertainment. Even Pervo in his *Profit with Delight* which has one of the clearest, most comprehensive definitions of the romance to date tends to stress the "delight" over the "profit" when comparing the romance with Acts. This seems more a result of emphasis than

---

[1] H. Cadbury, *The Book of Acts in History* (New York: Harper and Bros., 1955).

[2] R. Pervo, *Profit with Delight: The Literary Genre of the Acts of the Apostles* (Philadelphia: Fortress, 1987).

[3] E.g., D. Edwards, *Religion and Power: Pagans, Jews, and Christians in the Greek East* (Oxford: Oxford University Press, 1997); D. Edwards, "Surviving the Web of Roman Power: Religion and Politics in the Acts of the Apostles, Josephus, and Chariton's *Chaereas and Callirhoe*," in *Images of Empire* (L. Alexander, ed.; Sheffield: Sheffield Academic Press, 1991) 179–201.

[4] For bibliography D. Edwards, "Acts of the Apostles and Chariton's *Chaereas and Callirhoe*: A Literary and Sociohistorical Study" (Diss., Boston University, 1987).

[5] G. Sterling, *Historiography and Self-Definition: Josephus, Luke-Acts and Apologetic Historiography* (Leiden: E. J. Brill, 1992) 320.

misperception. Indeed, Pervo ventures that popular literature sought to please and to instruct.[6] And he posits that minimally Chariton must reflect local pride when he stresses the role of Aphrodite.[7]

Critical to most discussions of the romances is the interpreter's perception of the reader. Few would disagree that local elites in the Greek East or those associated with them comprised the primary reading audience. But how would such an audience react to Chariton's work: as a delightful work of entertainment,[8] as expressing their sense of isolation in a vastly expanded Hellenistic society,[9] as an aretalogy displaying the powers of the divine,[10] as a misconceived effort to write a *Mysterientext*,[11] as a Hellenistic operetta,[12] or, as one seventeenth century English translator of Chariton put it, as a history depicting the life of Hermocrates' daughter?

One must decide upon the "typical" reading audience at the time Chariton was written to fathom the most appropriate reading. Many New Testament interpreters (as well as classicists) *a priori* assume that *Chaereas and Callirhoe* functioned for readers in antiquity as entertaining, delightful, or pleasurable reading. Such arguments revolve primarily around the "erotic" motif, the travel of the protagonists and their bizarre adventures, and the interpreters' preconceived notion of the "sentimental" and "light-hearted" character of the story itself.

Interpreters generally ignore the role of religion in Chariton's work or inappropriately use a model dominated by a Christo-centered approach. This study suggests that Chariton of Aphrodisias reflects in his novel *Chaereas and Callirhoe* mythic and religious traditions that highlight the

---

6 Pervo, *Profit with Delight*, 13.

7 Pervo, *Profit with Delight*, 105–6.

8 Ben E. Perry, *The Ancient Romances: A Literary-Historical Account of Their Origins* (Berkeley: University of California Press, 1967) 45. Perry does suggest spiritual edification as a possible function but generally ignores it in his analysis.

9 B. P. Reardon, "Aspects of the Greek Novel," *G&R* 23 (1976) 118–31; *Courants littéraires grecs des IIe et IIIe siècles après J.-C.* (Annales littéraires de l'Université de Nantes 3; Paris: Les Belles Lettres, 1971) 309–412; "The Greek Novel," *Phoenix* 23 (1969) 291–309; "Novels and Novelties, or Mysteriouser and Mysteriouser," in *The Mediterranean World, Essays Presented to Gilbert Bangnani*, (Peterborough, Ontario, 1975) 78–100.

10 Gareth Schmeling, *Chariton* (TWAS 295; New York: Twayne, 1974) 129.

11 Reinhold Merkelbach, *Roman und Mysterium in der Antike* (Munich: C. H. Beck, 1962) 159, 339–40.

12 Graham Anderson, *Eros Sophistes: Ancient Novelists at Play* (Chico, CA: Scholars Press, 1982) 21.

power and prestige of Aphrodite. Further, Chariton's use of religious and mythic images mirrors similar efforts by local elites in Aphrodisias and in the Greek East as they sought to define their relation within the Roman 'web of power.'

Considerations on Method

How does one properly compare a text (especially an ancient novel) to its social and narrative context? How can one make statements about how the reading audience perceived the piece? In some circles it has become normal to argue that texts mirror interpreters and do not serve as windows through which one sees even dimly a real world. Narrative worlds exist apart from their author, and meaning is determined through an interaction with a reader/interpreter and the closed world of the text.[13] There is truth in this view. Ancient writers do not produce reality, no matter how hard they try, but rather a perception of reality. Narratives are self-contained and need not portray explicitly the author's real world.

Yet, no writer or reader operates in a literary or socio-cultural vacuum. Language, themes, and choice of images connect a text and its author with the world. Clarity about the social and cultural context in which a writer composes and a reader reads remains crucial. Modern interpreters invariably assume that readers (both ancient and modern) perceive the "meaning" of the text in some fashion. An explicit model that elucidates the initial social and cultural context(s) of an ancient text provides an interpretive framework from which to compare a narrative's language and orientation. It provides important (though not conclusive) clues as to how the narrative might have been read (a type of reader-response criticism).

But which local, regional, or general social and cultural patterns and which reading audience does one select? Local elites in the Greek East certainly provided at least one significant audience. Whether only women read it seems unproved. A close reading of Chariton's text indicates the major religious, political and social symbols, themes, or ideas of the author. An analysis of the civic and religious context of Aphrodisias and the Greek East provides the social and cultural context in which Chariton wrote.

---

[13] A fine discussion of this approach is by John J. Winkler, *Auctor and Actor: A Narratological Reading of Apuleius's The Golden Ass* (Berkeley: University of California Press, 1985) 1–24.

Few disagree that the religious element is present in Chariton's narrative.[14] No two interpreters stand in sharper contrast as to how religion
factors into an understanding of the ancient romance than Ben E. Perry
and Reinhold Merkelbach. Perry judged Chariton and the other Greek
romances as entertainment and secular literature, in contrast to Christian
romances (e.g., Acts of Paul or Pseudo-Clementines), which include
similar components but whose purpose intends "that simple souls might
be overawed and led into the way of salvation."[15] Merkelbach, however,
argues that romances such as Apuleius' *Metamorphoses* or Xenophon's
Ephesiaca reflect the symbolic death and rebirth of the initiate in the
mystery cults drawing on the myth of Isis' rescue of Osiris.[16] The
romances portray, according to Merkelbach, an attempt to address the
question and concerns of a new age ripe for the security and salvation
offered by the mystery cults.[17] B. P. Reardon's theory, that the novels are
myths depicting the isolated person in Hellenistic society read largely like
so many sentimental "ladies' magazines,"[18] straddles Perry's and Merkelbach's positions. Most interpreters fall somewhere between.

What characterizes these approaches is a tendency to overly "christian-
ize" the idea of religion. Both positive or negative evaluations of religion
in Chariton's work assumes a 'Christianizing' theory of religion that
stresses the role of religion as a guide through the personal crises of life
and as a means to salvation.[19] As Simon Price suggests, a more appropriate model for religion in antiquity focuses on how persons draw on

---

[14] A. D. Nock makes this observation in a review of K. Kerenyi's *Die griechisch-
orientalische Romanliteratur in religionsgeschlichtlichen Beleuchtung* where he states:
"Kerenyi is . . . probably in the right in emphasizing against Rohde the importance of
the explicit religious element in the plot of Chariton . . ." in "Greek Novels and
Egyptian Religion," in *Essays on Religion and the Ancient World* (Z. Stewart, ed.; 2 vols.;
Cambridge: Harvard University Press, 1972) 1.169–75, esp. 173. Nock does not agree
with Kerenyi's thesis that the religious component comes from the sacred myth of Isis
and Osiris.

[15] Perry, *The Ancient Romances,* 30.

[16] *Roman und Mysterium,* 79–80, 336ff.

[17] The exception in Merkelbach's scheme is Chariton who fails to understand the
proper significance of the mysteries (*Roman und Mysterium,* 159, 339). "Er war kein
grosser Geist, sondern nur ein kleiner Schreiber zu Aphrodisias in Kleinasien und hat
die Mysterien-romane, deren Hintersinn er nicht verstand, ziemlich sklavisch
nachgeahmt" (340).

[18] B. P. Reardon, "The Second Sophistic and the Novel," in *Approaches to the Second
Sophistic* (G. W. Bowersock, ed.; University Park, PA: American Philological
Association, 1974) 23–29, esp. 28.

[19] Price, *Rituals and Power,* 247.

religious myths and symbols to construct or define strategic power relationships (both real and perceived) between different parties.[20] The elite environment in which Chariton was written took religious and mythic imagery quite seriously. Religious myths and symbols permeated the ancient world. As Peter Brown has argued, "the cultural and religious aspects of the public life" of towns in the Roman empire were no "mere trappings which the urban elites could or could not afford. . . ."[21]

Setting the Stage: The Narrative World of Chariton

As a secretary to a local rhetorician, Chariton was affiliated with the local elite structure in Aphrodisias (1.1.1).[22] Chariton no doubt had knowledge of the administrative operation of a city in the Greek East; his novel also betrays values assumed by local elites in the Greek East.

Chariton's narrative underscores the relationship of the heroine Callirhoe with Aphrodite. The narration begins with a comparison of Callirhoe to the goddess and ends with Callirhoe praying at the base of her cult statue in Syracuse.[23] Throughout the narrative Callirhoe acts out on the human plane mythic and social roles of Aphrodite, roles that include Aphrodite's power to unite cities and nations,[24] her appearance as goddess of love,[25] her association with death,[26] and her close affiliation

---

[20] Price, *Rituals and Power*, 241–42.

[21] *The Making of Late Antiquity* (Cambridge: Harvard University Press, 1978) 34.

[22] For a sample of the inscriptions see *Monumenta Asiae Minoris Antiqua,* vol. 8 (W. M. Calder & J. M. R. Cormack, eds.; Manchester: Manchester University Press, 1962 [hereinafter *MAMA*]), 552 (Chariton), 437, 438, 462, 475 (Athenagoras). E. Rohde's conclusion that Aphrodisias in Caria is the site has carried the day, *Der griechische Roman und seine Vorläufer* (3d ed.; Leipzig: Breitkopf & Hartel, 1914) 522ff.; cf. K. Plepelits, *Chariton von Aphrodisias, Kallirhoe* (Stuttgart: Anton Hiersmann, 1976) 1–3; Schmeling, *Chariton,* 17–18; T. Hägg, *The Novel in Antiquity* (Berkeley: University of California Press, 1983) 5. C. Ruiz-Montero believes that the mention of a rhetor Athenagoras by Ammianus (*A.P.* 11.150) suggests that the Romance was written at the end of the first or the beginning of the second century; "Una observacion para la cronologia de Cariton de Afrodisias," *EstClas* 24 (1980) 63–69.

[23] 1.1.1–2; 8.8.15–16. Accurately observed by E. H. Haight, *Essays on the Greek Romances* (Port Washington, NY: Kennikat, 1943) 32, and Tomas Hägg, *Narrative Techniques in Ancient Romances* (Göteborg: Paul Astrom, 1971) 216.

[24] For opposing views that cities still had the right to make treaties, see Price, *Rituals and Power*, 126 n. 142.

[25] Readily available in literary sources such as Homer, which Chariton clearly uses in his work; see Blake's 'Index Analyticus,' 134ff. for Chariton's citations.

[26] Several tombs at Aphrodisias warn those who might disturb tombs of penalties that must be paid to Aphrodite; *MAMA* 8.547, 555, 565, 573, 576. See also Alfred Laumonier, *Les Cultes Indigènes en Carie* (Paris: E. de Boccard, 1958) 500. Lewis Farnell

with the sea.[27] Further, Chariton makes clear Callirhoe's membership in the local elite class. The daughter of Hermocrates, the Syracusan general, she is cultured (7.6.5), even-tempered (1.2.6), and well bred.[28]

Chariton describes Callirhoe as an absolutely amazing young woman,[29] the *agalma*[30] of all Sicily (1.1.1) whose beauty compares to that of Aphrodite Parthenos.[31] No work of stone, Callirhoe's human appearance embodies the *kallos* of the goddess Aphrodite (1.1.2).[32] In the ancient romances, comparisons of the human protagonist (both hero and heroine) with a deity are legion.[33] The portrayals of political figures in

presents evidence that Aphrodite was associated with death at various sites in Greece and Asia Minor in *The Cults of the Greek States* (5 vols.; Oxford: Clarendon, 1897) 2.652–53, 754–55.

[27] At Aphrodisias of Caria, a third century CE *aedicula* of Aphrodite features Aphrodite on a half shell held by two tritons drying her hair; see K. Erim, "Aphrodisias," *AS* 32 (1982) 9–13, esp. 13. Iris Love has shown that nearby Cnidos had an active cult to Aphrodite Euploia ("Knidos," *AJA* 82 [1978] 324). Farnell provides additional references to this aspect of Aphrodite (*Cults of the Greek States*, 2.636–38).

[28] See Johannes Helms, *Character Portrayal in the Romance of Chariton* (The Hague: Mouton, 1966) 45–66.

[29] *thaumastos ti chrema parthenou.*

[30] Kenneth Scott translates *agalma* as "cult image" ("Ruler Cult and Related Problems in the Greek Romances," *CPh* 33 [1938] 380–89, esp. 384), perhaps too extreme but more plausible than Warren Blake's 'admiration' (*Chariton's Chaereas and Callirhoe* [Ann Arbor: University of Michigan Press, 1939]), Georges Molinié's 'trésor,' (*Chariton: le roman de Chairéas et Callirhoé* [Paris: Budé, 1979]), or K. Plepelits' 'Entzücken' (*Kallirhoe*). Scholars generally consider *agalma* as an object placed in the temple and designed for worship; for references, see Nock, "Synnaos Theos," in *Essays*, 1.204 n. 5. Price, however, notes that translating *agalma* as cult statue assumes a cult association that does not always occur. Some private citizens did not receive public cult during the imperial period even though they had images (*agalmata*) placed in sacred locations, one even at Aphrodisias (*MAMA* 8.412) (Price, *Rituals and Power*, 178). This does not diminish the fact that the divine *kallos* of Callirhoe shines through the narrative. See also the discussion of the term by W. Burkert, *Greek Religion* (J. Raffan, trans.; Cambridge: Harvard University Press, 1985) 65, 91, 94, 187.

[31] Parthenos is an unusual ephithet for Aphrodite (although see *BCH* 32 [1908] 500). Marcel LaPlace plausibly suggests an allusion to Athena Parthenos ("Les Légendes Troyennes dans le "Roman" de Chariton Chairéas et Callirhoé," *REG* 93 [1980] 83–125, esp. 124–25). For discussions on the role of cult statues in antiquity see Nock, "Synnaos Theos," in *Essays* 1.202–51; Price, *Rituals and Power*, 170–206.

[32] Cf. Remy Petri, *Über den Roman des Chariton* (Beiträge zur Klassischen Philologie 11; Meisenheim am Glan: A. Hain, 1963) 11–12; and Helms, *Character Portrayal*, 42–45, who note the close relationship between Callirhoe and the goddess Aphrodite but who downplay its importance for the narrative. Peter Walsh cites the similar role played by Psyche in Apuleius' *Metamorphoses* in *The Roman Novel* (Cambridge: Cambridge University Press, 1970) 55 n. 2, 200.

[33] E.g., Xenophon's *Ephesiaca*, 1.2.6–8; 1.12.1; 2.2.4. Heliodorus, *Aethiopica* 1.2; 1.7;

Graeco-Roman society, especially in Asia Minor, were often identified with a god or goddess. Aggripina and Caligula's sister, Drusilla, were each called the New Aphrodite.[34] At Assos in Turkey a bath was dedicated to Julia Aphrodite (Livia).[35] Nock plausibly argued that such identifications depict ruling personages as another form of the deity.[36] The identification also helps maintain the political and social *status quo*. The practice began early. Price observes that the wife of Antiochus III, Laodice, established dowries for poor citizens' daughters; in her honor citizens established a new cult of Aphrodite Laodice. The "queen collocated with the goddess of love" and there occurred "a procession on the queen's birthday and sacrifices by all the brides and bridegrooms to the queen." Price concludes that these "cults established the king and queen at the center of civic life, both political and social."[37]

Several scenes exhibit Callirhoe's collocation of the civic and religious arenas.[38] Serving as the human vehicle for Aphrodite, Callirhoe's *kallos* overwhelms crowds and undoes the fortitude of political leaders. This is more than erotic, sentimental fare. In Syracuse her divine appearance amazes (*thaumadzein*) the crowd and many prostrate themselves before her (*proskynein*) (1.1.16). After the pirate Theron rescues Callirhoe from her tomb following her apparent death, he brings her to the country estate of Dionysius of Miletus in an attempt to sell her. Before presenting her, he uncovers her head and loosens her hair, actions that display her divine beauty.[39] Callirhoe's sudden entrance astounds (*kataplessein*) all

---

2.23; 2.39; 3.4; 10.9. The pattern goes at least as far as Homer who refers to individuals as "god-like" and "like unto Zeus in counsel."

[34] D. Magie, *Roman Rule in Asia Minor* (2 vols.; Princeton: Princeton University Press, 1950) 512.

[35] C. C. Vermeule III, *Roman Imperial Art in Greece and Asia Minor* (Cambridge: Harvard University Press, 1968) 457. See also A. Nock, "Synnaos Theos I," in *Essays* 1.226f.; J. Aymard, "Venus et les impératrices sous les derniers Antonins," *Mélanges d'Archéologie et d'histoire* 51 (1934) 178–96.

[36] "Synnaos Theos," in *Essays* 1.233–34. Nock calls this "a kind of association or comparison" (p. 235) although he believes it to be 'trite.'

[37] Price, *Rituals and Power*, 30.

[38] E.g., 1.1.11f; 1.1.16f.; 2.3.5.

[39] Cf. W. C. van Unnik's discussion of the important role of hair in "Les cheveux défaits des femmes baptisées," *VC* 1 (1947) 77–100. Further evidence for the importance of hair as a manifestation of the divine is indirectly provided by Athenaios who snidely remarks that Apelles' inspiration to paint his Aphrodite rising from the sea came from an incident involving a certain Phryne. "At the great assembly of the Eleusinia and at the festival of Poseidon in full sight of the whole Greek world . . . [Phryne] removed her cloak and let down her hair before stepping into the water"

who see her and they think they have seen a goddess since word had it that Aphrodite appeared (*epiphainein*) in the countryside (1.14.1; cf. 4.7.5).

The clearest example of Callirhoe's impact on crowds comes on her journey to Babylon. At each point of the way crowds turn out to see this "masterpiece of Nature, 'like unto Artemis or golden Aphrodite'" (4.7.5).[40] They were not disappointed as Callirhoe surpassed the reports. The journey concludes with her entrance into the city of Babylon. Despite Dionysius' attempt to hide Callirhoe under a *skene* or awning,[41] word of her beauty had gone before their entourage and "all of Babylon" poured out to see the sight. When Dionysius realizes that he cannot avoid the inevitable, he asks Callirhoe to come out. All in the crowd strain their eyes and their very souls (*psyche*). The result could easily fit a description of the Eleusinian mysteries. "Callirhoe's face gleamed with a radiance which held the eyes of all, just as when a great light is suddenly seen on a dark night."[42] Overcome with astonishment the Persians prostrate

---

(13.590); cf. Lucius' description of Isis' appearance as she rose from the water: "First she had a great abundance of hair, flowing and curling, dispersed and scattered about her divine neck" (*Metamorphoses* 11.3).

[40] Chariton compares Callirhoe to Artemis in order to highlight Callirhoe's divine appearance (cf. 1.1.16; 3.8.6; 4.7.5; 6.4.6). A close association existed between the cult statues of Artemis of Ephesus and Aphrodite of Aphrodisias. See the discussion by Robert Fleischer, "Artemis und Aphrodite von Aphrodisias," in *Die orientalischen Religionen im Römerreich* (M. J. Vermaseren, ed.; Leiden: E. J. Brill, 1981) 298–311. In *Chaereas and Callirhoe*, however, the emphasis falls on Callirhoe's relationship to Aphrodite. Indeed, Callirhoe's appearance before crowds at Syracuse, which is compared to Artemis' appearance before hunters (1.1.16), offers a contrast; Artemis appears to hunters in the country, Aphrodite's representative to crowds in the city.

[41] *Skene* is used several times in Chariton's narrative to describe a tent or awning from which someone suddenly emerges causing surprise, amazement and worship on the part of onlookers. These include Callirhoe's appearance before astonished crowds who prostrate themselves (*proskynein*) before her on her entrance into Babylon (5.3.9), Statira's return on the ship to the king (8.5.5), and Callirhoe and Chaereas who appear in regal trappings on their return to Syracuse (8.6.7–8). For a different use of the term compare 1.4.8.

[42] For a discussion of the Eleusinian mysteries with description of the effect on persons, see George E. Mylonas, *Eleusis and the Eleusinian Mysteries* (Princeton: Princeton University Press, 1961), and G. D'Alviella, *The Mysteries of Eleusis: The Secret Rites and Rituals of the Classical Greek Mystery Tradition* (Wellingborough, United Kingdom: Aquarian, 1981). Chariton's allusions to the mysteries (1.1.15; 4.1.9; 8.1.10) do not prove the existence of a mystery cult of Aphrodite at Aphrodisias. The discussion between Goodenough and Nock regarding the possible references to a Jewish mystery cult in Philo indicate the difficulty of identifying actual mystery practices on the basis of the literary evidence alone. See E. R. Goodenough, *By Light, Light: The Mystic Gospel of Hellenistic Judaism* (Amsterdam: Philo, 1969), and A. D. Nock,

themselves before her (*proskynein*) (5.3.9).[43] Callirhoe *qua* Aphrodite has conquered Babylon.[44]

Callirhoe has civic and religious import for Sicily and Syracuse.[45] Chariton indicates that lawful marriage and family mean stability and continuity in society, something stressed in the Roman empire. Callirhoe, daughter of Syracuse's most prominent political figure, marries Chaereas, son of the second most powerful figure, at the behest of the demos. Both families had feuded until the marriage united them (and the society as well). In contrast, disruption of the marriage disrupted society.

This is pointedly illustrated after Callirhoe's apparent death at the hands (or rather the foot) of her jealous and misinformed husband, Chaereas. Rumor quickly spread the word of her demise throughout all the city. The reaction? "From every side lamentations resounded, and the affair was very like the capture of a city" (1.5.1). At Chaereas' trial for the dastardly deed, he surprises everyone by refusing to defend himself. "Stone me to death in public. I have robbed our people of their crown (*apostephanoun*)" (1.5.5).

"The Questions of Jewish Mysteries," *Essays* 1.459–68. No evidence yet appears for mystery practices in connection with the cult of Aphrodite of Aphrodisias.

[43] Alexander Scobie has suggested that the act of *proskynesis* by the Babylonians reflects a practice "generally detested by the Greeks;" in *More Essays on the Ancient Romance and its Heritage* (Beiträge zur klassischen Philologie 46; Meisenheim am Glan: A. Hain, 1973) 24. Kenneth Scott agrees in part. "The attitude on *proskynesis*, freely paid the Great King or his wife by Persian subjects but refused by Greeks, is characteristic of the proud days when the Greek states were independent, and it is an attitude glorified in literary tradition. In the romances the gesture of adoration is often induced by gratitude, which, we know, was a common motive for the deification of a benefactor. Heroes and heroines are endowed with superhuman beauty which often wins them divine honors and causes people to regard them as epiphanies" (K. Scott, "Ruler Cult," 388–89). In *Chaereas and Callirhoe proskynesis* is performed before several different individuals by various groups and individuals; for a) Callirhoe as if she were a deity by Greek citizens at Syracuse (1.1.16); crowds on Dionysius' estate; people of Miletus; barbarians (Statira [5.9.1] and the crowds [5.3.9]); b) the cult statue of Aphrodite by Callirhoe and Chariton (once); c) the king by Dionysius, Mithridates, and subjects; and for d) the queen by servants and the crowd when she returns from her captivity.

[44] Cf. Kenneth Scott's assessment in "Ruler Cult," 386. This argues against G. Anderson's view that the mystery language appears only as incidental allusions. His statement that "even the nights at Eleusis or the Olympic Games fail to produce as much enthusiasm as Callirhoe's trial" (*Eros Sophistes,* 18) does not recognize that it is Aphrodite's power on display here. How better to express the excitement and awe that her power engenders than to allude to such experiences? cf. 1 Cor 9:24.

[45] Jacques Bompaire, "Le décor sicilien dans le roman grec et dans la littérature contemporaire (IIe siècle)," *REG* 90 (1977) 55–68.

When Callirhoe after her journeys returns to Syracuse, she appears before the citizens (demos) in the theater at Syracuse ". . . the people lifted their eyes to heaven, and praised the gods, feeling an even greater sense of gratitude for this day than for that of their victory" (8.7.2). Her reunion with Chaereas and subsequent return were more significant than the legendary victory over the Athenians in which the very existence of Syracuse was secured. The author's selection of similes places Callirhoe, as Aphrodite's representative, within the fabric of Syracusan society.[46]

But the reader also finds that the religious, political, and social dimensions of Aphrodite's power extend beyond the borders of Sicily.[47] In Miletus and, most particularly, the country estate of Dionysius, its leading citizen, Callirhoe prepares for her second marriage, this time to her former owner Dionysius. Returning from the temple of Aphrodite, Callirhoe approaches some sailors who prostrate themselves before (*proskynein*) her as if Aphrodite herself had appeared.[48] The city of Miletus is decked out for a sacred festival and each person sacrifices at home and the temple (not specified). The crowd (*plethos*) gathers at the temple of Homonoia, which Chariton states is the traditional site for bridegrooms to receive their brides.[49] Previously considering that beauty only "lay in nobility of fatherland (*patris*) and race (*genos*)," Callirhoe puts on the Milesian dress and bridal wreath. Only then does she turn and look (*apoblepein*) at the crowd. As one they shout "*he Aphrodite gamei*," "Aphrodite marries!" and give her all the attention of a deity or royalty, spreading purple cloth, roses, and violets before her and sprinkling her with perfume (3.2.15–17). The marriage between two individuals again represents the union of two leading members of the local elite classes and depicts East (Asia Minor/Miletus) meeting west (Syracuse); the common bond is Aphrodite as represented by Callirhoe. *Kallos* does not reside in

---

[46] Perry notes that the comparison of Callirhoe's death to the sacking of a city is meant seriously by Chariton; see his "Chariton and his Romance from a Literary-Historical Point of View," *AJP* 51 (1930) 93–134, esp. 129 n. 43.

[47] Callirhoe complains to Tyche that she has now become the talk of all Asia and Europe (5.5.3).

[48] This recalls Aphrodite's role as the goddess of the sea (Aphrodite Euploia); cf. 8.1.12. Kenneth Scott draws attention to the empress Domitia's association with Concordia/Harmonia, which he believes symbolizes the "harmonious relations within the imperial household" or "harmony in wedlock" (*The Imperial Cult under the Flavians* [Stuttgart: W. Kohlhammer, 1936] 85–86).

[49] Cf. Plutarch's statement that the "honor and charm, and mutual love and trust, that grow up daily [in a happy marriage] prove the wisdom of the Delphians in calling Aphrodite the goddess who joins together" (*Amat.* 769a).

nation or race but rather in Aphrodite's authority, which extends beyond political and social boundaries.

Aphrodite in Chariton's narrative works behind the scenes through her divine agent Eros, or through her often reluctant human agent Callirhoe to display her power. The author states that it is Aphrodite who arranges both marriages of Callirhoe (2.2.8; 2.3.5; 5.1.1), who reunites Chaereas and Callirhoe (8.1.3, 5), and who overrules the whims of Tyche (8.1.3).

Every incursion only leads inexorably to the final chapter, the reunion of those who have been separated. Even Tyche serves the final aims of Aphrodite, that is to test and train (*gymnadzein*, 8.1.3) the pair until they are prepared to be reunited. It is little wonder that the narrative concludes with Callirhoe in the temple of Aphrodite praying to Aphrodite that she never separate Callirhoe from Chaereas again (8.8.16). Callirhoe (and by this time the reader/hearer) knows where the power resides.

Callirhoe's wanderings from west to east may serve to create for members of the local elites in the Greek East a narrative full of suspense, novelty and excitement. But Chariton, like several other writers of ancient romances, depicts more than entertaining material.[50] Throughout his work, Chariton prominently displays for the reader the power and importance of Aphrodite. He does not stress internal changes or signs of 'conversion' experiences. Granted, Chaereas does come close in his move from suicidal, distraught, and jealous husband to one who, through his sufferings, has earned the forgiveness of Aphrodite and Eros and thus is reunited with Callirhoe, a changed man in heroic pose.[51] More significantly, Chariton portrays Aphrodite as part of a web of power that

---

[50] Michael Grant has stated it well:

Despite every incidental set-back, the gods are helping and guarding their special charges. Each writer tends to have a favourite god or gods of his own, and the general theme of attaining fulfillment through initiatory ordeals, described with almost formulaic uniformity, possessed obvious analogies to the ceremonials of salvation prescribed by the mystery faiths. Like the audience of medieval miracle plays we must put aside the modern idea that religion and entertainment are incompatible.

In *The Climax of Rome: The Final Achievements of the Ancient World AD 161–337* (Boston: Little, Brown, and Co., 1968) 130.

[51] Cf. the portrait of Chaereas in mourning (3.4.4), in chains (4.2.1ff.), and suicidal (1.6.1; 3.3.1.; 5.10.10) to his heroic appearance before his soldiers (7.3.10; 7.5.10–11) and the crowds at Syracuse upon his triumphant return (8.6.7). Perry has also observed this transformation in "Chariton and his Romance," 103–4.

encompassed aspects of ancient society, including bonds between nations and cities, creation of lawful marriage, display of proper social virtues, and control over the power of Fate.

Chariton's World and its Impact

How would Chariton's portrait of Chaereas and Callirhoe play with local elites in the Greek East? Here the environment in which the author wrote and the reader read is of paramount importance. Following is a brief sketch of one such environment.

Chariton wrote during or near the golden age of Aphrodisias, a city whose fortune prospered under the aegis of Rome. Thirty years of excavations substantiate Kenan Erim's claim that during the early centuries of this era, Aphrodisias "reached great fame and prosperity both as a religious site and as a center of art and culture."[52] One excellent example is the *Sebasteion* or imperial cult center at Aphrodisias that shows the intimate connection between Aphrodite of Aphrodisias, the Julio-Claudian house, and Rome from the perspective of local elites in the city.[53]

The imperial connection with Aphrodisias and its civic deity Aphrodite is also amply illustrated in a remarkable set of inscribed documents found associated with the theater wall at Aphrodisias. The inscriptions include copies of letters sent to the city by various Roman emperors.[54]

Descriptions of Aphrodite as "the goddess who is among them," (Doc. 8.1.38) 'ruler' (Doc. 18.1.4), 'founder' (Doc. 25.1.4), and 'source of the city's name' (Doc. 49.1.2) (allusions to her functions as the founder of Aphrodisias) indicate the long period of Aphrodite's close relationship with the civic identity of the city, particularly for local elites who received and later recorded the documents on the theater wall for all to see.[55] As late as the 3rd century, the Roman emperors Severus and Antonius state

---

[52] See K. Erim, "Aphrodisias" in *The Princeton Encyclopedia of Classical Sites* (R. Stilwell, ed.; Princeton: Princeton University Press, 1976) 68–70, esp. 68. See also Cornelius Vermeule, *Roman Art: Early Republic to Late Empire* (Boston: Museum of Fine Arts, 1978), who notes that Aphrodisias had a tradition of statuary and decorative carving beginning in the Hellenistic period and running through the time of Constantine (p. 173). See also *A Visual Dictionary of Art* (Greenwich, CT: New York Graphic Society Ltd., 1974) 83.

[53] K. Erim, "Aphrodisias," *AS* 33 (1983) 231–35, esp. 234.

[54] Joyce Reynolds' excellent work presents many of these documents with helpful analysis in her *Aphrodisias and Rome* (JRSMS 1; London: Society for the Promotion of Roman Studies, 1982).

[55] Cf. Reynolds' analysis, *Aphrodisias*, 80.

in official correspondence that Aphrodisias is "more closely related than others to the empire of the Romans because of [the goddess] who presides over your city, your existing polity and its laws which have survived unchanged up to our reign."[56]

As a protégé of Octavian, Aphrodisias received the rewards of freedom and local self-government with immunity from all Roman taxation.[57] The link between Aphrodisias and Rome, of course, drew initially on the Julio-Claudian claim to descend from Aeneas, the founder of Rome and son of Aphrodite.[58] The epithets of the various emperors in the documents found at the theater indicate the importance of Aphrodite in the bond between Rome and Aphrodisias, especially in the term *prometor* ("ancestral mother").[59]

The association is made explicit on a first century propylon that has the following inscription on its inner and outer faces: "To Aphrodite, the Divine Augusti, and the People." Greek cities, of course, often understood the emperor in the context of traditional deities. This may explain why the name of the deity is mentioned first.[60] As Joyce Reynolds observes "Aphrodite as first mother . . . presumably combined the concepts of first mother of all, first mother of the Aphrodisians, first mother of the Roman people and first mother of the Julian gens."[61] Aphrodite was a central symbol for the political and economic well-being of the city.

Some light is shed on Chariton's mention of the temple of Homonoia as the site of marriage for Callirhoe and Dionysius by a series of coin

---

[56] Reynolds, *Aphrodisias*, 127.

[57] Reynolds, *Aphrodisias*, 5.

[58] The link centered on the claim that Aeneas, son of Aphrodite, founded Rome; for a time it was strengthened by the relation of the first imperial dynasty to Aphrodite and, in a modified form, this outlasted the fall of that dynasty. Clearly demonstrated by G. Karl Galinsky, *Aeneas, Sicily, and Rome* (Princeton: Princeton University Press, 1969) 5ff.; see also Reynolds, Mary Beard, Charlotte Roueché, "Survey Article: Roman Inscriptions 1976–1980," *JRS* 76 (1981) 124–46, esp. 135; and Joyce Reynolds, "The Origins and Beginning of Imperial Cult at Aphrodisias," *PCPhS* 206 (1980) 70–80, esp. 70.

[59] Document 55.1.1.

[60] Cf. Price, *Rituals and Power*, 169.

[61] Reynolds, *Aphrodisias*, 184. In Document 32, Victory is said to always be with Caesar (Reynolds believes this is Julius Caesar) who is of divine descent (*theogenei*). Reynolds compares such use to an inscription from Ephesus in which Caesar is called a descendant of Ares and Aphrodite [*SIG* 1 347]. She suggests that "in Aphrodite's city it was not necessary to spell out details of the genealogy; there Aphrodite was the *theos par excellence*, and *theogenes* automatically meant her descendant" (p. 156).

issues from Aphrodisias. The coins feature the cult statue of Aphrodite of
Aphrodisias with those of other cities under the label *homonoia*. A coin
issued during the reign of Commodus, for example, shows an alliance
between Hierapolis and Carian Aphrodisias (*BMC Phyrgia* #25) that
depicts Aphrodite of Aphrodisias before a sacrificial altar with Apollo of
Hierapolis engaged in a *sacra conversazione*.[62] Other coin issues depict the
significance that Aphrodite played in the alliance with other cities and
Ephesus under Septimius Severus,[63] Antiochia,[64] Hierapolis,[65] and
Neapolis.[66] Such issues commonly expressed unity between cities during
the Imperial period. Although cities in Asia Minor probably had no real
power to make treaties,[67] the stress on harmony and kinship remained
and such gestures were important and serious for cities[68] who sought to
negotiate their power within the Roman empire's "web of power."

Aphrodisias' promotion of its goddess parallels (and probably benefits
from) a strong attraction to the goddess Aphrodite in the first two
centuries of this era. In the Greek East, magistrates often made
communal votive offerings to Aphrodite as their guardian or as a way to
contrast their particular duties. F. Sokolowski cites a number of votive
inscriptions from magistrates in Greek cities that stress Aphrodite as a
"patroness of friendship and of harmony."[69] Sokolowski notes Aphrodite's
close association with police officials, supervisors, naval commanders, and
those involved with penal facilities who "paid most frequently their
tribute to Aphrodite because of friendly relations existing among
themselves or between them and the people."[70] Magistrates often
dedicated to Aphrodite at the end of their military or civic service.[71] An
example of this in *Chaereas and Callirhoe* occurs when Chaereas offers

---

[62] Cornelius Vermeule, *Roman Imperial Art in Greece and Asia Minor* (Cambridge: Harvard University Press, 1968) 160–61.

[63] *BMC Caria,* vol. 18, #161, p. 53, plate 44.

[64] *BMC Caria,* vol. 18, #162, p. 53.

[65] *BMC Phrygia,* vol. 25, #166, p. 257.

[66] D. J. MacDonald, *Greek and Roman Coins from Aphrodisias* (BritARSup 9; Oxford: British Archaeological Reports, 1976) 31.

[67] Price, *Rituals and Power,* 126–27.

[68] Price, *Rituals and Power,* 127.

[69] F. Sokolowski, "Aphrodite as Guardian of Greek Magistrates," *HTR* 57 (1964) 1–8; cf. F. Croissant and F. Salviat, "Aphrodite gardienne der magistrats," *BCH* 90 (1966) 460–71.

[70] Sokolowski, "Magistrates," 2.

[71] Sokolowski, "Magistrates," 6.

sacrifices to Aphrodite at the end of his military ventures and before his return to Syracuse (8.2.8).

Aphrodisian elites apparently viewed Aphrodite's power as universal. The Aphrodisian cult statue, similar to that of Artemis at Ephesus, makes this clear.[72] The statue is typically divided into four zones. A colossal Aphrodite found at Aphrodisias serves as a good representative.[73] On the lower zone are displayed three erotes sacrificing incense, a frequent motif found on funerary reliefs.[74] The scene above it shows Aphrodite riding over the waves on a sea goat (or Capricorn) and accompanied by a dolphin. The third scene portrays Selene (moon) and Helios (sun) while the final scene has a picture of the three graces. These various zones indicate, according to G. Galinsky, mythic images of Aphrodite's power over the underworld, sea, sky, and earth.[75] Statues of Aphrodite of Aphrodisias have been found as far away as Portugal (Pax Julia) with a good number found at Rome itself.[76]

Some statues were dispersed in the first century BCE and Aphrodisians no doubt maintained their ties to the goddess of their home city when they became part of a strong influx of citizens from Asia Minor into Rome during this period. But most replicas of Aphrodite of Aphrodisias originate at sites in the second century CE, which coincides with the full blossoming and expansion of oriental cults across the Graeco-Roman world during the second century. Peter Noelke persuasively shows that the cult reached beyond the orbit of Aphrodisias and even of Asia Minor much like other oriental cults (e.g., the cult of Isis and Mithras, and Christianity).[77]

---

[72] Robert Fleischer, *Artemis von Ephesus und verwandte Kultstatuen aus Anatolien und Syrien* (EPRO 35 ; Leiden: E. J. Brill, 1973) 146ff.

[73] K. T. Erim, "Aphrodisias in Caria," *AS* 14 (1964) 25–28, esp. 26, gives his description of this statue. For photographic display of some of the many statues found see *Lexicon Iconographicum Mythologiae Classicae* (= LIMC) II.2 (Zurich and Munich: Artemis, 1984): 154–56.

[74] See Alfred Laumonier, *Les Cultes Indigènes*, 500.

[75] Galinsky, *Aeneas, Sicily, and Rome*, 217; see also Laumonier, *Les Cultes*, 497–98; R. Fleischer also observes that the statue of Aphrodite at Aphrodisias is similar to Artemis of Ephesus statues and that the decoration and zones depict the power of the goddess over nature, heavens, earth and water; a conception which he notes is late hellenistic/early Roman in "Aphrodisias," *LIMC* 2.1.2–154, esp. 153–54.

[76] Other sites include Ephesus, Athens, Salone, Leptis Magna, and a bronze statuette at Baalbek. See the summary and discussion of Peter Noelke, "Zwei Unbekannte Repliken der Aphrodite von Aphrodisias in Köln," *AA* 1 (1983) 107–31.

[77] Noelke, "Repliken," 129–30.

In short, Aphrodisias used the myths, symbols, and general popularity of Aphrodite to define itself amidst the Roman world of the first and second century CE. Aphrodite's appearance throughout the *oikoumene* in multiple forms (statues, coins) as well as throughout the pages of Chariton's text merely confirms for the reader the power, significance, and prestige of the city, its populace, and its goddess.

Conclusion

Chariton, like his city, intertwines religion and politics. Callirhoe, the heroine, highlights the power of Aphrodite as she travels across the landscape of the *oikoumene*. Each stage of her journey confirms for the reader the power and significance of Aphrodite over all aspects of the world order, especially the machinations of fate and social upheaval as represented by pirates, wayward politicians, disruption of proper marriage, separation from family, friends, country, and spouse. In addition, the text highlights that even the mightiest political figures are susceptible to Aphrodite's power. The latter of course appeals most particularly to local elites who interpret the social, political, and religious power networks existing in the Roman empire through the lens of Greek tradition and pride.

Chariton also stresses that persecutors of the hero/heroine consistently transgress the bounds of normal society and law. In contrast, the heroes or heroines, paradigms of local elites, present their law-abiding face before government officials, crowds, and the author's reading audience. Callirhoe maintains proper decorum through all tribulations, as does Chaereas later in the work; indeed, Chaereas argues against himself after he has 'killed' Callirhoe and robbed the people of their crown. He has broken the laws of society and argues for appropriate punishment. Chariton, a beneficiary of the local elite structure, makes clear that Aphrodite remains the final arbiter of power in the 'web of power' existing in the narrative world of Chaereas and Callirhoe. His narrative would resonate with members or aspiring members of elite groups at Aphrodisias and elsewhere who found attractive the notion that within even the Roman 'web of power,' the ultimate power broker remained Aphrodite.

Focalization in Xenophon of Ephesos' *Ephesiaka*[1]

Kathryn Chew
Drew University

Introduction

The *Ephesiaka* of Xenophon of Ephesos stands apart from the other Greek romances for the inconsistencies and infelicities of its construction. It has an uneven narrative texture, the length of its books and the story's pace vary quite a bit, and, compared with the other novels, it is inferior in composition. The quality of the *Ephesiaka* was first questioned by K. Bürger,[2] who maintained that the work is an epitome, following an observation made by E. Rohde that it read more like a synopsis than a novel.[3] This theory was used to account for the *Ephesiaka*'s narrative shortcomings: its brevity, the choppy pace, the general paucity of artistic expression and elaboration, the lack of motivation for certain events, the often abrupt introduction of characters or places, and even the lack of consistent divine providence. Epitomization is a popular theory.[4]

---

[1] I am indebted to the work of K. Bürger and especially T. Hägg, cited below. For my views on Xenophon's compositional technique, see "Inconsistency and Creativity in Xenophon's *Ephesiaka*," *CW* (forthcoming).

[2] K. Bürger, "Zu Xenophon von Ephesus," *Hermes* 27 (1892) 36–67.

[3] E. Rohde, *Der griechische Roman und seine Vorläufer* (4th ed.; Hildesheim: Georg Olms, 1960) 428–32; esp. 429: "Stellenweise liest sich diese Erzählung fast wie eine blosse Inhaltsangabe einer Erzählung; fast könnte man auf den Gedanken kommen, gar nicht einen voll entwickelten Roman, sondern nur das Skelett eines Romans, einen Auszug aus einem ursprünglich viel umfangreicheren Buche vor sich zu haben."

[4] For instance, Bürger, "Xenophon," H. Henne, "Le Géographie de l'Egypte dans Xénophon d'Éphèse," *RHPh* (1936) 97–106; G. Dalmeyda, "Auteur de Xénophon d'Éphèse," *BAGB* (1926) 18–28; and H. Gärtner, "Xenophon von Ephesos," *RE* 9 A2 (1967) 2055–2089, all argue for epitomization, while T. Hägg, "Die Ephesiaka des Xenophon Ephesios, Original oder Epitome?" *C&M* 27 (1966 [1969]) 118–61, concludes that the question is not capable of resolution. Most scholars, like G. Anderson, *Eros Sophistes. Ancient novelists at play* (Chico, CA: Scholars Press, 1982) 62, acknowledge the likelihood of epitomization. On the other side, C. Ruiz-Montero in her stylistic analysis "Una interpretación del "estilo kai" de Jenofonte de Éphesus,"

There is another significant way in which the *Ephesiaka* deviates from standard novelistic practice: the characters' adventures are not explicitly supervised by the gods, namely Eros and Tyche. In the other novels, Eros the god of love oversees the development of the love affair between the heroine and hero, and Tyche, Chance personified, is responsible for the bizarre circumstances which hinder the fulfillment of that love. For instance, in Chariton's novel, Eros instigates the love of the heroine and hero (1.1), which he then impedes by causing a succession of men to fall in love with the heroine, and Tyche causes events which prolong the lovers' separation—the heroine's pregnancy (2.8), the interception of an important letter (4.5), a war (6.8). And in Longus' novel's carefully controlled pastoral setting which is strongly identified with Eros' presence, Eros himself governs the heroine's and hero's erotic progress by contriving various events—the wolf chase (1.11) and Philetas' love lesson (2.3–8), while the influence of Tyche is apparent in events at and beyond the boundaries of that pastoral world—the pirate raid (1.28) and the war (2.20). Other gods do appear in the novels, but none with the consistency and frequency of Eros and Tyche. Though Eros is mentioned in the first book of the *Ephesiaka*, he drops out of the remainder of the novel, and Tyche personified does not enter the story at all. Other divinities do intervene, notably an unnamed god of Egypt and the Nile god at 4.2, and the god Apis delivers an oracle through children at 5.4, but their participation is incidental—and an assortment of other gods are named, though none enters the action of the *Ephesiaka*. In a novel in which the heroine must ward off eleven would-be rapists, and the Liebespaar must travel the *entire* known world, its author might be expected to reintroduce Eros and Tyche at key points to "refocus" the reader, but this does not happen. The *Ephesiaka*'s story abounds with the sort of activity that Eros and Tyche cause in the other novels, but the gods themselves are scarcely to be found. Is the novel's haphazard representation of Eros and Tyche explainable by means other than the epitome theory? This paper proposes to evaluate and account for the *Ephesiaka*'s treatment of Eros and Tyche using narratology, and then to apply the findings to the novel in general, resulting in an alternative to the epitome theory.

Emerita 50 (1982) 305–23, identifies elements of oral style . In this, Ruiz-Montero anticipates J. N. O'Sullivan, *Xenophon of Ephesus: his Compositional Technique and the Birth of the Novel* (New York: de Gruyter, 1995), who argues that the novel is a product of formulaic composition. For my treatment of O'Sullivan's thesis, see the article in n. 1.

The Epitome Theory

First, let us consider Bürger's epitome theory. It can explain the *Ephesiaka*'s brevity; not only is it the shortest of the Greek romances, with book four being noticeably shorter than the other books, but the *Suda* records ten books in this novel to the five we have.[5] It can explain the absence of gods; Merkelbach sees traces of Helios the sun god due to the significant rôle his temple plays in the reunion of the couple,[6] while others look for Isis the Egyptian all-purpose goddess, based on the reference to her in the oracle,[7] or also Eros, who as I have noted is usually an important figure in these romances. It can explain the missing motivation for some events: for instance, Habrokomes' journey to Italy in the fourth book and the human sacrifice of Anthia in the second book.[8] The epitome theory can explain the often terse and carelessly informal introductions of characters or places. For instance, the first mention of Hippothoos, the leader of the brigands, is unconventionally curt.[9] Usually introductions state the name of the person in the nominative case, often accompanied by τοὔνομα, and his or her national origin and occupation, for example, "there was this man named Hippothoos, who was from Perinthus, and fate had made him the captain of a gang of bandits. . . ." In the text, however, Hippothoos is acknowledged rather obliquely: ὑπὸ τῶν περὶ τὸν Ἱππόθοον τὸν λῃστὴν συνελήφθησαν—"[Anthia and the ship's crew] were captured by Hippothoos' robber band," with Hippothoos in the accusative case (2.11.11.3).[10] The robbers' cave is also casually used as a point of reference, when it has never been mentioned before: καὶ οὐ πρὸ πολλοῦ τοῦ ἄντρου τοῦ λῃστρικοῦ—"and not far from the robbers' cave . . ." (2.14.1.3). Such familiarity could imply some previously excised mention. And the epitome theory can also explain the

---

[5] Suda, s.v. "Xenophon Ephesios": ἱστορικός. Ἐφεσιακά· ἔστι δὲ ἐρωτικὰ βιβλία ί, περὶ Ἀβροκόμου καὶ Ἀνθίας· καὶ περὶ τῆς πόλεως Ἐφεσίων· καὶ ἄλλα.

[6] R. Merkelbach, *Roman und Mysterium in der Antike* (Munich: C. H. Beck, 1962) 91–113, and Gärtner, "Xenophon," argue that passages related to the cult of Helios were removed during epitomization.

[7] R. E. Witt, "Isis-Hellas," *PCPhS* 12 (1966) 48–69, associates Isis with Artemis. J. G. Griffiths, "Xenophon of Ephesus on Isis and Alexandria," *Hommages à M. J. Vermaseren* (EPRO 68; 3 vols.; Leiden: E. J. Brill, 1978) 1.409–37, with K. Kerényi, *Die griechisch-orientalische Romanliteratur in religionsgeschichtlicher Beleuchtung. Ein Versuch mit Nachbetrachtungen* (Tübingen: Mohr [Siebeck], 1927) argues that Artemis is a doublet of Isis.

[8] Bürger, "Xenophon," 47–48.

[9] Bürger, "Xenophon," 43–45.

[10] The Teubner text is used for quotations.

Ephesiaka's choppy pace and its scarcity of digression and elaborate description—both of which are hallmarks of a Greek romance. There are numerous places in the text where, as Bürger notes,[11] ripe opportunities for digression and ecphrasis are missed. Most notably, the shipwreck in book two is allotted but one sentence, whereas Achilles Tatius' novel lovingly devotes five chapters to its shipwreck. In addition, several of Anthia's would-be ravishers are disposed of rather summarily—granted, of course, that our heroine must defend herself against eleven rapists, while other heroines have merely two or three to deal with in twice or thrice the narrative time. But this brings up an important issue, which betrays the major weakness of Bürger's argument: this is the question of authorial design, that some scenes are shorter than others precisely because the author wrote them that way. Bürger attempts to circumvent this objection by asserting that the epitomization does not extend to the entire novel, but only to certain sections. He lists those places unscathed by the editor's axe as all of book one, the first half of book two, chapters two through ten of book three, the second chapter of book four and the end of book five.[12] It is tempting to call Bürger's epitome theory a catch-all for whatever problems bother a particular reader, but we will return to this analysis.

The Representation of Eros

Let us now turn to the representation of the god Eros in the *Ephesiaka*. The romance starts off conventionally enough with the introductions of the heroine and hero, both visions of loveliness and both committed to virginity. The hero is so enraptured with his own appearance that he neglects the worship of Eros, and thus engenders the god's enmity. Eros' interest in the couple's lives is thus motivated by his desire for revenge: ὁ δὲ Ἔρως ἔτι ὠργίζετο καὶ μεγάλην τῆς ὑπεροψίας ἐνενοεῖτο τιμωρίαν εἰσπράξασθαι τὸν Ἀβροκόμην—"but Eros was still furious and intended to take a terrible revenge on Habrokomes for his arrogance" (1.4.5.6–8). If the reader expects the standard divine revenge motif story, she will be disappointed. For Eros sets the couple's adventures in motion and then fades from the text. Yet his involvement is highly explicit in the first book: he becomes angered with the hero, he plans the pair's love and brings them into contact, he conquers their emotions and he sees them married.

---

[11] Bürger, "Xenophon," 41–43.
[12] Bürger, "Xenophon," 41.

The god's desire for further vengeance (as if falling in love is not punishment enough itself) is coordinated with the oracle at Kolophon, which foretells a long period of suffering and travels; this adventure part of the novel is heralded by the narrator's comment towards the end of book one: ἀλλ' οὐχὶ τὸ εἱμαρμένον ἐπελέλησто, [ἀλλ'] οὐδὲ ὅτῳ ἐδόκει ταῦτα θεῷ ἡμέλει—"but fate had not forgotten, nor had the god overlooked his plans" (1.10.2.3–4), which implies that Eros will have a further hand in the couple's story. This, however, is the final time Eros plays an overt role in the action, though he is mentioned twice more in the dialogue of the hero and heroine. The first of these instances is at the beginning of book two when Habrokomes, faced with the first of many oppressive erotic situations, echoes the god's intention: τιμωρίαν ἤδη με ὁ θεὸς τῆς ὑπερηφανίας εἰσπράττει—"the god is already taking revenge on me for my arrogance" (2.1.2.5–6). Anthia too recalls Eros' power; when she awakens in her tomb at the approach of the robbers: δυοῖν ἀνάκειμαι θεοῖς, Ἔρωτι καὶ Θανάτῳ—"I am a sacrifice to two gods, Eros and Death" (3.8.4.5–6).

Though Eros is no longer the acknowledged director of the couple's experiences, his complicity is strongly suggested by the highly erotic nature of their adventures and the frequency of suitor turnover. The most significant means by which the influence of Eros is implied is the physical mechanism of falling in love. This process never varies, and is common to all the Greek romances. The major component is the initial visual contact that inflames passion, that is, "love at first sight," which is followed by continual or habitual visual contact, which drives the lover to do wild and crazy things. For Habrokomes and Anthia, once Eros makes them see each other, they are overcome with love: "then they saw each other, and Anthia was captivated by Habrokomes, while Eros got the better of Habrokomes; he kept looking at the girl and in spite of himself could not take his eyes off her" (1.3.1.4–7). Likewise, the many people who fall in love with either of the couple always do so after explicit visual exposure, even though it is not expressly Eros who makes them fix their eyes. For instance, the brigand Korymbos falls for Habrokomes "from seeing him so often daily during the course of the voyage, and his contact with the boy inflamed him all the more" (1.14.7.4–7); and for the eirenarch Perilaus "the frequent sight of the girl led him to fall in love with her" (2.13.6.1–2). The notion of love, if not of Eros himself, is given a prominent position throughout the work.

Focalization

Why, then, does Eros disappear from the story at the end of book one? Is his rôle a hazard of epitomization? Is it that much easier to write "Polyidos fell in love with Anthia" rather than "Eros made Polyidos fall in love with Anthia"? The absence of Eros after the end of book one, and the paucity of active deities in general is striking in the *Ephesiaka* especially because it seems that the characters pass through the temple of a different god every page (actually eleven gods in all), though the narrative shows no deity stirring him or herself to participation. There is a change in the way the whole idea of love is portrayed after book one, and a change in the narrative's representation of action, but this, I propose, is due not to an abbreviation of the story, but to a shift in focalization.[13] Focalization is the perspective adopted by the narrator through which the story is told. A narrative can be focalized through one or more characters, or have no focalization at all. The first book is narrated with zero focalization. That is, the narrator relates the story from an external, omniscient point of view. Thus, possessing privileged knowledge unavailable to the characters, the narrator can depict the intentions and activity of Eros, who is naturally beyond the mortal characters' perception, and the narrator can also report the characters' intimate thoughts and feelings. Starting with the end of the first book, however, the narrator tells the story mainly from the mortal characters' points of view. With this variable internal focalization, the narrator no longer describes extrasensory phenomena, but restricts himself to a human perspective and understanding. Correspondingly, there is much less description of characters and surroundings—these elements are important for an omniscient narrator but not for a poor, suffering character. The intense character-oriented action does not accommodate the soul-searching soliloquies which abound in other Greek romances; characters in the *Ephesiaka* seldom take time to analyze their situations or fix blame upon any god for their troubles. If ever the characters vocalize their feelings, it is always regarding the human sphere of activity—a prayer for help, an expression of anxiety, a vow of chastity—characters almost never venture to attribute their sufferings to gods. After Eros is used to jump-start the story, and the tale is on its way, the narrator shifts

---

[13] See G. Genette, *Narrative Discourse, an Essay in Method* (J. E. Levin, trans.; Ithaca: Cornell University Press, 1980) 161–211, esp. 185–211, for definition and discussion of focalization.

into fast-paced action, the effect of which is heightened by focalizing through the characters.

Habrokomes and Anthia are concerned foremost with what is happening to them, and the immediacy of their individual plights is conveyed through the focalized narrative. For instance, book four, which covers Hippothoos' journey from Tarsos in Cilicia to Ethiopia, three thwarted erotic encounters for Anthia, and Habrokomes' trial, two near executions in Egypt and voyage to Italy, is given as much narrative time as the leisurely and detailed account of the couple's falling in love and marriage in book one. No longer is any disinterested hint given of impending events, but the characters deal with their experiences as they come. B. P. Reardon has characterized Xenophon's work as "breathless,"[14] and this indeed is what the reader feels like after reading it—the narrative careens from one character to the other and barely avoids several collisions before hopping the track once more. After making its shift to internally focalized narrative, the *Ephesiaka* returns once briefly to its original non-focalized, omniscient perspective, when the gods of Egypt intervene on Habrokomes' behalf and save him twice from death in book four.

What happens to Eros for the rest of the story? Although the god himself can no longer be a principal actor, because of the limited perspective of the narrative, his hand can be seen in love-inspired actions which occur throughout the story, especially in the operation of "love at first sight," and in the way that the succession of suitors is used to further the adventures of the couple, as Eros drives the other romances' storylines. The inconsistency in the composition of the *Ephesiaka* complicates its narratological analysis. Hägg emphasizes the narrator's distance from his narrative and his shifting among different characters' points of view.[15] While I characterize the narrative after book one as basically internally focalized and favor this reading because it explains the haphazard representation of the divine, M. Fusillo takes the focalization of the first book as a pattern for the rest of the novel, which he says has a zero focalization with occasional lapses into variable focalization.[16] This

---

[14] B. P. Reardon, *The Form of Greek Romance* (Princeton: Princeton University Press, 1991) 27.

[15] T. Hägg, *Narrative Technique in Ancient Greek Romances. Studies of Chariton, Xenophon Ephesius, and Achilles Tatius* (Stockholm: Almqvist & Wiksells, 1971) 120–124.

[16] M. Fusillo, "Textual Patterns and Narrative Situations in the Greek Novel," *GCN* 1 (1988) 17–31, esp. 25–26.

interpretation, however, explains none of the *Ephesiaka*'s narrative difficulties, and Fusillo seems to confuse point of view with focalization; T. Hägg, in fact, concludes that the question of epitomization cannot be answered and does not commit himself to either view.

Focalization and Tyche

The *Ephesiaka*'s handling of Tyche supports the case for internal focalization. The complete absence of Tyche from the narrative is extraordinary for this work in particular, for the *Ephesiaka* packs at least three times the action of Chariton's novel into less than half the text space. The density of action and event in the *Ephesiaka* might make one suppose that it relies heavily upon gods to manoeuvre its characters and organize its events. But this could not be further from the actual case. The premise of establishing Eros as the explicit cause of events is abandoned by the end of the first book, at which point one would expect Tyche to appear but she does not. Nevertheless, the *Ephesiaka*'s story progresses in the same vein as the other Greek romances—travel, adventures, numerous rivals for the affections of the heroine and hero. The novel seems to dispense with all divine causation, save what is convenient for the plot (for example, the Egyptian gods' double rescue of the hero). Other Greek romances use Tyche to render plausible and acceptable events which might otherwise strain the limits of credibility for the reader—for instance, in Chariton's novel Kallirhoe is ignorant of her pregnancy for two months until Tyche confronts her with a moral dilemma (2.8.5). Divine intervention legitimizes the event. In the *Ephesiaka* there are any number of suspect coincidences that obstruct the logical flow of the story, but that remain unjustified by divine providence. Yet Tyche is nowhere to be seen.

But the idea of chance is not wholly missing from the novel. When Habrokomes' and Anthia's problems are just starting, the brigand Euxinos tells the hero something which may be considered programmatic for the novel: δεῖ δέ σε τῇ τύχῃ πάντα λογίσασθαι καὶ στέργειν τὸν κατέχοντα δαίμονα—"but you must put everything down to Chance and accept the fate that rules over you" (1.16.3.4–5); then, the penultimate event in the story, Anthia's recognition of Leukon and Rhode, her long-lost servants, is prefaced by their asking her: ἀλλὰ τίς ἐνταῦθα ἄγει σε τύχη;—"but what Chance brings you here?" (5.12.5.4–5). The couple's adventures are framed by references to Tyche, which suggests her providence. In fact, Tyche is absent only in name; her presence is nearly palpable. How then can her conspicuous absence be explained? The point at which Tyche is expected to take over, namely, the end of book one as the characters' adventures get under way, is precisely the point at which the narrative's focalization shifts from an external to an internal perspective. Characters are no more privy to the workings of Tyche than they are to Eros' machinations. Thus, like Eros, Tyche's participation must be inferred through the sorts of events she is likely to cause. There is no shortage of unexpected circumstances worthy of Tyche, from the couple's capture by pirates at the end of book one, to Anthia's shipwreck in book two, to Habrokomes' shipwreck and enslavement in book three, to Hippothoos' timely and unwitting rescue of Anthia from the brothel in book five. The *Ephesiaka* is full of surprising situations and unpredictable twists in the action; in a typical non-focalized Greek romance, these occurrences would be the province of Tyche, but as the bulk of the *Ephesiaka* is focalized through its characters, Tyche's effects, rather than Tyche herself, are represented.

Focalization in the *Ephesiaka*

Thus in the *Ephesiaka*, gods are in control but their presence and operation are not explicit. This makes the action seem more chaotic and aimless than it otherwise might appear. For gods generally provide a framework, however loose, and contribute a sense of direction for the story. Even the events described in the oracle, which are usually programmatic for the story, become lost in the vast array of incidents. Without gods, this work could appear to be a disorganized collection of folktales, which has been proposed as an explanation for the *Ephesiaka*'s apparent disunity.[17] Narratological analysis restores the divine to its proper place in the story.

Shifting focalization can account for the unusual representation of the gods Eros and Tyche in the *Ephesiaka*. Can narratology also help to explain the work's many other narrative problems? I have already shown how the explicit participation of any god is precluded by the narrator's adopted perspective. Moreover, the often abrupt and cursory introduction of characters and places is a consequence of internal focalization; Habrokomes and Anthia are naturally limited by the boundaries of their human knowledge from the full background of any

---

[17] G. Dalmeyda, ed., *Xénophon d'Éphèse. Les Éphésiaques ou le roman d'Habrocomès et d'Anthia* (Paris: Les Belles Lettres, 1926) xxvii-xxxi, gives a good discussion of the folktale element in the *Ephesiaka*.

particular character they meet, unlike of course the narrator. Thus when Hippothoos is introduced by the clause "[Anthia and company] were captured by Hippothoos' robber band," this is giving all the information the heroine Anthia has at that moment: she has been abducted by robbers and their leader's name is Hippothoos; it would be ridiculous to expect the heroine to know more of the brigand's circumstances. Likewise, bringing the robbers' cave into the story for the first time as a point of reference might not be expected of an omniscient narrator, but seems perfectly natural coming from a character's point of view. The lack of motivation for certain events is also understandable; the reason for Anthia's sacrifice is not given precisely because the episode is told from her ignorant point of view, and not from that of the bandits.

The *Ephesiaka*'s choppy pace and the narrative's uneven texture are also attributable to the changes in focalization; the story's perspective shifts not only from Anthia to Habrokomes and back, but depending upon their individual situations, the narrative tempo varies as well. For instance, book three commences with four relatively slowly paced Teubner pages of Hippothoos telling his life story to Habrokomes, which is followed by four and a half pages of the more quickly paced tale of Anthia avoiding marriage to Perilaus by taking a drug, then awakening in her tomb and being stolen by robbers; the following two pages slow down the narrative, as Habrokomes learns about Anthia's supposed death and mourns her at her empty tomb, then the tempo speeds up as Habrokomes leaves in a rush for Alexandria; next there is a fast-paced half page of Anthia fending off the unwanted advances of the Indian Psammis who purchases her, which is succeeded by a very fast-paced one page account of Habrokomes' shipwreck, enslavement, dealings with the love crazy woman Kyno, her husband's murder and his own arrest. A more talented author might try to smoothe over the rough parts, but as it is, the *Ephesiaka* proceeds by fits and starts. The *Ephesiaka*'s capacity for artistic expression and description is also held in by the narrative's focalization, as I have discussed above. As the story is told from the characters' perspectives, it focuses upon what immediately concerns them, namely, what happens to them; Anthia is not going to pause to take note of the elaborate interior decoration of the brothel when she is intent upon guarding her chastity, nor is Habrokomes likely to keep a blow-by-blow account of his shipwreck when his own life is at stake. In fact, aside from the first book, the parts of the narrative which receive the most detailed treatment are the passages where the heroine or hero are least involved and thus have more attention to devote to observation. The *Ephesiaka*'s focalization constrains its length to a certain extent; granted, the work could have been longer if it had been told with zero focalization throughout, as in the first book, but how much longer is a question of creativity and ability. The character-oriented perspective limits the narrative's focus, compacting much more action than description into a short narrative time, and, as summary is more frequently employed than scene, much less attention is given to details and elaborations, such as digressions, character introductions and character motivation. All of these factors contribute to the frenetic quality of the narrative.

The Epitome Theory Reconsidered

I have tried to show that most of the *Ephesiaka*'s narrative infelicities can be explained apart from the epitome theory. But what of the epitome theory itself? The most convincing strike against it is its convenience, how it can be used at discretion to resolve any incongruities in the story. Unlike narratology, the epitome theory does not encompass a general explanation for the *Ephesiaka*, but serves mainly to cover up its blemishes. Moreover, as an epitome, the *Ephesiaka* would be a much worse job than as a novel, for inconsequential details, such as Anthia and the brigand Amphinomous feeding their dogs (note that this is in a passage Bürger thinks is epitomized) or Habrokomes' brief second trip to Sicily, are retained but potentially significant actions of gods (Isis, Helios or perhaps Eros) are excised. Stylistic analysis of the *Ephesiaka* also does not support epitomization: C. Ruiz-Montero, in "Una interpretación del "estilo kai" de Jenofonte de Éphesus," argues that the highly frequent and consistent paratactic use of καί in the *Ephesiaka* is a feature of oral style. Ruiz-Montero associates Xenophon's style with Herodotus and the Ionian writers, rather than with Homer, as J. N. O'Sullivan (see n. 4) who finds in the *Ephesiaka* features of formulaic composition a la epic. Furthermore, the *Suda*'s record of ten books to the five which make up the *Ephesiaka* as we have it need not be given too much weight; not only is the *Suda* notoriously unreliable, but numerals themselves are likely to become confused—in this case a scribe could have easily mistaken an upper case iota for an epsilon. The epitome theory also assumes a certain quality of work, which is probably unreasonable for this author. Consistency is not always a priority among the novelists (who did not have a bank of editors to scrutinize their every word), whereas telling an exciting story full of action and adventure is paramount. The epitome theory hinders rather than promotes understanding of this work.

Furthermore, comparison of Xenophon's work with known epitomes from Photios, the ninth century patriarch of Constantinople, locates the *Ephesiaka* stylistically between a novel and an epitome, but with more novelistic features.[18] Some rather obvious departures Photios makes from the novels, including Xenophon's, are his direct evaluations of style, content and quality of the work at hand, bibliographical material, and editorial introductory comments like "the twenty-fourth book presents . . ." (110b). Most striking about Photios' summaries is their lack of description, of places and actions, and especially of the Liebespaar: in his entry on Iamblichos' *Babyloniaka*, the only reference to Sinonis' and Rhodanes' appearances is καλὴ καὶ καλὸς τὴν ὄψιν (74a), whereas Xenophon spends his first chapter articulating how lovely Habrokomes is and what sort of effect his beauty has on others. All novels are quite generous with this particular detail. Photios not only excludes ecphrases,[19] but he also eschews description, and at times even acknowledgment, of emotions, which usually indicate characters' motivations for their actions. Instead, Photios focuses on action, and rarely includes any quotations, let alone dialogue,[20] relying on indirect statement where Xenophon and the other novelists use direct quotation. Photios' epitomes also contain much paratactic construction, both in the narrative and within indirect statement, listing long series of developments and incidents (cf. 51a, 76b–77a and 109b), a feature which Ruiz-Montero has observed in Xenophon's novel. Yet while Xenophon does cover narrative territory at a brisk clip, he does not encapsulate his characters' adventures in quite so cursory a form. For example, Anthia has one of her most brief encounters with Anchialos (4.5), but this scene is fleshed out in some detail, the narrator comments on Anchialos' disposition, his continual attacks upon her chastity and her reactions (including a quotation), and his final rape attempt at which Anthia defends herself and accidentally kills him. Though abrupt, this is nevertheless much more detailed than Photios' report of Sinonis' murder

---

[18] Of the five Greek romances, Photios provides a summary only of Heliodoros' novel, and mentions Achilles Tatius' novel only to criticize it for being ὑπέραισχρον καὶ ἀκάθαρτον (65b).

[19] Though he will note if they occur in the original (cf. 77a).

[20] Quotations are used only for clarity: cf. three times in the article on Iamblichos at 77b.

of Setapos under comparable circumstances in the Iamblichos section, which is allotted a mere one and one-half sentences (76b). Yet like Xenophon's, Photios' transitions are sometimes awkward: e.g., καὶ ταῦτα μὲν ὧδε προὔβαινε—"and things progressed in this way" (78a), or the ubiquitous favorite ἐν θ'—"meanwhile."[21] While Xenophon's *Ephesiaka* is not as plush as other novels, it is certainly a step or two above an epitome, and a Photian epitome at that.

Conclusion

The argument for the epitomization of the *Ephesiaka* is an argument from convenience, an attempt to explain away whatever bothers the arguer's sensibility. As I have just shown, the *Ephesiaka* more closely resembles a novel than an epitome. Narratology can explain more systematically the inconsistencies in this work, most of which result from a change in the *Ephesiaka*'s purpose and focalization: the first book carefully establishes Eros' revenge motif at a generous narrative pace, then starting with book two the novel quickly abandons Eros and instead begins to pack as much action as possible into the story. The oracle of the Egyptian god Apis in book five is an excellent example of divine machinations viewed from a character's perspective; Anthia prays to the god, but the god's response is conveyed through the medium of the children playing in front of the temple. The reduced role of the gods after book one accommodates the intense character-oriented action, which is accompanied by a shift from zero focalization to an internal focalization through the characters. Reading Xenophon's work as a novel told mainly from the characters' perspectives lets the narrative stand on its own merits. While the *Ephesiaka*'s artistry might not win him a Pulitzer in today's world, Xenophon would probably find himself deluged with offers for the movie rights.

---

[21] See Hägg, *Narrative Technique,* 164–72, for Xenophon's often unimaginative transitions.

Setting the Stage for Romances:
Xenophon of Ephesus and the Ecphrasis

Chris Shea
Ball State University

The *Ephesiaca* is the poor relation of the ancient romances, which are themselves the poor relations of a variety of literary genres. But perhaps the "incompetent" Xenophon (as Bryan Reardon calls him) has bungled his way into the wrong classification—as he has (apparently) bungled so much else.[1] It may be that the *Ephesiaca* is not just a bad *Daphnis and Chloe* or *Aeneid* or even a bad *Chaereas and Callirhoe,* it may belong to a rather different genre altogether.

One of the more curious aspects of this text is its handling of the story-line. The *Ephesiaca,* without much else to say—without a drive to pungent social commentary, for example—has surprising lapses in its remote, third-person narration. We might, in fact, call the *Ephesiaca* a kind of "content-depleted" text: in certain respects, the text has not even provided its audience with enough information for adequate under-standing.

Observe, for example, the case of the missing horse. In 2.12.3 Habrocomes is simply teleported from the scene without reference to the mode of his conveyance

ἔωθεν δὲ ἀναστὰς ἤλαυνε τὴν ἐπὶ Κιλικίας

This paucity of detail has disturbed Georges Dalmeyda, the French translator-editor of the 1926 and 1962 Budé editions, as it might well the general audience. He supplies the horse from 2.14.5

αὐτοὺς καὶ τοὺς ἵππους ἀνελάμβανον· ἦν γὰρ ⟨καὶ⟩ τῷ Ἱπποθόῳ
ἵππος ἐν τῇ ὕλῃ κρυπτόμενος

---

[1] B. P. Reardon, *The Form of Greek Romance* (Princeton: Princeton University Press, 1991) 127. Reardon's, as a straightforward literary study, is monumental in scope and certainly ranks among the most important contemporary studies of the genre of the ancient romance. But he is rather less useful in regard to Xenophon than to the other romance writers, as this comment betrays.

and translates

> . . . levé dès la pointe de jour, il prend [footnote], à cheval, la route de la Cilicie
>
> rising at dawn, he took, on horseback, the road to Cilicia.[2]

He then comments that earlier translators had simply rendered this *in Ciliciam progreditur* ("he made his way to Cilicia"), failing to note the method of transport specified at the end of the book.

He is quite right, of course, to point out Xenophon's lapse of attention here. After all, the closest modern equivalent in theme to this work would be some roistering "Adventures of Anthia and Habrocomes" mini-series, in which mounting up or being hauled off in a variety of conveyances would punctuate every big scene. There are other missed opportunities in this work: consider the mysterious case of Hyperanthes' hair. In 3.3.3 the bandit chief Hippothoos, bewailing to Habrocomes the death of his friend and lover Hyperanthes,

Λέγων ἐδείκνυέ τε τὴν κόμην καὶ ἐπεδάκρυεν αὐτῇ

finished speaking and showed the lock of hair and wept over it.

Just a few lines above (3.2.13), however, in telling the tale of Hyperanthes' drowning and burial,

Ἐγὼ δὲ τοσοῦτον ἠδυνήθην τὸ σῶμα διασῶσαι ἐπὶ τὴν γῆν καὶ θάψαι· καὶ πολλὰ δακρύσας καὶ στενάξας, ἀφελὼν λείψανα

It was all I could do to bring his body ashore and bury it; and I cried and moaned for a long time. I took up what was left . . .

Now, we might ask, what pulp fiction writer of any age would have neglected Habrocomes' horse and Hyperanthes' hair?[3]

Elsewhere, moreover, the author of the *Ephesiaca* is guilty of more than just a failure to exploit prime opportunities to stir his audience's interest. There are puzzling continuity errors to be encountered in this work: a neglected oracle (1.6.2), a dream-apparition (Habrocomes' father) who

---

[2] Georges Dalmeyda, *Xénophon d'Ephèse Les Ephésiaques, ou le roman d'Habrocomès et d'Anthia* (Paris: Les Belles Lettres, 1926[1], 1962[2]) 32. All quotations from the Greek text are drawn from the 1962 edition unless otherwise indicated. I have also relied on the edition of Petrus Hofman Peerlkamp (*Xenophontis Ephesii De Anthia et Habrocome Ephesiacorum libri V* [Harlemi: apud viduam Adriani Loosjes, 1818]) and, to a lesser extent, on the most recent edition, of Antonius D. Papanikolaou (*Xenophontis Ephesii Ephesiacorum libri V De amoribus Anthiae et Abrocomae* [Leipzig: B. G. Teubner, 1973]). In this, I follow Gareth Schmeling's recommendations (*Xenophon of Ephesus* [TWAS 613; Boston: Twayne, 1980] 173–74).

English translations are mine except where indicated.

[3] Dalmeyda (*Ephésiaques*, 32, 38–39) comments on these incongruities.

visits in vain (2.8.2), and such lapses as Perilaos' mysterious awareness of a Habrocomes whose existence Anthia has usually been at some pains to conceal (3.7.3; in 3.5.6–8 she had confided in Eudoxos, not in Perilaos).[4]

The text is replete with such examples, too many, in fact, to ascribe to authorial inattention. Until recently, most critics followed K. Bürger, who in an 1892 work, proposed that our *Ephesiaca* is an epitome of a smoothly constructed original.[5] A new generation of critics, however, is engaged in a re-exploration of ancient prose fiction in general, and the *Ephesiaca* has benefitted from the scrutiny of such astute critics as, among others, Tomas Hägg, Gareth Schmeling, Bryan Reardon, and Richard Pervo.[6]

It may be that one day some Egyptian farmer will upturn a copy of a "complete" *Ephesiaca*, demonstrating beyond doubt Bürger's thesis, but, until then, I prefer to join these latest commentators and begin with the assumption with which, no matter what their methodology, they can all agree: the text we have before us is, with minor adjustments, in the form in which its author intended us to experience it. What, then, can we make of this work?

---

[4] Dalmeyda offers each of these instances as evidence of the epitomizer's hand, as a convert to K. Bürger's point of view (see n. 5, below). For Bürger's influence on Dalmeyda's edition, see Tomas Hägg, "Die Ephesiaka des Xenophon Ephesios—Original oder Epitome?" *C&M* 27 (1966) 118–61, esp. 119–20n.

[5] Bürger first proposed this in "Zu Xenophon von Ephesus" (*Hermes* 27 [1892] 36–67).

For the opposing view, see inter al. Hägg, "Original oder Epitome?" 118–61; *Narrative Technique in Ancient Greek Romances: Studies of Chariton, Xenophon of Ephesus, and Achilles Tatius* (Stockholm: Acta Instituti Atheniensis, 1971); *The Novel in Antiquity* (Berkeley: University of California Press, 1983) 21. For point-by-point refutations of Bürger, see Hägg, "Original oder Epitome?" 124–38; James N. O'Sullivan, *Xenophon of Ephesus: His Compositional Technique and the Birth of the Novel* (New York: de Gruyter, 1995) 100–35.

The *Suda* ascribes to Xenophon of Ephesus a work of ten books, but the attributions of this ancient encyclopedia are now often regarded as suspect. The encyclopedia had rather more prestige in Bürger's day. On the *Suda*'s attribution, cf. Hägg, "Original oder Epitome?" 142–45.

[6] T. Hägg's "Original oder Epitome?," *Narrative Technique,* and *Novel in Antiquity* always provoke thought, but have rather less to say about this particular work.

I have benefitted greatly from my association with the Ancient Fiction and Early Christian and Jewish Narrative Group of the SBL (led by Ron Hock and Charles Hedrick) and recommend enthusiastically the work of two of my colleagues, Richard Pervo's *Profit with Delight: The Literary Genre of the Acts of the Apostles* (Philadelphia: Fortress, 1987) and Gareth Schmeling's *Xenophon of Ephesus.*

For vigorous literary criticism in the grand style, consult Reardon, esp. *Form of Greek Romance.* ("The Form of Ancient Greek Romance" in *The Greek Novel A.D. 1–1985*, [R. Beaton, ed.; London: Croom Helm, 1988] 205–16, has some refinements.)

In the case of other ancient texts, which have been demonstrated to be at least nearly complete, e.g., the *Iliad* and *Odyssey*, a failure of the text to supply or to edit details has been attributed to a stage in which the text was somehow not a text, i.e., was somehow not a written text as a modern reader would understand it, was somehow not a "novel," was not *Moby Dick* or *Wuthering Heights*. In the case of the Homeric epics, it would be generally agreed that such textual glitches might have arisen in a stage in which the text was transmitted through oral performance. Since a performer/singer cannot call back his voice, the argument goes, just such clumsy continuity errors as Habrocomes' "instant" horse must arise. A writer would, of course, reconcile such inconsistencies.

One recent commentator, James N. O'Sullivan, in a 1995 work, has boldly tackled the question of orality with regard to this text. He applies the theory of formulaic composition as refined by Milman Parry earlier in the century to demonstrate affinities between the process which generated the *Ephesiaca* and the oral processes which generated the *Iliad* and *Odyssey*.[7]

While I welcome O'Sullivan's critical stance as one which divorces consideration of the composition of the romances from the composition of the modern novel, I do not find Parry's methodology particularly instructive when applied to the composition of this work. Full-blown, the theory of oral composition of the Homeric works is predicated on the notion that the artist/performer (the song-stitcher) did not have access at once to the techniques of composition and transcription, i.e., the composers of the *Iliad* and *Odyssey* most likely could not have written their contributions to the text, as members of a pre- or proto-literate culture.[8]

The romances, by contrast, are firmly the product of a literate (and self-consciously literate) culture. It is not only that everyone in the romances—women, slaves, pirate chiefs, daughters of pirate chiefs—can read and write; most of the characters do read and write. In fact, letters

---

[7] O'Sullivan, *Xenophon of Ephesus, pass.*, but esp. chap. IV. Note also his remarks (99–100) on the application of his thesis. Cf. also Alexander Scobie, *Aspects of the Ancient Romance and Its Heritage* (Meisenheim am Glan: Anton Hain, 1969) 22.

[8] Parry's original contribution to the problem, made in his 1928 master's thesis for the *doctorat* at Paris, involved the formulaic analysis of noun-epithet combinations in the epics. It fell to his epigoni to extend his observations to formulaic phrases of greater length. A. B. Lord (*The Singer of Tales* [Cambridge: Harvard University Press, 1960]) supplied, from his field study of illiterate itinerant singers, the observation that the ability to write eroded the ability to sing. Among the foundational works of modern theories of oral composition, both of these depend heavily on the analysis of metrical texts.

which send some character haring off in a wrong direction or which file some false accusation could be thought to constitute a standard motif in the romances: consider, for example, the Phaedra and Hippolytus "plot-line."[9]

Moreover, although J. R. Morgan may be thought to have overstated the case a bit in claiming

> . . . these novels are desperately concerned to be part of Greek literature. Their whole fabric is shot through with motifs and patterns which their readers would recognize as deriving from the masterworks of the classical period,

such was the prestige of the Homeric epics at all times and at all levels of society that it might not be unreasonable to argue (as it were) *post Homerum, propter Homerum.*[10] This, it seems to me, is enough to account for the occasional parallel in theme or plot, and, while the language of the work is stylized, surely, "formulae" as applied to Parry's noun-epithet combinations, for example, is perhaps a bit of a misnomer.

I would contend, however, that O'Sullivan and other recent commentators have made an incalculably valuable contribution by their rigorous insistence on the integrity of the text as we have it and by their imaginative speculations on the nature of this unusual text.[11] O'Sullivan inspires me in fact to apply a rather different argument drawn from the work done on oral composition and Homer.

It is generally accepted that Homer made an appearance in the epics in the form of Demodocus, the bard of *Odyssey* 8.62–107, 266–366, and 469–586 and Phemius, the bard of *Odyssey* 1.153–155 and 325–352. This observation proved indispensable in ferreting out the compositional secrets of that work.[12] It occurs to me that Xenophon might have

---

[9] For the importance of letters in understanding the world of the ancient novel, see Ronald F. Hock, "The Greek Novel," *Greco-Roman Literature and the New Testament: Selected Forms and Genres* (D. Aune, ed.; Atlanta: Scholars Press, 1988) 141–42. In general, see Hock's work for his lucid commentary and detailed bibliography.

[10] J. R. Morgan, "Make-Believe and Make Believe: The Fictionality of the Greek Novels," in *Lies and Fiction in the Ancient World* (C. Gill and T. P. Wiseman, eds.; Austin: University of Texas Press, 1993) 175–220, esp. 223.

[11] See above, n. 6.

[12] For a complete discussion, see Alfred Heubeck, Stephanie West, and J. B. Hainsworth, *A Commentary on Homer's Odyssey* (Oxford: Clarendon, 1988) 340–350 *ad* 8.62, 103.

Demodocus is singing of the love of Ares and Aphrodite in 8.266–66.

followed Homer in this respect also and insinuated representations of the composition/presentation of the text into the text itself.

In 1.8.2–3 the newly-weds spend their first night together:

Ἦν δὲ αὐτοῖς ὁ θάλαμος ⟨οὕτως⟩ πεποιημένος· κλίνη χρυσῆ στρώμασιν ἔστρωτο πορφυροῖς καὶ ἐπὶ τῆς κλίνης Βαβυλωνία ἐπεποίκιλτο σκηνή· παίζοντες Ἔρωτες, οἱ μὲν Ἀφροδίτην θεραπεύοντες (ἦν δὲ καὶ Ἀφροδίτης εἰκών), οἱ δὲ ἱππεύοντες ἀναβάται στρουθοῖς, οἱ δὲ στεφάνους πλέκοντες, οἱ δὲ ἄνθη φέροντες· 3 ταῦτα ἐν τῷ ἑτέρῳ μέρει τῆς σκηνῆς· ἐν δὲ τῷ ἑτέρῳ Ἄρης ἦν οὐχ ὡπλισμένος, ἀλλ᾽ ὡς πρὸς ἐρωμένην τὴν Ἀφροδίτην κεκοσμημένος, ἐστεφανωμένος, χλανίδα ἔχων· Ἔρως αὐτὸν ὡδήγει, λαμπάδα ἔχων ἡμμένην. Ὑπ᾽ αὐτῇ τῇ σκηνῇ κατέκλιναν τὴν Ἀνθίαν, ἀγαγόντες πρὸς τὸν Ἀβροκόμην, ἐπέκλεισάν τε τὰς θύρας

And their bedchamber was arranged <thus>: a golden bed was strewn with purple bedclothes. And over the bed there was a canopy from Babylon embroidered with Erotes at play: some waiting on Aphrodite (there was a likeness of Aphrodite, too); some, making like cavalrymen, mounting sparrows; some plaiting crowns, some bearing flowers. These things were on one side of the canopy; on the other was Ares, out of armor, dressed for a love-bout with Aphrodite, crowned, wearing a fine cloak. Eros led him on his way, holding a lamp alight . . . Under this canopy they laid Anthia, bringing her to Habrocomes, and they closed the doors.[13]

Herewith an example of one of the fuller descriptions in the work, in the form of a rhetorical *ecphrasis*.[14] It purports to describe a bed-canopy depicting a Hellenistic commonplace: the love of Ares and Aphrodite.

But this ecphrasis rings an interesting change on the old rhetorical stand-by: it is really two ecphraseis. On the first level, it describes a bed-canopy embroidered with a scene dear to sentimental Hellenistic hearts. But when Habrocomes and Anthia are laid beneath the canopy, the whole forms another composition, another scene familiar to Xenophon's audience: Ares and Aphrodite beneath the bed-canopy, a standard of

---

[13] This is still a "content-depleted" description, one might argue: why is Aphrodite given such short shrift? Cf. Dalmeyda, *Ephésiaques* 11–12.

[14] For a complete discussion of the ecphrasis as a literary device (although not all pertains to the ancient variety), see Murray Krieger, *Ekphrasis: The Illusion of the Natural Sign* (Baltimore: Johns Hopkins University Press, 1992).

For ancient examples and theory, there is still no better discussion than that of Paul Friedländer (*Johannes von Gaza und Paulus Silentiarius: Kunstbeschreibungen justinianischer Zeit* [Leipzig: B. G.Teubner, 1912] 1–103). For epic in particular, see C. S. Byre, *Ekphraseis of Works of Art and Places in the Greek Epic from Homer to Nonnus* (Diss, University of Chicago, 1976).

bedroom wall-paintings and mosaics.[15] Our lovers have walked into a wall-painting, have entered another world, in fact, as the shutting of the doors would indicate.

In the classic *ecphrasis*, the shield of Achilles, for example, from *Iliad* 18, or the walls of Dido's temple in *Aeneid* I, or even Eumolpus and the boys in Trimalchio's picture-gallery (Petr. 83–89), the viewer and the reader occupy the same historical reality, we might say. Aeneas can see the Fall of Troy, a historical event, on a wall, and so can we—his perspective is ours.[16] We are asked to engage the narrative at Aeneas' level, feel his emotions, not the emotions of some onlooker—to look with Aeneas, not to look at Aeneas looking. But Anthia and Habrocomes were never in the same plane, as it were, with Aeneas and Eumolpus—they were always at a further remove.

Consider, for example, Xenophon's introduction of the lovers, Anthia

Ἦν δὲ τὸ κάλλος τῆς Ἀνθίας οἷον θαυμάσαι καὶ πολὺ τὰς ἄλλας ὑπερεβάλλετο παρθένους. Ἔτη μὲν τεσσαρεσκαίδεκα ἐγεγόνει, ἤνθει δὲ αὐτῆς τὸ σῶμα ἐπ᾽ εὐμορφίᾳ, καὶ ὁ τοῦ σχήματος κόσμος πολὺς εἰς ὥραν συνεβάλλετο· 6 κόμη ξανθή, ἡ πολλὴ καθειμένη, ὀλίγη πεπλεγμένη, πρὸς τὴν τῶν ἀνέμων φορὰν κινουμένη· ὀφθαλμοὶ γοργοί, φαιδροὶ μὲν ὡς κόρης, φοβεροὶ δὲ ὡς σώφρονος· ἐσθὴς χιτὼν ἁλουργής, ζωστὸς εἰς γόνυ. μεχρὶ βραχιόνων καθειμένος, νεβρὶς περικειμένη, γωρυτὸς ἀνημμένος, τόξα [ὅπλα], ἄκοντες φερόμενοι κύνες ἑπόμενοι. 7 Πολλάκις αὐτὴν ἐπὶ τοῦ τεμένους ἰδόντες Ἐφέσιοι προσεκύνησαν ὡς Ἄρτεμιν. Καὶ τότ᾽ οὖν ὀφθείσης ἀνεβόησε τὸ πλῆθος, καὶ ἦσαν ποικίλαι παρὰ τῶν θεωμένων φωναί, τῶν μὲν ὑπ᾽ ἐκπλήξεως τὴν θεὸν εἶναι λεγόντων, τῶν δὲ ἄλλην τινὰ ὑπὸ τῆς θεοῦ περιποιημένην· προσηύχοντο δὲ πάντες καὶ προσεκύνουν καὶ τοὺς γονεῖς αὐτῆς ἐμακάριζον· ἦν δὲ διαβόητος τοῖς θεωμένοις ἅπασιν Ἀνθία ἡ καλή.

---

[15] Cf., for example, a figured pavement mosaic, fragmentary, but showing a couple seated on a couch under a canopy supported by Erotes discovered in April 1937 in the "House of the Green Carpet" at Antioch. Doro Levi (*Antioch Mosaic Pavements* [2 vols.; Princeton: Princeton University Press, 1947] 1.315–16 and pls. LXXI a, CXXVIII) makes reference to this passage of Xenophon and to other similar scenes in art.

Of course the scene is equally familiar from literary sources, even as an *ecphrasis*; cf. Schmeling, *Xenophon,* 24.

[16] In fact, we are watching Aeneas compose a little ecphrasis of his own (*Aen* 1.459–463); he is not the object of vision.

So remarkable was the beauty of Anthia that she far outshone the other girls. She was fourteen years old, her body was blossoming to beauty, and the great perfection of her figure graced her youth. Her hair was light in color, let down for the most part, plaited a little, stirring at a movement of the breezes. Her eyes were fierce, shining because she was a girl, severe, because she was chaste. Her clothing was a purple tunic hiked up to the knee and let down on the arms. She was wrapped in a fawnskin, a quiver hanging down; she carried her arms, a bow and darts, hounds followed her. Many times seeing her in the sanctuary the Ephesians bowed low thinking she was Artemis. And when she was seen on this occasion, the crowd came out with a variety of exclamations about the sight: some, struck with awe, saying, "It's the goddess!" others saying, "No, it's some double provided by the goddess herself!" and all prayed and made obeisance to her, and they congratulated her parents. And a shout went up from the spectators, "Anthia the beautiful!" (1.2.5–7)

and Habrocomes

ὡς δὲ Ἀβροκόμης μετὰ τῶν ἐφήβων ἐπέστη, τοὐνθένδε, καίτοι καλοῦ ὄντος τοῦ κατὰ τὰς παρθένους θεάματος, πάντες ἰδόντες Ἀβροκόμην ἐκείνων ἐπελάθοντο, ἔτρεψαν δὲ τὰς ὄψεις ἐπ' αὐτὸν βοῶντες ὑπὸ τῆς θέας ἐκπεπληγμένοι, «καλὸς Ἀβροκόμης» λέγοντες, «καὶ οἷος οὐδὲ εἷς καλοῦ μίμημα θεοῦ.»

When Habrocomes appeared among the ephebes, although the spectacle of the maidens was beautiful, on seeing Habrocomes all forgot the girls and turned their eyes to him, shouting, inspired by the sight, "Oh beautiful Habrocomes," they cried, "no one can surpass him! In beauty he is the very image of a god!" (1.2.8)

Note the proliferation of words for the act of seeing, for gazing on, for being thunderstruck at the sight of—Anthia and Habrocomes. In some essential sense, they exist to be seen, their value lies in being seen. Thus, for example, it is not only that they fall in love with each other at first sight; all over the Mediterranean Anthia's sweet solicitude or Habrocomes' ferocious fidelity beg comment, while pirates and princes have only eyes for them. And we are invited to look at them, to experience their adventures at the audience's remove, at the level of the crowds at Tyre and Ephesus, for example, who worship them on sight.[17]

One might also note, in passing, that the picture of Anthia is, like the Babylonia bed-canopy, another double portrait. Xenophon is following fairly closely Vergil's introduction of Venus in *Aeneid* I.[18] But Venus is

---

[17] Eva Keuls (*Plato and Greek Painting* [Leiden: E. J. Brill, 1978] 42–44) has argued that this is the very essence of fiction in an ancient milieu influenced by Platonic aesthetics.

[18] Cf. Aeneas' encounter with his mother on the way into the city of Carthage (1.314–320). Vergil has clearly reworked *Od.* 6.102–109 (Odysseus meets Nausicaa and the girls) for the introduction of Dido (*Aen* 1.498–506), but, as for 1.314–320, I

disguised when her son Aeneas encounters her—as a devotee of Artemis. Observe the antitheses in Xenophon's description, the doubled and contradictory references to fierce self-sufficiency and soft invitation. Anthia is both goddesses—she makes sheep's eyes from her wolf's clothing. Xenophon's audience is unlikely to miss the reference to one of antiquity's best-sellers, but I might mention that the ancient reader had two ways to get this message: the book and the many wall-paintings, mosaics, etc., which captured moments or sequences of Vergil's text. In other words, Xenophon did not require the poet's narrative as his model; the painter's narrative might have served—and this description might also be an ecphrasis of a work of art.[19]

But this introduction of the major characters may give us another clue to the nature of this work: in what way would Anthia and Habrocomes differ from images of the gods? Hasn't Anthia been made by the goddess as another self?[20] Isn't Habrocomes the likeness of a god?[21] In some essential way, the two lovers are works of art—statues, perhaps. The author summoned them to life, softened the stone to flesh, like Pygmalion, spun them round the Mediterranean in an action-packed narrative, and then returned them to stone again, via the stele which is set up to commemorate their adventures in the last chapter of the work.

ἐνέθεσαν ἀναθήματα καὶ δὴ καὶ [τὴν] γραφὴν τῇ θεῷ ἀνέθεσαν
πάντα ὅσα τε ἔπαθον καὶ ὅσα ἔδρασαν

straightway they went to the temple of Artemis . . . and they set up a memorial and dedicated an inscription to the goddess detailing all they had done and all they had undergone. (5.15.2)

---

agree with R. G. Austin (*P. Vergili Maronis Aeneidos Liber Primus* [Oxford: Clarendon, 1971] 118 *ad* 314) that "Vergil's scene has nothing secondhand about it." Xenophon's, on the other hand, does, and, until the discovery of some source common to both, I believe Vergil is the model here.

Callimachus' charming hymn to the little girl Artemis may have influenced some details in Vergil's account; cf. *h.* 3.11–12.

[19] For the distinction between the author's narrative and the painter's, consider the "narrative" of the Aeneid found in a floor mosaic of the 4th cent. CE from Low Ham (Taunton, Castle Museum). In five "shots" (*emblemata*), the painter has made a romance of the "history" of Dido and Aeneas. Cf. Richard Brilliant, *Roman Art from the Republic to Constantine* (London: Phaidon, 1974) fig. III.15, 145.

Reardon, *Form of the Greek Romance, pass.*, is concerned to make the romance a purely Greek phenomenon, but even he makes an exception of the *Aeneid*.

[20] If this is indeed what 1.2.7 means; editors have had some difficulty with the text here.

[21] For *mimema* as "artistic representation" see Plato (*Lg* 669e, 796b). Platonic aesthetic theory and the concept of *mimesis* may have some bearing here; see below.

This work might have been imagined to be that inscription. Its author might have been imagined to be spinning a tale around some statuary of a nobler age which had long before lost its votive inscription in its adventurous journey from a plundered Greece to his dining room.

In some basic way, then, I would contend, this narrative not only has ecphraseis, like the *Aeneid* or the *Iliad* or the *Satyricon*, it is an ecphrasis, like *Daphnis and Chloe*. But, of course, this interpretation does not speak to the medium of this message and to the problems with narration which mar the work. To list but a few:

(1) a reluctant narrator who appears only to further the plot (rather than, for example, to comment on the follies of his day, the beauty of nature, the perfidy of big business, etc.);

(2) a narrator whose interventions, moreover, are so sparse or clumsy of detail as to have led a generation of critics to postulate an epitomizer;

(3) narration which occasionally seems to consist of outlines for potential dialogue scenes (descriptions of the characters' apostrophizing the absent lover, or praying, or confiding in a third-party, etc.), which could easily be expanded, with the addition of dialogue, into scenes from a drama;

(4) dialogue scenes where naturalism would decree narration "from on high" (as in the case of characters whose circumstances cannot possibly be imagined as permitting them to speak, or to be heard);[22]

(5) visible or audible (i.e., dramatic) manifestations of the characters' emotions;

(6) the author's indifference to description, of the appearance of most characters, for example, or of the physical setting;

(7) the author's carelessness in leaving uncorrected references to future events which never materialize (the author may be anticipating an audience which cannot refer back to some earlier point in the narrative, as a check).

If we put all these observations together and ask, what in our own world is this work? we would have an easy answer: a movie script, i.e., a work which is written, but not read; which can be experienced in solitary contemplation, but rarely is; which is dialogue-driven, even against the laws of nature (all that talk in the cockpits of open planes, for example); which has brief narrative passages which serve mainly to propel

------

[22] The speech of Habrocomes' attendant in 1.14.2 is a classic example, cf. Dalmeyda, (*Ephésiaques*, 18, xxx) and his comments on verisimilitude, and further, below.

characters into and out of various situations and locales; which tolerates lapses in continuity on the presumption its audience cannot refer back; and which is dependent for much of its descriptive coloring on the other arts which always attend it (set and costume design, photography, etc.).[23]

I would argue, then, that this might be a performancial text. Now, the connection between the ancient romances and drama has been long noted.[24] Xenophon, too, has his coups de théâtre; "theatremes" we might call them, suspensions of the conventions of prose narration (with biography or history as the model) for a temporary foray into the drama.[25] He even introduces some of them with a phrase which suggests the Aristotelian definition

Ἦν δὲ τὸ θέαμα ἐλεεινόν

It was a pitiable scene to see. (1.14.2, 2.6.3)[26]

But this explanation, although it goes some way, it seems to me, to answering questions raised by this "content-depleted" text, does not resolve all the difficulties. Consider this "theatreme" in 1.14.2–6 (introduced by the phrase cited just above): pirates have boarded the newly-weds' ship and have sorted its passengers into "best buys" and "remaindered." Habrocomes is deemed worthy of salvage from the burning ship, but not his old retainer. The old man, watching Habrocomes sail off, leaps into the sea, speechifying piteously. Now, it is not only that this would be ludicrously lacking in verisimilitude for a text composed as a straightforward prose narration, as Dalmeyda finds it, it would be over the top in a dramatic text, also.[27] Who is this character? Where was he in Book I? Can a dramatist be called competent who introduces a character just long enough for a bathetic star turn and then drowns him? As a collection of dramatic scenes strung together by some

---

[23] I wish to acknowledge Richard Pervo for his helpful comments on this point in the meeting of the Ancient Fiction and Early Christian and Jewish Narrative Group at which I first presented an abbreviated version of this paper.

[24] Cf. (among many) Scobie, *Aspects of the Ancient Romance* 20–39; Reardon, *Form of the Ancient Romance* 100–106, 130–135; Schmeling, *Xenophon* 46–51; J. W. H. Walden, "Stage-Terms in Heliodorus's Aethiopica," *HSCP* 5 (1894) 1–43, esp. 2–25 (s. "*drama*").

[25] Xenophon does not use the word *drama*, as Walden (n. 24) reminds us.

[26] This phrase accompanies the scene discussed just below, and Habrocomes' beating (2.6.3). In 4.2.5, in his prayer to the Nile, just before the spectacular crucifixion scene, Habrocomes expresses the wish that the Nile should not have had to see such a scene (*theama*) as the destruction of an innocent man.

[27] Dalmeyda, *Ephésiaques*, xxx.; see above, n. 22.

barebones narration and performed as a popular entertainment, this text would still raise doubts about its composition.[28]

Now I would propose to attribute these narratival inconsistencies not to an incompetent dramatizer, but to a dramatizer whose "money scenes"—their content and placement—have been dictated by something other than the stirrings of his own imagination. In other words, a work which depends on external referents for some of the details of its narrative. I would like to suggest that what we have before us is the script for a dramatic ecphrasis, as it were, a performance which "reads" a series of works of art, linking them into an (almost) coherent whole. This would go some way to explaining the case of the missing horse or of the missing lock of hair or of the missing Aphrodite—the narrator had no need to supply details which his audience could see in front of them.

If these were the only inconsistencies in this text, we might argue perhaps that it is a "script" written to accompany a book of illustrations, perhaps, for the performance of a professional rhetor.[29] But this text has difficulties beyond that (which I have compiled above), difficulties which give it the air of an improvisation. If a rhetor chose his own illustrations, for example, surely the text would be more harmonious. No, I'd like to argue that the performer had very little control over the "text" of his illustrations, and thus of his ecphraseis; this, I would contend, is the result of the circumstances of performance.

Perhaps we might appeal to the text for a hint to the venue for such a performance:

πολλὰ καὶ ποικίλα παρὰ πάντων τὰ διηγήματα, ὅσα τε ἔπαθεν ἕκαστος καὶ ὅσα ἔδρασε, παρεξέτεινόν τε ἐπὶ πολὺ τὸ συμπόσιον, ὡς αὐτοὺς ἀπολαβόντες χρόνῳ

> . . . after they had sacrificed on that day and after they had dined, many and colorful were the tales they told about everything each one had endured and everything each one had accomplished. And they extended the dinner party until

---

[28] Hägg (*Novel in Antiquity,* 21) prefers to see in these lapses "some contradictions and logical flaws . . . natural features of a simple adventure story though seldom noticed until the story in question is scrutinized under a magnifying glass, as the *Ephesiaca* has been." But, by contrast, consider Schmeling (*Xenophon,* 28) on the Babylonian bed-canopy, "Why put such a scene over the marriage bed of especially chaste lovers? Does Xenophon know what he is doing? do dirty scenes produce fertility? passion? or is a little humor intended?"

[29] As Eva Keuls once proposed in "Rhetoric and Visual Aids in Greece and Rome," in *Communication Arts in the Ancient World* (E. A. Havelock and J. P. Hershbell, eds.; New York: Hastings House, 1978) 120–34.

deep in the night, since they had been restored to each other after a long time. (5.13.5)

I'd like to suggest a context for a performance of a work like this—the Hellenistic symposium.[30] Let's think of this as a blueprint for an evening of entertainment, a "canned" dinner party, perhaps, for the host whose own guests lack the ingenuity to compose impromptu lamentations, or prayers, or apostrophes to an absent lover, or defenses on charges of adultery, or arguments to delay marriage for a year or to fend off your boss's wife—or any of the other rhetorical gems for which the novelistic narration provides but the settings.[31] Someone may be appointed an M. C. (a symposiarch), a "Xenophon," let's call him. The intelligentsia have their dinner-party handbooks—isn't that what Plato's *Symposium* is or Athenaeus' *Deipnosophistae*, whatever else they may be?—and the bourgeoisie, the koine-speakers, have theirs.

In this interpretation, the text we have before us is the script of a particularly good evening's improvisation, or a model for an evening's entertainment. In either case, I would argue, the episodes of the romance are suggested by the works of art "inhabiting" the patron's dining-room.

This would account for the structural anomalies in the text, for example: the "Xenophon" may not be completely in control of the details of the "external" narrative.

Is there evidence for such a practice? Lamentably, not much direct evidence, and that ambiguous; Eumolpus in the *Satyricon*, for example, seems to be doing something of the sort in Trimalchio's pinacotheca with his improvisation on a depiction of the Trojan War. But when we recall the explosion of narrative images on the walls of Imperial triclinia, it seems not unlikely.[32]

---

[30] Scobie has the fullest discussion of the possibilities for public performance of the romances. Cf. the introduction to *Aspects of the Ancient Romance*, 20–39.

[31] For the entertainment at dinner parties in general (and a riotous variety there is), see Christopher Jones, "Dinner Theater," in *Dining in a Classical Context* (W. J. Slater, ed.; Ann Arbor: University of Michigan Press, 1991) 185–98.

The prominence of certain texts in discussions of ancient dinner-parties (Plato's *Symposium*, Petronius' *Cena Trimalchionis*, the *Deipnosophistae*, etc.) tends to skew the evidence in the favor of upper-class sophisticates (or parodies thereof). For bourgeois dining, we might be better off picking and inferring our way through Plutarch. Scobie, *Aspects of the Ancient Romance*, 20–39, has done a bit of this.

[32] For the sheer volume of decoration and the wide array of subjects in the private homes of just one middle-sized town in the Empire, I can think of no better reference than the indices to K. Schefold's *Pompejanische Malerei Sinn und Ideengeschichte* (Basel: Benno Schwabe & Co., 1952).

We leave the text of Xenophon with one last "view of our lovers":

καὶ ταῦτα ποιήσαντες, ἀνελθόντες εἰς τὴν πόλιν τοῖς γονεῦσιν αὐτῶν τάφους κατεσκεύασαν μεγάλους (ἔτυχον γὰρ ὑπὸ γήρως καὶ ἀθυμίας προτεθνηκότες), καὶ αὐτοὶ τοῦ λοιποῦ διῆγον ἑορτὴν ἄγοντες τὸν μετ' ἀλλήλων βίον

And having done these things, they went up to the city, and erected great tombs for their parents (for it happened they had died of old age and despair), and, for the rest, they spent their life with each other celebrating a feast. (5.15.3)[33]

Here, Dalmeyda (76) and Papanikolaou (71) agree on ἄγοντες (Hercher), against Peerlkamp (42) who reads (with the codex, F) ἕξοντες. But, in view of the current hypothesis, I might, very tentatively, suggest we retain the manuscript reading here as a "future of artistic representation," i.e., as figures in a painting or statues in a group, they were "just-about-to-celebrate-a-feast" for the rest of their lives.

I do not hesitate to propose that this interpretation of Xenophon's text be tested with reference to Christian texts. Roman narrative painting spanned the Mediterranean from a period even much earlier than the Christian diaspora, and paintings with Roman-style linear elements have been found in the catacombs and in the synagogue at Dura-Europos.[34] But, perhaps more to the point, artists of the Roman style and their "Bilderbücher" conquered the Mediterranean in more portable media, as the source of exempla for illuminated manuscripts.[35] In any case, we

---

[33] Dalmeyda (64) finds in the contrast between the manner of death mentioned in 5.6.3 and this description evidence again of the dread epitomator. But I find his arguments here rather weak.

[34] The most telling examples here would be Roman narrative sarcophagi, the distribution of which (if only because made of more durable materials) is better demonstrated, but I prefer to limit this discussion to household art.

For Roman narrative painting, its relationship to the writing of history, and its linear sense of time, R. Brilliant is always perceptive and entertaining (*Roman Art from the Republic to Constantine* [London: Phaidon, 1974] chap. VI *et pass.*; *Visual Narratives: Storytelling in Etruscan and Roman Art* [Ithaca: Cornell University Press, 1984] *pass.*).

For Dura-Europos, see *The Excavations at Dura-Europos* (Final Report VIII, Part II; Kurt Weitzmann and Herbert L. Kessler, *The Frescoes of the Dura Synagogue and Christian Art* (DOS 28; Washington, DC: Dumbarton Oaks, 1990); for some precautionary remarks about the dangers of relating art to text, see Annabel Jane Wharton, "Good and Bad Images from the Synagogue of Dura Europos: Contexts, Subtexts, Intertexts," *Art History* 17 (1994) 1–25.

[35] For more on the relationship of wall-painting and manuscript illumination, see K. Weitzmann, *Illustrations in Roll and Codex: A Study of the Origin and Method of Text Illustration* (Princeton: Princeton University Press, 1947) esp. 30–45.

need not ask if Christians in the early period were likely to have encountered Pompeiian-style painting in a private setting, we might rather ask how they could have avoided it, whatever their theological convictions.

Thus, recent work of archaeologists and art historians cautions us against regarding Christianity as an anti-artistic culture because it is commonly regarded as aniconic. But, in any case, empty "sacral" landscapes such as those found at Pompeii do not violate the codes of aniconic religion—consider the architectural murals of Islam. Moreover, it might be argued, according to our thesis, that the "wall-illuminations" of the ancient romances are not only aniconic, in the sense of not "ficting" divinity, but are rather anti-iconic: in some basic sense images of the pagan gods are being rehabilitated, by being converted into images of human worshippers (cf. the introductions of Habrocomes and Anthia, above).

But to discuss whether such images fit into an understanding that early Christianity is rejecting the artistic creations of pagan culture on *theological* grounds is not to the point here. As Peter Brown, and the great Henri Marrou before him, have argued, it is not possible for even life-long Christians to escape a pagan culture which has invaded their dining rooms (for example), and one of the hallmarks of the grand outpouring of Greco-Roman civilization is the riotous celebration of the material culture.[36]

For the Christian period, illustrations of the Rossano Gospels (Syria, 6th cent., 188 fols., Rossano, Cathedral Library) may prove illuminating. Fols. 8r and 8v, depicting Christ before Pilate (or in a Roman context, I might note), were clearly copied from wall paintings, possibly 5th-cent. frescoes or mosaics from the Domus Pilati, Jerusalem (or so Loerke; further, cf. K. Weitzmann, *Age of Spirituality: Late Antique and Early Christian Art* [New York: Metropolitan Museum of Art, 1979] 492–93, no. 443).

"Cartoons and pattern-books travelled, and the same originals of ancient classical art inspired the artists of all provinces of the Roman Empire. We have cases of two or more replicas of the same original, sometimes found in places far apart; for example, the two mosaics with Centaurs fighting wild beasts: one found in Hadrian's villa at Tivoli and the other in Africa." (Levi, *Antioch Mosaic Pavements* I,9 and n. 43) For "Bilderbücher" see also Karl Schefold, *Vergessenes Pompeji: Unveröffentlichte Bilder römischer Wanddekorationen* (Bern and Munich: Francke, 1962) 44 and 78; R. Brilliant, *Visual Narratives,* esp. chap. 2.

[36] I highly recommend Peter R. L. Brown's splendid essay "Art and Society in Late Antiquity," in *Age of Spirituality: A Symposium* [K. Weitzmann, ed.; New York: The Metropolitan Museum of Art, 1980] 17–27]. He makes reference to a celebrated work on the "decadence" of antiquity, Henri Marrou's retraction ("Retractatio" 623–703) of earlier work grounded in a view of the disjunction of Christian and pagan culture (*Saint Augustin et la fin de la culture antique*[2]).

Thus, it seems to me, no aspect of the theory which I have advanced would necessarily be incompatible with the generation of early Christian texts: the earliest Christians are not so poverty-stricken, or so opposed to artistic representation, or so far from Roman influence that Xenophon might not have been invited to dinner for a dramatic ecphrasis of a Christian romance. I might add one further bit to this: I mentioned earlier that there is virtually no evidence for a private performance of the type I've described. There is some evidence, however, for ritual performances involving "readings" of narrative decoration in pagan sanctuaries and Mithraea. When we recall that in the Roman period, many of the rituals of the public sanctuaries simply moved into private homes, particularly into dining rooms (only to be converted back to public spaces in the Christian era), we might expect that members of a table-fellowship might be rather more familiar with such a performance.[37]

But if we can learn something about the early Christian texts from remembering that they were read at a dinner in what was essentially a dining hall, we may also be able to learn something about Greek prose fiction from recollecting those Christian dining halls. There is an example of the kind of performance I've been discussing attested from late antiquity (fifth century) from the heart of the Empire (Bologna). In a public dining hall, 14 (or possibly 10 or 11) wall images have been arranged in a sequential narrative. The artist has chosen to illustrate an event reported in several literary aretalogies, conflating the accounts and contributing details of his own. He may have used a book of sample illustrations. A performer, with no connection to the artist, perhaps, thus without approving or understanding the artist's decisions, leads a group of "diners" around the hall, performing a series of ecphraseis of the wall-panels. We call it the "Stations of the Cross."[38]

---

[37] For the dining room as sanctuary, see K. Schefold, "La peinture pompéienne Essai sur l'évolution de sa signification," *Collection Latomus* 108 (1972) 52–68.

[38] I offer this example a bit mischievously, I admit. The "Way of the Cross" has been attested as early as the fifth century in the Church of S. Stefano in Bologna. It is not known whether the original performance involved 14 or 11 or 10 images, all of which have occurred at other times in other places. This narrative, of course, has contained such elements as Veronica and her veil; in 1975 the number was standardized at ten depictions of the canonical gospel accounts.

A Nihilist Fabula: Introducing *The Life Of Aesop*[1]

Richard I. Pervo
Seabury-Western Theological Seminary

I. Promythium[2]

Aesop, the well-known fabulist from Phrygia, has justly been regarded a wise man, since he taught what it was salutary to call to mind and to recommend, not in an austere and dictatorial manner, as is the way of philosophers, but by inventing witty and entertaining fables he put into human minds and hearts ideas that were wholesome and carefully considered, while at the same time he enticed their attention.[3]

This quote from Aulus Gellius establishes Aesop as a proponent of "profit with delight" and thereby my own credentials to discuss him.[4] *The Life of Aesop* is one of the more important neglected sources of ancient popular literature, for it recounts in a generally unpretentious style[5] the career of a hero of the most humble origins who turns the world upside down, confounds the wisdom of the wise, and rises to a position of great honor, but perishes through a plot concocted by slighted antagonists, only to be vindicated after his death and venerated as a hero. The strategy of this paper is, after dealing in summary fashion with the standard

---

[1] This title plays upon *anilis fabula* ("old wives's tale"): Apuleius, *Met.* 4.27: *sed ego te narrationibus lepidis anilibusque fabulis protinus avocabo*, followed by the tale of Cupid and Psyche (and concluded with *Sic captivae puellae delira et termulenta illa narrabat anicula*, 6.25). I am most grateful to Niklas Holzberg, who supplied texts and made numerous useful corrections and suggestions.

[2] *Promythia* were set before ancient fables as reference guides to their particular "morals."

[3] A. Gellius *Attic Nights* 2.29.1, trans. J. C. Rolfe, *The Attic Nights of Aulus Gellius* (LCL; 3 vols.; Cambridge: Harvard University Press, 1927) 1.223–25.

[4] Cf. also the prologue to Phaedrus Book I, 3–4: *duplex libelli dos est: quod risum movet, / et quod prudenti vitam consilio monet.* "The dowry of the book is two-fold, it produces laughter and by prudent advice guides life."

[5] A software search indicates that the second English edition of Bauer's lexicon includes 120 references to the *Life of Aesop*. This is one mark of its stylistic proximity to early Christian narrative.

introductory questions and reflecting upon some features of its structure and plot, to read the *Aesop-Romance* like a "gospel."

Aesop, which is roughly the same length as the Gospel according to Mark, describes the life of the sixth century Aesop.[6] Centered, like *Callirhoe*, in Greek-speaking Ionia, its plot eventually embraces the various competing centers of power: Greek *poleis*, Lydia, Babylon, and Egypt.[7] Phrygian Aesop is a remarkably ugly slave, and speechless to boot.[8] Rusticated by his master to an estate, he is vulnerable to the machinations of fellow slaves, not least the manager (οἰκονόμος).[9] Aesop is able to thwart attempts to pin the blame for their own misdeeds on him. Thus, even while speechless, he displays the ingenuity that will lead to fame. The importance of this episode is to demonstrate that Aesop required no endowment of *intelligence*. Wisdom was there before the word.

As a reward for a simple act of hospitality to a minister of Isis, Aesop receives the gift of speech from that goddess and appropriate endow-

---

[6] Of the historical Aesop B. E. Perry says: "All that can be accepted as historically true in the ancient testimony about Aesop personally is this: that he came originally from Thrace, not from Phrygia; that he was at one time a slave on the island of Samos in the service of a man named Iadmon, who later freed him; that he was a contemporary of the poetess Sappho in the early sixth century B.C.; and that he was famed as a maker and teller of stories in prose . . ." (*Babrius and Phaedrus* [LCL; Cambridge: Harvard University Press, 1965] xxxv). Holzberg is more skeptical, and with reason. Although willing to consider the possibility that there was an historical Aesop, he is also prepared to regard him as the personification of a type: the hellenized oriental story-teller, one example of which would be slaves of oriental origin who served in the Ionian cities and transmitted in Greek fables long diffused in eastern cultures (*Die Antike Fabel: Eine Einführung* [Darmstadt: Wissenschaftliche Buchgesellschaft, 1993] 16–18).

[7] G. Anderson says: "It is as if a sage is allowed to dispense his precepts for princes and assorted pearls of wisdom all over the itinerary of the Alexander-Romance" (*Ancient Fiction: The Novel in the Graeco-Roman World* [Totowa, NJ: Barnes & Noble Books, 1984] 52). Like the Jewish novels (and "King Herod" in the Gospels and Acts), the romance employs standard names: Croesus (not too inaccurately), King Lycorus/Lycurgus of Babylon, Pharaoh Nectanebo of Egypt.

[8] Paul's letter to Philemon deals with an apparently Phrygian slave: Onesimus.

[9] The manager who figures in chs. 1–14 of *Aesop* illuminates Gospel parables about these figures, such as Luke 12:42–46; 16:1–8. The use of this term in 1 Cor 4:1; Tit 1:7, and 1 Pet 4:10 suggests that the parables apply to church leaders. *Aesop*'s Zenas is a text-book example of the bad manager. Managers are also found in romantic novels, for example *Leucippe* 5.17. A professional perspective on their treatment is provided by Varro, *Re Rust.* 1.17.4–7. Columella, *Re Rust.* 11, sets ideals for their training and behavior.

ments from each of the Muses who attend her.[10] No longer useless, he is of no use to the manager, who rightly regards him as a potential threat and sells him. In due course Aesop is taken to Samos, where he will manipulate the noted philosopher Xanthus into purchasing him.

Throughout the central, domestic, section of the novel (20–91) Aesop both educates and assists his hapless master, fornicates with his mistress, and, in general, keeps the household at a boil. When it seems that Xanthus has unjustly stymied Aesop's quest for manumission and brought the tale to an end, the outbreak of a civic crisis offers the slave an opportunity to manipulate his master into bestowing his freedom. Aesop then enters the public sphere.

He rapidly rises to become a diplomat and prime minister, a career followed, in modern fashion, by life as a public lecturer. Aesop emerges as a celebrated itinerant philosopher-sophist not unlike Dio of Prusa.[11] Slave has become like master, and more so, for if both Xanthus and Aesop enjoyed international reputations as lecturers, Aesop can go on tour and receives greater honors. Slaves become masters means that the world has been turned upside down. Conversely, it may mean that the pigs have begun to walk on their hind legs, to appropriate the image of a more recent animal fable.[12] Aesop shows proper gratitude to his beneficent patrons, the Muses, but not to their patron, Apollo, whose place of honor he usurps.[13] Pyramids are problematic, even for an engineer who outdoes the Egyptians. Apollo was not amused.

Aesop, like Jesus and Paul, sets out for his city of destiny, Delphi, with its oracle of Apollo. There he receives little recognition and turns upon the populace. His parabolic powers serve only to exacerbate the situation. Victimized by the old "slip a precious cup into the luggage" trick,[14] he is

---

[10] For Isis in the role of μουσαγωγός see P.Oxy. 1380, 62, 128. The editors refer to Plut. *De Isid* 3 (διὸ καὶ τῶν <ἐν> Ἑρμοῦ πόλει Μουσῶν τὴν προτέραν Ἶσιν ἅμα καὶ Δικαιοσύνην καλοῦσι). See also the references in F. Solmsen, *Isis among the Greeks and Romans* (Cambridge: Harvard University Press, 1979) 135 n. 3.

[11] The example of Dio is, of course, pertinent to the date of composition rather than to the (sixth-century) dramatic date. (Dio's discussion of slavery [Or. 14–15] is one of the longest of surviving philosophical treatments of the subject. See P. A. Brunt, "Aspects of the Social Thought of Dio Chrysostom and the Stoics," *PCPhS* 19 [1973] 9–34).

[12] *I.e.,* George Orwell's *Animal Farm.*

[13] For the text of chap. 110 see below.

[14] 127. There is a closely related motif in Gen 42:25–38 (money in the baggage). Real or alleged temple-theft is a driving narrative theme in Lucian *Toxaris* 28, and in

found guilty of sacrilege and compelled to die. In the wake of his death came plague and destruction that had to be appeased.

II. Introductory Issues

Text

The figure of Aesop is best known through fables still popular, not least as material suitable for children.[15] The *Romance* is not suitable for children and possesses, moreover, other attractions. With regard to Aesop's career there are, in addition to variations of his life, a number of traditions, not all of which are in concord.[16] The focus of this study is the Greek *Aesop-Romance*, at least two editions of which are attested. Until the middle of this century the only Greek recension available to modern European scholars was that produced by A. Westermann in 1845. This is known as W.[17] In 1929, near the beginning of his long and arduous labors in this field, Perry learned of a previously unknown manuscript in the Pierpont Morgan collection. Although mutilated in some places and inferior in others, this MS, known as G, is the chief source of the best edition of the romance.[18] G has considerably enhanced the standing of the *Aesop-Romance*, since it is a fuller, livelier, and better-organized text. By

---

the ass-story: Apuleius *Met.* 9.9–10//*Onos* 41, where the object in question is a golden φιάλη, just as in *Aesop.*

[15] For the most substantial collection, see B. E. Perry, *Aesopica. Vol. 1. Greek and Latin Texts* (Urbana: University of Illinois Press, 1952) 295–759, and idem, *Studies in the Text History of the Life and Fables of Aesop* (Haverford, PA: American Philological Association, 1936). Note also his *Babrius and Phaedrus*, which, with its introduction of 102 pages and appendix of 191 pages, is not typical of the Loeb series. On fables in the ancient world see also Holzberg, *Die Antike Fabel.*

[16] The *Testimonia* may conveniently be surveyed in Perry's collection, *Aesopica*, 211–247.

[17] In *Aesopica* Perry provides an edition of W, based upon more than a dozen MSS, 81–107, with variants 133–208. N. Holzberg advises, *per litt.*, that M. Papathomopoulos is preparing a new edition of W.

[18] Since 1952 there have been some additions to the G tradition (Perry, "Some Addenda to the Life of Aesop," *BZ* 59 [1966] 285–304). Papyri are also important, in particular, PBerol. 11623, PSI 156, POxy. 2083, 3331 +3720, PRoss. Georg. 18, which attest to the work's popularity in Graeco-Roman Egypt. These finds and subsequent reflection have culminated in the edition of M. Papathomopoulos, Ὁ βίος τοῦ Αἰσώπου Ἡ Παραλλαγὴ Γ Κριτικὴ ἐκδώση με Εἰσαγωγὴ καὶ Μεταφράση ('Ιωάννινα, 1990, corrected edition 1991.), of which the author most graciously and expeditiously supplied me with a copy, through the intercession of N. Holzberg.

contrast the W tradition is abbreviated, "secularized," and rationalized.[19] Although there is much to be learned from comparison of the various traditions, that based upon G (with supplements from W where G is lacunose) is primary.[20]

Genre

Aesop is, in my judgment, to be regarded as a novel. The grounds for this judgment will emerge in the following analysis. There are alternatives. The work has much in common with several types of lives, in particular lives of philosophers and authors, as well as affinities with the *Alexander-Romance*.[21] Failure to describe the subject's birth, childhood, and education is a feature shared by some ancient lives, including the Gospel of Mark. In response to the proposal that *Aesop* ought to be viewed as an admittedly legendary and essentially fictitious *bios* stand elements of form and contents. The romance, as will be argued below, is a carefully crafted work exhibiting a plot devised by the narrator rather than an outline dictated by a sequence of real or imagined events, or by a thematic arrangement.[22] In devising the work the narrator makes frequent and continual use of dialogue. Dialogue is a mark of novelists rather than of pseudo-historians or pseudo-biographers.[23] A survey of the contents reveals a substantial number of parallels to episodes in the

---

[19] On the character of W see the remarks of S. Merkle, "Die Fabel von Frosch und Maus: zur Funktion der λόγοι im Delphi-Teil des Äsop-Romans," in *Der Äsop Roman* (N. Holzberg, ed.; MSKP 6; Tübingen: Gunter Narr, 1992) 110–27, esp. 116 n. 18.

[20] For discussions of the text and its history see the bibliography in Holzberg, *Der Äsop-Roman,* 165–70. In addition to Perry and Papathomopoulos, one should note P. Marc, "Die Überlieferung des Äsopromans, *BZ* 19 (1910) 383–421, and C. Hower, *Studies on the So-Called Accursiana Recension of the Life and Fables of Aesop* (Diss., University of Illinois, Urbana, 1936). The translation of L. W. Daly (*Aesop Without Morals* [Thomas Yoseloff: New York, 1961], 31–90, supplements gaps in G from W. Daly states that B. E. Perry reviewed the translation.

[21] Note the titles in the MSS: In G it is (rather surprisingly) βίβλος Ξάνθου φιλοσόφου καὶ Αἰσώπου δούλου αὐτοῦ περὶ τῆς ἀναστροφῆς Αἰσώπου. The standard title in W is βίος Αἰσώπου τοῦ φιλοσόφου, with some interesting variants: Διήγησις (cf. Luke 1:1) Ἐσώπου, Διήγησις τοῦ Αἰσώπου, Βίος τοῦ πανθαυμάστου Αἰσώπου.

[22] Divergent *testimonia* indicate that different patterns could have been followed. It is due to authorial decision that the Aesop of the romance is a solitary figure, not a colleague of the Seven Sages, and without a lover—options supported by tradition. The exception proving this rule is his brief and unhappy association with an adopted son who will betray him (103–108).

[23] For a contrast in this regard see the *Historia Augusta.*

extant "realistic-comic" novels,[24] which are scarcely less prominent than are similarities to fictitious lives of philosophers and sages, such as Socrates, Ahikar, and Apollonius of Tyana, as well as themes, motifs, and techniques shared with romantic novels.[25] Since all novels are, in some way, fictional biographies, *Aesop* is aptly labeled as an historical novel, the fictional biography of a presumably historical individual. Comparison with the *Alexander-Romance* is particularly interesting, not simply because both center upon folk-heroes who died by murder, but because the Alexander of Pseudo-Callisthenes succeeds through the use of his wits.[26] The Alexander of the *Romance* has been transformed into a character like Aesop.[27] Therein appears a trait of "popular" narrative that is shared by such diverse figures as Alexander, Aesop, Apollonius of Tyana, Jesus, the apostles, and such characters as Daniel, Mordecai, and Tobit.[28]

Date and Provenance

The essential outline of Aesop's life as reported in the romance goes back to the early classical period.[29] Papyrological evidence suggests a second-century CE *terminus a quo*. As a popular, anonymous work, the romance was liable to frequent revision, including deletions, expansions, and abridgment.[30] In this case there is reason to suspect that longer editions were earlier. The text is almost devoid of hints that would locate it in a particular epoch, although it fits the social milieu of the early Roman imperial period. The book could derive from the first century, and is probably not later than the final third of the second century CE.[31]

---

[24] Some, but not all, of these affinities are indicated in the notes.

[25] Papathomopoulos discusses the genre of *Aesop* in ὁ βίος τοῦ Αἰσώπου, 11–12.

[26] On the theme in general see M. Detienne and J.-P. Vernant, *Cunning Intelligence in Greek Culture and Society* (J. Lloyd, trans.; Sussex: Harvester, 1976).

[27] See Richard Stoneman, *The Greek Alexander Romance* (London: Penguin Books, 1991) 1–28, esp. 17–22; "Riddles in Bronze and Stone: Monuments and their Interpretation in the *Alexander-Romance GCN* 6 (1995) 166–67; and "The Metamorphoses of the *Alexander Romance*," in *The Novel in the Ancient World* (G. Schmeling, ed.; Leiden: E. J. Brill, 1996) 601–12.

[28] One benchmark of the evolution of ancient culture is the increasing degree to which some figures become holy men and women.

[29] Herodotus 2.134–35; Aristophanes, *Wasps*, 1446–48.

[30] Precisely the same observation may be made about popular narratives known from the Jewish and Christian traditions, examples of which are Esther, Daniel, and the canonical and apocryphal gospels and Acts.

[31] Perry, *Studies*, 25–26, inclines toward the second century but concludes that "the most one may say with certainty is that the *Life of Aesop*, in the oldest form that we know it (i.e. in G), must have been composed, or rewritten, at some time between 100

There are reasons for suspecting that G, at least, derives from Egypt. These include its affinities with the *Alexander-Romance,* the role played by Isis, and the use of *Ahikar,* in particular, but temptations toward specificity are perhaps best resisted.[32] Many places in the late Hellenistic or Roman East could qualify as the site of the first edition, and each of the editions known (and unknown) may have a particular provenance.[33]

Sources[34]

Apart from traditions about Aesop, including written and/or oral legends, and fables attributed to him, the most readily detectable source of the romance is the frequently revised, widely translated, and often-plundered novel about Ahikar. Chapters 101–123 of the *Aesop-Romance* are borrowed from *Ahikar.*[35] Two observations arising from the use of this source:

1) To anticipate later arguments, the data have long been available to refute the notion that the romance is a mere conglomerate, for the Aesop-text both re-arranges and alters its sources to fit its own structure and viewpoint.

B.C. and 200 A.D." In *Babrius and Phaedrus,* however, he states that the life is "a product of the first century" (xxxvii). N. Holzberg appears to prefer a second or third century date (*Ancient Novel,* 15). Stefano Jedrkiewicz, *Sapere E Paradosso Nell'Antichità: Esopo E La Favola* (Roma: Edizioni dell'Ateneo, 1989) 158, opts for the first century.

[32] See Perry's comments in *Aesopica,* 3–4, with reference to M. Braun, *History and Romance in Graeco-Oriental Literature* (Oxford: Basil Blackwell, 1938). Since so much of the surviving "popular" literature comes from Egypt, the argument quickly takes on a circular quality.

[33] The testimonies report communication with Athens (Perry, *Testimonia,* 39, 224–25), an address to the Corinthians (ibid. 40, 225) and activities in Italy (ibid. 42, 225)—an itinerary approximating that of the apostle Paul. Different editions of the romance might have included visits to particular locales. Perry and others have speculated that G may be an "eastern" edition, W "western." A. La Penna ("Il Romanzo di Esopo," *Athenaeum* n.s. 40 [1962] 264–314) argues for a Syrian origin—a favored locale for the canonical gospels. On the question see also Jedrkiewicz, *Sapere,* 158 n. 4.

[34] For some intelligent proposals about the traditions underlying the romance see Jedrkiewicz, *Sapere,* 160–64.

[35] See Perry, *Aesopica,* 4–10, with a synopsis and discussion, as well as A. Lewis, R. Harris, and F. Conybeare, "The Story of Ahikar," in *The Apocrypha and Pseudepigrapha of the Old Testament* (R. H. Charles, ed.; 2 vols.; Oxford: Clarendon, 1913) 2.715–84, and, more recently, J. M. Lindenberger, "Ahiqar," in *The Old Testament Pseudepigrapha* (J. H. Charlesworth, ed.; 2 vols.; Garden City, NY: Doubleday, 1983) 2.479–507. Two of the essays in Holzberg's *Äsop-Roman* treat this subject: N. Oettinger, "Achikars Weisheitssprüche im Licht älterer Fabeldichtung," 3–22, and R. Kussly, "Achikar, Tinuphis und Äsop," 23–30.

2) The use of *Ahikar* in *Aesop* is a concrete example of the often hypothesized intersection between "oriental" and Greek fiction and, more specifically, this source links the *Aesop-Romance* with Jewish novels.[36]

III. Style, Structure And Narrative Technique

In the discussion of a text extant in two Greek editions it is appropriate to illustrate the importance of its structure by quoting two editions of another work: N. Holzberg's *Ancient Novel*. In the ancient (1986) German edition Holzberg devoted about ten lines to the *Aesop-Romance*, noting affinities with comic novels, but stressing that the author wished to provide no more than a framework for a series of fables.[37] The 1995 English edition of this work devotes a full page to the romance, with the assertion that it has a structural pattern *used* in fables, rather than being a mere shell for the presentation *of* fables.[38] Holzberg's 1986 observation was the kind of common opinion in which general introductions properly abound.[39] He has subsequently changed his mind. Once more I should like to make two consequent observations:

1) The "old view" of the structure of the *Aesop-Romance* is exactly like earlier judgments about the structure of the Gospels, in particular the Gospel of Mark, which (outside of birth narratives and passion stories) were viewed as random collections of material largely devoid of structure. The two cases are highly analogous and mutually illuminating. Behind this judgment lay the scholarly prejudice that popular narrative by definition lacks structure and generic features. For classicists that meant that the *Aesop-Romance* was unworthy of aesthetic analysis, even by B. E. Perry, who was willing to study such wretched specimens as the novel of

---

[36] Jews not only copied *Ahikar*, as the Elephantine papyrus demonstrates, but also borrowed his name in Tobit and Judith (as "Achior") and utilized the contents (Tobit). See L. M. Wills, *The Jewish Novel in the Ancient World* (Ithaca, NY: Cornell University Press, 1995) index, 271, *s.v.* "*Ahikar, story of.*"

[37] "Auch wenn die aus der Kaiserzeit stammenden Fassungen durch burleske Episoden und das niedrige soziale Milieu, in dem der Sklave Aisop sich bewegt, manche Berührungen mit der Welt des komisch-realistischen Romans aufweisen, dürfte es die ursprüngliche Intention des Verfassers dieser Vita gewesen sein, einen Rahmen für die Aneinanderreihung aisopischer Fabeln zu schaffen" (Holzberg, *Der Antike Roman: Eine Einführung* [Zurich: Artemis-Verlag, 1986] 23).

[38] Holzberg, *The Ancient Novel*, 15–16. See also his contribution to Schmeling, *The Novel*, 633–39.

[39] For examples of this position see the references in Holzberg's "Der Aesop-Roman: Eine strukturanalytische Interpretation," in *Äsop-Roman*, 33–75, esp. 33–35.

Chariton. For historians of Christian origins it implied assent to the judgments of F. Overbeck and K. L. Schmidt.[40]

2) Additional form-critical ramifications of this view emerge in the following remarks of Graham Anderson:

"In the Apocryphal Acts and their relatives one is simply conscious of juxtapositions of material rather than consciously artistic storytelling. The anonymous narrator is passing on received information to the best of his limited ability, and that is all that seems to matter to him. The Greek *Aesop-Romance* falls fairly obviously into this category, in so far as much of the material could have been presented to the same purpose in an arbitrarily different order. So, too in the various recensions of the *Alexander-Romance*."[41]

Anderson (who rejects Perry's efforts to exclude all but romantic novels from the realm of the ancient novel and who cannot be included among those who allow the genre only the narrowest of boundaries[42]), implicitly makes structure a generic requirement and would thus set aside the Apocryphal Acts, the *Aesop-Romance*, and the *Alexander-Romance* on the grounds that they have no real order and require none. If this perception of indifference to structure in those works is wrong, as it quite demonstrably is, then the grounds for relating such texts to romantic and other novels are considerably strengthened.

If one may be excused for taking his own rather undeveloped reflections of twenty years ago for something like a norm, I believe that those who read the romance in blissful ignorance of scholarly dogmas and look for structure will soon begin to discover inter-connections, cross-references, and parallels that will beg for the construction of an outline and will substantially enhance appreciation of the work.

The romance is not without some literary qualities. By any criterion irony, even if irony of only the most blatant sort, is a leading feature. Successive readings offer convincing proof of a well-developed and refined ironic sense. The first example is an incident that appears to engage the attention of most readers. When his master Xanthus is, like many characters in ancient novels, about to commit suicide, Aesop

---

[40] F. Overbeck's 1882 essay "Über die Anfänge der patristischen Literatur" is most accessible in a reprint: Darmstadt: Wissenschaftliche Buchgesellschaft, 1966. K. L. Schmidt formulated a position that remained dominant for fifty years: "Die Stellung der Evangelien in der allgemeinen Literaturgeschichte," in *Eucharisterion. Festschrift H. Gunkel* (H. Schmidt, ed.; Göttingen: Vandenhoeck & Ruprecht, 1923) 50–134.

[41] Anderson, *Ancient Fiction*, 132.

[42] Anderson, *Ancient Fiction*, 20 n. 6.

intervenes, although not, in approved novelistic fashion, until the very last second, and challenges him on his own grounds: "Master, where is your philosophy? Where is your boasted education? Where is your doctrine of self-control?"[43] This is a stinging application of the philosophical commonplace that deeds should match words. Yet when Aesop is condemned to death and the subject of a visit by a friend while imprisoned,[44] he hears these words from the anonymous supporter: "Where was your training? Where was your learning? You have given advice to cities and peoples, but you have turned out witless in your own cause."[45] Through formal and verbal parallels the author has underscored the irony of Aesop's situation: the *fabula* is now *de illo* (about himself).[46]

Retardation and the related device of foreshadowing indicate not only a capacity for elevating suspense but also an eye for larger narrative construction. The technique can be illustrated from a standard old American melodrama: just after the dastardly villain has tied the beautiful young daughter of an impoverished widow to the railroad tracks and the train is thundering toward her helpless form, the narrator says, "Meanwhile, back at the farm . . ."[47]

The anonymous narrator of *Aesop* (hereafter "the author")[48] demonstrates a well-developed sense of the uses of this technique. The famous philosopher Xanthus, who teaches his students[49] to pay no attention to women (24), is, in fact, hen-pecked.[50] Mme. X. (who, in accordance with

---

[43] 85.9–10, trans. Daly, p.73: Δεσπότα, ποῦ ἡ φιλοσοφία σοῦ, ποῦ σου τὸ τῆς παιδείας φρύαγμα, ποῦ σου τῆς ἐγκρατείας δόγμα; (For a similar use of anaphora see 1 Cor 1:20a ποῦ σοφός; ποῦ γραμματεύς; ποῦ συζητητὴς τοῦ αἰῶνος τούτου;)

[44] On this scene and its parallels with the socratic tradition see also below.

[45] 130.3–4, trans. Daly, *Aesop Without Morals*, 87: ποῦ σου ἡ παιδεία, ποῦ σου τὸ φιλόλογον, κ.τ.λ.

[46] Aesop does not dispute this. He responds by telling fables against himself.

[47] Some will wince at the association of retardation with foreshadowing, but the latter is also a means for raising questions that will not immediately be answered.

[48] Jedrkiewicz (*Sapere*, 171–82) has a number of astute proposals about the implied author of *Aesop* and his audience.

[49] σχολαστικοί/*scholastici* also play a prominent role in the *Satyrica*. In *Aesop* they form a sort of chorus against whom Aesop's words and deeds acquire greater intensity.

[50] The romance opens the door to much of the social reality behind the misogynist tradition, which, offensive as it is, may reflect more of the world as males boast that it is or argue that it should be, rather than what it often actually is. On three occasions she threatens to take her dowry and "go home to mother" (29, 31, 46). Control over this money provides her with considerable leverage against her husband (who, it

the polite tradition, remains anonymous), moved by the sight of handsome slaves,[51] requests that her husband Xanthus (who has been mentioned but not brought on stage) pick up a pretty young man on his way home from work (22). From the outset, then, a triangle is established among master, mistress, and slave. Aesop will play them as a *maestro* manipulates the violin, setting one against another, humiliating both, and yet ultimately preventing the dissolution of their marriage.[52]

When Xanthus brings home the promised slave, he is confronted with a chorus of female disappointment, as both mistress and servants had their hearts set upon an attractive male sexual object (29–31).[53] Not for the first or the last time, Aesop capitalizes upon his ugliness. What

should be noted, also seems to have genuine affection for her). The same theme is used in the *Acts of Philip*, 5.51.

[51] As an example of the different uses to which a motif may be put one may recall that a similar sight motivated Pope Gregory to send a mission to the Germanic inhabitants of England (Bede, *H.E.* 2.1).

[52] The author of 1–2 Timothy and Titus (the Pastoral epistles) has more in common with Xanthus's stated views about household management than would the heroes of the various Acts—or Jesus. In their first interchange following the purchase of Aesop Xanthus criticizes those who "go around upsetting decent households" with slander: ὁ ἐνέγκας σε πάντως τις τῶν εἰωθότων τὰς εὐσταθούσας οἰκίας διαβολαῖς ἀνατρέπειν and proceeds to detail the contents of such slander: . . . διέβαλέν με [ἀποκαλῶν] ὡς κακόδουλον ἢ πάροινον ἢ πλήσσοντα ἢ στομαχώδη ἢ ὀργίλον (28.8–10). Cf. 1 Tim 5:13 ἅμα δὲ καὶ ἀργαὶ μανθάνουσιν περιερχόμεναι τὰς οἰκίας, οὐ μόνον δὲ ἀργαὶ ἀλλὰ καὶ φλύαροι καὶ περίεργοι, λαλοῦσαι τὰ μὴ δέοντα. In addition to the theme of mistreating slaves there are two adjectives, ὀργίλον and πάροινον, which appear in the Pastoral Epistles as qualifications for leaders: Titus 1:7 δεῖ γὰρ τὸν ἐπίσκοπον ἀνέγκλητον εἶναι ὡς θεοῦ οἰκονόμον, μὴ αὐθάδη, μὴ ὀργίλον, μὴ πάροινον, μὴ πλήκτην, μὴ αἰσχροκερδῆ, 1 Tim 3:3 μὴ πάροινον μὴ πλήκτην, ἀλλὰ ἐπιεικῆ ἄμαχον ἀφιλάργυρον. Is Xanthus thus qualified to be a bishop? His words are not without irony, since anger and drunkenness are two faults that he will exhibit in the course of the narrative (anger: 55, etc.; drunkenness: 68).

[53] The sale of the ass in Apuleius, *Met.* 8.23–25 // *Onos* 35–36, has a number of interesting parallels to the purchase and advent of Aesop. The donkey, like Aesop, is unattractive to potential buyers (*Onos* 35). When Philebus, the new owner of Lucius-become-ass, arrives at his door he calls out "Girlies (κοράσια), I've bought you a handsome sturdy slave of Cappadocian stock" (*Onos* 36, trans. M. D. Macleod, *Lucian* [LCL; 8 vols.; Cambridge: Harvard University Press, 1967] 8.109). When one of Xanthus's slaves investigates Aesop, she returns and says, "Girls (κοράσια), I might just as well puncture your little dreams." (30.18–19, trans. Daly, *Aesop Without Morals*, 46). In both cases the κοράσια will be disappointed that the new slave is not a real man. In *Aesop* 30 a young slave exclaims joyfully that the master has bought her a husband. The ministers of Cybele state that Philebus has not acquired a slave but a bridegroom for himself (*Onos* 30). In retrospect these parallels do more than amuse, for they illuminate the status and fate of the slave.

mistress wants is the opportunity for adultery, as Aesop recites an insightful description of the seduction of a slave through intimate service: he will observe her in the bath, wrap a towel about her as she leaves the water, etc. (32).[54] Such conduct would shame mistress and master both. Readers have been given grounds for suspecting that Aesop is right.[55]

---

[54] In chap. 32 G develops irony through repetition of the ambiguous phrase ὁ καλὸς δοῦλος. Mme. X wants a good-looking slave who is *bad*. W is more blunt: she wants a slave who will serve her at the bath καὶ γυμνὴν βλέπειν σε (32.4, Perry p. 87). Ironically, when Aesop does accompany someone to the bath, it is his master (38). The problem of mistresses attended at the bath by male slaves is well summed up by K. Hopkins ("Novel Evidence for Roman Slavery," *P&P* 138 [1993] 3–27, 18): "The baths, cleanliness, heat and lust were a heady mixture; and the close association between powerful female mistresses and their male slave attendants in public and in private stimulated the anxieties of husbands, the malicious gossip of envious observers and of later Christian moralizers." For an example of the former see Martial, 7.35. On the latter see P. Brown in P. Veyne, ed. *A History of Private Life. Vol. I: From Pagan Rome to Byzantium* (A. Goldhammer, trans.; Cambridge: Belknap, 1987) 298. One apt example is Clement of Alexandria, *Paid.* 3.5: For dazzling thus those fond of display, they artfully try to win the admiration of their lovers, who after a little insult them naked. They will scarce strip before their own husbands, affecting a plausible pretence of modesty; but any others who wish may see them at home shut up naked in their baths, for there they are not ashamed to strip before spectators, as if exposing their persons for sale...The baths are opened promiscuously to men and women; and there they strip for licentious indulgence (for from looking, men get to loving), as if their modesty had been washed away in the bath. Those who have not become utterly destitute of modesty shut out strangers; but bathe with their own servants, and strip naked before their slaves, and are rubbed by them; giving to the crouching menial liberty to lust, by permitting fearless handling. For those who are introduced before their naked mistresses while in the bath, study to strip themselves in order to audacity in lust (*sic*), casting off fear in consequence of the wicked custom. See Rev. Alexander Robert, D.D., and James Donaldson, LL.D., eds., *The Ante-Nicene Fathers, Translations of the Writings of the Fathers down to A.D. 325* (Grand Rapids, MI: Wm. B. Eerdmans, 1989) 296–97.

In his exhortations to young men to avoid sex outside of lawful marriage and the purpose of procreation Musonius Rufus says, with regard to sex with slave-women: "If it seems neither shameful nor out of place for a master to have relations with his own slave, . . . let him consider how he would like it if his wife had relations with a male slave. Would it not seem completely intolerable not only if the woman who had a lawful husband had relations with a slave, but even if a woman without a husband should have? (*Frag.* 12, Lutz 86.35–38; trans. in C. E. Lutz, "Musonius Rufus, 'the Roman Socrates,' *YCS 10* [1947] 3–147, esp. 87).

[55] In 29 she reports a dream, sent by Aphrodite, in which Xanthus had acquired and presented her with a πάγκαλον σωμάτιον, a "real hunk." Relations between mistresses and slaves exhibit a contrast between romantic and comic fiction. In Xenophon's *An Ephesian Tale* rapacious mistresses threaten Habrocomes's future (2.5; 3.12). The former passage includes the following letter: Mistress, do as you will and use my body as the body of a slave; and if you want to kill me, I am ready; if you want to torture me, torture me as you please. But I could not come to your bed, nor would

They must wait for the other sandal to drop. Following a number of vicissitudes in her relation with both Xanthus and Aesop, it does. Aesop, who had been promised freedom, and wrongfully denied it, bore a grudge. He evidently permitted Mme. X. to discover him in the throes of auto-eroticism.[56] Rather than beg his pardon or speak of the dangers inherent in this practice, she promised him a new tunic in return for ten romantic passages at arms. This promise, too, was initially denied, on rather technical grounds (75–76, ironically resolved in his favor by Xanthus). Only then does he play the role of intimate body servant by *uncovering* her to the world.

While in charge of dinner preparations, Aesop, worried that the dog will eat the food, orders his mistress, who is resting upon a couch with her back to the table, to keep an eye on things.[57] She replies that she has eyes in her *derrière.*[58] Officious Aesop then drew up the robe of his sleeping mistress to facilitate this capacity. Xanthus and his students discovered her thus displayed. (77a). Between the naming of the possibility of adultery and its fulfillment, with revenge, appear all of Aesop's contacts with his mistress.[59]

I obey such a request even if you ordered me (Trans. by G. Anderson in *Collected Ancient Greek Novels* [B. P. Reardon, ed.; Berkeley: University of California Press, 1989] 141).

For Trimalchio sex with mistress (and master) is an opportunity to be exploited (*Sat.* 45). Aesop falls into the latter category. The most interesting parallel to *Aesop* in this regard is the fifth mime of Herodas. Iamblichus, *frag.* 35, speaks of a wife who told her husband that she had had sexual relations with a (blond) slave in a *dream.* Some other occurrences of this theme in ancient novels are Apuleius *Met.* 8.22 and Heliodorus, *An Ethiopian Story* 1.11.

[56] This chapter (75) is found in POxy. 3337. Perry (*Studies,* 7) states that the relevant page was "deliberately torn out of the codex, either by way of expurgation or for private circulation." The former seems more likely, given the frequency with which texts were censored and the relative ease with which a private copy of a single page could be produced.

[57] Like other forms of sexual abuse, adultery with a slave has its drawbacks. Aesop can give orders to his mistress because of the power he now holds over her.

[58] This line would gain force if it were a proverbial claim made about those whom nothing escapes, but a search of the collections has not yet confirmed this suspicion.

[59] A similar tension permeates *Daphnis and Chloe,* in a manner also illustrative of the different ways a theme may be played out in comedy and romance. Jedrkiewicz (*Sapere,* 170) points to the telling contrast between Chloe's feeling of desire (which she does not understand) while observing Daphnis in the bath (*Daphnis and Chloe* 1.12–13) and Mme. X.'s arousal when she sees Aesop masturbating (75).

Now public masturbation is rather "doggy" behavior.[60] No unflattering animal metaphor or epithet seems inappropriate to apply to the eventual teller of animal fables. When Aesop first arrived at Xanthus's house, the maid who answered the door[61] asked him where his tail was. He advised her that it was in front rather than behind. The adultery revealed his dogged endurance; exposure of his mistress's behind as an "evil eye" against the ravages of the dog closes this particular circle.

Almost. The dog-headed Aesop, a sexual rival of his master, sets up the household dog as a rival to the mistress (44–50a).[62] When he wishes to shame his master, he poses a silly riddle: "What do dogs shake?" (77b). His advice to his adopted son includes this exhortation: "Be affable and courteous to those you meet, knowing that a dog's tail gets him food and his mouth beatings."[63] This is not wisdom discovered in the study, for Aesop knows whereof he speaks. Finally, his initial animal fable relates how wolves deceitfully broke up an alliance between dogs and sheep. In the end the wolves will get Aesop.[64]

---

[60] There is an apophthegm about Diogenes of Sinope, who, according to Diogenes Laertius 6.69, was inclined to do all in public, both what pertained to Demeter and to Aphrodite: χειρουργῶν τ᾽ ἐν τῷ μέσῳ συνεχές, "εἴθε ἦν," ἔλεγε, "καὶ τὴν κοιλίαν παρατριψάμενον τοῦ λιμοῦ παύσασθαι·"

[61] Cf. Acts 12:12–16.

[62] This rivalry has a parallel in the *Satyrica*, where Trimalchio introduces his dog as his best friend and insults wives (64.7–8): Looking about for *delicias suas*, he saw the boy (Croesus) playing with a puppy.

"This sight reminded Trimalchio to send out for Scylax, 'protector of the house and the household.' (*praesidium domus familiaeque*) [cf. also the "*cave canem*" mosaic of 29, which fooled the narrator]. A hound of enormous size was immediately led in on a chain. A kick from the hall-porter reminded him to lie down and he stretched himself out in front of the table. Trimalchio threw him a piece of white bread remarking: 'Nobody in the house is more devoted to me' (*nemo, inquit, in domo mea me plus amat*). (J. P. Sullivan, trans., *Petronius: the Satyricon and the Fragments* [Baltimore: Penguin, 1969] 75).

[63] 110.2–3, trans. Daly, *Aesop Without Morals*, 81.

[64] Since intercourse with Aesop is like sex with an animal (and slaves are, in a sense, animals), it may be worth noting that one of the fables he tells against himself involves a man engaged in intercourse with a mule (131). That fable, in turn, suggests an element of the "Donkey-Romance" (Apuleius *Met.* 10.19–22//[?Ps.] Lucian *Onos* 50–52). In the latter Lucius, restored to human form, visits, with considerable anticipation, his former lover, only to be ejected because his transformation has been too complete for her taste. She had expected that he would preserve and wave his asinine credential (σύρειν τὸ μέγα τοῦ ὄνου σύμβολον), and labels the restored Lucius as a mere monkey (ἐς πίθηκον μεταμορφωθεῖς(56). Compare the more formidably endowed Aesop and his tail (30).

Chapters 44–50, in which Aesop capitalizes upon vague instructions to precipitate a family quarrel, also exhibits retardation. The climax might have come promptly in 46, but is delayed by a return to the symposium in 46–48, which postpones the confrontation. In the closing chapters the execution of Aesop, announced as imminent in 132, is retarded through a series of six fables, the last on the very verge of death. Readers certainly know how the story will end, but this delay arouses suspense and heightens pathos.

The initial scenes present a brief and effective example of retardation. Aesop gives, as it were, a cup of cold water to a minister (ἱεροφόρος) of Isis who has lost her way. She prays that he will be rewarded. After a narrative summary of her petition (4), the narrator supplies her verbatim prayer offered upon finding the right road.[65] The goddess listened to his prayer. Of this Aesop was, of course, ignorant. For him it was time for his blessed siesta.[66] There follows in chapter 6 an elegant purple patch, a charming ecphrasis that both delays the resolution and foreshadows all

---

Comparison with the ass-story reveals how similar the fates of Aesop and Lucius are. Aesop and his fellow slaves must serve as pack-animals (17–19), as does the ass (and the foolish Socrates, *Met.* 1.7. Cf. also Seneca, *ep.* 47.5). Both are beaten, abused, accused of crimes of which they are not guilty, unable to defend themselves, locked up for their alleged misdeeds, and given promises that are not fulfilled. Slaves are animals.

[65] However understood in the narrative context, this prayer is an expression of genuine piety: διάδημα τῆς ὅλης οἰκουμένης, Ἴσι μυριώνυμε, ἐλέησον τόνδε τὸν ἐργάτην, τὸν κακοπαθοῦντα, τὸν εὐσεβῆ, ἀνθ᾽ ὧν εὐσέβεσεν, οὐκ εἰς ἐμέ, δέσποινα, ἀλλ᾽ εἰς τό σὸν σχῆμα. καὶ εἰ μὴ πολυτάλαντον τὸν βίον αὐτοῦ διορθώσασθαι βούλει, ὃν ἄλλοι θεοὶ ἀφήρηνται, τὸ γοῦν λαλεῖν αὐτῷ χάρισαι· δυνατὴ γὰρ σὺ καὶ τὰ ἐν σκότει πεπτωκότα πάλιν εἰς φῶς προ<αν>ελέσθαι. ("Oh, crown of the whole world, Isis of many names, have pity on this workman, who suffers and is pious, for the piety he has shown, not to me, Oh mistress, but to your appearance. And if you are unwilling to repay this man with a livelihood of many talents for what the other gods have taken from him, at least grant him the power of speech, for you have the power to bring back to light those things which have fallen into darkness." 5.3–8, trans. Daly, *Aesop Without Morals*, 33). Both the form of the prayer and the role of Isis as restorer of fallen humans invite comparison with Apuleius *Met.* 11.1–6. The difference is, of course, that in *Aesop* Isis appears at the beginning and never again, although her services would have been useful. In Apuleius's novel, she effects the rescue that brings about a happy ending. Nonetheless, the gift of speech effectively transforms Aesop from animal to genuinely human existence.

[66] The contrast between this scene and Lucian *Philopseudes* 22, where bored and wealthy Eucrates leaves his workers to their chores and wanders off into the woods, there to encounter a divine being (who is awesome, half a stade in height, and accompanied by an earthquake and thunder), underlines the status of Aesop. For slaves epiphanies must, so to speak, be restricted to periods of permitted leisure.

manner of pleasant things.[67] Moment and scene are idyllic. Early Christian literature also relates healing miracles, but none of them is adorned with *this* sort of "novelistic detail."[68] Hitherto "nature" has been nothing but soil requiring wracking labor. The ecphrasis is an epiphany of an almost joycean sort, the first light of a sun that will bring transformation.[69] Its utopian quality is congruent with a theology that views Isis as the source of earth's beauty and fruits; in its depiction of natural beneficence chapter 6 foreshadows the story of Mother Nature's care for her step-children (37).[70] Its rhetorical quality[71] foreshadows the verbal gifts Aesop will receive.[72]

---

[67] On this passage see E. Mignogna, "Aesopus Bucolicus: Come si 'mette in scena' un miracolo (Vita Aesopi c.6)," in Holzberg, *Äsop Roman*, 76–84. She demonstrates that the best parallel to this passage is Hesiod, *Op. et Dies* 582–596. Hesiod is certainly an apt allusion for a scene that will bring an epiphany of the Muses to a rustic figure. It should be noted that *Works and Days* belongs to the tradition of ancient popular wisdom and is therefore a suitable resource for the story of Aesop the sage.

[68] The differences between G and W at this point are considerable. Both refer to a minister or priests of Isis, but W is much shorter, omits the ecphrasis of chap. 6, and assigns the epiphany to Tyche alone, without the Muses. Elimination of the Muses is almost certainly secondary. Which came first? Tyche or Isis? On the one hand Tyche is more Hellenistic, appropriate to New Comedy and the like. On the other hand she is relatively colorless and is less objectionable to Christian readers, who were familiar with her statues in their cities. W might derive from the scholarly activities of ninth-century Byzantines, who returned to the earlier standards of Greek historiography, in which Fate plays a prominent part. The most decisive factor is, however, the role of Isis (and Serapis) with healing miracles. Tyche was not a healing goddess. Still, it is a nice problem. See Jedrkiewicz, *Sapere*, 178–180, and Holzberg, "Äsop-Roman," 45 n. 59 with references.

[69] The closing words are: ἐφ' ὧν ψυχαγωγούμενος ὁ Αἴσωπος εἰς ἡδὺν ὕπνον κατήγετο (6.17–18).

[70] On chs. 34–37 see also below. Since chap. 6 would not be out of place in *Daphnis and Chloe*, the reader may also detect here a sophisticated irony in the strong contrast between the tone and content of these two novels. The utopian coloring will gain meaning in the graces bestowed upon Aesop. His animal fables (e.g., 97, 99, 133) often refer to the golden age when humans and animals shared the same speech (cf. Gen 3).

[71] One of the book's most successful combinations of literary style and psychological insight emerges in the account of Aesop's discovery that he can speak (8), as he joyfully names the objects before him. The asyndeton effectively communicates his excitement: "Now there is a mattock; that is an ox. . . ."

[72] Effective retardation also marks the story of how Aesop met the challenge of king Nectanebo to build a tower that touches neither earth nor heaven, broached in 105 and resolved in 116. At the outset Lycurgus is helpless. There follows the news that Aesop is alive (107). Following his rehabilitation and attempt to instruct his nephew, Aesop makes his preparations (107–111). In chap. 112 he arrives at Memphis, where his display is delayed by a series of challenges (112–115).

The events of the beginning are artfully echoed in the final chapters. First and foremost, as Niklas Holzberg observes,[73] Aesop is to all intents and purposes "speechless" at Delphi, for his words might as well have been addressed to the wind, so ineffective were they. Healed in response to his hospitality to a representative of a god (4), he dies when the Delphians will not respect a shrine and Zeus Xenios, the god of strangers. The priestess required assistance because she had gone astray. Aesop's penultimate fable is about a farmer who had gone astray (140). That farmer, like Aesop, found no helper.[74] Another of his Delphic fables tells of a woman who prayed that her daughter might acquire intelligence, echoing the pious prayer of the priestess. This prayer, too, is answered, but not as she wished, because of mistaken literalism, one of the book's ironic leitmotifs (131).[75] Finally, of course, the shrine in which the condemned Aesop seeks refuge is dedicated to the *Muses*, his initial benefactors (7; 134). With the exception of the reference to Muses, none of these correspondences is exact, wooden, or particularly contrived. Artistry of this quality does not suggest a narrator who arbitrarily arranged assembled traditions.

The romance redounds with skillful plotting. Chapter 67 initially appears to be an independent scatological *chreia*. Xanthus is at a symposium and well into his cups when nature calls.[76] As a slave Aesop must stand near to hand with water and towel. Xanthus poses a conundrum: why do people examine their bowel movements? Aesop answers with an etiological story about a prince who, due to his excesses, was so devoted to defecation that he discharged his own brains. On this account

---

[73] Holzberg, "Äsop-Roman," 71.

[74] The final fable concerns a man who sent his wife into the country so that he could abuse his daughter (141). In the opening chapter Aesop, unsuitable for urban service, is sent to the country and becomes the target of abuse. In turn he engages in illicit sex with his mistress. Isis would not approve: her inspired priest reproves Lucius for having sex with a slave (Apuleius *Met.* 11.15).

[75] A fragment from the *Acts of Peter*, preserved in Pseudo-Titus *De Dispositione Sanctimonii*, tells of a farmer who prayed that Peter would do what was "fitting" for his daughter. In response, she fell dead. Since this did not please the father, Peter revived her. Within a few days she eloped with a guest. (The text was edited by D. de Bruyne, *Revue Bénédictine* 25 [1908] 151–52. See also de Santos Otero in *New Testament Apocrypha* [W. Schneemelcher ed.; R. McL. Wilson, trans.; 2 vols.; Louisville: Westminster/John Knox, 1992] 2.53–74 and W. Schneemelcher, *Apocrypha*, 279, 287.)

[76] Vocations of this character are not excluded from ancient narrative fiction. Examples include Heliodorus, *An Ethiopian Story*, 2.19, Iamblichus, 74b, *AAndr* 13, and, far from least, Apuleius *Met.* 7.28.

Xanthus need not worry; he has no brains to lose.[77] This is no isolated anecdote, but part of a unit that extends through chapter 74. Xanthus returns to the party where it soon becomes clear that he *has* lost his wits. The subject is the same: conundra. Aesop seeks to warn his master with a theological story, but to no avail. Xanthus is so drunk that he wagers all of his *bios* that he can drink up the sea and pledges his ring as a token.

The following morning Xanthus is performing his morning ablutions, with Aesop and pitcher once more in attendance, when he notices the missing ring and inquires as to its whereabouts, whereupon his slave reveals the grim truth. This narrative technique is one means by which authors weave isolated incidents into an artful plot, "the figure in the carpet," to borrow a phrase from Henry James. Xanthus's ignorance about the ring is a synecdoche for his oblivion and a metaphor for his missing brains.[78] These chapters display more the hand of a skillful narrator than the thumb-print of a collector of anecdotes.

Our author knows something of rhetoric, as well as philosophy. 51–56 describe one of the many symposia Xanthus gives for his students. Following a number of humiliating experiences about the use of precise language, Xanthus simply orders Aesop to provide something good and attractive (ὀψ<ών>ησον εἴ τι χρηστὸν ἐν τῷ βίῳ 51.3). Xanthus cannot

---

[77] Aesop's first experience with his new master deals with appropriate techniques for micturation (28). Anderson (*Ancient Fiction*, 211) finds "the motif . . . understandably rare in literature" and urges attention. He notes that Trimalchio first comes into view while relieving himself: in *Sat.* 27.5–6 Menelaus says, after they have observed Trimalchio in the bath,

"This is the man you'll be dining with . . . in fact, you are now watching the beginning of the dinner." No sooner had Menelaus spoken than Trimalchio snapped his fingers. At the signal the eunuch brought the chamber pot for him, while he went on playing. With the weight off his bladder, he demanded water for his hands, splashed a few drops on his fingers and wiped them on a boy's head." (Trans. Sullivan, *Petronius*, 45.) Xanthus preferred to perform this duty on the road. One may observe that Hesiod, one of the author's favorite poets, introduces the θεῖος ἀνήρ to western literature with the observation that those so characterized will not piss against the wind: ἑζόμενος δ' ὅ γε θεῖος ἀνήρ, πεπνυμένα εἰδώς, ἢ ὅ γε πρός τοῖχον πελάσας εὐερκέος αὐλῆς. (*Op. et Dies* 731–32). Xanthus is no "divine man." Aesop's response sheds light on the status of slaves bound to masters with high standards: he will have to defecate on the fly. In the light of that remark, chap. 67 acquires some irony.

[78] Not long thereafter the city of Samos will lose its seal and Xanthus will be unable to explain the significance of the event (81). For his part Aesop will be betrayed by his own signet ring (104).

cure himself of indefinite references to the singular.[79] Aesop acquires pigs' tongues and prepares them in three different ways. The guests are soon nauseated and admit that they have been vanquished by tongues—a relatively clever pun. Aesop replies with a bit of conventional epideictic rhetoric:

A. τί οὖν ἐστιν ἐν τῷ βίῳ γλώσσης χρησιμώτερον ἢ μεῖζον; μάθε ὅτι

B. διὰ γλώσσης πᾶσα φιλοσοφία καὶ πᾶσα παιδεία συνέστηκεν.

C. χωρὶς γλώσσης οὐδὲν γίνεται,
οὐδὲ δόσις, οὐ<δὲ> λῆψις, οὐδὲ ἀγορασμός (triad)

C'. ἀλλὰ διὰ γλώσσης πόλεις ἀνορθοῦνται, δόγματα καὶ νόμοι ὁρίζονται (triad)

B'. εἰ οὖν διὰ γλώσσης πᾶς βίος συνέστηκεν,

A'. γλώσσης οὐδέν ἐστι κρεῖττον (53.5–10).

"What can one imagine finer or greater than the tongue? You must observe that all philosophy, all education, depends on the tongue. Without the tongue nothing gets done, neither giving, nor receiving, nor buying. By means of the tongue states are reformed and ordinances and laws laid down. If, then, all life is ordered by the tongue, nothing is greater than the tongue."[80]

1 Corinthians 13 is one of many examples of the type. Aesop's point is made. On the next day Xanthus orders Aesop to produce the worst (54). What does he buy? Tongue, naturally. When challenged, it becomes clear that the cat has not got his tongue.

A. καὶ τί χεῖρον διὰ γλώσσης οὐκ ἔστιν;

B. διὰ γλώσσης ἔχθραι, διὰ γλώσσης ἐπιβουλαί, ἐνεδρεῖαι, μάχαι, ζηλοτυπίαι, ἔρεις, πόλεμοι,[81]

A. οὐκοῦν χεῖρον οὐδέν ἐστι τῆς μιαρωτάτης γλώσσης (55.3–6).

"What is there that is bad which does not come about through the tongue? It is because of the tongue that there are enmity, plots, battles, rivalry, strife, wars. Is it not, then, true that there is nothing worse than this most abominable tongue?"[82]

---

[79] In 39 he asked Aesop to cook lentil for himself and his guests. Aesop made a soup from one lentil. Gal 3:16 is an example of the use of this differentiation in dialectic.

[80] Trans. Daly, *Aesop Without Morals,* 57.

[81] This catalogue of vices is not unlike those found in early Christian literature. Cf., for example, Gal. 5:20 (ἔρις κ. ἔχθρα); James 4:1, 4 (μάχη κ. ἔχθρα); Rom 13:13 (ζῆλος κ. ἔρις). Such parallels emphasize the extent to which early Christian ethics utilized the language of civic discourse.

[82] Trans. Daly, *Aesop Without Morals,* 58.

Topoi such as these are normally used to provide a contrast.[83] By applying the techniques of praise and blame to the same object Aesop mocks rhetoric and dialectic, which can present equally convincing arguments for both sides of a question. His much learning threatens to drive students and professor mad.[84] The conclusion to this episode introduces the theme of the next: the rarity of those who do not mind other people's business.

Holzberg has made a detailed study of the structure of the romance with a careful detection of its patterns.[85] Holzberg notes the prominence of triplets[86] and observes that the entire work conforms to one type of fable pattern in which the protagonist first does something right, then something wrong, and thus comes to a bad end. Moreover, each of the three major sections of the work features a particular type of teaching: direct speech, solution of enigmas, and fables.[87] However much some may wish to criticize components of his analysis or to propose alternatives,

---

[83] Cf. 1 Esdr 4:34–40 "Gentlemen, are not women strong? The earth is vast, and heaven is high, and the sun is swift in its course, for it makes the circuit of the heavens and returns to its place in one day. [35]Is he not great who does these things? But truth is great, and stronger than all things. [36]The whole earth calls upon truth, and heaven blesses her. All God's works quake and tremble, and with him there is nothing unrighteous. [37]Wine is unrighteous, the king is unrighteous, women are unrighteous, all the sons of men are unrighteous, all their works are unrighteous, and all such things. There is no truth in them and in their unrighteousness they will perish. [38]But truth endures and is strong for ever, and lives and prevails for ever and ever. [39]With her there is no partiality or preference, but she does what is righteous instead of anything that is unrighteous or wicked. All men approve her deeds, [40]and there is nothing unrighteous in her judgment. To her belongs the strength and the kingship and the power and the majesty of all the ages. Blessed be the God of truth!" (RSV).

[84] Cf. Acts 26:24.

[85] Holzberg, "Äsop-Roman."

[86] Triplets are equally important in such early Christian narratives as Mark, for example the three-fold pattern built about Jesus's three predictions of his death in chs. 8–10, each of which is followed by an assertion of misunderstanding, a lesson on discipleship, and a wonder.

[87] The core of Holzberg's outline is:
1. Prologue. (1–19)
2. Aesop and Xanthos. (20–9)
2.1 Aesop arrives in Xanthus's household as a slave. (20–33)
2.2 Aesop plays tricks on his master. (34–64)
2.3 Aesop helps his master. ([65–67] 68–91)
3. Aesop helps the Samians. (92–100)
4. Aesop helps king Lycorus of Babylon. (101–123)
5. Aesop in Delphi: he cannot help himself (124–142)

it will henceforth be extremely difficult to contend that the romance lacks structure.

IV. Aesop as "Gospel"

Introductory Remarks

In seeking to read Aesop as a "gospel"[88] I desire neither to assimilate it to Christian (or religious) literature in an imperialistic way nor merely to demonstrate its relevance for the study of early Christian literature, but rather to raise questions about its viewpoint and "message" while expanding the literary and cultural horizons of those who focus upon early Christian narrative. The project is justified on general grounds in that the romance is a popular, anti-establishment account of the life and death of a teacher of wisdom who preferred short figurative stories to long-winded rhetoric, dialectic, and metaphysics. Historical justification stems from the use of *Ahikar.* The story of Ahikar is one of the earliest (and best attested) Semitic texts that combines a life-story with teaching. Tales of the vindication of the suffering righteous person provided the model for the framework of Christian accounts of the passion of Jesus.[89] The *Aesop-Romance* shares these roots but develops them from a quite different perspective and views them through different cultural and ideological lenses. If one can see in Mark a "gospel as parable,"[90] one can likewise read *Aesop* as a "gospel in fable."

The broad structure of the romance reveals similarities and differences from the canonical gospel pattern. Chapters 1–19 constitute a prologue, in which Aesop is equipped for his vocation and established in a household. Estimates about the extent of the prologues to the various Gospels differ, but only Luke devotes a comparable amount of text to events prior to the public ministry. More than one half of *Aesop* relates to his "private" experience in the household of Xanthus (20–91), a home in which he lacks honor and freedom. Thereafter Aesop is a free and public figure, moving from a local to an international stage (92–123), and finally electing to go to the city of his destiny and nemesis, Delphi (124–142). In

---

[88] For the purposes of this study "gospel" is to be construed in a very wide sense, not exclusive of the various acts nor even of hagiography.

[89] See G. W. Nickelsburg, "The Genre and Function of the Markan Passion Narrative," *HTR* 73 (1980) 153–84.

[90] J. R. Donahue has proposed reading gospels as "parable." See, for example, *The Gospel in Parable: Metaphor, Narrative, and Theology in the Synoptic Gospels* (Philadelphia: Fortress, 1988).

broad terms, the beginning and end resemble those of the story of Jesus; the middle is different.

Even in this central section similarities can be noted, not just in that Aesop has come to set members of the household against one another and corrode the foundations of social order,[91] but also in that much of his service takes place in the context of intellectual symposia at which issues of etiquette and questions of philosophy have more or less equal weight.[92] The numerous symposia in the Gospel of Luke come to mind.[93] Preparation of a commentary on the social and intellectual significance of the meals in *Aesop* would be a rewarding exercise. These scenes add to the considerable literature parodying symposia.[94]

Aesop as Social Gospel

That major difference noted between the stories of Aesop and Jesus is important. Both engage the microcosm (family) and macrocosm (city) of social life, but Aesop the slave is depicted as living within the microcosm and Aesop the freedman plays an important role in civic life. The romance deals with the basic themes of political life, including the well-being of the polis and its survival under imperialism. *Aesop* is in this sense genuinely and fundamentally Hellenic. The Jesus tradition provides but bits and glimpses of city life, with a preference for outdoor teaching in rural areas and stories about village existence. The *Aesop-Romance* takes place within the world inhabited by the apostle Paul, and its hero, like the

---

[91] Cf. Luke 12:49–53 and parallels.

[92] Although substantial drinking is characteristic of these meals, the food is expected to be simple and there are no professional entertainers or elegant servants. To this extent Xanthus would receive high marks from the philosophical tradition. The exception comes in 57–64, where Xanthus is seeking to prove to Aesop that anyone can become a περίεργος. The symposia of this section, which abound in comparisons with the banquet of Trimalchio in the *Satyrica*, involve a number of varied courses and presume the presence of a cook and a baker, who can expect punishment for their shortcomings. Elsewhere cooking is Aesop's responsibility. Chapters 57–64 may have been adopted from one or more comic sources without particular regard for a lack of consistency. It is clear that the narrator of *Aesop*, like many popular narrators, is not worried about *some* inconsistencies. This selective indifference does not, however, justify the conclusion that the narrative is uniformly careless or devoid of structure.

[93] For example: Luke 5:17–29; 7:36–50; 10:38–42; 11:37–54; 14:1–24; 19:1–10; 22:14–38.

[94] On symposia see R. Pervo, "PANTA KOINA: The Feeding Stories in the Light of Economic Data and Social Practice," in *Religious Propaganda and Missionary Competition in the New Testament World: Essays Honoring Dieter Georgi* (L. Bornmann et al., eds.; Leiden: E. J. Brill, 1994) 164–94, and the references there.

Paul of Acts, can move easily in the courts of the mighty. If the behavior of Aesop evokes the Jesus of the apophthegms,[95] the "ethics" are closer to the exhortations of Paul regarding community life.[96]

If one can imagine "Paul of Tarsus" and Jesus of Nazareth reading and discussing this book, it is thus likely that Paul would have found more merit in its themes than Jesus would have, although the latter might have been somewhat more appreciative of its earthy humor. Keith Hopkins has provided an illuminating reading of *Aesop* as a source of views about slavery.[97] Most of the tensions and anomalies of slavery are cleverly exposed: in the field slaves are subject to the vicious brutality of supervisory fellow slaves; at home they are ever-present targets for arbitrary humiliation and abuse.[98] The promise of manumission is often advanced and just as often withdrawn. Injustice prevails on both fronts.

One subject of considerable interest to historians of early Christianity and of ancient social life is the fantasy picture of the absent good κύριος (master).[99] This fantasy is prominent in *Aesop* 1–15, especially chapters 1–3, and 9–12. In 13 Aesop makes an explicit contrast between his master κατὰ φύσιν and the manager.[100] The same theme governs the parable of Luke 12:42–46//Matt 24:45–51. *Aesop* permits readers to hear the words of an absent master: He instructs his manager Zenas to sell Aesop, give him away if he cannot be sold, and beat him to death if no one will take him *gratis.* So much for fantasy. Nonetheless, Hopkins rightly views the novel as non-revolutionary. One might call it moderately reformist in viewpoint.

---

[95] For example, Luke 7:36–50 (Mark 14:3–9), Mark 7:1–23.

[96] Note the comments on the catalogue in 55.3–5, n. 81.

[97] "Novel Evidence."

[98] 13.9–16 offers a telling critique of slave life: Aesop threw his mattock down and said, "What a wearisome thing it is being a slave to a slave! What's more, it must be evil in the sight of the gods. 'Aesop, lay the table. Aesop, heat the bath. Aesop, feed the livestock.' [Cf. Luke 17:7–10]. Anything that's unpleasant or tiresome or painful or menial, that's what Aesop is ordered to do. So I have the power of speech the gods gave me, don't I? The master will come, and I'll be right there to accuse this fellow and do him out of his stewardship. But now I must knuckle under. (Trans. Daly, *Aesop Without Morals,* 36–37.) The crucial phrase is παραδεδομένη δουλεία, translated by Daly as "being a slave to a slave." Other renditions ("slavery betrayed") are possible, but what is essential is that he does not say that slavery is absolutely and unconditionally evil. For similar sentiments see Appendix 20 to the fables, quoted in n. 102 below, and Herodas *Mime* 8.1–15, where the master awakens a female slave with language that would earn the admiration of a drill-sergeant.

[99] Hopkins, "Novel Evidence," 15, identifies this theme.

[100] This phrase makes explicit the view that slavery belongs to the realm of φύσις (nature) rather than to that of νόμος (convention).

Masters who mistreat their slaves are likely to pay a price; Xanthus was cuckolded on one (extended) occasion and humiliated on any number of others. Uppity slaves are also liable to punishment. Aesop does die in the end, after all. Manumission, the dream of most slaves, may not satisfy all of the claims advanced on its behalf:[101] "The irony is that once freed Aesop no longer has the protection of his master. Freedom exposes the ex-slave to fresh dangers."[102]

Aesop may become the master of Xanthus (28),[103] but he will be beaten for his achievements.[104] The *Aesop-Romance* is a cautionary tale for

---

[101] The social function of manumission in Roman imperial slavery as a benefit to masters is helpfully illuminated by K. R. Bradley, *Slaves and Masters in the Roman Empire* (New York: Oxford University Press, 1987), who built upon the earlier work of K. Hopkins, *Conquerors and Slaves* (Cambridge: Cambridge University Press, 1978). The relevance of this for the study of early Christian social thought is ably set forth by A. J. Harrill, *The Manumission of Slaves in Early Christianity.* (HUT 32; Tübingen: Mohr (Siebeck), 1995). In sum: modern researchers incline to view manumission as motivated by liberal principles. If Paul, for example, favors manumission (1 Cor 7:21), he is a liberal. In the Greco-Roman world, however, manumission was a conservative technique, the carrot used to elicit good behavior, just as the stick punished bad behavior.

[102] Hopkins, "Novel Evidence," 14, with references to Epict. *Diss.* 4.1.35 and Phaedrus, *Appendix* 20, which is not a fable of the traditional type: "A slave running away from a master of cruel disposition met Aesop, to whom he was known as a neighbour. 'What are you excited about?' asked Aesop. 'I will tell you frankly, father—and you deserve to be called by that name—since my complaint can be safely entrusted to your keeping. I get a surplus of blows and a shortage of rations. Every now and then I am sent out to my master's farm without any provisions for the journey. Whenever he dines at home I stand by in attendance all night long; if he is invited out I lie in the street until daybreak. I have earned my liberty, but I am still a slave though gray-headed. If I were aware of any fault on my own part, I should bear this with patience. I have never yet had my belly full, and besides that I have the bad luck to suffer tyranny exercised by a cruel master. For these reasons, and others which it would be too long to recount, I have decided to go away wherever my feet shall take me.' 'Now then, listen,' said Aesop, 'these are the hardships that you suffer, according to your account, when you have done no wrong; what if you commit an offence? What do you think you will suffer then?' By such advice the man was deterred from running away. (Trans. Perry, *Babrius and Phaedrus*, 401–403.) The relevance of this to such passages as Luke 12:35–38; 17:7–10 is noteworthy.

[103] The name Xanthus, "golden boy," is one of the ironies of the romance, as it is a common name for slaves. When Aesop publicly exposes Mme. X.'s fantasies about the new slave, he describes him as ξάνθος, blond.

[104] Aesop receives beatings in 58 and 77; the last is brutal but cut short, in good novelistic fashion, by a *deus-ex-machina*. Sadistic fascination with flagellation is manifest in Herodas, *Mimes* 3 and 5, and is characteristic of martyrological literature, as in 2 Macc 7:1; 4 Macc 6:3, 6; 9:12 (cf. Acts 16:23; 22:25) and novels (Pervo, *Profit*, 48–50, with a quote from A. D. Nock).

masters and slaves, with particular reference to the latter. This text could be read aloud in a household of masters and slaves during Saturnalia. Everyone would have a good time, some steam could be released, and then things could get back to normal. Aesop is, when all has been said and done, a *loyal* slave who repeatedly helps his master when he appears, in the eyes of modern readers, to have no moral obligation to do so. Stuck with a master unwilling to reward his service with manumission, Aesop found occasion to gain freedom by simultaneously helping his master.

The literary function of potential manumission is to provide suspense: when and how will Aesop be able to achieve freedom? It drives the plot in the same manner that worry about when the couple will be re-united functions in romantic novels.[105] That the story does not end with the manumission of Aesop to live happily ever after is no less important to appreciation of its literary structure and sophistication.

Aesop the Teacher

As teachers Jesus and Aesop have much in common, including a down-home sort of wit that exposes pretensions and clarifies issues through the telling of simple stories and the use of proverbs.[106] Aesop could be called a "narrative 'theologian,'" one who answers questions and resolves problems by telling stories. In both cases their stories will issue in the death of the protagonist. Elements of the Cynic and Socratic traditions that are more latent in the Jesus-tradition play, as might be expected, a more overt role in the story of Aesop.[107]

---

[105] Perhaps an even more apt example is the simultaneous fear and hope of the reader that Daphnis and Chloe will learn how to make love. Cf. also n. 59.

[106] Perry (*Aesopica* 261–289) lists 179 aphorisms and proverbs attributed to Aesop in two collections. In the romance proverbs may be applied by the narrator (e.g., 4) or uttered by the protagonist (e.g., 26).

[107] There is a detailed and perceptive analysis of the comparisons between Aesop and Socrates by M. Schauer and S. Merkle, "Äsop und Sokrates," in Holzberg, *Der Äsop Roman*, 85–96, a theme to be discussed below. Among the more specific affinities with Diogenes, in addition to his canine lack of discretion while engaging in the private relief of sexual tension, are Aesop's quest for someone who minds his own business (57–64), reminiscent of Diogenes's search for a good person (D.L. 6.41); his witticisms in the slave market, where he offered himself to those who would purchase a master (D.L. 6.29; 74); and the anecdote about true men in the baths (*Aesop* 66; D.L. 6.40). Diogenes had difficulty interpreting the voice of Delphi (D.L. 6.20–21) and regarded temple theft as acceptable (D.L. 6.73—although food seems to be the issue, as it is in POxy. 1800). These motifs highlight the more general role of Aesop as a critic of superficial culture and apparent wisdom like Diogenes.

With regard to his prophetic qualities Aesop has rather more in common with Daniel (and with the ideal sage of Sirach 39:1–6) than with Jesus. Like Daniel he receives honor and advancement, serving a Babylonian king as διοικήτης (101).[108] Like Daniel he is a diviner. Divination, including the interpretation of dreams and omens, is one of this novel's pervasive themes. The task is a presumed function of philosophers (who thereby likewise take on the role of the ideal sage of Sirach 39:1–6).[109] The uses and limits of divination constitute one of the perduring and subtly unifying themes of the romance.[110] This theme gains in force when Aesop's conflict with Apollo is taken into account.

As Aesop stands liminally at the door of his new home Mme. X. announces that she has dreamed of a beautiful new slave.[111] Xanthus assures her that she will see "an *Apollo,* or an Endymion or a Ganymede," a trio that could serve as the cast for a female version of the judgment of Paris. Her dream will not come true.[112] Aesop resolves the dilemma with an explanation of the origin of true and false dreams.[113] The latter, it transpires, arose because the patron of the *Muses,* Apollo, suffered from *hybris.* This angered Zeus, who inaugurated divination through dreams. In due time Zeus forgave Apollo and devised false dreams as a means for restoring the popularity of Apollo's oracle (33).

In the immediate context this explanation mollified Mme. X. It also foreshadows much of the plot and names many leading themes: ugly

---

[108] Both Daniel and Aesop, as well as Mordecai (Esther), participate in the literary tradition reflected in *Ahikar,* of course, but this is a source the author of *Aesop* chose to use and to integrate into the account.

[109] Nowhere is the "popular" viewpoint of the romance more apparent than in its picture of philosophers, who can best serve the public as wizards but who are generally incompetent and hypocritical. (The birth of philosophy and the stereotype of the absent-minded professor appear to have been simultaneous, witness the story about Thales's fall into an irrigation ditch [Plato, *Theaetetus* 174a]. Aristophanes's *Clouds* provides an apt comparison as well as a contrast illustrative of social and cultural change: *Aesop* is a narrative written in a generally simple style for a broad public.)

[110] Various types of divination serve varied and vital functions in ancient novels. For some examples see Pervo, *Profit,* 72–74, 164–165.

[111] 29, on which see above.

[112] Artemidorus *Onirocriticon* 1.78 (p. 88, 8–10 Pack) states that dreaming of being penetrated by a domestic slave is not good, as it signifies that the dreamer will be scorned and injured by that slave. If the text is not exclusively androcentric—as it probably is—the advice would have profited Mme. X.

[113] The distinction between true and false dreams was a general problem that engaged the attention of ancient specialists in dream theory and interpretation.

Aesop vs. beautiful Apollo, the role of Delphi, the Muses, the *saeva ira* (fierce anger) of a deity, and the supreme lordship of Zeus.[114] Later (ch. 77) Xanthus boasts of his acumen as an interpreter of omens. A pair of crows, it seems, would augur particularly good luck. Sent to observe the signs, Aesop spots a pair of crows by the door and so reports. Between cup and lip there was a vital slip, as one of the birds had flown away before Xanthus could arrive. For his "false" reporting Aesop receives a thorough whipping,[115] after which he denounces the whole business of divination as vain (εἰς μάτην, 77.4).

Like Daniel, Aesop can read the handwriting on the wall, specifically a grave, decoding the (allegedly) mysterious A B Δ O E Θ X in three different ways, each varying according to circumstances, but uncovering a buried treasure nevertheless.[116] The playful variations of his existential exegesis are not without their critical implications for all such mystification and its interpretation (78–80). Nor is its reward: confinement.[117]

These omens and puzzles have set the stage for a portent of public interest. In the midst of civic elections at Samos an eagle sweeps down and steals the city seal. Seers and priests can offer no solution. Bible readers would know that in situations like this it is time for the coach to put Daniel into the game.[118] In fact the Samians will get a Joseph.[119] An astute elder observes that Xanthus, the noted philosopher, is on hand and well qualified for this duty. As in the case of his wife's dream, etc., he

---

[114] Note also the long fable of chs. 134–139.

[115] One experience Aesop shares with the characters of a wide range of ancient fiction is frequent condemnation without proper investigation or trial: 11, 77, 104, and 132.

[116] Stoneman ("Riddles in Bronze and Stone," 159–170, 166–167) points out the parallel with the dedicatory inscription of Alexandria (*Alex.-Romance* 1.32), together with a number of interesting observations about the function of omens and other divinatory materials in the two works. The discovery of gold through an inscription also occurs in Iamblichus, 74a.

[117] 78–80 provide a revealing commentary on the status of slaves. Aesop has found a treasure. His master is welcome to half and is to free Aesop who will take the balance, but emancipation would leave Aesop free to betray Xanthus for appropriating the treasure of a king. Aesop gets neither freedom nor gold and is locked up for his pains. Holzberg ("Äsop-Roman," 49) places chs. 34–37 and 78–80 as a frame around material depicting Aesop's victories over his master. Each of these passages includes the theme of divine aid and providence.

[118] Cf. Daniel 2.

[119] Cf. Gen 41 (in which sexual relations between mistress and slave also play a large role).

was hapless.[120] Aesop must be released from captivity to give the solution (81–91). By pinning Xanthus in a corner bounded by honor and shame he wins his freedom. The civic assembly provides a public forum in which Aesop can achieve what private negotiations could never achieve.[121]

After interpreting an omen regarded by all as anything but vain, Aesop the freedman takes up a new style of teaching: in fables.[122] Whereas the ancient collections of Aesopic fables were prepared and indexed as resources to help rhetors find illustrations to enliven their speeches (much on the order of modern "sermon illustrations," or anecdotes for speakers),[123] fables and the like constituted for Aesop the essential, if not the entire, content of his reported addresses. Many will be reminded of the use of the parables of Jesus in the gospel tradition. This comparison alone indicates the extent to which gospel and *Aesop-Romance* can illuminate their respective cultural settings. Furthermore, both the parables of Jesus and the fables of Aesop acquire interpretation from their narrative contexts. Outside of these settings, their meaning is frequently ambiguous.[124] Fables and parables can have similar functions: through an analogy presented in the form of a brief story hearers are given opportunity to detach themselves from emotional and other prejudices so as to be able to view the situation in a fresh light that often reveals an obvious solution.[125] Since, however, the stated task of this essay

---

[120] Xanthus had, in fact, already lost his own seal once and could not remember it. Aesop's personal seal is used to his disadvantage in 104.

[121] Aesop's risible price forms an *inclusio* around his ownership by Xanthus (27 and 90).

[122] The Prologue to Phaedrus, Book 3, 32–37, states that slaves invented the fable as a means for veiling their actual thoughts and thus evading punishment for insolence or impudence. Mark 4 advances the theory that Jesus spoke in parables as a form of unintelligible code. In the romance fables are not veiled communication but more often a means for communicating in ways that people *can* understand without taking offense or blaming the messenger. Some of the Delphi fables (123–142) are offensive, but their meaning is not veiled.

[123] Perry, *Babrius and Phaedrus*, xv, Holzberg *Antike Fabel*, 26–29.

[124] A recent study of the parables stressing such ambiguities is Charles W. Hedrick, *Parables as Poetic Fictions: The Creative Voice of Jesus* (Peabody, MA: Hendrickson, 1994).

[125] It may be accounted as either a weakness or a strength of the romance that no explanation is offered for the change in form. One might presume that audiences, for whom the name Aesop was synonymous with fable, have been waiting expectantly for the frequent use of the form. He has had this capacity from the beginning, for the Muses bestowed upon him λόγων εὕρεμα καὶ μύθων Ἑλληνικῶν πλοκὴν καὶ ποιήσεις (7.11–12. on πλοκή note Apuleius *Met.* 1.1 . . . *varias fabulas conseram*. See also the textual difficulties, Papathomopoulos, ὁ βίος τοῦ Αἰσώπου, 45). In the narrative there has been much λόγων εὕρεμα, but few "Greek stories." In retrospect

is narrative comparison, it may be high time to get back to our maiden tied to the railroad tracks.

In the Beginning

Beginnings are for authors both a problem and an opportunity. How should gospels begin? With a promise of revelation: "These are the secret sayings that the living Jesus spoke and Didymos Judas Thomas recorded" (*GThom.* 1)? With the awesome claim of an omniscient narrator: "In the beginning was the Word, and the Word was with God, and the Word was God (John 1:1)? At another beginning: "The beginning of the gospel of Jesus Christ, [the Son of God]" (Mark 1:1)? *Aesop* begins in reasonably good Greek fashion: "The story-teller Aesop, whose contributions to human life were of the greatest value, was by fate a slave, by birth a Phrygian of Phrygia."[126] Said fashion is nonetheless not unlike that of Mark, who also guides the reader by making high claims for his subject, and not much less shocking, since neither Galilean artisans nor Asian slaves were the normal stuff of which dreams were made.[127]

The narrator then describes Aesop's appearance. This, too, is customary.[128] The gospel tradition shows no interest in the appearance or habits of Jesus.[129] We shall never know his favorite foods, hair color, or

---

the "message" of the novel is that the gift of crafting fables requires freedom for its implementation and that telling fables is a symbol of Aesop's freedom.

[126] 1.1–2 ὁ πάντα βιωφελέστατος Αἴσωπος, ὁ λογοποιός, τῇ μὲν τύχῃ ἦν δοῦλος τῷ δὲ γένει φρὺξ <ἐξ Ἀμορίου> τῆς φρυγίας, reveals the narrator's desire to pack as much characterization as possible into a few words.

[127] Philosophers could be of servile origin, as was the Cynic Menippus, introduced by Diogenes Laertius as follows: "Menippus, also a Cynic, was by descent a Phoenician—a slave, as Achaicus in his treatise on *Ethics* says." (6.99, trans. R. D. Hicks, *Diogenes Laertius* [LCL; 2 vols.; Cambridge: Harvard University Press, 1925], 2.103.)

[128] Of Zeno Diogenes reports: "He had a wry neck . . . he was lean, fairly tall, and swarthy . . . he had thick legs; he was flabby and delicate. . . . They say he was fond of eating green figs and of basking in the sun." (D.L. 7.1, trans. Hicks, *Diogenes Laertius*, 2.111, with authorities removed.)

[129] The earliest such description is that of Paul: μικρὸν τῷ μεγέθει ψιλὸν τῇ κεφαλῇ ἀγκύλον ταῖς κνήμαις [*Latin: cruribus elegantibus* = εὔκνημον] εὐεκτικὸν σύνοφρυν μικρῶς ἐπίρρινον [*Latin: naso aquilino*] χάριτος πλήρη . . . (*APl* 3.3). J. K. Elliott (*The Apocryphal New Testament,* [Oxford: Clarendon, 1993] 364) translates: "small in size, bald-headed, bandy-legged, of noble mien, with eyebrows meeting, rather hook-nosed, full of grace." B. J. Malina and J. H. Neyrey include a full discussion of this passage in their *Portraits of Paul* (Louisville: Westminster John Knox, 1996) 101–52.

attitude toward sun-bathing.[130] Readers learn that Aesop is ugly, not homely, but hideous: προγάστωρ, προκέφαλος, σιμός, λορδός, μέλας,[131] κολοβὸς βλαισός, γαλιάγκων, στρεβλός, μυστάκων, ἡμεριὸν ἁμάρτημα, "potbellied, misshapen of head, snub-nosed, swarthy, dwarfish, bandy-legged, short-armed, squint-eyed, liver-lipped—a lucid monstrosity."[132] To top it off he is unable to speak. The narrator's comment is confirmed by nearly everyone who encounters Aesop in the first two-thirds of the novel.[133] The kindest comparisons are to animals;[134] some of the epithets are vegetable (turnip)[135] or mineral (jug).[136] The portraits of Socrates come quickly to mind.[137] Aesop and Socrates are text-book examples of the contrast between inner and outer beauty, appearance and reality.[138] In the romance, however, Aesop's ugliness

---

[130] A Canon of Coventry relates a story about two elderly women of humble status who, walking about the modern cathedral, gazed upon the famous tapestry of Christ in glory that dominates the east wall. After some reflection, one of these good ladies said to her companion: "Don't look a bit like 'im, does it?"

[131] Since the narrator characterizes Aesop as Phrygian, readers would presumably understand μέλας as "dark" rather than African.

[132] 1.2–6, trans. Daly, *Aesop Without Morals,* 31 (corrected to reflect the text of Papathomopoulos).

[133] See chs. 1, 14, 16, 19, 21, 24, 26, 30–31, 87, 98. References to Aesop's unpleasant appearance disappear once he enters the service of royalty.

[134] One of the nicer ironies of the romance is that Aesop, who tells fables about talking animals, looks like an animal who talks. Cf. chap. 10.

[135] "Garbage" (περικάθαρμα, e.g., 14) brings 1 Cor 4:13 to mind.

[136] The most complete catalogue comes at a dramatically apposite point: from the citizens of Samos, when Aesop is introduced as an interpreter of omens: "Is he a frog, or a hedgehog, or a pot-bellied jar, or a captain of monkeys, or a moulded jug, or a cook's gear, or a dog in a basket?" (87, trans. Daly, *Aesop Without Morals,* 74). Since drinking, cooking, and dogs have been featured in the narrative, those epithets are ironic. In his response Aesop turns the image against them: "When did anyone ever decide on a jar of wine by looking at it rather than by taking a taste?" His tricolic conclusion: "The Muse is judged in the theater and Aphrodite in bed. Just so, wit is judged in words" (88, trans. Daly, *ibid.*) has its own ironies. Aesop, client of the Muses, is speaking in a theater and has recently demonstrated his prowess in bed.

[137] For details see Schauer and Merkle, "Äsop und Sokrates," 90–91.

[138] For example, compare *Aesop* 26 and Alcibiades's description of Socrates in Plato's *Symposium,* beginning at 215a. Alcibiades says that Socrates is like the statues of Silenus, and that he resembles the satyr Marsyas (215B). In the romance Aesop shares the fate of Marsyas (100), on which see below. Contrasts between outside and inside are also found in the Jesus-tradition (e.g., Mark 7:1–23) and elsewhere in early Christian literature (e.g., 1 Pet 3:1–4).

does not merely place him in opposition to some gymnasium heart-throb: it serves to contrast him with Apollo and the values he represents.[139]

Whatever its hue, Aesop's skin is thick. Insults roll off him like water.[140] The slave can even claim that his appearance, which can frighten children, is a quality that will enhance his market value.[141] This is something other than platonic ontology. If Aesop looks like a dog, it is possible that he will have the sexual prowess of that species. He does.[142] When Aesop neglects Apollo and incurs the god's wrath, he symbolizes who he is and what he means. I propose that the romance embodies a "Hellenistic" protest against the Hellenic cult and ideal of beauty, law, and order encapsulated in the myths and depiction of Apollo. *Aesop* is a prose epic featuring a Thersites in the role of wandering hero who comes finally not back to his home but to a foreign land where jealous rivals will crush him.[143] That which by classical Greek standards is *eo ipso* barbarous, useless, and gruesome, a veritable index of shame, is here presented as πάντα βιωφελέστατος.[144] Something good can come from Nazareth.[145]

---

[139] The Hellenic version of the Latin proverb *mens sana in corpore sano* ("a sound mind in a sound body") would be "a beautiful mind in a beautiful body." Aesop has a sound mind in an ugly body. By analogy with the mime-tradition Aesop is a character with a frightful mask who reveals ugly truths. Such characters are likely to suffer.

[140] 21, 87. Public mockery, Aesop's indifference to this, and invocations of the contrast between outside and inside are thematic markers of major transitions: Aesop's purchase by Xanthus and his emancipation: 21, 24, 26 and 87–88. Jesus, too, meets mockery with silence during the passion (Luke 23:9; John 19:9).

[141] Chapters 15–16.

[142] Chapters 30 and 75, discussed above.

[143] On the parallels between Thersites and Aesop see G. Nagy, *The Best of the Achaeans: Concepts of the Hero in Archaic Greek Poetry* (Baltimore: The Johns Hopkins University Press, 1989), 259–265, 279–281, 309, and 313.

[144] Affinities in Hellenistic art are shown by Barbara Hughes Fowler in her chapters on "The Burlesque" and "The Grotesque" (*The Hellenistic Aesthetic* [Madison: University of Wisconsin Press, 1989] 44–78). She prints, as fig. 31, p.45, "The Thorn Remover from Priene," now in Berlin. On p. 44 Fowler comments that this statue of c.100 BCE "Is a parody of a late-third-century B.C. statue, probably in bronze, of a handsome nude youth serenely performing the same task. The terra-cotta version is of a prematurely aged street boy, perhaps black, somewhat stunted in his growth, with puffed-up cheeks, squinting eyes, puckered lips, and wrinkled nose and brow." The description resembles that of Aesop. A similar parody is included in the procession of Isis worshipers (Apul. *Met.* 11.8), which includes an ape dressed up like Ganymede, complete with gold cup.

[145] Cf. John 1:46. Malina and Neyrey (n. 125) locate such descriptions within the social code of the rhetorical tradition.

To remain within the realm of popular prose narrative, the contrast with the opening of the romantic novels, whose protagonists are free, high-born, rich and surpassingly attractive, is nearly absolute. Consider Aesop and Callirhoe at the time of sale.[146] The owners of both set out for wealthy markets: those who kidnapped Callirhoe to Ionia, Aesop's purchaser to Samos.[147] Callirhoe is prime goods, worthy of a home visit for a private transaction.

> As he approached the country house, Theron [the pirate who has abducted our heroine] thought up the following move: he uncovered Callirhoe's head, shook her hair loose, and then opened the door and told her to go in first. Leonas and all the people in the room were awestruck at the sudden apparition—some of them thought they had seen a goddess, for people did say that Aphrodite manifested herself in the fields.[148] There they were awestruck when Theron came in behind, went up to Leonas [agent for the prospective buyer] and said, "Get up and see to receiving the woman; she is the one you want to buy." General joy and amazement followed.[149]

Aesop is one of three slaves exhibited at Samos. The others are a tutor and a musician, whom the owner dresses in the most flattering manner possible.

> But he couldn't cover up or prettify Aesop, since he was a completely misshapen pot, and so he dressed him in a sackcloth robe, tied a strip of material around his middle, and stood him between the two handsome slaves. When the auctioneer began to announce the sale, many noticed them and said, "Bah, these fellows look fine enough, but where did this awful thing come from? He spoils their appearance, too. Take him away."[150]

Divine comparisons also occur when Xanthus brings home his new slave Aesop: his wife offers thanks to Aphrodite and he promises an epiphany of Apollo. Those who want to read about beautiful people had

---

[146] Little is known about the marketing of slaves in the Greco-Roman world. See Harrill, *Manumission*, 36 and his references.

[147] *Callirhoe* 1.11; *Aesop* 20.

[148] The relation of this passage to early Christian literature is discussed in M. Parsons and R. Pervo, *Rethinking the Unity of Luke and Acts* (Minneapolis: Fortress, 1993) 90–94.

[149] *Callirhoe* 1.14, trans. B. P. Reardon in *Collected Ancient Greek Novels*, 37.

[150] *Aesop* 21.7–3, trans. Daly, *Aesop Without Morals*, 40. The closing words, ἆρον ἀπ' αὐτῶν τὸν μέσον, resemble the demands for Jesus's crucifixion, as in John 19:15 ἐκραύγασαν οὖν ἐκεῖνοι· ἆρον ἆρον, σταύρωσον αὐτόν. For parallels in the sale of the ass see n. 53. Another child of wisdom sold as a slave is the apostle Thomas, who, Jonah-fashion, has resisted his assigned mission territory (*Acts of Thomas* 2). Like Aesop he builds castles in the air, so to speak (*ibid.* 17–22; *Aesop* 111–116, following *Ahikar*). With the deed of Aesop compare the ingenuity of Alexander in constructing a flying machine (*Alex.-Rom.* 2.41).

better stick with *Callirhoe.* Aesop is an epiphany of an entirely different sort.[151] An epiphany he could certainly use, and an epiphany he will get, a visitation from Isis *avec les Muses* that will not transform him from a speechless animal into a free, handsome, and articulate human being, but one that will give him both speech and power. In short, the romance begins with a story-teller who cannot speak.[152] That subject presently becomes the recipient of a twin benefaction. Isis heals his disability; verbal gifts come from the Muses.

Both healing and verbal endowment are common enough. The latter is a typical call-story. Like Hesiod (*Theog.* 22–23), Moses (Exodus 3:10), and Amos (Amos 1:1; 7:14) Aesop is visited in a rural setting, far from the well-known vices and distractions of city life. Like Isaiah (Isaiah 6:5–8) and Moses (Exodus 4:10) he receives rhetorical capacity.[153] The obvious corollary in the story of Jesus is his Baptism, which endowed him with prophetic and oratorical gifts.[154] None of these persons required healing. Despite the availability of ready and reasonable answers, the initial disability of Aesop and his cure are not easy to explain. He is far from a sinless new Adam; Aesop has fallen very far indeed. In the beginning Aesop is sub-human, *instrumentum vocale vocis non capax* (a speaking tool incapable of speech).[155] He begins with less than rags and will rise to more than riches. In the beginning was the wordless one.

---

[151] In 16 one of his fellow slaves suggests that he is an apotropaic device to ward off the evil eye. In 77a he will make an apotropaic device of his mistress's "eyes."

[152] In this he resembles Zechariah, who was temporarily punished for obstinacy (Luke 1:20–64). Aesop's misfortune is attributed to divine displeasure in general (5, 10) but is not otherwise explained.

[153] Of these parallels, the *Theogony* is primary, both because of the role of the Muses and because of the evocation of Hesiod in the preceding context.

[154] This is most explicit in Luke 3–4 but implicit in Matthew and Mark.

[155] Varro reports that some authorities make a gallic division of the means by which land is worked: *alii in tres partes, instrumenti genus vocale et semivocale et mutum, vocale, in quo sunt servi* ("others into three: the class of instruments which is articulate, the inarticulate, and the mute; the articulate comprising the slaves"). The other *instrumenta* are cattle and vehicles. (*Re. Rust.* 1.17.1, trans. W. D. Hooper, rev. H. Ash, *Marcus Terentius Varro On Agriculture* [LCL; Cambridge: Harvard University Press, 1935], 225.) The source is Aristotle: ὁ δοῦλος κτῆμά τι ἔμψυχον. (Slaves are animate instruments, *Pol* 1.2.4, cf. *Nich. Eth.* 8.13, 1161). Roman law did not subscribe to this view: *Dig.* 1.6.2 (Ulpian), and Gaius, *Institutes* 1.53. The fundamental tension of slavery, property that must at the same time be human to be useful is the motive force that drives the middle section of *Aesop*'s plot (Hopkins, "Novel Evidence"). Aristotle perceived the problem. In chap. 13 of *Politics* 1, where he turns to the moral basis for household life, Aristotle raises the question of whether slaves are to have other virtues than as tools or service. Can they can possess the four cardinal virtues? Either answer

The Aesopic Passion Narrative

Graham Anderson seizes upon *Aesop* to expose the prejudices of the academy: "It is perhaps a comment on the social pre-judgement of scholars that this text is usually denied any entitlement to be considered as literature at all, let alone as romance: the hero is a slave, physically handicapped, and black as well."

He then observes that, after overcoming all obstacles, Aesop is "martyred for no religion."[156] This may sound virtuous in an age when no religion is probably better than any, but it is not precisely accurate. Aesop was healed of his disability as a reward for piety and died calling upon Zeus Xenios while seeking asylum in a shrine of the Muses. Irreligious he was not. Aesop was executed for impiety, but then so were Socrates and, according to the Gospels, Jesus.[157] Aesop knew the gods to whom he was indebted, and to them he offered homage. At Samos Aesop sacrificed to the Muses and erected a shrine in their honor, neglecting their patron, Apollo (100). In Babylon, King Lycorus caused the erection of a golden statue of Aesop with the Muses and sponsored a big celebration in recognition of his wisdom.[158] Immediately thereafter the narrator reports that Aesop left on tour, desirous of seeing Delphi,[159] with a promise to return and settle permanently in Babylon. The final phrase removes any hint of danger and sparks in the reader a sense of pathos.

Why does Aesop wish to visit Delphi? The text has not specified any Greek cities that he visited. Does he go as an innocent, unaware, unlike the reader, of the wrath of Apollo? Or is he throwing down the gauntlet before Apollo's face? In classical terms the question concerns the nature of Aesop's *hybris*. The romance does not give a straightforward answer to this question, but it does provide some hints and expose its own motives.

---

is problematic, for, if they possess those virtues, slaves will not differ from free persons. On the other hand they are rational human beings (1259b 18ff.). *Aesop* reads like a commentary on this dilemma.

[156] Anderson, *Ancient Fiction,* 101.

[157] Mark 14:64.

[158] 123.5–7: ἐκέλευσεν οὖν ὁ Λυκοῦργος ἀνδριάντα χρυσοῦν ἀνατεθῆναι τῷ Αἰσώπῳ μετὰ καὶ τῶν Μουσῶν καὶ ἐποίησεν ἑορτὴν μεγάλην ὁ βασιλεὺς ἐπὶ τῇ τοῦ Αἰσώπου σοφίᾳ. ἀνατεθῆναι is used of religious offerings. Note that the text does not speak of statues of Aesop and the Muses, but of Aesop, "with the Muses, also," subordinating the latter.

[159] Cf. Luke 9:51; Acts 19:21.

The first hint appears in chapter 33, where Aesop explains the nature of dreams in a story that is not entirely flattering to Apollo.[160]

A second hint transpires in chapter 100, when Aesop erects a shrine featuring the Muses, and, evidently, himself[161] "—Not Apollo." Apollo became angry with him as he had become angry with Marsyas."[162] Marsyas was a Phrygian (or Asian) godlet, identified as a satyr or silenus in the Greek tradition who, having picked up a flute discarded by Athena (who had invented it but did not care for the way it altered her noble countenance), grew competent enough to challenge Apollo to a musical contest. Apollo won and took as his forfeit the life of Marsyas.[163] The Marsyas comparison has had no small influence on the Aesop-tradition. According to Perry "Aesop became a Phrygian instead of a Thracian because he was conceived on the analogy of the Phrygian Marsyas."[164] The implication of those three words, ὡς τῷ Μαρσύᾳ (100.14), is that Apollo was angry because Aesop had the *chutzpah* to challenge him to a contest. The same three little words also constitute a foreshadowing of the end, a "passion prediction," as it were. The ugly asiatic marsyases of this world will be torn to pieces by its apollos.[165] When it comes to a

---

[160] This incident is described in part II, above.

[161] The text of 100.12–14, questionably emended by Perry to read στήσας μέσον αὐτῶν Μνημοσύνην is improved by Papathomopoulos to τόνδε Αἴσωπος θυσίαις ταῖς Μούσαις ἱερὸν κατασκευάσας ἔστησε μέσον αὐτῶν αὐτὸν μνημόσυνον, οὐκ Ἀπόλλωνα.

[162] 100.14:<δι'> ὁ Ἀπόλλων ὠργίσθη αὐτῷ ὡς τῷ Μαρσύᾳ

[163] On Marsyas see H. v. Geisau in *Der Kleine Pauly* 3:1050–51 and the references there. By imperial times the death of Marsyas could be viewed as a form of crucifixion, as an apparent execution of Leucippe shows: "One of the attendants laid her on her back and tied her to stakes fixed in the ground, as sculptors picture Marsyas bound to the tree." (*Leucippe* 3.15, trans. J. Winkler in *Collected Ancient Greek Novels*, 216). Ovid (*Met.* 6:382–400) spares no sensibilities in his description of the punishment: As he screams, his skin is stripped off the surface of his body, and he is all one wound: blood flows down on every side, the sinews lie bare, his veins throb and quiver with no skin to cover them: you could count the entrails as they palpitate, and the vitals showing clearly in his breast (387–391, trans. F. J. Miller, *Ovid, Metamorphoses* [LCL; 2 vols.; Cambridge: Harvard University Press, 1916] 1.315.) At 386 Marsyas screams: "*a! piget, a! non est,*" clamabat "*tibia tanti.*" Aesop might agree with the second part of this sentiment; life is of more value than a flute. Repent, however, he does not.

[164] Perry, *Babrius and Phaedrus*, xl–xli. Perry argues that the historical Aesop came from Thrace. *Testimonia* 4–12 (*Aesopica*, 215–217) relate to Aesop's native land. Jesus, according to Matthew and Luke (but not John), had to be born in Bethlehem.

[165] Perry (*Studies*, 15) states that Aesop, like Marsyas is "a champion of the native talent of the common folk as opposed to the formal learning of the aristocrats and academicians whose god is Apollo."

contest between the chicken and the fox, wise bettors will lay their money upon the fox.[166]

The motives of the romance emerge in the finale. Aesop, the great deflator of philosophical pretensions, has, as observed, become himself an itinerant sophist more than willing to accept the financial tribute of his appreciative hearers. The Delphians were appreciative but not forthcoming. Swarthy Aesop then chastises their pale skins and upbraids them for their unworthiness (124–125).[167] Like Jesus in John 8:31–59, he makes unflattering statements about the ancestry of his audience: they are slaves.[168] With these unkind words the ex-slave prepared to knock the dust from his sandals and leave. At that point Apollo took a hand: "But the officials (ἄρχοντες), seeing how abusive he was, reasoned to themselves, 'If we let him go away, he'll go around to other cities and damage our reputation.' So they plotted to kill him by a trick (ἐβουλεύσαντο οὖν <αὐτὸν> ἀνελεῖν δόλῳ, 127.3–4)." With the connivance of Apollo, who was angry with Aesop because of the insult on Samos in not honoring him up along with the Muses, the Delphians, not waiting for a reasonable pretext, devised a villainous scheme so that the other visitors could not help him.[169]

The situation is not unique:

---

[166] Cf. Luke 13:31–35.

[167] The jibe (pallid complexion presumably suggests a lack of "manliness") makes apt use of a trite Homeric tag referring to the shortness of human life. This, too, has its ironies.

[168] John 8 is set in the Temple at Tabernacles. In v. 33 the crowd says: "We are descendants of Abraham and have never been slaves to anyone. What do you mean by saying, 'You will be made free'?" Note also vv. 39–44, in which the hearers are characterized as offspring of the devil, and the climax in v.59, an attempt to stone Jesus.

[169] 127.1–8 trans. Daly, *Aesop Without Morals,* 86. The text of one sentence (ll. 4–10) is basic for the determination of cause and effect. It is also uncertain. The text emended by Perry and accepted by Papathomopoulos begins with a genitive absolute: καὶ τοῦ Ἀπόλλωνος μηνίοντος διὰ τὴν ἐν Σάμῳ ἀτιμίαν where the participle refers to Apollo's anger. G, however, reads μηνύοντος δὲ τὴν, which suggests that Apollo supplied information about Aesop's conduct at Samos. If the Delphians learned of this, they do not bring it up. Something like Daly's supplied "connivance" is required to bring sense from the text, but it constitutes a tacit emendation. One possibility is to repoint the text by placing a comma after δόλῳ, and rendering: "They therefore plotted to kill him by deceit, since Apollo was also angry because of the dishonor at Samos, when he [Aesop] did not erect a statue of him [Apollo] with the Muses, but, as they lacked a good reason, they devised a wicked scheme . . ." (Papathomopoulos resolves the problem by adding, from W, after δόλῳ καὶ: <ὡς ἱερόσυλον αὐτὸν καταδικάσαι, καὶ> τοῦ Ἀπόλλωνος . . .

"It was now two days before the Passover and the feast of Unleavened Bread. And the chief priests and the scribes were seeking how to arrest him by stealth (δόλῳ), and kill him; for they said, 'Not during the feast, lest there be a tumult of the people.'" (Mark 14:1–2, RSV)[170]

Like Jesus, Aesop has gone to the lair of the fox; like Jesus, Aesop loses the favor of the people and is accused of sacrilege; like Jesus, Aesop falls victim to a priestly plot and is framed; like Jesus, Aesop angers people (and leaders) by telling stories; like Jesus, Aesop is willing to pray that the cup be taken from him; like Jesus, Aesop warns his attackers that they will be punished; like Jesus, he will receive post-mortem vindication. Quite unlike Jesus, however, Aesop actively seeks his own acquittal and escape. Jesus is described as finding his fate inevitable: Jerusalem kills prophets.

Socrates did not pray that the cup be taken from him.[171] A three-way comparison of the "passions" of Aesop, Socrates, and Aesop shows how ideology shapes narrative reports.[172] These traditions are not independent. According to Schauer and Merkle Plato[173] knew and criticized the Aesop tradition. The romance, for its part, echoes Plato, while the Socratic tradition influenced, however indirectly, early Christian portrayals of the fates of Jesus and others. Moreover, since the canonical passion stories are at considerable variance with one another, it is not possible to make a precise comparison unless one account is taken as the model. If, for example, John were the basis of comparison, Jesus would much more closely approximate Socrates, especially if the farewell dialogues of John 13–17 are included. The Lucan Jesus is also serene and active. Mark's picture is quite different. A comprehensive study would require analysis of all of the variant traditions about Aesop, Socrates, and Jesus and would constitute a monograph. The present endeavor is no more than a preliminary exploration.

Aesop, Socrates, and Jesus are presented as victims of injustice. Western civilization reads the trial of Socrates through the eyes of Plato's

---

[170] Hopkins ("Novel Evidence," 24) says that Aesop was finally forced to die by "an unholy alliance between a jealous God (Apollo), local dignitaries and the free citizens." The evangelists state that Jesus was forced to die by an unholy alliance between the misguided, jealous agents of God, local officials, and the citizenry.

[171] Καὶ ἅμα ὤρεξε τὴν κύλικα τῷ Σωκράτει· καὶ ὃς λαβὼν καὶ μάλα ἵλεως, *Phaedo* 117B. "At the same time he [the executioner] offered the cup to Socrates. He took it, and quite graciously."

[172] The relevant Platonic dialogues are *Euthyphro, Apology, Crito,* and *Phaedo.*

[173] Schauer and Merkle, "Äsop und Sokrates," with a summary conclusion at p.96. The following observations are much indebted to this study.

Apology.[174] The story of Jesus is known through equally apologetic texts. The *Aesop-Romance* is no apology of the typical sort. Aesop was condemned by vote at a trial to which he was not invited, the verdict of which he learns in prison (132). His defense speeches must be given in other contexts (as, in fact, were those of Jesus). Common to all three is the rather necessary feature of arrest and detainment.

Both Aesop and Socrates are visited by friends in prison.[175] In the case of Jesus there were no such visits, not only because the nature of his incarceration was not of the sort that leaves scope for visiting hours, but also because all of his (male) friends had, in the Marcan tradition, fled the scene.[176] The Gospel tradition thus had to manage things differently.[177] Mark 13 presents an address to a small band dealing with the future of nation and community; shortly thereafter Jesus and his followers gather for a final meal, a major theme of which is betrayal.[178] Socrates also devoted the final hours with his friends to questions of ultimacy, in particular the immortality of the soul. Because of this doctrine he could accept death with more than equanimity: it is liberation. The Christian accounts, in either Mark (and parallels) or John, speak not of the fate of individuals but of communities. These differing perspectives bring to the fore the social contrast between belief in the immortality of individual souls and faith in resurrection as the vindication of God's people. For Aesop neither belief was a source of comfort. He saw nothing to welcome in his coming death. He blamed no one but himself. Rather than discourse serenely about the beauty of existence freed from the body, Aesop related two "naughty" tales, one

---

[174] The journalist I. F. Stone devoted his final years to a revisionist effort: *The Trial of Socrates* (Boston: Little, Brown, 1988).

[175] Since this friend (131) is announced without the suggestion that Aesop was accompanied by or had gained friends while in Delphi, the view that the narrator sought to contrast his hero with Socrates is strengthened.

[176] The apocryphal acts remedy this deficit, for example *APl.* 3.18–20 (Thecla); 7 (Ephesus).

[177] Re: the chicken and the fox (Luke 13:31–35): In the passion of Jesus the cock-crow announces his betrayal (Mark 14:72 and parallels). Socrates's final words are a request to Crito that a cock be offered to Asclepius (*Phaedo* 118). He has been healed.

[178] John 13–17 has no apocalyptic address but does include reflections upon the last things. Note the use of "friends" in John 15:13–14. Aesop is no stranger to betrayal. Often betrayed by his master, he must experience the ultimate betrayal: condemnation to death through the intrigue of an adopted son (103–104, through the use of Aesop's seal, a motif found also in 69 and 81, discussed above). For his part, Jesus expresses despair at abandonment by his father (Mark 15:34, below).

about death, the other about losing one's wits through gaining them.[179] In psychological terms, he is "depressed" at the thought of death.

The Jesus of Mark is rather more like Aesop than Socrates. Alone in a garden he begs relief but accepts the will of God.

Jesus: "Abba, Father, for you all things are possible; remove this cup from me; yet, not what I want, but what you want (Mark 14:36, NRSV)

Aesop: Finding no means of saving himself, Aesop said, "Now how can I, a mortal man, escape what is to be?" (128.11)[180]

Abandoned by his friends, Jesus cries out that he has also been abandoned by God, only to be misunderstood yet once more (15:34—the only "word of Jesus from the cross" in Mark). Of both it can be said that they saved others but cannot save themselves, although for Jesus this comes from mockers, rather than from a consoling friend (Mark 15:31; *Aesop* 130).[181]

Socrates dies in serene confidence; Jesus dies because it is God's will, in agony or serenity, depending upon the source; Aesop dies because he has no choice. The first two resolutions are satisfying. The third is less so. Readers would like to see Aesop "play the man" and accept death with a bit more fortitude.[182] Disturbing as his cowardice may be to one's tastes in protagonists, it is not accidental. Aesop is a "classic" anti-hero because he has no belief in immortality and no desire to perish as a glorious martyr, scapegoat,[183] or victim of injustice. The finale of Aesop's life is not lacking

---

[179] On this scene see above. One of the tales is a variation of "The Widow of Ephesus," *Satyrica* 111–112, Phaedrus, *Appendix* 15. The fable of 131 echoes that of 67.

[180] Trans. Daly, *Aesop Without Morals,* 87. (For the phrase see the saying of John the Baptizer, Luke//Matt 3:7.)

[181] Holzberg stresses this paradox, "Äsop-Roman," 69, and elsewhere.

[182] In G Aesop does, "when push comes to shove," throw himself from the cliff (142). In W he is thrown. *POxy.* 1800 (which is not a fragment of the romance, but of a collection of lives in very brief form, rather on the order of desk encyclopedia entries) states that he was first stoned and then thrown from the cliff. It seems likely that G is secondary because it makes Aesop a bit more heroic. Luke 4:29–30 (cf. John 8:59) presents Jesus as (miraculously) evading a similar fate for a similar crime.

[183] For the understanding of the legend of Aesop's death as the story of a scapegoat (φαρμακός), see Perry, *Babrius and Phaedrus,* xlii-xliii, and Nagy, *Best of the Achaeans,* 279–290, both of whom make use of the published form of A. Wiechers's dissertation: *Aesop in Delphi* (Meisenheim am Glein: A. Hain, 1961). In the *Onos* the robbers who have acquired Lucius the ass propose at one point to hurl him over a cliff as a purification (καθαρισμόν) for their group (22; cf. also 25). J. D. Crossan explores the relation to the Israelite scapegoat tradition as background to the passion narratives in *Who Killed Jesus? Exposing the Roots of Anti-Semitism in the Gospel Story of the Death of Jesus* (New York: HarperSanFrancisco, 1995).

in a kind of unsentimental and gritty realism that characterizes modern literature.[184] As a slave he could scorn the rich, but when opportunities for honor and wealth came, he seized them. Life was good, and he had no desire to bring it to a close. Far from being, like Peregrinus, a "new Socrates,"[185] our hero is an anti-Socrates whose message implies that metaphysics is nonsense.[186] Aesop is more a cynic in the modern than in the ancient sense, but he is a gentle cynic who used his knowledge of human nature to help others, and he was genuinely blind to social barriers.

Chapters 35–37 exhibit this quality. When a gardener seeks from Xanthus an answer to the problem of why weeds grow without care, Xanthus brushes him off with the Stoic platitude that all things are governed by divine providence (πάντα τῇ θείᾳ προνοίᾳ διοικεῖται, 35.14).[187] Aesop scoffs at this. Xanthus brags "I studied at Athens under philosophers, rhetoricians, and philologists. And do you have the effrontery to set foot on the *Muses'* Helicon?"[188] Unknown to Xanthus, Aesop has every right to do just that, and he will best Xanthus in all three categories. Xanthus then appeals to the mysteries of nature into which not even philosophers dare to penetrate. In the end Aesop is given the assignment.[189] He does so by relating a similitude that likens weeds to the natural children of Mother Earth and cultivated plants to step-children.[190] In this incident Aesop exposes both the intellectual pretensions and the social snobbery of professional philosophers, who despise the unwashed multitude and their practical questions, questions that they cannot, in fact, answer. The story itself is revelatory: Aesop is an ugly weed, as is the gardener. The gods care for such. Even when wronged, he exacted

---

[184] To state the matter succinctly: If Erich Auerbach had read the *Aesop-Romance*, book he would have had to revise some of the statements in *Mimesis*, in particular those about the uniqueness of the Gospels.

[185] For the characterization of Peregrinus as a Christian "New Socrates," see Lucian, *Peregrinus* 12.

[186] Similarly, Schauer and Merkle ("Äsop und Sokrates," 69, 93) who describe the Aesop legend as a foil to the Socrates of Plato on the death of the true sage, and suggest conclusions like mine.

[187] Aesop will, in due course, be placed ἐπὶ τῆς διοικήσεως (over the administration) of the Babylonian empire, 101.7–8.

[188] 36.6, trans. Daly, *Aesop Without Morals,* 49, (with emphasis added).

[189] For a similar dodge by Xanthus see 86.

[190] Matt 13:24–30 and Mark 4:26–29 have a similar content.

vengeance of a limited sort most often intended to instruct.[191] Like the glorified Christ—and unlike the Jesus of the Gospels—Aesop is an agent of reconciliation. He is, however, most humanly not reconciled to his own fate.[192]

The plot of *Aesop*, then, operates on two levels: Aesop is responsible for his own fate. He has become a philosopher who collects fees, a pig who walks, an ex-slave who insults non-paying Delphians by calling them slaves. This is a purely human and rational narrative plane: the death of a salesman of wisdom. On the divine horizon flashes the wrath of Apollo. Aesop has neglected to give that god honor. In theological terms he has, like Marsyas, entered into an ἀγών (contest) with the god of Delphi, freely dispensing revelation and wisdom to gardeners and monarchs in prose stories accessible to all. Such behavior is risky and leads to conclusions from which general morals may be drawn. The post-ultimate irony is that this anti-hero was heroized after his death.

When Is the End Not an End?

Like Jesus, Aesop informed his attackers of the consequences of their action (133–139).[193] They remained unmoved. Vengeance was two-fold: a plague[194] (resolved by an oracle of *Zeus*, not of Apollo) and punitive military expeditions. This edifying conclusion, reminiscent of the *Iliad* (an account of a punitive military expedition that opens with a plague sent by Apollo), as well as of the Synoptic Apocalypse,[195] raises interesting

---

[191] This quality is most apparent in his relations with Xanthus; from the perspective of the novel even his adultery with Mme. X. is harmless because he did not inform on her. His goodness is most tellingly portrayed in his refusal to take vengeance upon his adopted son (108–109), a notable alteration of *Ahikar*, where revenge is cruelly extracted (death by whipping accompanied by sapiential instructions). The son's name is also changed. In G it is "Helios," an apt allusion to the Apollo who will exact full and perfect revenge. (Helios/sun also appears in chs. 113–115.)

[192] In 33 Aesop agrees to be reconciled with Mme. X. Having brought about her departure, he then effects her return to Xanthus (50a). Later he becomes an ambassador who effects political reconciliation (100). Yet his antepenultimate fable features a tumblebug who would not be reconciled with a rapacious eagle (135–139).

[193] An interesting parallel to the traditions about the death of Aesop is the "Daulis" fragment edited by S. A. Stephens and J. J. Winkler, *Ancient Greek Novels: The Fragments* (Princeton: Princeton University Press, 1995) 375–88. Daulis leads a barbarian army in an attack on Delphi designed to kill the prophet of Apollo and thus rid the world of false oracles.

[194] Daly (*Aesop Without Morals*, 90) nods here, translating "famine," having evidently mistaken λοιμός for λιμός.

[195] Wars: Mark 13:7–8; Pestilence: Luke 21:11.

questions about the relations between "romance" or "gospel" and history, for "the *Life of Aesop* tradition actually presents the death of Aesop as a *cause* of the First Sacred War, but the institutional reality that Aesop reproaches—namely, that the people of Delphi are sacred to Apollo—is a lasting *effect* of the First Sacred War."[196] Metonymies of this nature permeate the gospel tradition, where effects of the First Jewish Revolt and the separation of Christians from Jews are thrust back into the life of Jesus and viewed as causes of his death.[197]

Aesop was thus vindicated: Jerusalem has been destroyed in punishment, as it were. Was he also exalted to heaven? On Aesop's own post-mortem fate the romance is not quite explicit, although Nagy shows that atonement for his death required the establishment of a hero-cult for Aesop and that cultic terminology is present in the tradition.[198] *Aesop* concludes, as it were, with Mark 15:37. This is a truly post-modern gospel, all the more noteworthy since traditions permitted, indeed, may be said to have expected a different end. For others reported that Aesop returned to life.[199] One of these accounts refers to a bodily resurrection: "Aesop, slain by Delphians, came back to life and fought together with the Greeks at Thermopylae."[200] The remaining notices refer to the ascent or reincarnation of his soul. For a socratic anti-Socrates to whom the romance ascribes no belief in immortality and whose death accords with that belief, this is the absolutely final irony.

Conclusion

In form the *Aesop-Romance* resembles the apocryphal acts, in that it relates in relatively simple style the career of a charismatic hero who seems to overcome one obstacle after another until the last episode, when he is killed. Like several of the apocryphal acts the relatively simple style

---

[196] Nagy, *Best of the Achaeans,* 283–284.

[197] A prime example of this is the charge that Jesus will destroy the temple (Mark 14:58).

[198] See Nagy, *Best of the Achaeans,* 285, 8n1, who extracts data from G, W, and other traditions, together with context from the history of religions.

[199] Perry, *Aesopica, Testimonia* 45–47, p. 226. Aesop, like many characters in ancient fiction, experiences *Scheintod.* The Babylonian king ordered his execution in chap. 104, but the delegated officer did not obey and is therefore able to bring him back from the dead to rescue his beleagured monarch. He announces: Αἴσωπος ζῇ. In accordance with the tradition King Lycorus meets this news with a mixture of skepticism and joy.

[200] Ptolemaeus Hephaestus in Photius, *Bib.* cod. 252 (= Perry, *Testimonia* 47).

derives from authorial decision rather than from sheer inability. As in the case of at least two of the apocryphal acts,[201] the judgment that *Aesop* lacks structure is erroneous. *Aesop*, like much early Christian narrative, *is* "popular," not because its author and audience are uniformly ἄνθρωποι ἀγράμματοι καὶ ἰδιῶται (unlettered laypersons, Acts 4:13), but because it takes a stand apart from elite culture and ideology.

On the formal level this distance emerges in its relation to classical genres and modes. In so far as the romance is epic it parodies epic by presenting a hero more like Thersites than Achilles.[202] The domestic scenes of bourgeois life suggest analogies with New Comedy.[203] With regard to its type of humor, however, *Aesop* is a repristination of *Old Comedy* (and mime). Old Comedy humor placed in New Comedy settings and cast in episodic prose narrative is one way of characterizing the "realistic" comic novel. *Aesop* strengthens the conviction, fueled by accumulating papyrus data,[204] that there were a number of such novels in Greek, most of which did not survive aesthetic and moral disdain.[205]

In the end *Aesop* is not comedy, old or new, but something akin to tragedy, the fall of a flawed hero. The "new types of heroes" (and heroines) of gospel, acts, and romance are bourgeois and sometimes even cowardly, but they do not have lethal faults, only, in some cases, defects that may be remedied by amendment of life.[206] Gareth Schmeling

---

[201] Both the *Acts of Thomas* (the only complete specimen of the group) and the *Acts of Andrew* exhibit structural sophistication. Were the others complete, it is likely that they would be seen as the products of careful design.

[202] On Thersites see n. 143. Holzberg ("Äsop-Roman," 39 n. 35) suggests possible parody of epic diction in 21, 34, 36–37, 51–53. Dennis MacDonald argues that the *Acts of Andrew* are a Christian parody of epic, *Christianizing Homer* (New York: Oxford University Press, 1994). Epic parody is a staple of the comic novel, most notably in the *Satyrica*.

[203] Holzberg, "Äsop-Roman," notes these analogies.

[204] For the impact of fragments upon the understanding of the limits of ancient novels see Stephens and Winkler, *Ancient Greek Novels*, 3–19. The *Onos* attributed to Lucian and the lost *Metamorphoses* of Lucius of Patrae also belong or are indebted to the comic tradition, as do the Latin novels of Petronius and Apuleius.

[205] Similarities between the *Aesop-Romance* and comic novels are most usefully set forth in Anderson, *Ancient Fiction*, 211–16 and 227–28, and J. J. Winkler *Auctor & Actor: A Narratological Reading of Apuleius's Golden Ass* (Berkeley: University of California Press, 1985) 276–91.

[206] Paul is intemperate before his conversion (Acts 8:3; 9:1–2). Chaireas distrusts his wife and assaults her (Chariton, *Callirhoe* 1.4). Habrocomes despised Eros, but was quickly converted (Xenophon, *An Ephesian Tale*, 1.4). Aseneth despised men (*Aseneth* 2.1). Each of these heroes must pay a penalty for their previous failings, "suffer for their sins," to be sure, but they are blemishes cleansed and expiated rather than fatal

says that "Under pressure, the new heroes of comedy and the novel yield to powerful forces and survive to live happily ever after. The classic Greek hero does not yield; he breaks."[207] Of Aesop it may be argued either that he does or that he does not yield. He certainly does not repent. No matter, for he will be broken. This is neither good comedy nor orthodox tragedy. In its behalf one may note that it is true to the lives of many.

Aesop is an integrated work, not the result of a narrator who switched masks in the final scene, but a comico-tragedy (vs. tragicomedy) with strong satiric features, the tale of a hero whose protagonist trembles at death yet faces it by telling dirty jokes.[208] Freedom from generic constraints has its rewards. And, yes, for those who demand it, Providence will play the last card, but readers will find little joy in her revenge. With that last last card providentially comes my last word: when read as a gospel, *Aesop* turns out to be a pretty good novel.

Epimythium[209]

A certain person had recited to Aesop some poor compositions, in the course of which he had inappropriately sounded his own praise at great length. Wishing, therefore, to know what the old man thought of it, he said: "I hope I have not appeared to you to be too proud of myself? The confidence that I feel in my own genius is no illusion." Aesop, who was completely worn out by listening to the miserable volume, replied, "For my part, I emphatically endorse your bestowing praise on yourself; for it will never come to you from any other source."[210]

---

flaws. Apuleius, not atypically, is more sophisticated in this matter, for his Lucius will pay stiff and enduring penalties for his sins before the conversion and redemption that will rescue him in the final book of the *Metamorphoses*.

[207] G. Schmeling, *Xenophon of Ephesus* (TWAS 613; Boston: Twayne, 1980), 122 (with a reference to T. B. L. Webster). In this there is a contrast between Aesop and the Alexander of the Romance, as the latter more closely resembles the tragic hero in his general unwillingness to unbend.

[208] This conclusion is similar to the views of Holzberg, "Äsop-Roman," 72–75, which should be consulted.

[209] An *epimythium* is the still familiar concluding "moral" to a fable.

[210] *Appendix* 9, trans. Perry, *Babrius and Phaedrus*, 383.

Why New Testament Scholars Should Read Ancient Novels[1]

Ronald F. Hock
University of Southern California

For a number of years I have been an avid reader of the Greek romances—prompted initially by their entertaining and informative stories that my students could enjoy and at the same time learn about various aspects of social life in the Greek East of the early Roman Empire, the context for much of Paul's missionary efforts, not to mention much of earliest Christianity once it spread beyond Jerusalem, Judea, and Samaria. My interests in the romances thus originated in their considerable value for illuminating the New Testament and other early Christian literature,[2] but I am increasingly focusing on the romances in and for themselves.[3]

Consequently, I was delighted when Professor Charles Hedrick of Southwest Missouri State University sought my help among others in seeking to incorporate these romances more directly into the program of

---

[1] Earlier versions of this paper were presented at the Annual Meeting of the SBL in San Francisco, November 1992; at the International Meeting of the SBL in Leuven, Belgium, August 1994; and at the Pacific Coast Regional Meeting of the SBL in Berkeley, March 1997.

[2] See, e.g., "The Greek Novel," in *Greco-Roman Literature and the New Testament* (D. Aune, ed.; SBLSBS 21; Atlanta: Scholars Press, 1988) 127–49; "A Support for his Old Age: Paul's Plea on behalf of Onesimus," in *The Social World of the First Christians: Essays in honor of Wayne A. Meeks* (L. M. White and O. L. Yarborough, eds.; Minneapolis: Fortress, 1995) 67–81; "Social Experience and Beginning of the Gospel of Mark," in *Reimagining Christian Origins: A Colloquium Honoring Burton L. Mack* (E. Castelli and H. Taussig, eds.; Valley Forge, PA: Trinity Press International, 1996) 311–26; and *The Infancy Gospels of James and Thomas* (The Scholars Bible 2; Sonoma, CA: Polebridge, 1996) 25–27.

[3] See "An Extraordinary Friend in Chariton's *Callirhoe*: The Importance of Friendship in the Greek Romances," in *Greco-Roman Perspectives on Friendship* (J. T. Fitzgerald, ed.; Atlanta: Scholars Press, 1996) 145–62, and "The Rhetoric of Romance," in *Handbook of Classical Rhetoric in the Hellenistic Period, 330 B.C.–A.D. 400* (S. Porter, ed.; Leiden: E. J. Brill, 1997) 445–65.

the Society of Biblical Literature. His efforts—and they were primarily his—led eventually to the formation of the Ancient Fiction and Early Christian and Jewish Narrative Group.[4]

1. The Romances: Hottest Property in Town

The formation of this SBL Group comes at a very auspicious time, for the romances, long neglected and often despised among classicists, have experienced a renaissance of late. Indeed, one recent assessment asserts that they have become "one of the hottest properties in town."[5] Five romances have survived intact, and papyrus fragments of a number of others have come to light from the sands of Egypt, which, when combined with references to and summaries of several others in later literature, suggest that romances were one of the typical literary productions of the early Roman Empire. At any rate, recent scholarship has made these romances more readily available than ever before and has provided them with a growing, varied, and sophisticated secondary tradition. The five romances as well as the major papyrus fragments and some related narratives are now available in English in a single volume: *Collected Ancient Greek Novels*, edited by B. P. Reardon.[6] Critical texts of the romances continue to appear, highlighted recently by the inclusion of Chariton's *Callirhoe* in the Loeb Classical Library,[7] whereas the papyrus fragments have at last been edited in a single volume.[8] In addition,

---

[4] For details, see C. Hedrick, "Ancient Fiction and Early Christian and Jewish Narrative Working Group," *PSN* 24 (1994) 6–7.

[5] See E. L. Bowie and S. J. Harrison, "The Romance of the Novel," *JRS* 83 (1993) 159–78, esp. 159.

[6] B. P. Reardon, ed., *Collected Ancient Greek Novels* (Berkeley: University of California Press, 1989).

[7] *Chariton, Callirhoe* (G. P. Goold, ed. and trans.; LCL; Cambridge: Harvard University Press, 1995). Other recent editions of the romances: *Xenophontis Ephesii Ephesiacorum libri V de Amoribus Anthiae et Abrocomae* (A. Papanikolaou, ed.; Leipzig: B. G. Teubner, 1973); *Longus, Daphnis et Chloe* (2d ed.; M. D. Reeve, ed.; Leipzig: B. G. Teubner, 1986); *Chariton, Le roman de Chairéas et Callirhoé* (A. Billault, ed. and trans.; Paris: Les Belles Lettres, 1989); and *Achille Tatius d'Alexandrie, Le roman de Leucippé et Clitophon* (J.-P. Garnaud, ed. and trans.; Paris: Les Belles Lettres, 1991). A Teubner edition of Chariton is being prepared by B. P. Reardon (so Bowie and Harrison, "Romance," 161–62).

[8] See *Ancient Greek Novels: The Fragments* (S. A. Stephens and J. J. Winkler, eds.; Princeton: Princeton University Press, 1995). Cf. also R. Kussl, *Papyrusfragmente griechischer Romane* (MSKP 2; Tübingen: Gunter Narr, 1991).

introductions to the romances proliferate;[9] and specialized studies, primarily from literary and social perspectives,[10] are appearing at an increasing rate—all of it carefully and handily recorded in G. Schmeling's *Petronian Society Newsletter.*[11]

2. The Romances: Sources for Thick Description of the Greco-Roman World

But it is more than just an auspicious time to read the romances. A more important reason to do so are the contents of the romances themselves. To be sure, their principal interest is love, which is most capably treated by D. Konstan.[12] But this theme hardly exhausts the contents of the romances, for they also provide the reader with a remarkably detailed, comprehensive, and coherent account of the social, economic, and religious institutions of the people and regions that witnessed the spread of Christianity into the Greek East of the early Roman Empire.

---

[9] See, e.g., T. Hägg, *The Novel in Antiquity* (Berkeley: University of California Press, 1983); J. R. Morgan and R. Stoneman, eds., *Greek Fiction: The Greek Novel in Context* (London: Routledge, 1994); N. Holzberg, *The Ancient Novel: An Introduction* (C. Jackson-Holzberg, trans.; London: Routledge, 1995); and *The Novel in the Ancient World* (G. Schmeling, ed.; Leiden: E. J. Brill, 1996). Among older works, see esp. E. Rohde, *Der griechische Roman und seine Vorläufer* (3d ed.; Leipzig: Breitkopf & Hartel, 1914); B. E. Perry, *The Ancient Romances: A Literary-Historical Account of their Origins* (Berkeley: University of California Press, 1967); and B. P. Reardon, *Courants litteraires grecs des IIe et IIIe siècles après J.-C.* (Paris: Les Belles Lettres, 1971) 309–403. For short accounts, see esp. B. P. Reardon, "The Greek Novel," *Phoenix* 23 (1969) 291–309; E. L. Bowie, "The Greek Novel," in *The Cambridge History of Classical Literature. Vol. 1. Greek Literature* (P. Easterling and B. Knox, eds.; Cambridge: Cambridge University Press, 1985) 683–99.

[10] Literary analyses are legion, see, e.g., G. Anderson, *The Novel in the Graeco-Roman World* (Totowa, NJ: Barnes & Noble, 1984), and B. P. Reardon, *The Form of Greek Romance* (Princeton: Princeton University Press, 1991). For social analysis, see, e.g., H. Kloft, "Imagination und Realität: Überlegungen zur Wirtschaftsstruktur des Romans *Daphnis und Chloe,*" *GCN* 2 (1989) 45–61; K. Hopkins, "Novel Evidence for Roman Slavery," *P&P* 138 (1993) 3–27; B. Egger, "Women and Marriage in the Greek Novels," in *The Search for the Ancient Novel* (J. Tatum, ed.; Baltimore: Johns Hopkins University Press, 1994) 260–80; and A. M. Scarcella, "The Social and Economic Structures of the Ancient Novels," in *Novel in the Ancient World*, 221–76.

[11] Published yearly in April, *The Petronian Society Newsletter* celebrated its 25th anniversary in 1995 and provides comprehevnsive bibliographies on all sorts of ancient fiction as well as news of conferences and other information of interest to scholars in the field.

[12] See D. Konstan, *Sexual Symmetry: Love in the Ancient Novel and Related Genres* (Princeton: Princeton University Press, 1994).

The romances are set in Antioch, Tyre, Tarsus, Ephesus, Miletus, Alexandria, Paphos, Xanthus, and Tarentum, to name just a few of the cities also mentioned in the New Testament, and in these cities we observe first-hand all sorts of people in ordinary and extraordinary situations—from the activities of the leading aristocratic families in the πόλις to those of the most marginalized shepherds and brigands in the χώρα and ἔρημος.

To illustrate the richness of the data, let me describe briefly the mosaic that can be pieced together from the aristocratic families that appear in the four romances most contemporary with the New Testament[13]—Chariton's *Callirhoe*, dated from the late first century BC to the early second century AD;[14] Xenophon's *Ephesian Tale* and Achilles Tatius' *Leucippe and Clitophon*, both dated to no later than the mid-second century;[15] and Longus' *Daphnis and Chloe*, dated to the late second or early third century.[16]

These romances follow twelve aristocratic families and the households they occupied and managed, but there are more limited, but often complementary, data on eleven others. The resulting mosaic is a surprisingly "thick description" of the members of these households and their many activities. For example, we see householders hosting symposia,

---

[13] For a more general account of aristocrats in the romances, see M.-F. Baslez, "L'idée de noblese dans les romans grecs," *DHA* 16 (1990) 115–28.

[14] For dating Chariton to the period 25 BC to AD 50, see Goold, *Chariton*, 2; for a mid-first century dating, see K. Plepelits, *Chariton von Aphrodisias, Kallirhoe* (Stuttgart: A. Hiersmann, 1976) 4–9; and for the early second century, see C. Ruiz-Montrero, "Aspects of the Vocabulary of Chariton of Aphrodisias," *CQ* 41 (1991) 484–89. For recent discussion of the issues involved with this novel, see Ruiz-Montrero, "Chariton von Aphrodisias: Ein Überblick," *ANRW* 2.34.2 (1994) 1006–54, and B. P. Reardon, "Chariton," in *Novel in the Ancient World*, 309–35.

[15] For the dating of Xenophon, see H. Gärtner, "Xenophon von Ephesus," *RE* 9A2 (1967) 2055–89, esp. 2086–87. For discussion of the issues involved with this novel, see, besides Gärtner's Pauly article, C. Ruiz-Montrero, "Xenophon von Ephesus: Ein Überblick," *ANRW* 2.34.2 (1994) 1088–1138, and B. Kytzler, "Xenophon of Ephesus," in *Novel in the Ancient World*, 336–60. The dating of Achilles Tatius has recently been pushed back, from the late second century (so, e.g., Reardon, *Courants*, 334 n. 56), to the first half of that century, prompted by the discovery of a papyrus fragment of this novel (see H. H. Willis, "The Robinson-Cologne Papyrus of Achilles Tatius," *GRBS* 31 [1990] 73–102). For issues involved with this novel, see K. Plepelits, "Achilles Tatius," in *Novel in the Ancient World*, 387–416.

[16] For the dating, which is hardly secure, see R. L. Hunter, *A Study of Daphnis and Chloe* (Cambridge: Cambridge University Press, 1983) 3–15. For issues involved with this novel, see Hunter's "Longus, *Daphnis and Chloe*," in *Novel in the Ancient World*, 361–86.

offering sacrifice, visiting rural properties, speaking in the theatre, taking on public duties, arranging marriages, and making wills; we see their wives attending religious festivals, praying in temples, punishing slaves, and fleeing the ravages of war; we see their sons attending the gymnasium, hunting in the countryside, participating in religious processions, and visiting a hetaira; their daughters playing the lyre, walking in the garden adjacent to the house, making seductive overtures to newly purchased slaves, and participating in religious festivals. We see domestic slaves managing households, guarding doors, pouring wine, delivering letters, exposing babies, purchasing slaves, grooming horses, letting in adulterers, receiving their freedom or suffering abuse and excruciating corporal punishment. In addition, we see parasites enjoying the daily and extravagant board of their hosts, friends and freedmen accompanying the householder on trips, relatives being welcomed for visits, and even shipwrecked victims taken in and later provided with money and supplies for the return trip home. Finally, we see the slaves and tenants on the aristocrats' rural properties herding sheep and goats, digging pits to capture wolves, picking grapes and making the new wine, fighting off the attacks of brigands, counting the grains of wheat after a harvest, playing the pan-pipes under a tree or swimming in the rivers, catching birds with bird-lime, greeting the Nymphs each morning, and turning brigand when an occasion arises. For many of these activities the romances are sufficiently detailed to provide vivid descriptions of the conventions of thought and behavior that governed these activities.

Similar summaries are possible for any number of specific social institutions—for example, slavery, brigandage, travel, burials, symposia, trials, public and private festivals, hunting, and harvests. And many intellectual activities receive their due as well—from learning letters to becoming familiar with literature, from mastering the skills needed to compose simple fables to the expertise required to compose and deliver complex prosecution and defense speeches. In short, the romances are virtually an unparalleled, if underused, source for a wide range of social and intellectual institutions that characterized life in the Greco-Roman world during the New Testament period.

3. The Romances: Illuminating the New Testament

And yet, for New Testament scholars the real reason for reading the romances, however good the secondary tradition or detailed their narrative worlds, is their ability to clarify and illumine early Christian (and Jewish) literature. And even here the romances do not disappoint. They supply a wealth of data that not only corroborate and clarify various details and formal literary features in the New Testament but also illumine such central concerns as Christological titles, as I have tried to show elsewhere regarding the title Son of God in the opening verses of Mark (1:1–15) and the confession that Jesus Christ is Lord in the Philippians hymn (Phil 2:6–11). For the former title the social conventions governing the visit of a householder to his estate, which are nicely detailed in Longus' account of the visit of Dionysophanes (4.1–15), illumine why Mark characterized John the Baptist as a slave-messenger (1:2, 7) and Jesus as Son of God (1:1, 11) as well as arranged them in strict sequence (1:14).[17] For the latter title the conventions governing slaves and masters clarify the language, structure, and plausibility of the Philippians hymn.[18]

Here, however, I wish to illustrate the value of the romances for understanding the New Testament in other ways: first by sampling briefly the variety of parallels that the romances supply for reading the New Testament, and then by discussing at greater length a single New Testament passage and bringing to bear a number of parallels from the romances that provide new insight into its meaning.

3a. Romancing the New Testament

First, then, a sampling of parallels—linguistic, grammatical, literary, and behavioral:

1) A grammatical construction that is rather frequent in the gospels is the partitive use of ἀπό or ἐκ with a suppressed τινές (e.g., Matt 23:34; Mark 12:2; John 7:40). This construction is sometimes identified as an example of Biblical Greek, originating in the LXX. But this genitive also appears in Longus: ". . . they sent Daphnis *some of what they were eating* (ἀπ' ὧν ἤσθιον)" (4.15.4).

---

[17] See further Hock, "Social Experience," 314–24.
[18] See further Hock, "Greek Novel," 142–44.

2) Mark's use of ἀρχή (1:1) to signal "the beginning" of the fulfillment of Isaiah's prophecy (vv. 2–3) in the preaching of John the Baptist matches the use of ἀρχή in the romances. Early in Xenophon's story, for example, Habrocomes and Anthia receive an oracle from Apollo (1.6.2), whose dire predictions, however, do not find immediate fulfillment. But later in the story, when the sailors on board the ship they are on become drunk and allow a pirate ship to attack, Xenophon notes that this incident represented the "beginning" (ἀρχή) (1.12.3) of the oracle's fulfillment (cf. also Chariton, 1.6.5; Achilles Tatius, 1.3.1).

3) In addition, the oracle in Xenophon has a formal structure that parallels the passion predictions in the Synoptics (Mark 8:31; 9:31; 10:32 and pars.). The oracle (1.6.2) reads as follows (using the private translation of my colleague E. N. O'Neil):

> Why long to learn their illness' end and cause?
> One illness holds both, hence relief's at hand.
> But dire the sufferings (δεινὰ πάθη) I see for them
> And endless toils: both will flee o'er the brine,
> Madly pursued, and be distressed by chains
> 'Mid sea-consorting men. For both a grave
> And wasting fire will be a bridal chamber,
> And afterwards besides the flowing Nile
> Offer rich gifts to Isis, holy savior;
> Yet after woes they'll have a better fate (ἀρείονα πότμον).

What is of interest in this oracle are the use of the word "sufferings" (πάθη) to characterize all the hardships they will endure as well as the structure of the oracle in which sufferings dominate until a more positive note is struck at the very end: a better fate. Jesus' passion predictions also include the same word for suffering; indeed, Mark's "suffer much" (πολλὰ παθεῖν) (8:31) is very close to what Anthia will say later, namely that "she had suffered much" (πέπονθα πολλά) (5.9.5). In addition, the passion predictions have the same structure of suffering being dominant until a brief mention of a better outcome is sounded at the end, as is especially apparent in the third passion prediction (Mark 10:32):

> The son of man will be handed over to the chief priests and the scribes,
> And they will condemn him to death and hand him over to Gentiles,
> The latter will mock him and spit upon him and scourge him and kill him,
> But after three days he will be raised up.

4) Mark says that Herod listened gladly to John the Baptist (6:20: ἡδέως αὐτοῦ ἤκουεν), an expression that appears several times in Chariton (2.1.5; 5.9.3: ἡδέως ἤκουεν; cf. also 4.6.2; 5.9.2). In addition, we find its opposite. Callirhoe, when told by Plangon of the difficulties she

will face raising her baby should she decide to give birth, listened despondently (2.10.2: βαρέως ἤκουσεν).

5) Mark's formulation of Jesus' charge against the temple authorities—"You have turned the temple into a cave for brigands" (ὑμεῖς δὲ πεποιήκατε αὐτὸν [scil. τὸν οἶκον=τὸ ἱερὸν] σπήλαιον λῃστῶν) 11:17)—is very close to the accusation against Clitophon, Leucippe, and her father for spending a night in the temple of Artemis: "You have turned the temple of Artemis into a temple of Aphrodite" (τὸ τῆς Ἀρτέμιδος ἱερὸν Ἀφροδίτης πεποιήκατε) (Achilles Tatius, 8.10.6).

6) Mark's direct address to his readers—"Let the reader understand" (ὁ ἀναγινώσκων νοείτω) (13:14)—is paralleled in Chariton who admits that his last chapter will be most enjoyable to his readers (τοῖς ἀναγινώσκουσιν) (8.1.4).

7) Luke's use of ψυχή ("soul") as a means of self-address in the parable of the rich fool (12:19) also appears in Chariton in a soliloquy by Dionysius (3.2.9).

8) That the father in the parable of the prodigal son (15:11–32) should run to meet his returning son (v 20: δραμών) has struck interpreters as most unusual, as beneath the dignity of an old man, but in the romances such precipitous behavior seems conventional for greeting people long thought to have died. Thus, Callirhoe's father Hermocrates runs on board the ship his daughter is at long last returning on to Syracuse (Chariton, 8.6.8: καταδραμών), and Astylos, Daphnis' brother, runs to greet him when he learns the latter's true identity (Longus, 4.23.1; cf. 2.30.1; 4.36.3; Achilles Tatius, 1.4.1; 7.16.3). Indeed, the language used of the prodigal—of being lost and now found (vv 24, 32: ἀπολωλὼς καὶ εὑρέθη) is also used by Longus of Daphnis (4.22.3: εὑρεθεὶς ἀπωλώλει Δάφνις). And, as in the parable, there follows a joyful celebration (Luke 15:22–25; Longus, 4.25–26; cf. 2.30–37), complete with dancing (Luke 15:25; Longus, 4.25.2; cf. 2.36–37) as well as addressing the delicate matter of reassuring the son who had always been at home (Luke 15:25–32; Longus, 4.24.3–4).

9) Paul's description of his native Tarsus as "no mean city" (οὐκ ἀσήμου πόλεως) (Acts 21:39) is repeated by Clitophon for his native Tyre (Achilles Tatius, 8.3.1), and the chant of the Ephesians—"Great is Artemis of the Ephesians" (μεγάλη ἡ Ἄρτεμις Ἐφεσίων)—that is heard when Paul threatens the livelihood of silversmiths in that city (Acts 19:28) is also heard in the romances—both in Xenophon (1.11.5) and in Achilles Tatius (8.9.13).

10) Paul's most elaborate use of imagery from the gymnasium (1 Cor 9:24–27) finds a parallel in the comment of a young man in Chariton's story. He says that only one of the competitors in a contest receives a crown (1.2.2–4; cf. 1 Cor 9:24).

11) Paul's letters share various epistolary conventions with letters that appear in the romances, including closing greetings (Rom 16:3–16; Phil 4:21–22; cf. Chariton, 8.4.6), the authenticating signature (1 Cor 16:21; Phlm 19; cf. Chariton, 8.4.6), and arrangements for delivery and oral messages (Col 4:7–8; cf. Chariton, 4.5.1–2; 8.4.7–9; Xenophon, 2.12.1; Achilles Tatius, 5.21.1).

3b. Romancing the Good Samaritan

This sampling, as brief as it is, should suffice to indicate the variety of ways that the romances can clarify the New Testament. But there is a second way to underscore the value of the romances, and that is to analyze more fully a single New Testament passage by bringing to bear a variety of parallels from the romances that cumulatively reveal the meaning of the passage—indeed, a meaning not previously proposed. Such a prospect is exciting, indeed, and one place to begin is with the parable of the Good Samaritan (Luke 10:30–37).

The literary context of this parable in Luke is a conversation between Jesus and a lawyer (vv. 25–29). It begins with the lawyer's question about what he must do to inherit eternal life (v. 25). Jesus has the lawyer himself answer (v. 26), which he does by combining two passages from Jewish scripture (Deut 6:5 and Lev 19:18) to form the familiar *Doppelgebot*: love of God and love of neighbor (v. 27; cf. Matt 22:37; Mark 12:29–30). Jesus agrees with this answer, adding only an admonition: "Do this and you will live" (v. 28). The lawyer, however, extends the conversation by asking a further question: "Who is my neighbor?" (v. 29). It is this question that provides the bridge between the conversation and the following parable, for Jesus answers by telling of a traveler to Jericho who is attacked by brigands and left for dead (v. 30); of a priest and Levite who pass him by (vv. 31–32), and of a Samaritan who has compassion, stops to help, and then takes him to an inn for recuperation (vv. 33–35). Jesus then asks the lawyer which of the three had acted as a neighbor to the victim of brigand atttack (v. 36). The lawyer's answer—"the one who showed him mercy" (v. 37a)—prompts Jesus' concluding admonition: "Go and do likewise" (v. 37b).

This parable has attracted enormous scholarly attention, but only a few illustrative studies need concern us here,[19] for my interest is limited to questions of the parable's connection to its literary context, its narrative focus, and its subject matter. For example, scholars have often posited a tradition history for this parable that detaches it from its immediate Lukan context—in large part due to a troublesome inconsistency between the questions of vv. 29 and 36, the former asking who the neighbor is and the latter who acted as a neighbor. This inconsistency—characterized by J. D. Crossan as a shift from the lawyer's passive question (who is to be treated as a neighbor?) to Jesus' active one (who behaved as a neighbor?)—has persuaded scholars to suspect a seam in the Lukan presentation.[20] Scholars, accordingly, have followed Crossan and hypothesized that the parable (vv. 30–35/36) did not originally belong to the dialogue between Jesus and the lawyer.[21]

The consequence of this literary analysis is, of course, to interpret the parable apart from its context. Crossan is again typical: "The parable of the Good Samaritan in <Luke> 10:30–36 was originally independent of its present context and must be interpreted therefore apart from that later framework." Once extricated from its Lukan context, however, scholars have had to posit other interpretive frameworks—for example, in terms of Jesus' concept of the Kingdom of God,[22] a general theory of parable as metaphor,[23] or a socio-political backdrop of peasant *mentalité*.[24]

The problem is that none of these frameworks leads to a persuasive interpretation. To be sure, a number of details in the parable have been adequately explained over the years—the real life danger of brigand attack on the road from Jerusalem to Jericho, the differentiation and roles of priest and Levite, the animosity between Jews and Samaritans, the

---

[19] For a summary of recent interpretations of this parable, see C. W. Hedrick, *Parables as Poetic Fictions: The Creative Voice of Jesus* (Peabody, MA: Hendrickson, 1994) 95–100.

[20] See J. D. Crossan, "Parable and Example in the Teaching of Jesus," *NTS* 18 (1972) 285–96, esp. 288–91.

[21] See, e.g., J. A. Fitzmyer, *The Gospel according to Luke* (2 vols.; AB 28–28A; Garden City, NY: Doubleday, 1985) 882–83. For good discussion of the issues involved, see I. H. Marshall, *The Gospel of Luke: A Commentary on the Greek Text* (Grand Rapids, MI: Eerdmans, 1978) 445–46.

[22] See, e.g., Crossan, "Parable," 295–96.

[23] See, e.g., R. W. Funk, "The Good Samaritan as Metaphor," *Semeia* 2 (1974) 74–81.

[24] See, e.g., D. E. Oakman, "Was Jesus a Peasant? Implications for Reading the Samaritan Story (Luke 10:30–35)," *BTB* 22 (1992) 117–25.

medicinal properties of oil and wine, the purchasing power of two denarii, and so on.[25] Nevertheless, the resulting interpretations remain unsatisfactory, even misleading. For example, D. E. Oakman's appeal to peasant *mentalité* leads him to say that Jesus' audience would have sympathized with the brigands(!), since, he claims, brigands "in Jesus' day were perceived by the Jewish peasantry as social bandits and thus considered heros [sic] in the villages."[26] Similarly, R. W. Funk's emphasis on the parable as metaphor which reveals a fantasy about a new order of reality called the Kingdom of God leads him to exaggerate the novelty of the Samaritan's behavior, since, Funk asserts, he acts "in an altogether unexpected way."[27] And J. Jeremias distracts us when he understands the lawyer's answer—"The one who showed him mercy" (v. 37a)—to be a way of avoiding "the hateful term Samaritan."[28]

The problem with these contemporary interpretations is that none of them gives adequate attention to what is clearly the focus of the parable—namely, the narrative detail lavished on the Samaritan's actions (vv. 34–35). Crossan's literary analysis will illustrate why the Samaritan's actions deserve attention. He divides the parable into seven sections (with word counts) as follows:

1. Man travels to Jericho (v. 30a) (10 words)
2. Brigands attack (v. 30) (10 words)
3. Priest passes by (v. 31) (14 words)
4. Levite passes by (v. 32) (12 words)
5. Samaritan has compassion (v. 33) (10 words)
6. Samaritan provides help (vv. 34–35) (50 words)
7. Jesus asks who has acted as a neighbor (v. 36) (13 words).[29]

Clearly, the fifty words used to describe the Samaritan's actions far exceed those for any other section and thus deserve explanation, and not simply explanations of specific details of his behavior, such as Jeremias' comment that the oil would mollify and the wine disinfect (v. 34).[30] No, what is called for is a conceptual understanding of the Samaritan's actions as a whole. Scholars have been too content to use vague or

---

[25] See, e.g., Jeremias, *Parables*, 202–5. The practice continues: Hedrick, *Poetic Fictions*, 103–9.

[26] Oakman, "Was Jesus a Peasant?" 121.

[27] R. W. Funk, *Honest to Jesus: Jesus for a New Millennium* (San Francisco: Harper San Francisco, 1996) 176–77.

[28] Jeremias, *Parables*, 205.

[29] Crossan, "Parable," 293.

[30] Jeremias, *Parables*, 204.

modern categories to describe the Samaritan's behavior—for example, "neighborliness" or "goodness." But how would Jesus' first century hearers or Luke's readers have conceptualized this behavior? What term would they have used? On this question scholars are clueless.

The clue, I submit, comes from the romances, which is not surprising since the characters in the romances often travel and suffer misfortunes that include brigand attack. A closer look at the romances, moreover, will reveal that the apposite term for the Samaritan's behavior is φιλανθρω-πία. But to arrive at this conclusion involves a rather circuitous and complex argument.

I begin with an authorial comment by Longus. The area on Lesbos where Daphnis and Chloe are herding their flocks is attacked by brigands who kidnap Daphnis, steal some cattle, murder their cowherd, and head out to sea (1.28). Chloe, however, took up the cowherd's pan-pipes and played a melody that caused the cattle to capsize the boat and allow Daphnis to swim safely to shore (1.29–30). Longus then comments: "In this way Daphnis was saved from two dangers beyond all hope—the danger of brigands and the danger of shipwreck" (1.31.1).

Longus' comment prompted me to think of comparable incidents in the New Testament, such as the brigand attack in the parable of the Good Samaritan and the shipwreck of Paul and his companions off Malta in Acts 27:39–44. In the latter, Paul and all aboard make it safely to shore where the local inhabitants warm them before a fire, offer them hospitality until spring, and supply them with provisions for continuing their trip to Rome (28:1–10). Luke's comment on the inhabitants' behavior is that they displayed "no ordinary φιλανθρωπία" (28:2).

The extraordinary φιλανθρωπία shown Paul and the others reminded me of the extensive care extended by the Samaritan to the victim of a brigand attack in the parable, prompting the question whether φιλανθρωπία is not also the implicit term that defines the Samaritan's conduct. At any rate, the term φιλανθρωπία seemed worthy of further investigation, and one definition in particular, that is, one focusing on behavior, has proved fruitful. This definition, attributed to Plato, identifies three kinds of behavior as characteristic of φιλανθρωπία. The definition reads as follows:

There are three kinds of φιλανθρωπία. One occurs through greetings—for example, when some people greet everyone they meet by extending their right hand and offering greetings. Another kind occurs whenever someone is helpful to anyone who is unfortunate. Another kind of φιλανθρωπία characterizes those who enjoy hosting dinners (φιλο-δειπνισταί). Therefore, φιλανθρωπία includes giving greetings, offering benefactions, and hosting dinners and promoting social discourse (DL 3.98).

The Platonic definition is useful because it permits us to identify philanthropic individuals, and no better example emerges than the hunters Dio Chrysostom encountered after a shipwreck off the treacherous Hollows of Euboea. Dio's lengthy account of his experiences (*Orat.* 7.1–80) forms a προλαλία to his oration on what to do with the urban poor and is worth a detailed summary.[31] After reaching land, Dio says, he started wandering along the shore and met a hunter chasing down a deer that had fallen from a cliff to its death on the shore below. The hunter greets him (7.5). Then, he invites him back to his lodgings to recover from the ordeal and to wait for a break in the weather (7.5); once back at the lodgings Dio is fed (7.64, 67–76) and in the course of the meal learns of an upcoming wedding to which he is invited to stay on for the celebrations and feast (7.79). In other words, the hunter exhibits all three philanthropic behaviors mentioned by Plato—giving greetings, providing food and lodging, and extending an invitation to dinner.

Dio, moreover, is not the only one shown such φιλανθρωπία. While walking back to the hunter's lodgings, he learns of other victims of shipwreck who were treated just as well by the hunter, his brother, and their families. Indeed, such help had become a habit with the hunter, for he tells Dio: "Many times (πολλάκις) I showed mercy (ἠλέησα) to shipwrecked victims who came to my lodgings; I welcomed them, gave them something to eat and drink, and helped them in any way I could; then I accompanied them back to civilization" (7.52).

One of these shipwrecked victims later stood up in defense of the hunter at a trial and related how he and his traveling companion were helped by the hunter. His account of the hunter's help recalls that shown by the Samaritan. At any rate, the man says that, after being shipwrecked, getting to land, and wandering about,

> we came to some structures and stood shouting. This hunter came out and took us inside and lit a fire. . . . He himself rubbed one of us, his wife the other, with animal fat, since they had no olive oil. Next, they poured warm water over us until they revived us since we had been shivering with cold. Then they made us recline, wrapped us in what they had, and set before us wheat bread to eat, while they themselves ate boiled millet. They gave us wine to drink (while they drank water)

---

[31] For text and commentary, see D. A. Russell, ed., *Dio Chrysostom, Orations VII, XII, and XXXVI* (Cambridge: Cambridge University Press, 1992) 29–158.

as well as roasted and boiled venison. On the next day when we wished to leave they held us back for three days. Then they escorted us to the plain, and when we left them they gave to each of us meat and a very nice animal skin. And when he saw that I was still doing poorly after the ordeal he put a tunic on me, taking it from his daughter who then wrapped herself in some rag. I gave it back, though, when I reached the village (7.56–58).

Dio's hunters were truly philanthropic individuals, but the conventions also work in reverse, identifying their opposite, the misanthrope. For example, in Menander's *Dyskolos*, whose alternate title, incidentally, is Μισάνθρωπος, the main character Knemon greets nobody (*Dysk.* 726; cf. 427–28), refuses to help Sikon who has forgotten a cooking utensil for a sacrifice at Pan's shrine near Knemon's house (456–80, 500–14), and refuses to go to a dinner, much less host one (911–58). In other words, the behavioral characteristics of both φιλάνθρωπος and μισάνθρωπος were conventional, so that Luke's readers, and even Jesus' hearers, might be supposed to have conceptualized the Samaritan's considerable aid to a victim of brigand attack as being φιλανθρωπία.

That such a suppositon is, in fact, probable emerges from a closer look at the usage of a word used by the lawyer to Jesus' question. The latter asks: "Which of these three do you think acted as a neighbor to the victim of brigand attack?" (v. 36). The lawyer responds: "The one who showed him mercy (ὁ ποιήσας τὸ ἔλεος μετ' αὐτοῦ)" (v. 37a).

The noun ἔλεος ("mercy"), it turns out, is often used as a synomym for φιλανθρωπία, as is already apparent from what the hunter said (Dio, *Orat.* 7.52: ἐλέησα). In other words, the lawyer is not to be understood, as Jeremias thinks, as trying to avoid saying the hated word "Samaritan" and thus resorts to circumlocution; in fact, Jeremias' interpretation distracts us from sensing the crucial clue to understanding the Samaritan's behavior. Luke, who uses φιλανθρωπία in Acts 28:2, uses here the synonym ἔλεος for characterizing the Samaritan's aid of someone who has fallen into misfortune.

A few illustrations of ἔλεος (and its verbal form ἐλεεῖν) used as synonyms for φιλανθρωπία should prove conclusive. The romances are particularly helpful here. Longus, for example, narrates two similar incidents in which a herder comes to the aid of the most unfortunate of people—an exposed infant. The goatherder Lamon finds an exposed baby boy being nursed by one of his she-goats (1.2.1–3.2), and the shepherd Dryas likewise finds an exposed baby girl being nursed by one of his ewes (1.4.1–6.3). Longus notes both herders' reflections on the animals' behavior. Lamon, for example, thought first of taking only the valuables set out with the infant, but then was ashamed that he would not equal the φιλανθρωπία of the goat; consequently, he picked up everything—the tokens, the baby, and the goat—and took them home to his wife (1.3.1–2). Dryas, too, learns a lesson from his ewe in showing mercy (ἐλεεῖν) and likewise picks up the infant girl and takes her home (1.6.1–3). Here we have identical behavior—animals nursing exposed infants—which Longus characterizes in one case as illustrating φιλανθρωπία (1.3.1) and in the other as showing mercy (ἐλεεῖν) (1.6.1).

The interchangeability of these terms, moreover, receives confirmation in other romances—five times in Chariton alone (1.10.2 and 4; 3.4.9–10; 4.214; 5.4.7; 6.5.10). Consequently, Luke's use of ποιεῖν τὸ ἔλεος in the parable of the Good Samaritan (v. 37a) and φιλανθρωπία in Acts 28:2 are thus two ways of speaking about the same, that is, philanthropic, behavior.

Further confirmation, however, comes from the appearance of yet other words in the parable which likewise appear in philanthropic contexts, such as ἡμιθανής ("half-dead") (v. 30),[32] ἐπιμελέομαι ("take care of") (v. 35),[33] and πλησίον ("neighbor"), the very term that prompted the parable in the first place and then is repeated at its conclusion (vv. 29, 36). With respect to the last word, note, for example, that Callirhoe, when she hears that her husband Chaereas is reported to have been murdered while anchored off shore in the vicinity of a temple of Aphrodite, prays to the goddess, complaining that she had shown no mercy (οὐκ ἠλέησας) toward one who had sailed on her account and had even watched a handsome young man being murdered near (πλησίον) her temple (3.10.6). Conversely, the most famous misanthrope, Timon of Athens, is reported to have said: "I am happiest when no one is my neighbor (μηδενός μοι πλησιάζοντος)" (Lucian, *Timon* 35).

It should now be clear that the parable of the Good Samaritan (Luke 10:30–36/37) is about φιλανθρωπία. The detailed description of the Samaritan's coming to the aid of one who suffered a misfortune (vv. 34–35); the use of the word ἔλεος to describe this conduct; and the use of other words that appear in philanthropic contexts, including πλησίον (vv. 29, 37), all point to conventions used in discussing φιλανθρωπία in the romances and elsewhere in Greco-Roman literature.

---

[32] See, e.g., Chariton, 3.3.16; 4.6; 5.4.

[33] This word is virtually synonymous with philanthropic behavior. See, e.g., Chariton, 1.13.10; 2.2.2; 2.6.4; 3.3.17; 4.6; 5.8.9; Xenophon of Ephesus, 1.15.2; 2.2.5; 10.3–4; 4.2.10; 5.2.6; 9.13; 10.12.

If this reading is correct, then several implications for the interpretation of the parable emerge:

1) The central figure in the parable is the Samaritan, not Funk's "man in the ditch"[34] and certainly not Oakman's brigands.

2) The hostile relations between Jews and Samaritans are not as central to the parable as Crossan's claim that the literal point of the parable was to get Jews to speak the unspeakable: combining "good" and "Samaritan";[35] rather, the victim of brigand attack, while implicitly a Jew, is portrayed more as an unfortunate person, one who is a potential recipient of philanthropic aid;[36] at most, Jesus' Jewish audience would have been ashamed that a Samaritan proved more philanthropic than the priest and Levite, much as Lamon was ashamed at being bested by a goat in φιλανθρωπία, or Dio's city dwellers by the rural hunters.

3) The Samaritan's behavior, when examined in terms of φιλανθρωπία, does not appear so novel, as Funk thinks, and certainly not so "frighteningly idealistic" that it must be seen as a satire of the late Jewish ideal of a righteous person;[37] on the contrary, the Samaritan's behavior becomes rather conventional, as Dio's hunters' repeated and exhaustive help of shipwreck victims shows.

4) The standard literary analysis that isolates the parable (vv. 30–35/36) from its Lukan context (vv. 25–29, 36–37) becomes more problematic, for the obvious, if implicit, use of philanthropic conventions in the parable argues for a greater unity of parable and context than is usually allowed. This unity, however, will become apparent from one last glance at the romances.

Chariton narrates a meeting between Callirhoe and Dionysius that is illuminating in this regard. Dionysius has recently, if only briefly, seen the beautiful Callirhoe, his newly purchased slave, but even in that brief encounter has fallen in love with her. Consequently, he wants to see and talk with her again, and at this next meeting he introduces himself as follows: "I am Dionysius, the leading citizen of Miletus and perhaps of all Ionia, widely known for piety (εὐσέβεια) and φιλανθρωπία . . ." (2.5.4).

Dionysius is trying his best to impress Callirhoe and thus emphasizes his high social status and his good moral character, the latter summarized in two words, one for his relation to the gods (εὐσέβεια) and the other

---

[34] See Funk, "Metaphor," 78.

[35] See Crossan, "Parable," 295–96.

[36] Hedrick (*Poetic Fictions*, 116) goes too far in reducing the man to a nobody.

[37] So Hedrick, *Poetic Fictions*, 115–16.

for his behavior toward people (φιλανθρωπία). This pair of behaviors—piety toward the gods and love for mankind—echoes what Jesus expected the lawyer to say in order to gain eternal life. Though couched in the language of Jewish scripture, the lawyer's summary is the same: "You shall love the Lord your God with all your heart, soul, strength, and mind, and your neighbor as yourself" (v. 27; cf. Deut 6:5; Lev. 19:18).

In other words, this pairing of εὐσέβεια and φιλανθρωπία as a shorthand way for describing a good person, Samaritan or otherwise, is thereby conventional and, moreover, places the parable more coherently in its present literary context. The parable, it turns out, interprets the command to love the neighbor (Lev 19:18) since, in the lawyer's mind, the one word "neighbor" is not clear. The parable achieves clarity by understanding "neighbor" in the broadest possible terms, those implicit in φιλανθρωπία, or love of mankind. In other words, the lawyer now knows what is required of him: to be a good person he must, like Dionysius, love God unconditionally and be philanthropic. The latter requirement, we now know, is not some vague moral category, such as "the late Jewish ideal of the righteous man," as C. Hedrick proposes,[38] but a clear and specific moral obligation: accepting a limited number of responsibilities toward an unlimited number of people—specifically three responsibilities: greeting everybody, aiding anyone who is unfortunate, and being gregarious, as shown in attendance at symposia.[39]

Even if the parable were only secondarily put in its present context by Luke, it nevertheless fits this context rather well, for it clarifies the second half of the *Doppelgebot* by appeal to φιλανθρωπία, the conventional partner of piety, loving God, as encapusalating the essence of a good person.

Conclusion

It should now be abundantly clear why New Testament scholars should read ancient novels. They are, in a word, indispensable—for corrobo-

---

[38] See Hedrick, *Poetic Fictions,* 114–16. So many behaviors are included that such an ideal becomes analytically hopeless.

[39] Incidentally, when so phrased, φιλανθρωπία is the complement of φιλία, or friendship, which calls for an unlimited number of responsibilities to a limited number of people, as ably illustrated in the romances, esp. in Chariton's portrayal of Polycharmus (see my "Extraordinary Friend," 147–57). The friendship ethic provides the content of the Johannine love command (see John 13:33–35; 15: 12–17; 1 John 3:11–17, 23; etc.).

rating and clarifying any number of details in the New Testament and for gaining new insights into the central interests and claims of the New Testament, whether Christological or moral, as indeed we discovered in the case of the latter in the parable of the Good Samaritan. The romances have pointed the way to seeing φιλανθρωπία as the implicit meaning of the Samaritan's behavior. Consequently, we now know both what love of neighbor means and why we rightly put "good" before "Samaritan."

Secrecy and Recognitions in the *Odyssey* and Mark: Where Wrede Went Wrong[1]

Dennis R. MacDonald
Claremont Graduate University

In the Gospel of Mark Jesus avoids publicity, silences those he heals, and muzzles demons who recognize him. Unfortunately, the earliest evangelist never states why Jesus maintained secrecy. William Wrede considered it damage control to explain why Jesus himself had never claimed to be the Messiah. Jesus avoided the title because it was inappropriate prior to the resurrection, as Mark seems to imply by having Jesus command Peter, James, and John, "to tell no one what they had seen" on the Mount of Transfiguration, "until after the Son of Man had risen from the dead."[2] I will analyze Mark in the light of secrecy and recognitions in the *Odyssey*, where these motifs play a dominating role.[3] When viewed from this comparative perspective, Mark's so-called "Messianc Secret" looks dramatically different.

One of Penelope's suitors scolded another for abusing a beggar, who actually was Odysseus in disguise: "what if perchance he be some god come down from heaven? And the gods do, in the guise of strangers from afar, put on all manner of shapes, and visit the cities, beholding the violence and the righteousness of men."[4] This dictum depicts the gods as guardians of the moral order, who, in disguise, visit mortals to test their

---

[1] *The Messianic Secret* (J. C. G. Greig, trans.; Greenwood, SC: Attic, 1971).

[2] Mark 9:9.

[3] The best treatment to date of secrecy and recognition in the epic is that of Sheila Murnaghan, *Disguise and Recognition in the Odyssey* (Princeton: Princeton University Press, 1987). Secrecy and recognitions, so prominent in *The Odyssey* and Mark, play a far less significant role in Matthew and Luke, even when they are recasting Mark. For example, Matthew omits Jesus' silencing the demons in Mark 1:34 (Matt. 8:16), and Luke omits the silencing in Mark 3:12 (cf. Mark 3:11–12 and Luke 6:18–19).

[4] *Od.* 17.484–87. All translations of the epic are taken from the LCL edition.

treatment of strangers. For example, when Athena appeared, she took the form of Mentes, or Mentor;[5] or a maidservant, or a young shepherd.[6]

Odysseus had just returned to Ithaca when she appeared to him as a young man in order to test him. She then transformed herself into her own likeness, so that Odysseus would recognize her,[7] but then disguised Odysseus as a beggar, so that the suitors would not recognize him.[8] His impenetrable disguise made possible a sequence of πεῖραι, 'tests,' in which he ascertained the faithfulness or treachery of his servants and family.[9] The warning of the suitor was not far wide of the mark: the beggar was indeed like "some god come down from heaven," like the gods who "put on all manner of shapes, and visit the cities, beholding the violence and the righteousness of men."[10]

Should his foes unmask him, they would kill him, so he repeatedly lied to conceal his identity and had to curb himself, lest, by performing remarkable feats of strength, he arouse suspicions among the suitors that he was no ordinary old beggar.[11] Because the reader knows crucial information about the identity of the hero unavailable to most characters within the narrative, he or she repeatedly detects irony throughout the end of the epic.

Once Odysseus had tested the loyalty of his household, he could safely reveal himself, but now he might be put to the test and have to produce a sign (σῆμα) that he was who he said he was. The most memorable of these signs was his boyhood scar on his thigh, but he had other signs as

---

[5] *Od.* 1.105 and 2.268.

[6] *Od.* 6.22, 13.222, and 20.31; cf. 16.157–58.

[7] *Od.* 13.287–310.

[8] *Od.* 13.397–403; cf. 13.190–93. Earlier in the epic, too, Odysseus kept his identity a secret when in a hostile environment (*Od.* 4.244–56 and 7.14–45).

[9] In each of these situations, Homer used the cognate verbs πειρᾶν and πειρητίζειν, both meaning 'to test.' For the testing of Penelope see *Od.* 13.333–38 (πειρήεαι; 336); of the servants see 15.304–6 (πειρητίζων; 304), 16.305–7 (πειρηθεῖμεν; 305), 313 (πειρητίζων), and 319 (πειράζειν); and of Laertes 24.214–21 (πειρήσομαι and πειρητίζων; 216 and 221) and 235–40 (πειρήσαιτο and πειρηθῆναι; 238 and 240).

For a brief but useful discussion of testing in the epic, see Agathe Thornton, *People and Themes in Homer's Odyssey* (London: Methuen, 1970) 47–51.

[10] On Odysseus's disguise as an imitation of divine disguises see Albert B. Lord, *The Singer of Tales* (Harvard Studies in Comparative Literature 24; Cambridge: Harvard University Press, 1960) 175; Murnaghan, *Disguise*, 11–13, 20, 53, 59, and 67–68; and especially Emily Kearns, "The Return of Odysseus: A Homeric Theoxeny," *CQ* 32 (1982) 2–8.

[11] *Od.* 14.191–3, 17.419–44, 18.94;19.106–248 and 261–307, and 24.301–14.

well. For example, Penelope tested him by making a false statement about their bed.[12] He immediately recognized her mendacity and described his crafting of the bed down to its supporting thongs. "Thus do I declare to you this sign (σῆμα)."[13] "[H]er knees were loosened where she sat, and her heart melted, as she recognized the signs (σήματ'[α]) . . . which Odysseus showed her."[14] Laertes, his father, refused to accept his son's self-disclosure without an accompanying sign (σῆμα).[15] Odysseus bared his telltale thigh and accurately described the fruit trees and vines that his father had given him in his youth.[16] Then Laertes "recognized the signs (σήματ'[α]) which Odysseus showed him without error."[17] Prior to the slaying of the suitors, Odysseus invariably insisted that those who learned his true identity maintain utter silence so that he could continue to avoid detection by his enemies.

Similarly, at the beginning of Mark's gospel the reader gains information not available to characters within the narrative apart from Jesus himself and the demons; namely, that Jesus of Nazareth actually is God's Son.[18] The discrepancy between the reader's understanding and that of other characters in the gospel creates irony, just as we have observed in the epic.[19]

As God's Son, Jesus possesses superhuman powers which function as signs of his identity, leaving him vulnerable to discovery by the Jewish authorities. It is worth noting that Mark accused these authorities of seeking the places of honor at banquets and devouring the houses of

---

[12] *Od.* 23.173–81; cf. 114: πειράζειν.

[13] *Od.* 23.202.

[14] *Od.* 23.205–6. See also 19.215–50.

[15] *Od.* 24.329.

[16] *Od.* 24.330–44.

[17] *Od.* 24.346.

[18] Mark 1:1 and 11. The discussion of secrecy in Mark presumes that Heikki Räisänen is correct in distinguishing between Mark's secretive parable theory and the role of secrecy in the narrative (Heikki Räisänen, *The 'Messianic Secret' in Mark* [C. M. Tuckett, trans.; Studies of the New Testament and Its World; Edinburgh: T. & T. Clark, 1990] 76–141 and 242–43).

[19] According to David Rhoads and Donald Michie, "The characters in the story are blind victims of the irony of the situation, while the reader sees the ironic contrast between what the speaker says and the way things really are. For example, when the opponents ridicule Jesus for claiming to be king of the Jews, the reader sees that the statements which they intend to be ironic sarcasm really are true: Jesus can prophesy; he really is king of the Jews; his death will secure the destruction of the temple; and he cannot save himself except by losing his life" (*Mark as Story: An Introduction to the Narrative of a Gospel* [Philadelphia: Fortress, 1982] 60).

widows,[20] criticisms altogether apt for Penelope's suitors. They had made Jesus' "house" a "den of robbers,"[21] and when he confirmed to the Sanhedrin that he was indeed "the Messiah, the Son of the Blessed One," they condemned him to death. Throughout the gospel, then, Jesus maintained secrecy concerning his identity as Messiah/Son of God by necessity. His ability to perform miracles, especially his exorcisms and raising the dead, were signs of his true identity and therefore had to be hidden from his rivals.

This understanding of secrecy deviates from most other interpretations, including Wrede's, by proposing that the disclosure of the secret takes place not at the empty tomb but at the Sanhedrin trial. In support of this hypothesis, I will argue the following four theses. First, when Jesus is among friends, he is least prone to require secrecy. Second, when he is in public among Gentiles, he shows somewhat more caution, but even here he seldom insists on silence. Third, Jesus is most cautious about publicity in Jewish environments when the authorities themselves are not present. Fourth, in passages where Jesus and the Jewish leaders appear together, he never insists on secrecy. His opponents themselves had witnessed everything. Instead, he cleverly clouds his identity in ambiguous titles, metaphors, allegories, and counter-questions and thus provides his opponents insufficient grounds for killing him. Only at his trial does he reveal himself as the Messiah/Son of God.

Thesis One. When Jesus was among his most reliable associates, he seldom insisted on secrecy. One finds no such commands after Jesus healed Peter's mother-in-law,[22] after he stilled the storm,[23] after he walked on water,[24] or after he withered a fig tree with a curse.[25] The only ones who witnessed these miracles were the disciples. Commands to secrecy also do not appear in the two stories of the feeding of multitudes, probably because only the disciples themselves actually witnessed the multiplication. The only two instances of Jesus' silencing his disciples follow unambiguous identifications of Jesus as the Messiah or Son of God, which greatly heighten the risk of disclosure.

---

[20] Mark 12:39–40.

[21] Mark 11:17.

[22] Mark 1:29–31.

[23] Mark 4:35–40.

[24] Mark 6:47–52.

[25] Mark 11:12–14 and 20–24.

Midway in the narrative, Jesus asked his disciples who people thought he was.[26] Their answers show that his attempts at remaining incognito successfully kept the masses baffled about his identity, for they suspected he might be John the Baptist, or. Elijah, or another of the prophets.[27] Jesus then asked the disciples directly, "But who do you say that I am?" and Peter answered, "'You are the Messiah.' And he sternly ordered them not to tell anyone about him."[28] Jesus silenced Peter not because he answered wrongly, but precisely because he answered correctly. If broadcast, this identification might come to the attention of the authorities.

Peter's so-called confession might better be called his recognition. In fact, the scene resembles Eurycleia's recognition of Odysseus from the scar on his leg. "Surely, you are Odysseus, dear child, and I did not know you, until I had handled all the body of my master."[29] Odysseus then grabbed Eurycleia by the throat and said, "[W]hy will you destroy me? . . . [B]ut now since you have found me out and a god has put this in your heart, be silent for fear some one else in the house may learn about it."[30] Peter and Eurycleia both recognized the identities of their masters, articulated their recognitions in the second person singular, and were told in no uncertain terms to keep silent about it.

The other silencing of Jesus' intimates occurs after his Transfiguration, where three of the disciples heard a voice from heaven declaring Jesus to be God's Son. "[H]e ordered them to tell no one about what they had seen, until after the Son of Man had risen from the dead."[31] This statement need not mean that the empty tomb was the revelation of

---

[26] Mark's selection of Caesarea Philippi for this scene and the scenes that follow until 9:29 probably is due to its proximity to Mount Hermon, a favorite location for epiphanies, of which the transfiguration on "a high mountain" would be an example. I am grateful to George Nicklesberg for this observation.

[27] Cf. Mark 6:14–15.

[28] Mark 8:29b–30.

[29] *Od.* 19.474–75. Odysseus's scar figures prominently later in the epic: "I will show you a manifest sign (σῆμα ἀριφραδές)" (21.217 [spoken by Odysseus] and 23.73 [spoken by Eurycleia, referring to her recognition of the scar in 19.386–475]).

[30] *Od.* 19.482 and 485–86. Later Eurycleia summarized this incident to Penelope in order to explain why she had not informed her mistress earlier that Odysseus had returned: "This [scar] I noticed while I washed his feet, and was eager to tell it to you as well, but he laid his hand upon my mouth, and in the great wisdom of his heart would not allow me to speak" (23.75–77). See the discussion of Eurycleia and Homeric recognition scenes generally in N. J. Richardson, "Recognition Scenes in the *Odyssey* and Ancient Literary Criticism," *Papers of the Liverpool Latin Seminar* 4 (1983) 219–35.

[31] Mark 9:9.

Jesus' secret. It could also mean that only after the resurrection would the disciples have understood Jesus' Transfiguration; only then would they comprehend "what this rising of the dead could mean."[32]

Thesis Two. When in a public Gentile setting, Jesus shows only mild anxiety about rumors of his miracle working. In fact, after exorcising the Gerasene, he said, "Go home to your friends, and tell them how much the Lord has done for you, and what mercy he has shown you."[33] In "the region of Tyre" he did not want people to know he was there, but when he exorcised the daughter of the Syrophoenecian woman, he did not insist she keep silent.[34] Only once in a Gentile environment did he command by-standers "to tell no one":[35] the healing of a deaf man.

Thesis Three. In Jewish contexts where their leaders are absent, Jesus is most likely to insist on silence. While he was teaching at a synagogue at Capernaum, a demoniac identified him as "'The Holy One of God.' But Jesus rebuked him, saying, 'Be silent, and come out of him!'"[36] The placement of this exorcism in a synagogue increases the danger; the authorities might learn from the participants that demons proclaimed Jesus as the Son of God.

Again in Jewish Capernaum, Jesus healed many, "and cast out many demons; and he would not permit the demons to speak, because they knew him."[37] Later, large numbers of people thronged to him, both Jews and Gentiles, and again he healed and exorcised. "Whenever the unclean spirits saw him, they fell down before him and shouted, 'You are the Son of God!' But he sternly ordered them not to make him known."[38]

Jesus cured a blind man and ordered him to go home; "Do not even go into the village,"[39] viz. Jewish Bethsaida. Jairus, "one of the leaders of the synagogue," asked Jesus to heal his daughter. When Jesus learned that the girl had died, he took with him only his three closest companions, Peter, James, and John; on arriving at the girl's home, he commanded everyone to leave except for her parents; after he revived her, "He strictly

---

[32] Mark 9:10.

[33] Mark 5:19.

[34] Mark 7:24–30.

[35] Mark 7:36.

[36] Mark 1:24–25.

[37] Mark 1:34.

[38] Mark 3:11–12. In Mark 6:53–56 gives a summary of miracles performed in a Jewish environment without requiring silence, but even here it might be assumed, especially in light of its parallel summary in 3:7–12.

[39] Mark 8:26.

ordered them that no one should know this."[40] Jesus must use these extreme precautions here because of the girl's grave condition, death, and the consequent magnificence of Jesus' action. If Jairus were to broadcast the girl's revival, word might get to the authorities. Even though Jesus does not insist on secrecy after every miracle in a Jewish environment,[41] he does so far more consistently than when among Gentiles.

This interpretation of Jesus' secrecy might explain the curious exchange between Jesus and a leper: "A leper came to him begging him, and said to him, 'If you choose, you can make me clean.' Infuriated, he stretched out his hand and touched him, and said to him, 'I do choose. Be made clean!' Immediately the leprosy left him." Readers ancient and modern have puzzled over why Jesus would have been angry at the leper. I suggest the answer pertains to his desire for anonymity, for if he were to heal the leper, he would necessarily expose his powers to the authorities. According to Torah, this was the only cure that required a demonstration of purity before a priest and the observance of a public ritual.[42] By healing a leper, then, Jesus risked exposing his powers to the very authorities he wanted to keep in the dark.[43] Despite the risk and still infuriated, Jesus healed him.[44] "After growling at him, he thrust him out at once, saying to him, 'See that you say nothing to anyone; but go, show yourself to the priest, and offer for your cleansing what Moses commanded, as a testimony to them.'"[45] Apparently the leper was not even to tell the priest who it was who had healed him but merely to demonstrate that he had indeed been healed. "But he went out and

---

[40] Mark 5:43a.

[41] There are no such commands after the healings at Gennesaret or the healing of Bartimaeus.

[42] Lev. 14:2–32.

[43] Leprosy often was seen as a living death and its cleansing as a revivification (Num. [LXX] 12:10–15, 2 Kings 5:7, 4 Kgdms [LXX] 5:14, Josephus, *Ant.* 3.11.3, and *b. Sanh.* 47a). See also Robert H. Gundry, *Mark: A Commentary on His Apology for the Cross* (Grand Rapids: William B. Eerdmans, 1993) 95. In the light of this identification leprosy/death, Jesus' cleansing of the leper might point to him as a supreme divine agent, further endangering him. Q lists the cleansing of lepers among the miracles that would demonstrate the identity of "the coming one" (Q 7:22).

[44] The healing itself may have been informed by 2 Kings 5:1–14.

[45] Mark 1:43–44.

began to proclaim it freely, and to spread the word, so that Jesus could no longer go into a town openly, but stayed out in the country."[46]

Thesis Four. When Jesus and the authorities do come into direct confrontation, he keeps them flummoxed concerning his identity by means of evasion, metaphors, and sheer wit, much like Odysseus among the suitors. Even though he seems to have understood that his miracle working might blow his cover, he healed a paralytic in the presence of "some of the scribes,"[47] healed a man with a withered hand on the Sabbath while "the Pharisees" were in the synagogue,[48] and cast out a demon in the vicinity of "some scribes."[49] These are the only miracles Jesus performs in the presence of the authorities, and quite appropriately none of them ends with a command to silence. Those from whom Jesus wanted most to keep his identity a secret had themselves observed his powers.

He also refused to produce miracles as signs of his identity before his opponents. "The Pharisees came and began to argue with him, asking him for a sign (σημεῖον) from heaven, to test him (πειράζοντες αὐτόν). And he sighed deeply in his spirit and said, 'Why does this generation ask for a sign (σημεῖον)? Truly I tell you, no sign (σημεῖον) will be given to this generation.'" Mark's σημεῖον is the Koine equivalent of Homer's σῆμα. In the *Odyssey*, characters test the hero by asking for signs that he was who he said he was, and he complied, but only for those who had proven to be faithful. In the presence of his enemies, however, he avoided all revealing utterances and acts. Similarly, Jesus knows that the Pharisees who ask for a sign are unreliable, and for this reason he refuses to produce a sign.[50]

---

[46] Mark 1:45. In Greek the subject of the first phrase probably is the leper, but could also be Jesus himself. See the arguments of James K. Elliott ("The Conclusion of the Pericope of the Healing of the Leper and Mark 1:45," *JTS* ns 22 [1971] 153–57, and "The Healing of the Leper in the Synoptic Parallels," *TZ* 34 [1978] 175–76).

[47] Mark 2:1–12.

[48] Mark 3:1–6.

[49] Mark 9:14–29. It is not certain that the scribes themselves witnessed the exorcism; see vs. 25, where Jesus seems to speed up the exorcism to avoid detection.

[50] Mark uses the verb πειράζειν again twice; in both cases in controversies with Jewish authorities who test him on matters of torah-observance (10:2 and 12:15; Matthew and Luke both take Mark 12:28–34 as a testing concerning the law [Matt. 22:35: πειράζων; and Luke 10:25: ἐκπειράζων]). Mark 13, the so-called Synoptic Apocalypse, is a testing of sorts, apparently modeled after Penelope's testing of Odysseus in *Odyssey* Book 19. The disciples come to Jesus asking him for a sign

Early in Mark, the Jewish authorities decided to rid themselves of Jesus, knew he threatened their authority, and witnessed his powers of exorcism and healing, but prior to the trial they had never heard from him an unambiguous declaration of his identity.[51] They heard it for the

(σημεῖον) when the temple will be destroyed, and he obliges them with a speech similar to Odysseus's to Penelope.

This interpretation of Mark 8:11–12 may explain Mark's omission of the reference to Jonah in the version of the saying about signs known to Q. Compare the following:

Q/Luke 11:29–30	Mark 8:11–12
When the crowds were increasing,	The Pharisees came and began to argue with him,
he began to say,	asking for a sign from heaven, to test him.
"This generation is an evil generation;	And he sighed deeply in his spirit and said, "Why does this generation
it asks for a sign,	ask for a sign? Truly I tell you,
but no sign will be given to it	no sign will be given to this generation."
except the sign of Jonah.	
For just as Jonah became a sign to the people of Nineveh, so the Son of Man will be to this generation."	

In Q, Jesus speaks to the crowds, not to his opponents as in Mark. More important, in Q Jesus does indeed give them a sign, not a miracle but the example of Jonah who preached repentance to non-Jews. In Mark's version, Jesus gives his interlocutors no sign whatsoever. Any sign to his enemies would be dangerous.

Parallels with Q also illumine this hypothesis in connection with the Beelzebul controversy. In Q 11:20 Jesus claims, "if it is by the finger of God that I cast out demons, then the kingdom of God has come upon you." This statement is missing in Mark, presumably because had Jesus made it to the religious authorities, he would have raised further suspicions concerning his identity: in him God's rule has arrived. Notice also that the Son of Man appears in the Q version of the saying about blasphemy. Q 12:10: "And everyone who speaks a word against the Son of Man (τοῦ υἱοῦ τοῦ ἀνθρώπου) will be forgiven"; Mark , however, seems to alter the tradition in order to deflect attention on Jesus as the Son of Man: "The sons of men (τοῖς υἱοῖς τῶν ἀνθρώπων) will be forgiven all the sins and blasphemies they utter" (3:28).

[51] Scholars who oppose this interpretation of secrecy in Mark often cite as counter evidence the healing of the paralytic in 2:1–12, in which Jesus seems carelessly to risk detection by openly defending his authority to act as an agent of God. Here Jesus secretly entered Capernaum, but the crowds somehow discovered that he was staying in a particular home and there they thronged, including "some of the scribes." Unable to enter for the crowd, four men dug through a roof and lowered a paralytic to Jesus, who then pronounced his sins forgiven and healed him.

When Jesus told the paralytic "your sins are forgiven," he nearly exposed his identity to his enemies, who rightly asked, "Who can forgive sins but God alone?" Mark expects the reader to answer, "God's Son can, too." But this is precisely what Jesus cannot say, for then his secret would be revealed at the beginning of his career and the authorities would almost certainly shorten it.

In order to get Jesus out of this perilous situation, Mark supplies him with cleverness that might have impressed a trickster like Odysseus. Jesus asked the scribes, first and only time at his trial, a scene that resembles Odysseus's revelation to the suitors.

All "the chief priests, the elders, and the scribes were assembled" and "were looking for testimony against Jesus to put him to death; but they found none."[52] Their inability to secure witnesses suggests that Jesus' identity remained a secret. "[T]he high priest asked him, 'Are you the

---

and take your mat and walk?'" (2:9). Telling the paralytic to stand obviously is the more difficult of the two statements insofar as it is verifiable in a manner impossible for a mere declaration of forgiveness. By healing the paralytic, then, Jesus demonstrated that he had the "authority" to forgive sins. Jesus did not say that he had authority to forgive sins as the Son of God, but as the Son of Man, employing a notoriously ambiguous title that applies even to Jewish prophets in the Bible. To be sure, Jesus came dangerously close to revealing his identity to his opponents, but at least for the moment he cleverly avoided the charge of blasphemy, a capital offense, and demonstrated healing powers and compassion that shamed his quibbling detractors and kept them baffled about his identity.

This orientation toward secrecy also may help settle a long-standing problem in translating v. 10, which the NRSV renders as though Jesus continued to address the scribes as follows: "'But so that you may know that the Son of Man has authority on earth to forgive sins'—he said to the paralytic—'. . .'" The dashes placed around the phrase "he said to the paralytic" attempt to rescue the awkwardness of the Greek. Mark frequently employed substandard syntax (e.g., the anacoluthon in v. 1: εἰσελθὼν . . . ἠκούσθη), but the sentence as it stands makes perfectly good sense if one sees it as an address not to the scribes but to readers: "But so that you [readers] may know that the Son of Man has authority on earth to forgive sins, he said to the paralytic . . ." (For a defense of this interpretation, see George H. Boobyer, "Mark 2:10a and the Interpretation of the Healing of the Paralytic," *HTR* 47 [1954] 115–20, and Robert M. Fowler, *Let the Reader Understand: Reader-Response Criticism and the Gospel of Mark* [Minneapolis: Fortress, 1991] 102–3.) This reading not only rescues Mark's Greek but further advances the interpretation of secrecy advocated here. If v. 10a addresses the scribes, one could argue that Jesus wanted to demonstrate his unique authority to them, but if the verse addresses the reader, the demonstration of authority to forgive sins was for the sake of those who would read the Gospel, not for the scribes, who could have used this information against him. By ending the address to the scribes at v. 9, Jesus silences them with a clever counter question, which leaves them speechless and in the dark about his identity. All they know is that Jesus pronounced the paralytic's sins forgiven and healed him, which surely would have aroused further suspicions about him, but did not unambiguously disclose his identity as God's son.

Scholars note, however, that if 10a addresses the readers instead of the scribes, it would be the only place where Mark's narrator and not Jesus himself uses the title Son of Man. Indeed, it would be unique among all the Gospels. Furthermore, Matthew and Luke seem not to have been offended by Mark's Greek for they retained the construction, and it is unlikely that they, too, intended to address their readers (Matt. 9:6 and Luke 5:24). Mark's construction certainly is awkward when taken as a continuation of Jesus' speech, the argument goes, but he somehow had to indicate that Jesus turned his comments from the scribes to the paralytic.

52 Mark 14:56.

Messiah, the Son of the Blessed One?' Jesus said, 'I am; and "you will see the son of Man seated at the right hand of the Power," and "coming with the clouds of heaven."'"[53] Mark's Jesus obviously alludes to Dan 7:13 (LXX): "and behold, he was coming with the clouds of heaven like a Son of Man." In the Gospel, however, this scriptural allusion functions as a revelation and in that respect it resembles the self-disclosure scenes in the *Odyssey*, where the hero identifies himself in the first person singular as the one who at last has come home.

> To Telemachus: "I here, I (ἐγώ), . . . after sufferings and many wanderings, have come (ἤλυθον) in the twentieth year to my native land."[54]

> To Eurycleia: "[A]nd now after many grievous toils I am come (ἤλυθον) in the twentieth year to my native land."[55]

> To his faithful servants: "At home now in truth am I here before you, my very self (αὐτὸς ἐγώ). After many grievous toils I am come (ἤλυθον) in the twentieth year to my native land."[56]

> To the suitors: "[Y]ou thought that I should never more come home (οὔ μ' . . . οἴκαδ' ἱκέσθαι) from the land of the Trojans, seeing that you wasted my house."[57]

> To Laertes: "That man am I (αὐτὸς ἐγώ), father, myself, standing here, of whom you ask, come back (ἤλυθον) in the twentieth year to the land of my fathers."[58]

Jesus' self-disclosure to the Sanhedrin and Odysseus's to these characters share some expression of self-identification (εἰμί, ἐγώ, or με + infinitive), an expressed or implied predicate ("the Messiah, the Son of the Blessed One," "myself," or "that man . . . of whom you ask"), and a statement concerning the hero's return: Odysseus at last had returned; Jesus would return in the future. When speaking of Odysseus's return, Homer once used a form of ἱκνέομαι; otherwise he used a poetic form of ἔρχομαι (ἤλυθον). Mark's word for Jesus' return is ἐρχόμενον. The Jewish authorities would "see the son of Man seated at the right hand of power, . . . coming with the clouds of heaven"; that is, he would return in judgment, as Odysseus did against the suitors.

---

53 Mark 14:60–62.
54 *Od.* 16.205–6.
55 *Od.* 19.483–84.
56 *Od.* 21.207–8.
57 *Od.* 22.35–36.
58 *Od.* 24.321–22. See also 9:19 and 16.187–88.

These examples do not require one to think that Mark had particular passages of the *Odyssey* in mind. Perhaps one should say no more than that Mark borrowed the motif from the epic as he was able to recall it from memory. If one were to make the dependence more directly literary, one would have to advance a parallel sufficiently distinctive in vocabulary, or order of presentation, or function. Mark's account of the Transfiguration satisfies these criteria when compared with Odysseus's revelation to Telemachus.

Odysseus the beggar had taken refuge in the miserable hut of Eumaeus the swineherd when Telemachus returned from the Peloponnese. By treating the stranger graciously, Telemachus proved his fidelity.[59] Athena came to Odysseus and said, "now tell your son your secret and do not hide it."[60] She touched him with her wand and transformed his appearance into "his youthful bloom." When Telemachus saw him in this form, he

> marveled, and, shaken, turned his eyes aside for fear it was a god. And he spoke, and addressed him with winged words:

> "Of different sort you seem to me now, stranger, than a while ago, and the clothes you wear are different, and your color is no longer the same. Truly you are a god, one of those who hold broad heaven. Be gracious, then, that we may offer to you acceptable sacrifices and golden gifts, finely wrought; and spare us."[61]

Odysseus's transformation functions as a sign that he was not a beggar, but Telemachus understandably misinterpreted the sign as an epiphany. He asked for mercy for fear the stranger may have disguised himself in order to test his hospitality of strangers.[62] He had reason to worry: he had not invited the stranger to his magnificent home. There he was with a god on his hands in the hut of swineherd!

In Mark's account of the Transfiguration, Jesus took his three most intimate associates up to a mountain, where he was transformed. Like Odysseus, Jesus had a divine launderer.

---

[59] *Od.* 16.40–45 and 68–89.

[60] *Od.* 16.168.

[61] *Od.* 16.178–85.

[62] Kearns, "The Return of Odysseus," 5.

Odyssey 16.172–74	Mark 9:3
Athene touched him with her golden wand. **A well-washed cloak and tunic** she first of all put about his breast, and she increased his stature and his youthful bloom.	And he was transformed before them, and **his clothes became dazzling white,**[63] **such as no fuller on earth could bleach them.**

Like Telemachus, Peter was terrified, overinterpreted what he saw, and offered exceptional hospitality.

Odyssey 16.178–80 and 181–85	Mark 9:5–7
And his staunch son marveled, and, **shaken,** turned his eyes aside, for fear it was a god. **And he spoke. . . :** "Of different sort you seem to me now, **stranger,** than a while ago, and the clothes you wear are different, and your color is no longer the same. Truly you are a god, one of those who hold broad heaven. Be gracious, then, **that we may offer**	**And Peter said** to Jesus, **"Rabbi,** it is good for us to be here;

---

[63] The phrase translated here "his clothes became dazzling white" represents τὰ ἱμάτια αὐτοῦ ἐγένετο στίλβοντα λευκὰ λίαν. The participle στίλβοντα, 'dazzling,' 'glistening,' is a *hapax* in the New Testament; Matthew and Luke each deleted it. Within Greek literature at large, στίλβω is not particularly rare (it occurs several times in the LXX), but Homer uses it once in the *Odyssey* in a context similar to the passages here discussed.

At the beginning of Book 6, Odysseus, having suffered shipwreck, washed up on the shore of the Phaeacian island, Scheria, entirely nude, and in this compromised condition asked for hospitality from maidens washing clothes at the shore. "[T]errible he seemed to them, all befouled with brine, and they fled in fear" (6.137–38). All fled but princess Nausicaa, who offered hospitality and some newly washed clothing. After he washed himself and put on the clothing (εἵματα = ἱμάτια, Mark 9:3), Athena transformed him into a marvelous sight—taller than before and festooned with cascading curls. Here and in the lines that follow, Athena's transfiguration of Odysseus strongly resembles his transfiguration before Telemachus in 16.172–74, cited as a parallel to the transfiguration of Jesus.

[T]he goddess shed grace upon his head and shoulders. Then he went apart and sat down on the shore of the sea, gleaming (στίλβων) with beauty and grace; and the maiden marveled at him, and spoke to her fair-tressed handmaids, saying:

"Listen, white-armed maidens, to what I am about to say. Not without the will of all the gods who hold Olympus does this man come among the godlike Phaeacians. Before, he seemed to me uncouth, but now he is like the gods, who hold broad heaven." (6.235–43)

Like Jesus in Mark's transfiguration, Odysseus is transfigured to glisten with glory such that those who saw him took him for a god. In light of the rarity of στίλβω in early Christian literature, the similar usages of this verb as a participle to describe characters transformed into divine glory, one might suspect some literary connection between them.

| to you acceptable sacrifices and golden gifts, finely wrought;

and **spare us**." | **let us make three tents**, one for you, one for Moses, and one for Elijah."
He did not know what to say,
for **they were afraid**. |

In both columns, the motivation for the gift was fear, and the solitary speaker, Telemachus or Peter, uses a verb in the first person plural aorist subjunctive when offering the gift.[64]

Odysseus would not let Telemachus give him anything: "I am no god; why do you liken me to the immortals? No, I am your father."[65] In Mark, on the other hand, the voice from the cloud revealed that Jesus was indeed divine, God's "beloved son." The disciples were to listen only to him and not liken him merely to Elijah and Moses. Both the *Odyssey* and Mark have their heroes decline the gifts and both rebuke someone for attributing divinity to a mortal. Telemachus must be certain to tell no one that his father had returned, not even family members. Similarly, Jesus told Peter, James, and John to tell no one, not even the other disciples.

Odyssey 16.301–3	Mark 9: 9–10a
[L]et no one hear (μή τις) that **Odysseus is at home**; neither let Laertes know it, nor the swineherd, nor any of the household, nor Penelope. [Telemachus kept the secret as instructed.]	As they were coming down the mountain he **ordered them to tell no one** (μηδενί) **about what they had seen**, until after the Son of Man had risen from the dead. So they kept the matter to themselves.

The combination of motifs in *Odyssey* 16.172–303 and Mark 9:2–10 are too close to be accidental. In both a god transforms the hero into glory befitting a deity, including the transformation of clothing: a "well-washed cloak" and "clothes . . . dazzling white, such as no fuller on earth could bleach them." The transformation produces terror and the offering of gifts in order to appease the one who was transformed. The gifts offered in both accounts were refused, the recipients of both transfigurations were scolded for making mortals divine, and the heroes in both accounts insist on total secrecy.

In conclusion, the disclosure of Jesus' secret takes place on Maundy Thursday, not Easter Sunday, as Wrede thought. Mark's model for his use of secrecy and recognition was the *Odyssey*, where the hero, disguised as

---

64 *Od.* 16.184: δώομεν; Mark 9:5: ποιήσωμεν.

65 *Od.* 16.187–88. Cf. 16.205–6: "I here, I (ἐγώ), . . . after sufferings and many wanderings, have come (ἤλυθον) in the twentieth year to my native land."

beggar, planned the destruction of his enemies. When others did learn his identity, he strictly charged them to maintain silence. Homer's recognition scenes also involve testings, the use of signs to prove the beggar was the master, and the suppression of feats of strength that would alert his foes of his identity.

Similarly, Jesus avoided publicity because the authorities would have dispatched him out of jealousy as soon as they suspected that he claimed to be the Messiah or Son of God. They sought to test him by asking for a sign of his identity, but he refused to perform one and sought to suppress the publicity of his miracle working. He did not require silence equally of everyone. Instead, he most consistently insisted on silence when in a public, Jewish environment, where the authorities were absent. He never insisted on silence when the authorities were present, because they had seen everything for themselves. Once they cornered him into claiming to be the Messiah/Son of God, they wasted no time in seeing to his destruction on the charge of blasphemy.[66] Mark seems to have borrowed from Homer the motifs of disguise, testing, signs, recognitions, disclosure, and silence, and, as in the *Odyssey,* the use of these motifs permits situational irony in which the reader, knowing the identity of the stranger, enjoys the narrative at a level inaccessible to the characters themselves. The so-called Confession at Caesarea Philippi may well call to mind the recognition of Eurycleia while washing and anointing Odysseus's feet. The Transfiguration seems to echo the transfiguration of Odysseus to Telemachus. The parallels between the two works suggest Mark's deliberate imitation.

---

[66] David Rhoads, a New Testament scholar, and Donald Michie, a literary critic, interpret secrecy in Mark in much the same way, though without citing analogies in Homer or other ancient literature.

> Jesus must deal with the authorities, once they have turned against him . . . . Jesus does not explicitly make public claims that he is the anointed one or the son of God; he commands the demons (who call him the son of God) to shut up; and when the disciples identify him as the anointed one, he tells them to keep quiet. At his trial we discover why Jesus hides his identity. Upon openly declaring who he is, the authorities condemn him to death for blasphemy. The dilemma for Jesus is this: how can he inaugurate God's rule, yet evade the effort of the authorities to trap him? (*Mark as Story,* 84)

Mark 14:61–62 has been considered the disclosure of the messianic secret also by John R. Donahue (*Are You the Christ? The Trial Narrative in the Gospel of Mark* [SBLDS 10; Missoula, MT: Scholars Press, 1973]), Norman Perrin ("The High Priest's Question and Jesus' Answer [Mark 14:61–62]," in *The Passion in Mark: Studies in Mark 14–16* [W. H. Kelber, ed.; Philadelphia: Fortress, 1976] 81–82), and B. L. Mack (*A Myth of Innocence: Mark and Christian Origins* [Philadelphia: Fortress, 1988] 263 and 281).

Creating Plot in Episodic Narratives:
The Life of Aesop and the Gospel of Mark

Whitney Shiner
George Mason University

The Gospels can be read in at least two distinct ways. They can be read as a series of self-contained episodes, and they can be read as a continuous narrative. The former approach is taken by ecclesiastical readings from the lectionary and was emphasized by the approach of the form critics. In reaction to the form critical emphasis on the independence of the short forms, literary critics have emphasized the latter approach, analyzing the Gospels as narrative wholes. To the extent, however, that this narrative criticism has taken its models from twentieth century literary criticism, a criticism that has been primarily concerned with the analysis of modern novels, it has de-emphasized, at least in theory, the episodic nature of the Gospels in order to delineate the plot development and the characterization of various figures. A unity or linearity of development is often a presupposition of modern critical theory.

The analysis of ancient narratives and ancient literary theory has shown a number of ways in which ancient narrative differs from modern novels and short stories. One distinction that may be made is a greater tolerance for and appreciation of an episodic narrative style.[1] Episodic narrative has two primary characteristics. First, the narrative is developed to a considerable extent by the use of more or less self-contained episodes. Second, the reader's or listener's interest is concentrated on each episode as it occurs, and pleasure is derived to a substantial degree from the effect of the individual episodes. In reading the Gospels as episodic narrative, one must see the narrative as simultaneously episodes and as extended narrative. The extended narrative is built from more or

---

[1] This has been noted by Mary Ann Tolbert in her discussion of Mark as popular literature (*Sowing the Gospel: Mark's World in Literary-Historical Perspective* [Minneapolis: Fortress, 1989] 70–78)

less self-contained blocks. Continuity in the extended narrative is found not so much in the continuity of detail in action and characterization between episodes as in continuity in the overall impact of the episodes. To take an analogy from art, extended episodic narrative is like a mosaic. The effect is derived from the pattern of episodes or stones, and one does not necessarily expect the details of the stones to align.

Like the Gospels large portions of *The Life of Aesop* are built from narrative episodes that are largely independent.[2] Although there are, as in the Gospels, notable exceptions, for the most part the individual episodes retain their interest even in isolation from the plot of the narrative as a whole. This is especially true of the most extensive section of the *Life*, in which Aesop repeatedly outwits his master, the philosopher Xanthus. Much of the macronarrative structure of *Aesop*, such as Aesop's sale to the philosopher, his manumission, and his entering into service to Lycurgus, serve largely to move the narrative from one type of episode, appropriate to Aesop's earlier situation, to a different type of episode, appropriate to the new plot situation. A comparison of a Gospel narrative with the narrative of Aesop will help to delineate the common features of episodic narrative as well as to throw into relief the unique features of each narrative as the authors adapt the episodic style to their own purposes. The Gospel of Mark is a work that is extremely interesting in the effects it creates from episodic patterning and will serve as our Gospel example.

K. L. Schmidt's famous comparison of the Markan narrative to pearls loosely strung together was a recognition of the episodic narrative style of the Gospel.[3] Schmidt concluded from the episodic style of Mark the existence of independent units of oral tradition, and this conclusion formed the basis for the form-critical investigation of the history of the pre-existing units. More recent studies have suggested a great deal more

---

[2] For the Greek text of *The Life of Aesop*, see Ben Edwin Perry, *Aesopica: A Series of Texts Relating to Aesop or Ascribed to Him or Closely Connected with the Literary Tradition That Bears His Name, Vol I: Greek and Latin Texts* (Urbana: University of Illinois Press, 1952). Unless noted, all English translations from *The Life of Aesop* are taken from the translation of Lloyd W. Daly (*Aesop Without Morals: The Famous Fables, and a Life of Aesop* [New York and London: Thomas Yoseloff, 1961] 29–90).

[3] Karl Ludwig Schmidt, "Die Stellung der Evangelien in der allgemeinen Literaturgeschichte," in *EUCHARISTERION: Hermann Gunkel zum 60. Geburtstag* (H. Schmidt, ed.; 2 vols.; FRLANT 19; Göttingen: Vandenhoeck & Ruprecht, 1923) 2.50–134, esp. 127.

authorial freedom in the production of episodic units.[4] It is now generally acknowledged that Schmidt and the form critics who built on his observations underestimated the narrative and rhetorical sophistication of the Synoptic writers. Joanna Dewey, for example, has likened Mark to an interwoven tapestry rather than a string of pearls.[5] Nevertheless, the episodic style is undeniable. To understand the narrative effect of Mark careful consideration must be given to the episodic style, how it is constructed, what constraints it places on an author, and what its appeal and purpose might be.[6]

Episodic Style in Ancient Narrative

The *Life of Aesop* is not a particularly sophisticated piece of writing, but it should be emphasized that in antiquity the episodic writing style was not necessarily a sign of lack of sophistication. Many biographies contain episodic material loosely connected into an overall narrative. The *Progymnasmata* of Hermogenes of Tarsus distinguishes two types of independent episodes that might be told to characterize a person, the *chreia* and the *apomnēmoneuma* or reminiscence. The *chreia* is a short, self-contained saying or anecdote. The *apomnēmoneuma*, on the other hand, might be of any length (*Progymn.* 3 [p. 6, 15–17 Rabe]).[7] Either one could appear as an independent unit, or they could serve various functions within larger works. The art of manipulating *chreiai* was taught to students in the early stages of rhetorical study.[8]

---

[4] While I assume that both Mark and the author of the *Life of Aesop* made use of significant amounts of pre-existing material, I have for the most part left aside the question of the source of the episodic units. Certainly narrative can generate episode just as episode can generate narrative, and one cannot simply assume from the episodic style that the units circulated independently.

[5] Joanna Dewey, "Mark as Interwoven Tapestry: Forecasts and Echoes for a Listening Audience," *CBQ* 53 (1991) 221–36.

[6] For a discussion of the episodic style of Mark in relation to the repetition of feeding stories in 6:34–43 and 8:1–9, see Whitney Taylor Shiner, *Follow Me! Disciples in Markan Rhetoric* (SBLDS 145; Atlanta: Scholars Press, 1995) 223–26.

[7] Found in Ronald F. Hock and Edward N. O'Neil, *The Chreia in Ancient Rhetoric, Vol. I. The Progymnasmata* (SBLTT 27; Atlanta: Scholars Press, 1986) 174–75. A collection of *chreiai* providing a clear indication of the scope of their use in written sources is found in Vernon K. Robbins, *Ancient Quotes & Anecdotes* (FFNT; Sonoma, CA: Polebridge, 1989).

[8] Ronald F. Hock, "General Introduction to Volume I," in Hock and O'Neil, *Chreia,* 9–22.

Clearly literary audiences in the ancient world were fond of both short forms and did not particularly expect them to be ordered into an extended narrative. Some of the *Lives of the Eminent Philosophers* by Diogenes Laertius consist of little more than haphazard collections of *chreiai*. In other cases, as in Iamblichus' *Pythagorean Life*, *chreiai* or *apomnēmoneumata* were grouped according to various virtues that they illustrate. Chapters twenty-eight through thirty-three of that work present in sequence illustrations of piety, wisdom, justice, temperance, courage, and friendship. The individual episodes and sayings are connected with varying amounts of discursive material.

Much of Philostratus' *Life of Apollonius of Tyana* is similarly written in an episodic style.[9] However one might judge Philostratus' ability as a writer, he certainly cannot be charged with lack of sophistication. He was thoroughly acquainted with the high literature of his time and the best of contemporary rhetoric. Yet portions of his work, especially those parts dependent on other sources, are largely collections of episodes collected according to geographical provenance. Even in the portions of the *Life*, such as the travel narratives to India, Egypt, and Ethiopia, where Philostratus seems to have little if any constraint on his writing from facts or sources, he often strings together pearls of sophistic declamation as the passing sights suggest to Apollonius various ways of displaying the author's erudition. Philostratus combines a complicated macronarrative of Apollonius' travels and confrontations with the good and evil emperors of his time with a great deal of episodic narrative and rhetoric.

Several scholars have noted the episodic nature of early Greek narrative. B. A. van Groningen labeled the style paratactic composition, emphasizing the loose connection between the episodes.[10] The episodic style of Homer was noted as early as Aristotle, who refers to the *Iliad* as πολύμυθον, containing many stories, in the *Poetics* (1456a.12). James A. Notopoulos cites as post-Homeric examples Hesiod, Alcman's *Partheneion*, Xenophanes, Semonides, Pindar, Empedocles, Parmenides, and Herodotus.[11] Notopoulos linked the paratactic style of early Greek literature to the effects of oral composition.[12] As oral composition gave

---

[9] Shiner, *Follow Me!* 137–38

[10] B A. van Groningen, "Eléments inorganiques dans la composition de l'*Iliade* et de l'*Odyssée*," *REH* 5 (1935) 3–24.

[11] James A. Notopoulos, "Parataxis in Homer: A New Approach to Homeric Literary Criticism" *TAPA* 80 (1949) 1–23, esp. 10–11.

[12] Notopoulos, "Parataxis," 14–23.

way to written composition, he argues, narrative based on loosely connected episodes gave way to a conception of a work of literature as a single organic whole. This conception is expressed as an ideal by both Plato (*Phaedrus* 264c, 270d) and Aristotle (*Poetics* 1459a).[13]

The examples from the philosophical biographies indicate that, at least in the biographical genre, episodic composition remained common, even when authors sought to meld the episodes into a general unity. The episodic style may have survived in biography and history even when supplanted by a more continuous, organic narrative in drama because it was felt to be more appropriate for showing the nature of a life. A drama may revolve around a single action, but lives consist of multiple actions, and a person's character is revealed in various incidents that may have no particular interconnection. The episodic style is arguably truer to life than the imposition of a continuous narrative on events as found in most modern biography.

In spite of the arguments of Plato and Aristotle, it appears that for ancient audiences the episodic style, far from showing the limitations of an author, was a source of considerable pleasure. The episodic style was a way of extending and complicating plot in the absence of the character development or psychological complication that drives many modern narratives. It provided the readers or listeners with material easily adapted for their own purposes, whether teaching their children, entertaining others with borrowed anecdotes, or displaying their own erudition. It is certainly well suited to group readings, where members of the audience might miss certain portions of the narrative.[14]

Composition of Episodes in the *Life of Aesop*

Many of the episodes in *Aesop* bear a striking resemblance, both in content and outline, to the self-contained *chreiai* told about philosophers and other famous persons. Since they are presented with fairly elaborate narrative detail, most of the episodes of the *Life of Aesop* are too long to qualify as *chreiai* by the classic definitions of the form. Stripped of their narrative detail, however, many of the episodes of the *Life of Aesop* might be stated in a sentence or two in a form having no connection with either the figure of Aesop or the narrative of the *Life*. Several *chreiai* concerning Aesop are found in Phaedrus' metrical versions of Aesop's fables (2.3; 3.3,

---

[13] Notopoulos, "Parataxis," 2–7.

[14] James A. Notopoulos, "Continuity and Interconnexion in Homeric Oral Composition," *TAPA* 82 (1951) 81–87.

5, 14, 19; 4.5) and in other sources,[15] although none of the known *chreiai* appears as episodes in the *Life*.

One incident in the *Life*, Aesop's report to his master that there was only one man at the crowded bath (65–66), is very similar to a *chreia* concerning the Cynic Diogenes reported by Diogenes Laertius (6.40).[16] Diogenes Laertius reports the *chreia* in two terse sentences:

> To one who asked as he was leaving the public baths if many men were bathing he said no. But to one who asked if there was a large crowd he said yes.

The expansion of this *chreia* in the *Life* gives a good indication of the narrative technique of the author. The incident is transferred into the narrative of Aesop by having Xanthus the philosopher send Aesop, who is the philosopher's slave at this point, to the bath to determine if it is crowded. The author provides a rationale for the determination that most of those in the crowd do not deserve the title of men, showing that they are too lazy to move a stone causing people to stumble at the entrance. Aesop's correct but misleading report to Xanthus that there is one man in the bath is used in the narrative as one of a series of disputes between Aesop and his master turning on the precise meaning of words. When Xanthus returns with Aesop he is put out by what he takes to be Aesop's false report, and Aesop explains why his report is correct. The *chreia* is transformed into one more instance of Xanthus' failure at philosophy. The incident is particularly effective in condemning Xanthus' philosophical skill since many in the audience would recognize the motif to be connected with Diogenes, and thus indirectly Xanthus is condemned by the founder of Cynicism as well as by his own slave.

Several other episodes from the *Life of Aesop* might similarly be compressed into a sentence or two in the typical style of a short *chreia*. For example, chapters 35–37: When asked why weeds spring up faster than cultivated crops, X replied, "Because the earth loves her own natural

---

[15] Perotti's Appendix to Phaedrus 9, 13, 17, 20; the Augustana recension of prose fables of Aesop 8; Aristophanes, *Wasps* 1401 ff; Themistius, *Orat.* 32. All these *chreiai* may be found in Ben Edwin Perry's edition of *Babrius and Phaedrus* (LCL; Cambridge: Harvard University Press, 1965), that of Aristophanes on p. 503; Themistius, p.505. In addition, a number of fables are given settings from the life of Aesop in various collections.

[16] A similar incident is reported concerning Diogenes' visit to Olympia (Diogenes Laertius 6.60). A connection between Aesop and Diogenes was made by other writers. Phaedrus includes a *chreia* about Aesop in which he carries a lamp through the forum during daylight hours and replies, when asked why, that he is looking for a man (3.19). This is apparently an adaptation of the well-known *chreia* concerning Diogenes (Diogenes Laertius 6.41).

children more than those she is forced to adopt." Other episodes elaborate material that might be, in its simplest form, an aphoristic saying or a riddle. "A wife will leave at the smallest slight, but a dog remains loyal even when beaten" (44–49). "What is the finest and most worthless thing in the world? The tongue" (51–55).

Since the author of *Aesop* presents such material as extended narratives, it appears that the expansion of detail was experienced by the audience as pleasurable ornamentation. The high estimation of an author's ability to complicate and expand is suggested by the Muses' gift to Aesop of the skill of πλοκή, or complication of plot (7). Aristotle's *Poetics* contrasts πλοκή with λύσις, loosing or plot resolution (1456a).[17] Πλοκή applies a metaphor of twisting or weaving to the construction of plot. It seems in Aristotle to be equivalent to δέσις, a metaphor of binding together, as with sticks in a bundle or stones in a wall.[18] In Aesop's fables, πλοκή would refer to Aesop's ability to set up unexpected reversals. In a short *chreia*, πλοκή would be restricted to the setting of a saying or action. Through more extensive πλοκή a short *chreia* may be converted into an expanded *chreia*, and with even greater complication, it may become an *apomnēmoneuma* and serve as a plot episode in an extended narrative. Students learned to expand *chreiai* in the early stages of their rhetorical training. Such an exercise is included in Theon's *Progymnasmata*.[19] Although Theon's example is much less extensive than the expansions in *The Life of Aesop*,[20] it seems likely that such school exercises would prepare an audience to appreciate the skill involved in the expansion and manipulation of *chreiai* into plot episodes such as those found in the *Life.*

The episodes in Mark's narrative tend to be shorter and less elaborately detailed. While the less extensive episodes would not produce the same sort of pleasure derived from the detailing of the episodes in *Aesop*, they allow Mark to create more forceful effects through the juxtaposition of episodes. The Markan world view is one of hidden

---

[17] The text appears to be out of place, and following the suggestion of Susemihl, is often transposed to 1455b, 18.3.

[18] LSJ, s.v.

[19] Hock and O'Neil, *Chreia* 100–103.

[20] To expand (ἐπεκτείνειν or ἐκτείνειν) a *chreia* means to fill out the *chreia* in a narrative mode and is distinguished from ἐργασία, elaboration according to a set sequence of argumentation, as described in Hermogenes' *Progymnasmata* 3 (pp. 7, 10–8, 14 Rabe). On the latter, see Burton L. Mack, "Elaboration of the Chreia in the Hellenistic School" in Burton L. Mack and Vernon K. Robbins, *Patterns of Persuasion in the Gospels* (Sonoma: Polebridge, 1989) 31–67.

meanings, in parables, in miracles, and in history. Mark has masterfully adapted the episodic style to the expression of this view of the world by allowing the audience to find implied meaning in the patterning of episodes and the interconnections between them. The terseness of the individual episodes facilitates the creation of implied meaning since the rapid pace of the narrative keeps the memory of previous episodes fresh in the reader's or listener's mind.

Purpose of Episodic Style in Aesop and Mark

The episodic style is particularly well suited to the apparent purpose of the writer of the *Life of Aesop*. While Aesop was known as one of the seven sages, he was famous primarily as the composer of fables. Yet fables occupy only a minor part of the *Life*. They are mentioned as one of the gifts of the Muses (7), it is stated that Aesop wrote a book of fables (100), and nine examples of the use of fables in disputes may be found in the latter part of the book (94, 97, 99, 129, 131, 133, 135–39, 140, 141). The central focus of the book, however, is Aesop's wit rather than his ability in composing fables. The pleasure found in reading the *Life* is largely that of seeing Aesop repeatedly outwit a number of antagonists. In many ways Aesop corresponds to the trickster figures familiar in many cultures. Tricksters are often populist figures in the sense that they unmask the foibles of the elite. Aesop, the embodiment of folk wisdom in the form of a misshapen slave, is certainly no exception. The writer of the *Life* has given a particular twist to the trickster motif by making the principal victim of Aesop's wit the philosopher Xanthus. The *Life* is primarily a satire on perceived pretensions of philosophy, as the street smart Aesop proves for all to see that the intellectual elite is, like the famous emperor, wearing no clothes. It is easy to imagine boys, sent by their fathers to learn philosophy, circulating *Aesop* among themselves, all the while getting a good laugh at their own teacher. Even Aesop's brief career as a philosophical lecturer (101) shows the superiority of native wit to the learnedness of the school philosophers. It is telling that no details are provided of Aesop's career as a lecturer, as detailed description might well make the folk-sage look too much like the school philosophers that the *Life* satirizes. Aesop's activity as a lecturer simply continues the satire, with Aesop presumably collecting large fees for his wit, now dignified with the title philosophy. Even in the latter part of the narrative there is little in Aesop's speech that reflects the philosophy of the philosophical schools. The closest is the collection of aphorisms that comprise Aesop's instruction to his son (109–110), but the aphorisms are more reminiscent of wisdom teaching than that of the philosophers.

That Xanthus, and thus philosophy, was seen to be the primary focus of the *Life* is reflected in one of the two titles given to the work, *The Book of Xanthus the Philosopher and Aesop His Slave*. The section in which Xanthus is Aesop's chief antagonist occupies the bulk of the work (20–90), while the beginning (1–19) establishes Aesop's wit and its divine source and the end (91–142) attaches Aesop to the existing story of his life as a teller of fables who met his end at Delphi. The section between Xanthus and Delphi, largely borrowed from the Ahiqar romance, continues the populist theme by showing Aesop besting the hired wise men of the greatest kings of his time.[21] Xanthus is from beginning to end a catalog of character defects. He is shown to be cheap, henpecked, and unable to control his slave. He is unable to learn from experience, repeating the same mistakes in his losing battle of wits with Aesop. He puts forward Aesop's ideas as his own and reneges on an agreement with Aesop. He allows himself to be cuckolded and blindly encourages Aesop to repeat his crime.

The ludicrous figure of the philosopher who does not live up to his teachings was a standard figure of satire in the ancient world. Lucian's *Philosophies for Sale* is a well-known example, but the figure can be found as well in works sympathetic to philosophy, where the false philosopher serves to set in high relief the integrity of those true to their calling. The *Life of Apollonius*, for example, shows Apollonius overcoming the disadvantage of having such a teacher, proving his natural aptitude for living the truth (1.7), while Euphrates, also portrayed as a false philosopher, becomes Apollonius' chief antagonist, denouncing him to the Emperor Domitian (5.31–39; 8.3).

The *Life*'s mocking of philosophy goes beyond Xanthus' defective character with several satirical jibes at the nature of philosophy itself. One line in particular illustrates the author's attitude toward philosophy. When a gardener seeks Xanthus' advice on a question, the philosopher incredulously demands to know, ". . . how anything I say can help you as a gardener. I'm no craftsman or smith to make you a hoe or a leek slicer; I'm a philosopher" (35). The philosopher, of course, is not even aware that he has condemned his vaunted knowledge as irrelevant. Proud of having studied in Athens under philosophers, rhetoricians, and

---

[21] The connection between the two was natural, since Ahiqar, like Aesop, composed fables.

philologists (36) and of having debated in many great halls (37), he is unable to teach anyone how to live or how to understand the nature of the world.

The philosophers' concern with careful definition comes in for extended satire in a series of episodes in which Aesop literally carries out imprecise orders given by Xanthus, taking an empty flask to the bath when Xanthus does not specify taking oil (38), cooking a single lentil for dinner when Xanthus uses the singular form (39–41), and bringing dainties from a banquet to the philosopher's dog when Xanthus sends them to "the one who loves me" (44–50). These obvious absurdities are specifically linked by Aesop to the concern of philosophers for precision of statement when he claims that it will help Xanthus to make better presentations in the classroom (43). Philosophy's concern with careful definition and apparent quibbling over words is made to look ridiculous through Aesop's responses to Xanthus.

Since the long central section of *Aesop* is concerned primarily with satirizing philosophy, the character of Aesop himself is a secondary concern. Aesop is no hero of the moral life as is Apollonius, and the failings of Xanthus do not, like the failings of Apollonius' teacher, serve to underline his own rectitude. Aesop's shameless affair with his master's wife (75–76), for example, hardly places Aesop in a good light, but it affords the audience pleasure to see the intellectual Xanthus once again play the fool. The author of the *Life* is content to let his hero unmask the failings of others without himself offering an alternative example. This portrayal of Aesop is not out of keeping with the fables attributed to him nor with the *chreiai* attached to his name, both of which satirize human failings without often offering an alternative model of life.

The satirical attack on philosophy is well suited to the episodic narrative style. The alleged foolishness of philosophy is best demonstrated through repetition, and the audience's pleasure is derived through repeatedly seeing the pretentious intellectual bested by his slave. As in a Roadrunner cartoon, the audience is conditioned to expect Aesop to outwit the philosopher. There is no sense of tension about who will triumph in the repeated conflicts. The audience's interest instead centers on how Aesop will prevail. Since the audience knows the outcome in advance, they are placed in a position superior to that of Xanthus from which he appears even more foolish. Like Wiley Coyote he is doomed to begin with and appears foolish even to enter the fray. There is very little that plot complication might do to further that primary pleasure.

In both Mark and *Aesop* the episodic style works well to accomplish the purposes of the narratives because in both repeated action is extremely important. In *Aesop* the essential point of the narrative is that the protagonist repeatedly and consistently outwits his antagonists. Mark's plot is more complex, but it can only show many essential points about Jesus through repeated action. Jesus' ability as a healer or miracle worker can be shown only through repeated healings and miracles. The futility of trying to understand Jesus on a human level can be shown only through the repeated failure of those closest to him to understand his words or identity. Jesus' superiority to his opponents can be shown only by his repeatedly outwitting them.

As Robert Tannehill has pointed out in a discussion of smaller units within the Synoptic tradition, a repetitive pattern of particulars suggests to the audience that the series is open ended.[22] Similarly, the repetition of similar episodes suggests that such episodes are typical of the activity of the hero, his antagonists, or the other characters concerned. Jesus becomes the one who can heal, who defeats his opponents in dispute, and so on. Aesop becomes the one who outwits the philosopher, who can solve all riddles, who excels in fables.

If, as I have argued, the primary pleasure in reading or hearing the *Life of Aesop* is that of seeing the pretentious look foolish, it is possible that the dispute material in the Gospels has a similar function. The disputes between Jesus and various religious authorities play a prominent role in the Synoptic Gospels and have often been analyzed for their ideological or doctrinal content as well as for their place in the narrative development of the Gospels. Their entertainment value has been less frequently commented upon. The use of dispute material in *Aesop* raises the possibility that the audience of the Gospels may have expected the dispute material to function as entertainment as well as a source of doctrine. The audience of Mark would thus experience the dispute material as examples of the stupidity of Jesus' antagonists, most often members of various Jewish political, religious, or intellectual elites, and the material would give Mark's audience a good laugh at the expense of the Pharisees. The repeated failure of Jesus' opponents in their disputes with Jesus, like the repeated failures of Xanthus in the *Life of Aesop*, has a certain slapstick quality akin to the trials of Wiley Coyote in Roadrunner cartoons. The fact that Jesus' opponents, like most of Aesop's, are from

---

[22] Robert C. Tannehill, *The Sword of His Mouth: Forceful and Imaginative Language in Synoptic Sayings* (SBLSS 1; Missoula, MT: Scholars Press, 1975) 42.

the elite adds a populist strain to the depiction. Since it is quite likely that Mark's audience did not have first hand experience of the Pharisees, the actual butt of the jokes may be all those who oppose Jesus and the church.

Importance of Macronarrative in Mark and *Aesop*

Although the individual episodes provide significant pleasure as they are individually experienced by the reader or listener, the authors of both Mark and *Aesop* have added another level to that pleasure through the development of a continuous macronarrative. The macronarrative is more important and more elaborate in Mark than in *Aesop*, in part because the Markan narrative has a clear narrative goal, the death and resurrection of Jesus, and narrative preparation for that goal, as well as Mark's christological concerns that are deeply entwined with the death of Jesus, creates pressure for macronarrative elaboration. For example, Mark demonstrates early on the antagonism of certain groups toward Jesus that makes his final death comprehensible in the realm of human causation. The misunderstanding of the disciples helps make comprehensible the misunderstanding of the antagonists. The parables and miracles are models of the difficulty of understanding. The messianic secret allows Mark to portray the divine reality in spite of human misunderstanding.

In the *Life of Aesop*, on the other hand, the macronarrative does not move so clearly toward a set goal. The death of Aesop at Delphi has been part of the story of Aesop from at least the time of Herodotus.[23] It does not seem, however, to have been part of the essential understanding of who Aesop was. On the contrary, it seems curious, even after repeated readings, to see the ever clever Aesop so helpless and lacking in resources. Up to the final scene there is some narrative coherence as the reader or listener sees Aesop's social, economic, and political situation gradually enhanced. Niklas Holzberg argues that the increasing rank and success of Aesop is matched by an increasing hubris which leads to his death.[24] While his death does seem to be caused by his insulting the god Apollo, that insult appears to be an isolated incident rather than part of a

---

[23] Herodotus 2.136.

[24] Niklas Holzberg, "A Lesser Known 'Picaresque' Novel of Greek Origin: The *Aesop Romance* and Its Influence," in *GCN* 5 (1993) 1–16, esp. 10–11. For a more thorough discussion of the structure of *Aesop*, see *idem*, "Der Äsop-Roman: Eine strukturanalytische Interpretation," in *Der Äsop-Roman: Motivgeschichte und Erzählstruktur* (N. Holzberg, ed.; MSKP 6; Tübingen: Gunter Narr, 1992) 33–75.

pattern. The rest of the episodes are not crafted to reinforce the point. Thus the incident seems more designed to explain Aesop's death than to provide an overall structure for the narrative.

Divine Causation and Narrative Plausibility

One limitation of episodic narrative is that the relative independence of the episodes is not well suited for developing causal connections that build plausibility into the narrative. To a certain extent ancient audiences seem to be less concerned with causal connections than are modern audiences. Nevertheless, some plausibility structure seems to be necessary for narrative success. A common way of showing plausibility in ancient narrative is to show divine causation. A related feature of ancient narrative, the use of oracles to provide an audience with a guide to coming events, has been discussed by J. Bradley Chance.[25] It seems likely that reliance on divine causation in ancient narrative is not merely a literary device but reflects a shared understanding of the nature of causation in the world. This is another important factor that supports the use of episodic narrative. If the cause of human events were found in the human realm, then the type of causal links that can be traced in connected, nonepisodic narrative would be important. As long as the true cause of human events exists in the divine realm, however, it is relatively less important to trace those causal links, and too careful a tracing of such links would imply a false understanding of causation.

Both Mark and *Aesop* use divine causation to enhance the plausibility of the narrative. The two pivotal points in the narrative of *Aesop*, the bestowal of the gift of language upon Aesop and his death at Delphi, are the result of divine intervention. The first episode of the *Life* shows Aesop as a mute slave (1–3). In this episode, where he escapes from a plot to blame him for a theft, he demonstrates the same resourcefulness that is typical of his character in the later narrative. He does not possess, however, the power of language that won him fame as a writer of fables and that is essential for his success in his disputes with Xanthus and in posing and solving riddles when he rises to the level of royal competitions. These gifts are bestowed upon him by the goddess Isis and the Muses in the second episode of the plot as the result of a kindness shown to a priestess of Isis by the slave (4–8).

---

[25] J. Bradley Chance, "Divine Prognostications and the Movement of Story: An Intertextual Exploration of Xenophon's *Ephesian Tale* and the Acts of the Apostles," in this volume pp. 219–34.

The death of Aesop at Delphi appears to result from the anger of Apollo that resulted from Aesop's erecting a shrine to the Muses and himself while ignoring Apollo, who had a claim to be honored as the leader of the Muses (100).[26] Although no explicit link is noted, the connection seems clear. Certainly nothing on the purely human level can explain how Aesop, after repeatedly extricating himself from tight situations and besting everyone he meets in argument, suddenly becomes so ineffectual in dealing with the population of Delphi (124–42). The people of Apollo's city are simply expressing the wrath of the god. While these two important events, the creation of Aesop through the gift of language and his destruction at Delphi, are linked to the divine realm, the divinities and a sense of their intervention remain in the background for most of the *Life of Aesop*.

In Mark, on the other hand, a sense of divine preordination pervades the narrative, in spite of Jesus' repeated attempts to overcome it. One method that Mark employs to create this sense of divine inevitability is the appearance of prophecy at crucial points. The chain of prophecy and fulfillment in the Markan prologue (1:2–3 and 1:4–8; 1:7–8 and 1:9–11) present the audience with an inexorably progressing divine plan from the very beginning.[27] Other important prophecies include the three passion predictions, predictions of tribulation and the parousia in chapter thirteen, and Jesus' predictions of his betrayal (14:18), the disciples' falling away (14:27–28), and Peter's denial (14:30).

Prophecy is a way of overcoming the randomness of episodic narrative, but Mark is such a master of the episodic style that the apparent lack of connection in episodic narrative becomes integral to the sense of divine inevitability. The sense of an unfolding divine plan created by the prophecy and fulfillment of the Markan prologue is immediately reinforced by the immediate and unexplained response of the disciples to Jesus' call (1:16–20), the immediate appearance in the synagogue of the demon-possessed man testifying to Jesus' identity (1:21–28), the immediate presentation of Jesus to Simon's sick mother-in-law that initiates Jesus' healing ministry (1:29–32), and Jesus' reference to the purpose of his coming (1:35–39). Through this rush of events, Mark masterfully creates the sense of an unfolding destiny, and the episodic

---

[26] This seems to be the meaning of the text, though Perry emends the Greek text in his edition to make the statue one of Mnemosyne, the mother of the Muses.

[27] Norman R Petersen, *Literary Criticism for New Testament Critics* (Philadelphia: Fortress, 1978) 52–53.

style is central to the effect. The appearance of a series of discrete events with relatively little causal connection between them that, nevertheless, immediately propel Jesus in less than a day to a position as a renowned teacher, healer, and exorcist is admirably designed to provoke a sense of wonder at the invisible hand of God working in apparently random events.

Building Narrative from Episodic Units

In spite of this difference in the complexity of the macronarrative, the authors of both *Aesop* and Mark share several strategies as they weave their episodes into a continuous plot.

(1) *Similar episodes are repeated to develop a point.* As shown above, this method is very useful in developing characterization. Mark groups healings, for example, in chapter one to show by cumulative effect Jesus' ability to heal. The short repeated episodes more effectively establish the point than either an extended single healing or a summary statement. *Aesop* similarly groups similar material. As the slave of Xanthus, Aesop is shown to outwit his master in varieties of dispute material. Within this section similar material is grouped as well, such as the episodes in which Aesop literally follows the directions of Xanthus (38–50). When Aesop gains his freedom, he speaks both to the crowd of Samos and to King Croesus with fables (94–99). A section of aphorisms is used to illustrate Aesop's philosophical teaching to his adopted son (109–110). After establishing himself in Lycurgus' court, his wit is employed solving and posing riddles (111–23). His final argument with people of Delphi is carried out by means of fables (129–42).

(2) *Within the plot as a whole discrete sections are created that are, in terms of size and content, amenable to episodic development.* There seems to be a natural limit to the number of similar episodes that may be grouped before an audience loses interest. In the case of extended episodes with greater narrative elaboration, such as are found in *Aesop*, the narrative bulk of such a group may be much greater. In Mark 1:21–2:12, for example, a healing section includes one exorcism, three healings, one summary of healing and exorcism, and another summary of exorcism. In *Aesop* the hero uses three fables in succession to extricate himself from difficulties and establish his position with Croesus (93–100). This section ends with a generalizing episode in which Aesop writes down his fables. Holzberg has analyzed the large central section of *Aesop* in which Aesop is owned by Xanthus into a section of exposition (20–33), episodes based

on direct instruction (34–64), and episodes based on the solution of a difficult problem (65–91).[28] These sections may then be broken into more manageable subsections through the grouping of material such as episodes in which Aesop literally follows the direction of Xanthus (38–50).

(3) *The discrete sections are ordered to suggest a coherent plot development from one to the other.* The healings of Mark 1 lead, through a combined healing/dispute to the dispute material of chapter two ending in one more healing/dispute, leading after a short interlude to the dispute about the meaning of the exorcisms that explains the tension between the acclamation of the crowd and the opposition of the authorities. Through the parable theory chapter four introduces a general understanding of meaning by which the ambiguity of the exorcisms can be understood. A similar method may be observed in *Aesop.* For example, Aesop's sale by his first master (10–12) is prepared for by an episode showing why the steward wanted to get rid of the slave (9). Aesop's manumission (90) is prepared for by Xanthus' offer to let Aesop buy his freedom, which he later withdraws (80).

(4) *Sustained conflicts between the hero and another person or group are established and episodes are used to illustrate the conflict.* In Mark the conflict between Jesus and various authorities is an obvious example. The conflict is established through a series of episodes early in the Gospel (2:1–3:6). The first of these episodes (2:1–12) points forward to the charge of blasphemy brought against Jesus at his trial; the last of them (3:1–6) ends with the decision of the authorities to kill Jesus. Another series of episodes near the end of the Gospel (11:27–12:40) reiterates the conflict and sets the stage for the passion narrative. In between, single episodes of various length and complexity appear to develop more completely some aspects of the conflict. In 3:22–28, for example, the tension between the exorcisms that have brought the acclamations of the crowds and the authorities' rejection of Jesus is explored. In 7:1–23, Mark introduces a more programmatic attack on the position of the Pharisees. The Pharisees are used to introduce the relationship between Jesus' miracles and signs in 8:11–13 and to introduce the question about divorce in 10:2–12, in which Jesus publicly claims authority to set aside the law of Moses.

The *Life of Aesop* is more centrally focused on conflicts between Aesop and others. Some, such as the opening episode of the stolen figs, are

---

[28] Holzberg, "'Picaresque' Novel," 9

limited to single episodes, while others, such as Aesop and Xanthus, extend through many episodes. Most of these conflicts are continuous in the sense that almost all of the episodes in a particular section focus on the conflict. The subplot of the conflict between Aesop and Xanthus' wife, on the other hand, shows an intermittent conflict much on the same pattern as the conflict between Jesus and the authorities in Mark. Xanthus' wife instigates the purchase of a slave (22). On arriving home with Aesop, Xanthus proves to be intimidated by his wife, but Aesop tames her by charging her with lewd intentions (29–32). This episode points forward to the resolution of the conflict between Aesop and the philosopher's wife, when the wife does in fact demand to have sexual relations with Aesop (75–76). The conflict reappears several times in between. The lost material between 37 and 38 clearly contains some conflict between Aesop and Xanthus' wife. In another episode Aesop gives delicacies sent by Xanthus to his wife to his dog, promoting conflict between the philosopher and his wife (44–46; 49–50). When Aesop is challenged to find a person who is not a busybody, Xanthus' wife is indirectly humiliated by Aesop as she becomes a pawn in a contest between the philosopher and his slave. Xanthus has demanded that Aesop produce someone who would not interfere in other people's business. When Aesop presents a rustic as such a person, Xanthus makes his wife act below her station by washing his feet and finally threatens to burn her alive in an attempt to get the rustic to interfere with his unseemly behavior (61–64).

(5) *Episodes of various lengths are presented to create variety.* In general, the *Life of Aesop* develops episodes into much more extensive narratives than does Mark. Occasionally, however, short self-contained interchanges appear, as in chapter forty, which contains two short incidents that help to develop the theme of imprecise instructions. The aphoristic teaching of Aesop to his adopted son (109–10) provides a similar break from more elaborated material.

Mark displays more variety in narrative development of individual episodes and skillfully places episodes of varying length within the narrative. For example, the opening chapters use short episodes to establish quickly various aspects of Jesus' identity and the conflict between Jesus and the authorities. The more extensive miracle stories in 4:35–8:10, on the other hand, slow the narrative down and enhance the impression of Jesus as a miracle worker by emphasizing the extraordinary nature of individual miracles. This same section of the Gospel includes extended narratives of the death of John the Baptist (6:14–29) and a conflict with the Pharisees (7:1–22). With the entry into Jerusalem, Mark begins another section dominated by less developed episodes (11:1–12:44), creating a headlong rush toward the passion, which is appropriately arrested by the eschatological discourse (13:1–37) that points beyond the rush of human events to the future goal of God.

(6) *Narrative within episodes is elaborated to enhance the narrative quality of the whole.* As already mentioned, narrative elaboration seems to be highly valued by the author and audience of the *Life of Aesop,* and most of the episodes are highly elaborated. In Mark, on the other hand, such elaboration is more rare. The greatest amount of elaboration is found in the passion narrative, where elaboration is necessary to provide appropriate narrative bulk for these events. Certain other events, such as the healing of the demoniac possessed by the legion (5:1–20) and the death of John the Baptist (6:14–29), are related with considerable narrative detail. These elaborated narratives are essential in creating the effect of sustained narrative for the Gospel as a whole.

(7) *Discrete episodes are interwoven to extend narrative tension or to provide keys for interpretation.* Mark's technique of inserting one episode within another is well known.[29] In Mark's narrative, the intercalations often appear to suggest connections between the episodes so that one interprets the other, often suggesting a hidden meaning for an event. Thus the intercalation of the cursing of the fig tree and the temple incident (11:12–25) has been interpreted as indicating a withering of the temple and its rejection as the place of divine worship.[30] The death of John the Baptist that replaces the expected description of the disciples' journeys of preaching and healing suggests that the true mission of the disciples is one that includes death and suffering as well as exorcism and healing (6:6b–31). The brave testimony of Jesus at his trial contrasts with the cowardly denial of Jesus by Peter, setting both into higher relief (14:53–72). The intercalation of the dispute about the meaning of Jesus' exorcisms and Jesus' dispute with his family explains for the audience

---

[29] Recent discussions include: James Edwards, "Markan Sandwiches: the Significance of Interpolations in Markan Narratives," *NovT* 31 (1989) 193–216; Geert Van Oyen, "Intercalation and Irony in the Gospel of Mark," in *The Four Gospels 1992: Festschrift Frans Neirynck* (BETL 100; 3 vols.; Leuven: Leuven University Press, 1992) 2.949–74; Thomas Shepherd, "The Narrative Function of Markan Intercalation," *NTS* 41 (1995) 522–40.

[30] Donald Juel, *Messiah and Temple* (SBLDS 31; Missoula, MT: Scholars Press, 1977) 135–56.

how Jesus' family could understand Jesus to be beside himself as well as how the Jewish leaders, represented by the Pharisees, could be passed over by God in favor of those who do the will of God (3:20–35).

A very similar technique of intercalation is used in *Aesop,* primarily as a method of retarding the narrative. The episode in which Aesop cooks a single lentil (39, 41) is extended by the insertion of two short interchanges between Aesop and Xanthus where Aesop follows directions in a similarly literal manner (40). The episode in which Aesop gives the delicacies intended for Xanthus' wife to his dog (44–46, 49–50) is also prolonged by the insertion of some witty sayings of Aesop at the banquet (47–48). An interchange between Aesop and the governor, in which Aesop is momentarily sent to jail for claiming not to know where he was going, is used to retard the development of the incident in which Aesop reports there is only one man at the bath (65). In contrast to Mark, the intercalated episodes do not seem to be used to suggest deeper or more spiritual meanings. If they have any connection, they seem to be similar in a straightforward manner, showing examples of similar activity. The special Markan use of the intercalation technique represents an adaptation of the technique to his view of the activity of Jesus as parabolic, holding within it a deeper meaning only grasped by those with ears to hear or eyes to see.

(8) *Similar episode plots are presented at different places in the narrative to recall earlier episodes and to suggest an underlying unity of theme or plot.*[31] In Mark, for example, one finds a section of narrative early in the Gospel that portrays the conflict between Jesus and various Jewish authorities (2:1–3:6). Shortly afterwards Mark presents an episode that helps the audience interpret that conflict (3:22–30). The main thrust of the plot then turns in other directions, focusing on parables and miracles and the relationship between Jesus and the disciples. At certain points within the narrative, however, conflict episodes (7:1–23; 8:11–12; 10:1–12) or sayings referring to conflict (8:15; 9:12–13) occur which keep that conflict fresh in the mind of the audience and often link it to current plot developments. The dispute in 7:1–23, for example, contains a parable that the disciples fail to understand. The demand for a sign (8:11–12) raises the question of whether or not the miracles of Jesus are signs. Then just before the passion narrative, when the conflict with the authorities becomes once again central to the coherence of the plot, a new section of conflict episodes reestablishes the theme (11:27–12:44).

---

[31] Mark's use of this technique is discussed in detail in Dewey, "Tapestry."

In *Aesop* there is less weaving together of narrative sections, but one finds a recurrence of certain motifs that create patterns of familiarity within the narrative. One recurrent motif important for the development of the narrative is Aesop's narrow escapes from various dangers. The repeated escapes—from being punished for stealing figs (2–3), from possible death at the hand of his overseer (9–11), from being beaten by Xanthus (56–64), from being sent to jail (65), from the anger of King Croesus (95–99), from a sentence of death due to a false accusation (104)—establish an impression of invincibility that is suddenly reversed with Aesop's death at Delphi when his cleverness fails him (127–42). Holzberg has shown that this motif is developed by two converging patterns of Aesop being held prisoner for no good reason (80, 104, 128) and Aesop being three times wrongly accused of theft (3, 42, 128), both of which culminate in the final death scene.[32]

By means of these and other strategies, a skillful narrator can create the effect of a relatively continuous narrative while working, for the most part, with discrete episodic units. The result is particularly effective for reading aloud, since the discrete individual episodes keep the listener's attention focused while the larger plot develops. The style can be particularly effective in suggesting connections between various episodes or types of episodes when an exact chronological account is of secondary importance. The author of Mark has been particularly skillful in exploiting this possibility of episodic narrative, showing by the placement of episodes and by developing verbal connections between them the relationships between parable, miracle, dispute, teaching, and passion.

Reading and Hearing Episodic Narrative

Just as the composition of episodic narrative requires the use of somewhat different strategies from those employed in the composition of continuous narrative, reading or hearing episodic narrative involves somewhat different moves on the part of the reader or listener from those used when reading continuous narrative. The most important difference is the way in which individual incidents within the story are constructed into a whole. The distinction is far from absolute, but in general episodic narrative requires that the reader or listener allow a greater degree of independence to the episodes than is expected in continuous narrative. To a great extent the episodes themselves in their

---

[32] Holzberg, "'Picaresque' Novel" 9–10.

individual impact on the listener are the building blocks of the narrative, not the details of the particular occurrences within the episodes. While ancient audiences, because of their familiarity with episodic narrative, would expect episodes to be relatively independent and would have experience in creating narrative from episodic blocks, modern audiences have expectations created by continuous narrative that may have to be modified before they can experience episodic narrative in the way it was originally heard.

The relative independence of episodes correlates with the understanding of character found in Greco-Roman literature. In a modern novel or short story it is often the psychological twists and turns of one or more characters that hold the reader's interest. As E. M. Forster says, in a novel we can get to know a person more fully than we ever can in real life.[33] Modern readers are trained to use the events in the story to construct the psychology of the characters and see how that psychology develops as characters react to those events. Ancient audiences, on the other hand, tended to see character as more static. Characters were often treated in terms of moral types.[34] The popularity of the *chreia* form and of collections of *chreiai* about famous persons in part reflects this understanding of character. The individual saying or episode is understood to be revelatory of a person's character understood as a relatively unchanging entity. A person's character is understood through the sum of these revelatory moments.

If the reader or listener tries to make psychological sense out of the entire chain of an episodic narrative in the same way that modern readers approach modern novels, the results may be incongruous. I have argued elsewhere that the two feeding stories in the Gospel of Mark would have been heard as relatively independent, and while each is illustrative, among other things, of the disciples' lack of insight, modern readers' concern with how the disciples could utterly forget the first feeding is misplaced.[35] The construction of the character of Xanthus in the *Life of Aesop* is rather similar. Both Xanthus and the Markan disciples suffer from lack of insight, but if individual episodes are read as continuous

---

[33] E M. Forster, *Aspects of the Novel* (San Diego: Harcourt Brace Jovanovich, 1985) 47.

[34] For discussions of characterization in ancient literature, see Theodore J Weeden, Sr., *Mark—Traditions in Conflict* (Philadelphia: Fortress, 1971) 15–18; Tolbert, *Sowing the Gospel* 76–78.

[35] Shiner, *Follow Me!* 222–26.

narrative, their density becomes hard to explain. For example, Xanthus does not seem to learn from past experience as he is repeatedly caught by Aesop following his directions in an overly literal way or following ambiguous directions in a way he did not intend. It is hard to understand what might be going through his mind when, after the first all-tongue dinner party, Xanthus again gives Aesop an open-ended direction, and this time to serve the worst rather than the best that he can find (51–55)! When taken as snapshots of the respective characters of Xanthus and Aesop, however, the episodes create a coherent picture.

Episodic narrative needs to be appreciated on its own terms if we are to be able to understand the episodic narratives of the ancients. It has different conventions from modern continuous narrative, but skillfully employed it can achieve effects as dramatic or as subtle as those created in the continuous narrative style. The more fully we can understand the episodic style, the closer we can come to hearing the Gospels and other ancient narrative with ears that hear as the ancients heard.

Conceiving the Narrative:
Colors in Achilles Tatius and the Gospel of Mark

Charles W. Hedrick
Southwest Missouri State University

Introduction

Achilles Tatius was a late second-century CE novelist[1] whose novel *Leucippe and Clitophon* enjoyed a wide popularity in Egypt, to judge from the number of manuscripts (seven) that have been discovered.[2] While the narrative clearly focuses on the romance of Leucippe and Clitophon and their problems, the narrator frequently wanders from this story line with vivid and fulsome descriptions, whose excessiveness in themselves have no apparent connection to the plot. There are also digressions with lengthy narrative asides on a variety of unrelated subjects. Most of the descriptive material and commentary is on the surface gratuitous in terms of the romantic adventures of Leucippe and Clitophon; the excessive description in itself does nothing to further the action, rather it tends to slow it down.[3] On the other hand, in keeping with the author's expressed "fascination with passion" (2.1)[4] and interest in "tales of love" (2.3)[5] such vivid description can only be seen, at least in part, as a deliberate attempt to enhance the reader's visual image.

---

[1] John J. Winkler, "Achilles Tatius, Leucippe and Clitophon," in *Collected Ancient Greek Novels* (B. P. Reardon, ed.; Berkeley: University of California Press, 1989) 170.

[2] Winkler, "Achilles Tatius," 170.

[3] See Thomas Hägg, *Narrative Technique in Ancient Greek Romances. Studies of Chariton, Xenophon Ephesius, and Achilles Tatius* (Stockholm: Almqvist & Wiksells, 1971) 103–8, but compare for an opposite analysis Shadi Bartsch, *Decoding the Ancient Novel. The Reader and the Role of Description in Heliodorus and Achilles Tatius* (Princeton: Princeton University Press, 1989).

[4] Translation by Winkler, "Achilles Tatius," 177. I am using the divisions in *Achilles Tatius* (S. Gaslee, trans.; LCL; Cambridge: Harvard University Press, 1961).

[5] Translation by Winkler, "Achilles Tatius," 177.

This phenomenon is called ἔκφρασις (description) in the handbooks on rhetoric of the second century and later.[6] Until recently ἔκφρασις has been viewed as "irrelevant and excessive" by those who have studied the ancient novel.[7] In 1989, however, this consensus was challenged by Shadi Bartsch. Bartsch argues that these passages "necessarily figure as crucial tools in the author's narrative strategy. . . ."[8] The narrator never tells the reader how the descriptions are related to the plot, but is inviting the reader to reflect on them in terms of the story. See Bartsch's discussion on the painting of the "Abduction of Europa" that opens the tale.[9] Because of its position at the very beginning of the narrative, readers may well suspect that it will play some specific interpretive role in the narrative but no clarification is ever given. Consequently Bartsch argues that readers "are lured by their own expectations into producing vague conjectures about the relationship of painting to narrative. . . .but cannot guess at its extent or validity. . . ."[10]

According to Bartsch, what has been called "gratuitous" description, when read in the light of the rhetorical techniques of the second century and later, is a deliberate narrative strategy inviting readers to ponder the significance of the descriptions, but without presenting them with authoritative interpretations. It is a technique to solicit the readers' engagement with the narrative.

By comparison, Mark's narrator seems almost ascetic when it comes to the use of visually enhancing language in the narrative. In few places does Mark's narrator digress or deliberately use descriptive language to enhance the reader's visual imaging of the story. There are few descriptions that could be considered "excessive" in the style of Achilles Tatius. As a rule Mark is quite wooden in the use of description. Enhancement for Mark is usually "more" and "bigger." Mark routinely misses opportunities to enhance the reader's visual imaging of the events of the narrative.

I. Description in Achilles Tatius

Achilles Tatius frequently delays the progress of the narrative, digressing to provide the reader bits of anecdotal information, to

---

6 Bartsch, *Decoding the Ancient Novel*, 7–10.

7 Bartsch, *Decoding the Ancient Novel*, 4–5.

8 Bartsch, *Decoding the Ancient Novel*, 6–7.

9 Bartsch, *Decoding the Ancient Novel*, 44–45, 48–50.

10 Bartsch, *Decoding the Ancient Novel*, 44–45.

moralize on various subjects, to portray various entities and address issues by means of elaborate, graphic, and garnished description. In the passages that advance the plot, on the other hand, the narrator less frequently employs language enhancing the reader's visual experience.

A. *Anecdotal Digressions and Narrator's Asides*[11]

For example, the narrator digresses with a brief unrelated anecdote: "On the Discovery of Purple" (2.11.4–8). In this instance, the anecdote is connected to the narrative by the barest connective (2.11.4).[12] When the anecdote concludes, the narrator abruptly recommences the story of Leucippe and Clitophon with no transition. Generally there is no transition into and out of these digressions.[13]

Some digressions are accommodated by inclusion in the speeches of personae in the novel,[14] and some are not digressions in the narrow sense that one is aware of a break in the story, but digressions only in the sense that they wander from the topic.[15] On occasion, the narrator moralizes in these anecdotes and digressions.[16] Throughout the narrative there are shorter anecdotes and asides; for example, an anecdote about beauty:

---

[11] See Bartsch, *Decoding the Ancient Novel,* 12–13, note 12, for another list of digressions.

[12] Gaslee, *Achilles Tatius,* 75.

[13] See the following anecdotes and digressions: On Providence, 1.3.2–3; On Wounds, 1.6.2–4; On the Origins of Wine, 2.2–3.1; On Eros and Dionysos, 2.3.3; On the Kiss, 2.8.2; On the Egyptian Ox, 2.15.3–4; On Shame, Grief, and Anger, 2.29.1–5; On Weeping, 3.11.1–2; On the Egyptian Clod, 3.13.3; On Pity, 3.14.3; On the Nile Horse, 4.2.1–3; On the Nile River, 4.11.3–8; On Egyptians, 4.14.9; On the Crocodile, 4.19.1–6; On Tears, 6.7.4–8; On Anger and Love, 6.19.1–7; On the Water of the Styx 8.12.1–9.

[14] On Women, 1.8.2–8; On the Lovelife of the Palm, 1.17.4–5; On the Lovelife of Rivers and Fountains, 1.18.1–2; On the Lovelife of Vipers and Eels, 1.18.3–5; On Miraculous Sights, 2.14.7–10; The Fable of the Lion and the Gnat, 2.21.1–5; The Fable of the Lion and the Gnat, 2.22.1–7; On the Phoenix, 3.25.1–7; On the Elephant, 4.4.2–8; On the Source of the Elephant's Sweet Breath, 4.5.1–3; On the Kiss, 4.8.2–3.

[15] On Capturing the Nile Horse, 4.3.1–5; On Nile Water as a Beverage, 4.18.4–6; On Rumor and Slander, 6.10.4–5; On Wounds and Tears, 7.4.4–5; On the Pan Pipes, 8.6.1–15.

[16] These tend to be rather brief: On Love Stories, 1.5.6; On the Lewd, 2.13.1; On Shame, 2.24.3; On Great Dangers, 3.3.5; On a Slow Death at Sea, 3.4.5–6; On Eros' Attack, 4.6.1; On Those in Love, 4.10.3; On Time as the Medicine of Grief, 5.8.2; On Athena's Judgments, 8.8–9.

"For beauty wounds deeper than any arrow and strikes through the eyes into the soul; the eye is the passage for Love's wound."[17]

B. Decorative Description[18]

Frequently the narrator suspends the action to provide the reader lengthy decorative descriptions of various objects,[19] locations,[20] people,[21] topics,[22] and events.[23] These lengthy descriptions[24] play no immediately obvious role in furthering the story. For example, the narrator digresses to give a rather elaborate description of a large vessel used for mixing wine on the occasion of the festival of Dionysos:

> My father, wishing to celebrate it with splendour, had set out all that was necessary for the dinner in a rich and costly fashion; but especially a precious cup to be used for libations to the god, one only second to the famous goblet of Glaucus of Chios. The material of it was wrought rock-crystal; vines crowned its rim, seeming to grow from the cup itself, their clusters drooped down in every direction: when the cup was empty, each grape seemed green and unripe, but when wine was poured into it, then little by little the clusters became red and dark, the green crop turning into the ripe fruit; Dionysus too was represented hard by the clusters, to be the husbandman of the vine and the vintner. As we drank deeper, I began to look more boldly and with less shame at my sweetheart.[25]

---

[17] See also for briefer anecdotes and asides: On Egypt, 3.5.5; Melite's Joke, 5.14.4; On Hope, 5.22.8; On Eros, 5.26.3–4; On Eros as a Master of Rhetoric, 5.27.1; On Eros, 5.27.4; On the Mind, 6.5.5; On the Face as Reflecting the Mind, 6.6.2–3; On the Eyes, 6.6.3; On Jealousy, 6.11.2; On a New Love, 6.17.4; On Lovers' Talk, VI.18.3; On Misfortune, 7.2.3; On Fear and Memory, 7.10.4; On Dionysos as Father of Freedom, 8.4.2.

[18] See Bartsch, *Decoding the Ancient Novel*, 12–13, note 26, for another list of descriptions.

[19] The Painting of Europa 1.1.2–13; The Bucking Horse, 1.12.3–4; Calligone's Wedding Dress, 2.11.2–4; Two Paintings by Evanthes: Andromeda, 3.6.3–7.9 and Promethus, 3.8.1–7; The Painting of Philomela, 5.3.4–8 and Its Explanation, 5.5.1–9.

[20] The Port of Sidon, 1.1–1; The Garden of a House, 1.15.1–8.

[21] The Musician, 1.5.4–5; Melite, 5.13.1–2.

[22] The Merits of Homosexual versus Heterosexual Love, 2.35.2–38.5.

[23] Leucippe's Song, 2.1.1–3; A Sacrifice, 2.14.1–3; The Sailing of a Ship, 2.32.1–2; Menelaus' Story, 2.34.1–7; A Shipwreck, 3.1.1–5:5; Clinias' Escape, 5.9.1–10.7.

[24] There are also brief narrative digressions that do not further the story in any direct or overtly indirect way. Compare the following: a grove, 1.2.3; a woman in a dream, 1.3.4; Leucippe, 1.4.3–4 and 1.19.1–2; a servant, 2.17.3; Leucippe's boudoir, 2.19.2–3; Conops, 2.20.1; Zeus, 3.6.1; robbers, 3.9.2; robbers and horse, 3.12.1; Nile celebration, 4.18.3; City of Alexandria, 5.1.1–6; the festival of Zeus Serapis, 5.2.1–3; Lacaena, 5.17.3; what tears do to eyes, 6.7.1–3; tears, 6.7.4–8.

[25] 2.3.1–3: Gaslee, *Achilles Tatius*, 60–61.

The description of the cup is merely a meandering detail in the progress of the narrative. At most, the elaborate description, clearly designed to enhance the reader's visual image, serves only on the surface to inform the reader of the plush nature of the festival. There is no obvious connection to the love story.

Bartsch, however, sees in the description a metaphor for the "outcome of the romance" between Clitophon and Leucippe.

> The ripening of the fruit, the change of color from pale to a deep red, and the erotic and Dionysian associations of this crop itself provide on the one hand a metaphor for the simultaneous progression of the mutual attraction of hero and heroine. . . .On a deeper level, the description, in which the vessel is filled with red wine and undergoes a corresponding change in color, also suggests itself as a parallel for the physical process of sexual arousal.[26]

Perhaps! Absent any clear guidance from the narrator, how could anyone know what was in the mind of the author? And even with guidelines, who would presume to read the author's mind? Readers should be careful not to attribute too quickly to the author what may only be a creative reading; or to say it differently: readers should be aware of the "affective fallacy": that is, confusing the text's affect on a given reader with the intention of the author.[27]

C. The Use of Color as Visually Enhancing Description

The narrator uses language that appeals to the reader's senses of hearing,[28] smelling,[29] feeling,[30] tasting,[31] and especially seeing. The narrator's use of colors to describe the visual character of objects, particularly in the descriptive digressions, is quite elaborate, and is distinctive of

---

[26] Bartsch, *Decoding the Ancient Novel*, 146–57.

[27] See D. O. Via, Jr., *The Parables. Their Literary and Existential Dimension* (Philadelphia: Fortress, 1967) 73–88; W. K. Wimsatt, Jr. and M. C. Beardsley, *The Verbal Icon. Studies in the Meaning of Poetry* (Lexington: University of Kentucky Press, 1954) 3–18 and id., "The Intentional Fallacy," *Swanee Review* 54 (1946) 466–88.

[28] "Whistling of flutes, banging of doors," 1.8.3; "bubbled," 1.15.6; "chirping," 1.15.7; "hisses," 1.18.4, "crunched," 2.11.5; "trills like a string, sings like a lyre," 2.14.8; "wind whistles tunefully," 5.16.5; "Buzzing," 2.7.3 and 2.21.4; "clear divine note, musical sound" 8.6.13; "Loud," 2.7.2.

[29] "Sweetest savor," 4.5.3; "sense of smell," 2.2.5.

[30] "Rough and hard," 2.11.5; "cold as snow," 1.2.3 and 2.14.7; "tender hands," 4.9.4; "wrinkled, scaly, and hard as stones," 4.19.2; "slippery," 6.10.4; "cold," 2.2.5; "kisses sting," 2.7.7.

[31] "Taste was sweet and cool," 4.18.4.

this author's narrative style.[32] For example, compare the narrator's description of Leucippe:

> An eye at once piercing and voluptuous; golden hair in golden curls; black eyebrows—jet black; pale cheeks, the pallor shading in the centre into a ruddy hue, like that stain wherewith the Lydian women tint ivory; and a mouth that was a rose—a rosebud just beginning to uncurl its petals.[33]

The use of colors in this particular segment just quoted is designed to give the reader a certain visual image of Leucippe, in the "mind's eye" as it were. The colors themselves are not really significant for the plot. The narrator could have described her great beauty (which *is* significant to the plot) in other ways, however. Hence, the colors have only one function: to enhance the reader's visual experience.

Generally the use of color in the narrative is descriptive,[34] although occasionally color is used to distinguish one thing from other like things.[35] Also the narrator of this story can use color figuratively; i.e., not literally.[36]

In one instance the narrator describes Clitophon standing before the court after previously having been condemned to death: "instead of his fetters he is wearing a white robe (στολή), and the prisoner is standing in the ranks of those who are free."[37] It is not immediately clear why it should be a "white" robe, rather than simply a robe, or a blue robe for example.

When Clitophon was arrested he was wearing Melite's clothing that had enabled him to get out of the lady's bedroom undetected (6.1.1–3; 6.5.1). After he was convicted of murdering Leucippe and sentenced to death, he was stripped naked and hung up in chains (7.12.4). Later he received a reprieve from the execution because the priest of Artemis

---

[32] *Pale, whitened, white:* 1.1.7; 1.1.9; 1.15.5–7; 2.1.2; 2.11.3–4; 3.7.4–5; 4.19.3; 4.7.1–3; 7.4.4; *Red:* 1.1.8–9; 1.15.5–7; 2.3.2; 2.11.3–4; 3.25.2; *Blue:* 1.1.8–9; *Purple:* 1.1.10; 2.1.4; 2.11.3–4; 2.11.6–8; 2.7.4–5; *Green:* 2.3.2; *Gold:* 2.11.3–4; 3.25.2; *Black:* 2.11.3–4; IV.5.2; 4.5.3; 4.19.3; 6.7.1–3.

[33] 1.4.3–4: Gaslee, *Achilles Tatius,* 14–15.

[34] Clearly the dominant use is to enhance the reader's visual experience: 1.1.8–9; 1.4.3–4; 1.14.2; 1.19.1–2; 2.3.2; 3.7.3–5.

[35] For example, 1.1.10; 1.15.5; 2.2.2.

[36] For example, "growing pale" (ὠχρίασεν), 1.8.1; grew pale, then reddened (ὠχρίασα . . . ἐφοινίχθεν), 2.6.1; the color of blood for purple dye (τὰ χείλη τοῦ κυνὸς ἡμαγμένα), 2.11.5–6; the rose growing in the cheeks (ῥόδον δὲ ἐμπεφυτεῦσθαι ταῖς παρειαῖς), 5.13.1.

[37] 8.8.4: Gaslee, *Achilles Tatius,* 412–13.

declared a holy sacrifice. The priest then bailed him out of jail (8.16.2) and subsequently he became a suppliant (ἱκέτης) of Artemis.

Possibly the "white robe" is intended to contrast Clitophon's new situation with his former prisoner status; i.e., "instead of fetters he now wears a white robe" (λευκὴν . . . στολήν)—and in that case the white robe would appear to describe what ordinary people (i.e., non-prisoners) wear on formal occasions. But why then should its color also be given? Why not just say "wearing a robe," if the reason were to distinguish Clitophon's new dress from prison garb?

Possibly the white robe is the "uniform," as it were, worn by the suppliants of Artemis; and Clitophon, as a suppliant of Artemis, is therefore appropriately dressed in a *white* robe. Yet when Leucippe prepares for the "ordeal of the Pan pipes," she is clad in "customary" dress (κεκοσμημένη στολῇ τῇ νενομισμένῃ, 8.6.12–13), which turns out to be a "sacred robe" (στολή) that is further described as "a long tunic (χιτών) of linen (ὀθόνης)." It is not described as white (8.13.1), though undyed linen may have appeared as off white.[38]

D. The Use of Colors in Narrative

In English there are at least four different ways that colors can be used in narrative. (1) The usual use of colors is to describe, or to distinguish one thing from another like thing. (2) A second use is figurative or symbolical; for example, to use an expression such as "the man is yellow" to mean that he is a coward. Other figurative uses of color are: "blue" for sad; "seeing red" to mean angry; "green" with envy, etc. (3) In some cases while a color retains something of its descriptive function, it is nevertheless well on its way toward being incorporated into the *nomen* of the thing it previously described. Compare, for example, the following: "yellow pages," "brown bag lunch," the "silver screen," a "yellow cab," the "green grocery," etc. (4) In other cases the color has been totally subsumed into the thing it formally modified so that the color function is lost and the color has instead become the thing itself; note, for example, "to blackmail" someone, the "blackmarket," government "white papers," the "White House," the "black board," the German "Black Forest," etc.

---

[38] According to Yigal Yadin, *The Finds from the Bar Kokhba Period in the Cave of Letters* (Jerusalem: Israel Exploration Society, 1963) 252, linen is difficult to dye, though its natural pale yellowish color might have appeared "white."

In *Leucippe and Clitophon* the narrator's use of colors is limited to (1) and (2) above. It would be difficult to identify (3) and (4) in ancient languages, since these categories are conceptual.

E. Inadvertence of the Author

Another possible explanation for the use of the modifier "white" for Clitophon's robe is that it is due to simple inadvertence on the part of the author, and hence the word is redundant.[39] It seems to be a consensus that during the Roman Republic and early Empire the usual color of the tunic worn by upper class males was white (Juvenal, *Satire* 3.179).[40] The general holiday dress of the populace was white,[41] and the dress for formal occasions was likewise white (cf. Theophrastus, *Char.* 21.11, and Aeschines, *Ctesiphon* 77). In fact, the white toga was the characteristic garment of the Roman male "for a thousand years." Treated with fuller's chalk, it could be given a "dazzling brilliancy." A garment so treated was called the *toga splendens* or *candida.*[42] In the Roman Empire there were even attempts by the emperors to coerce the wearing of the toga (i.e., white) for formal and holiday occasions.[43] Working men, however, wore darker colors, since they would not need to be cleaned as frequently.

The *stola* (στολή) was basically a longer tunic that in the Greek period was worn by both men and women.[44] In Josephus, for example, the

---

[39] For an example of an oversight on the part of this author see 2.19.4–6. Leucippe's mother apparently always kept the keys to the suite of rooms that included the bedrooms for her and her daughter. She followed the elaborate practice of locking the doors from the inside and the outside—the keys then being passed back to her by the servant who locked the door from the outside through a hole for that purpose. Yet Satyrus obtained a second set of keys. The reader is never told how that happened, or how it was possible to unlock the inside lock from the outside, when it took both an inside and outside person to lock the double doors.

[40] L. M. Wilson, *The Clothing of the Ancient Romans* (Johns Hopkins University Studies in Archaeology 24; Baltimore: Johns Hopkins University Press, 1938) 66, 68, 69; H. W. Johnston, *The Private Life of the Romans* (Chicago: Scott/Foresman, 1903) 158–82, and especially sections 236–38, 240, 246–47, 270; W. W. Fowler, *Social Life at Rome in the Age of Cicero* (New York: Macmillan, 1909) 53; G. Showerman, *Rome and the Romans. A Survey and Interpretation* (New York: Macmillan, 1937) 62.

[41] Wilson, *Clothing of the Ancient Romans*, 67.

[42] Johnston, *Private Life of the Romans*, 161, 166.

[43] J. Carcopino, *Daily Life in Ancient Rome. The People and the City at the Height of the Empire* (E. O. Lorimer, trans.; New Haven: Yale University Press, 1940) 155. This is a good indication that the custom had begun to change.

[44] W. C. F. Anderson, "Stola," in W. Smith, W. Wyate, G. E. Marinden, eds., *A Dictionary of Greek and Roman Antiquities* (3d ed. rev. and enlarged; 2 vols.; London: John Murray, 1901) 2.716–17; Carcopino, *Daily Life in Ancient Rome*, 153–56, Wilson,

(στολή) is used as a generic word for clothing or garments (*Ant.* 2.134; 5.37; 11.327; 18.361); it is used to describe a woman's garment (4.301; 8.266; 18.78) as well as a man's garment (13.46; 19.87, 97, 123, 270). However, there must have been some difference in the actual design of the garments, since Josephus can also describe men not wearing a woman's στολή (4.301), and both Ammonius (12.108) and Gaius (19.30) tried to conceal themselves in the στολή of a woman, suggesting that one at that time could tell a difference.[45]

In the Roman period the *stola* was adopted by the Roman matron as the garment she wore in public; it was her formal wear by which she was distinguished.[46] Josephus, for example, describes an occasion on which a husband had his wife remove her στολή and "put on the dress of a simple woman" (*Ant.* 8.266). As long as she did not select a loud or brilliant color, the *stola* of the Roman matron could be any color she desired. Loud colors were considered immodest for the Roman matron.[47]

In the light of such information, it is at least possible that the use of "white" to describe Clitophon's στολή before the court (8.8.4) is due simply to the way the author conceived it in that situation and thus the color "white" has no significance beyond the author's conception of it in that way. It was simply a redundant description of what the author saw in the mind's eye. It is likely for the same reason that the tunic (χιτών) is described as white at two other locations in the narrative (1.1.10 and 3.7.5). When Leucippe went through the ordeal of the Pan pipes

---

Clothing of the Ancient Romans, 155. In Achilles Tatius it is a garment worn by both men and women.

[45] Wilson (*The Clothing of the Ancient Romans*) describes the difference between the male and female χιτών in the Roman period: the female χιτών had longer sleeves, was longer in length, and the skirt was fuller (152). This agrees with Josephus' description of the female χιτών "in ancient times" (*Ant.* 7.171). But it should be noted that priests also wore full length tunics (Josephus, *Ant.* 20.6). See also Yadin, *The Finds From the Bar Kokhba Period,* 219–40: In the twenty-five ἱμάτια (mantles) or parts thereof, found in the cave, Yadin determined that the men's mantles were lighter in color (white/yellow), while the women's were more colorful. The garments were distinguished by notched bands (male) and gamma-shaped patterns (female) on the garments. Josephus (*War,* 4.561–63) describes John of Gischala and the Galileans dressing in women's apparel (γυναικείας ἐσθῆτας ἀναλαμβάνοντες) which were "dyed (βεβαμμένων) mantles (χλανιδίων)." Since Josephus was deliberately describing women's clothing, it suggests that women's clothing was dyed, while male clothing was not.

[46] Wilson, *Clothing of the Ancient Romans,* 155.

[47] Wilson, *Clothing of the Ancient Romans,* 163.

(8.13.1), however, the author omits a color designation for her στολή although the author also may well have visualized it as white or off white.

In short, designating a color, on the one hand (8.8.4; 1.1.10; 3.7.5), and the lack of color, on the other hand (8.13.1), are not necessarily due to the author's desire to send the reader some arcane signal or symbolic message, but rather both can reasonably be attributed to the author's conceptualizing of robes and tunics. Conceiving it as white, the author idly designates it so in one instance, but does not bother to do so in another, although it is likely still conceived as white. In any case the author really does not have to specify a color, since a reader likely would have visualized the στολή as white, unless told differently.

For an analogous situation in English compare how people will refer to traffic signals: as "traffic lights," or simply "lights," or sometimes as "red lights," "green lights," or "stop lights." In such a designation the use of the color "red" or "green" has little function as color, but only as a designation for the traffic signal. Another similar redundant use of color is how caution lights are described. In our culture caution lights are always yellow; yet sometimes we will say "yellow caution light" and at other times simply "caution light."

II. Description in the Gospel of Mark

Mark's narrator, on the other hand, never digresses from the issue before the reader to provide lengthy descriptions of anything. The only lengthy digression in the text is the narration of John's arrest and death at the hands of Herod (6:17–29), but the "description" can scarcely be called "visually enhanced." Mark is generally quite unimaginative in the way events and people are described.

A. Description in Mark Is Usually "More and Bigger," or "More Emphatic"

Everyone is familiar with Mark's use of εὐθύς "immediately"[48]—usually regarded as somewhat equivalent to a narrator's "and then." But in the light of the way Mark enhances language descriptively in the narrative, readers should perhaps take the word more seriously as a deliberate sequential connective meaning "quickly." Note Mark's "immediately with haste" (6:25) as an example of the tendency to elaborate/intensify.

---

[48] J. C. Hawkins, *Horae Synopticae. Contributions to the Study of the Synoptic Problem* (2d ed. revised and supplemented; Oxford: Clarendon, 1968) 12. Hawkins lists Mark's 38 uses of εὐθύς to Matthew's 18 and Luke's 7.

In Mark everything is large, loud, and bigger.⁴⁹ There is no such thing as a small crowd, for example.⁵⁰ Mark tends to emphasize for effect,⁵¹ or to exaggerate for effect.⁵²

B. Specific Descriptive Digressions in Mark

In contrast to Achilles Tatius, Mark digresses only three times for the purpose of providing the reader visually enhancing description. In Mark 1:6 the reader is provided with a description of John the Baptist: "John was clothed with camel's hair, had a leather girdle around his waist, and ate locusts and wild honey." In 6:8–9 the reader is provided with a list of those items the Twelve were authorized to take with them on their preaching mission: "a staff, no bread, no bag, no money in their belts, to wear sandals, and not put on two tunics." In 14:51–52 Mark again digresses to describe a young man who had followed Jesus. He had on "nothing but a linen cloth about his naked body." When he was seized "he left the linen cloth and ran away naked."

There are several other longer descriptions with visually enhanced language that are not digressions in a narrow sense: the healing of the deaf mute around Tyre (7:33–34), the healing of the blind man at Bethsaida (8:23), the healing of the spirit possessed boy (9:18, 20, 26),

---

⁴⁹ Compare Mark's use of πολύς, 1:45; 2:2; 5:24, 38, 43; 6:13, 20, 34; 8:1; 9:14, 26; 12:5, 37; 15:41 (πλεῖστος, 4:1); μέγας, 1:26, 39; 13:2; 15:37 (μεῖζον, 4:1); περισσός, 6:51, and ἱκανός, 10:46.

⁵⁰ Compare Mark 4:31: "smaller (μικρότερον) than all seeds on earth," but even this is an intensification: it was not small, but rather "smaller."

⁵¹ 1:35, exceedingly (λίαν); 1:43, sternly charge (ἐμβριμησάμενος); 1:45, openly (φανερῶς); 6:20, 12:37 gladly (ἡδέως); 6:26, exceedingly distressed (περίλυπος); 6:32, lonely place (κατ᾽ ἰδίαν); 6:48, painfully (βασανιζομένους); 7:35, plainly (ὀρθῶς); 8:12, groaned deeply in spirit (ἀναστενάξας); 8:25, looked intently (διέβλεψεν), saw everything clearly (ἐνέβλεπεν τηλαυγῶς ἅπαντα); 9:6, terrified (ἔκφοβος); 9:15, greatly distressed (ἐξεθαμβήθησαν); 12:4, treat shamefully (ἠτίμασαν); 12:14, truly (ἀληθής); 12:32, well and truly (καλῶς . . . ἐπ᾽ ἀληθείας); 14:31, vehemently (ἐκπερισσῶς); 14:33, greatly distressed (ἐκθαμβεῖσθαι); 14:45, at once (εὐθύς).

⁵² 1:5 (all the country of Judea, Jerusalem and [all] were baptized); 1:32–33 (all who were sick or possessed, whole city at the door); 2:8 (perceiving in his spirit); 3:20 (could not even eat); 5:20 (all men marvelled); 6:20 (all that they had done and taught); 6:33 (ran on foot from all the towns); 6:55 (ran about the whole region [χώραν]); 6:56 (wherever he came villages, cities, or country); 12:33 (all whole burnt offering); 12:43 (poor widow gives more than anyone else, gave her whole living); 13:19 (such tribulation as has never been or will be); 14:9 (in the whole world); 14:53 (all chief priests, elders, and scribes); 15:16 (whole battalion assembled); 15:33 (over the whole land).

and the description of the days after the tribulation (13:24–25). Most of
the descriptive material in Mark is comprised of brief isolated phrases
and it generally does not involve visually enhancing language.[53]

Perhaps Mark's most effusive description is that of the nard with which
Jesus was anointed in the house of Simon, the leper; it was an "an
alabaster flask of ointment of pure nard, very costly" (14:3). Only Mark's
description of Jesus on the mount of transfiguration rivals it. "His
garments became glistening, intensely white as no fuller on earth could
bleach them" (19:3). These two passages together represent Mark's most
creative and imaginative indulgence, if it can be called that, into visually
enhancing description.[54]

C. The Use of Color in Mark

Mark, like Achilles Tatius, also makes use of descriptive colors in the
narrative, although Mark's use of colors is not as effusive as that of
Achilles Tatius. With the exception of Mark 9:3, where one can see a
deliberate use of the color white (λευκά) as a description of Jesus'
garments, the reason for their use in the text is not always immediately
clear: the instances are 6:39 green (χλωρός); 15:17, 20 purple
(πορφύρα); 16:5 white (λευκός).

1. Purple

The use of purple for the robe of Jesus in 15:17, 20 seems to be a
deliberate ironic twist by Mark. Mark Chapter 15 ironically portrays Jesus
as king. Pilate asks Jesus, "Are you king of the Jews" (15:2) and twice
offers to release Jesus "the king of the Jews" for the crowd (15:2, 9). The
crowd, however, wants him crucified, so he is led away. The soldiers
mockingly clothe him in purple, the symbol of royalty, rank, and high

---

[53] 1:10, descending like a dove; 6:34, crowd like a sheep without a shepherd; 7:14,
vessels of bronze; 8:24, men like trees walking; 9:2, kingdom come with power; 11:2,
colt on which no one ever sat; 11:4, colt tied at the door out in the street; 11:20, fig
tree withered away to its roots; 12:6, beloved son; 12:38, scribes who like to go about
in long robes; 12:41–43, rich/poor; 13:1, wonderful buildings; 14:6, beautiful thing;
14:13, man carrying a jar of water; 14:35, a little further; 14:40, eyes were heavy; 14:54,
Peter warming himself by the fire; 15:21, Simon coming in from the country; 15:36,
sponge put on a reed; 15:43, Joseph a respected member of the council; 15:46, linen
shroud, tomb hewn out of a rock; 16:4, stone was very large; 16:5, sitting on the right
side.

[54] I do not include Mark's use of specific numbers in the text, for example: 5:1
(2000 pigs); 6:37 (200 denarii); 6:43 (12 baskets); 6:44 (5000 men); 6:48 (fourth
watch of the night); 8:9 (4000 people); 14:5 (300 denarii).

social status in the Roman Republic and early Roman Empire,[55] and also properly provide him (as king) with a "crown" (of thorns, 15:17). They salute him as "king of the Jews" (15:18), and mockingly kneel down in homage before him (15:19). They lead him out and crucify him with an inscription indicating his crime—"the king of the Jews" (15:26). The chief priests mock him as the "king of the Jews" who cannot save himself (15:32).

2. Green

Mark 6:39 describes the grass on which Jesus commands the 5000 to sit as "green" grass (χλωρῷ χόρτῳ). As used in the pericope, the use of the color seems unnecessary and in some ways redundant. It would have been sufficient simply to say "on the grass," as Matt 14:19 has it, or simply "sit down" as Luke 6:14 has it. John also omits the color (6:10).

Mark had used χόρτον (4:28) earlier without the modifier "green": "The earth automatically produces—first the χόρτον (the "grass," i.e., tiny shoots, blades), then the spikes of wheat, then the full (i.e., ripened) grain (σῖτον) in the spike." The image sets out the full reproductive cycle of wheat. The young tender shoots appear first followed by the "spike," and then the ripened grain in the spike. There can be no question that Mark *conceived* the first "blades" to pierce the earth as tender, green, or "living," though it is not so described. In 6:39 Mark clearly "conceives" the area where the people sit as carpeted with "living" or green grass, since it is described as χλωρός. The modifier "green" creates a visual image of the area where the people recline as being carpeted with "living" grass rather than dry, withered, or dead grass. Such a distinction between kinds of grasses (i.e., dry/living) seems to be a common use in the Hebrew Scriptures (Ps 37:2; 90:5–6; 2 Kgs 12:26; Ezek 20:47; Isa 15:16; 37:27; 40:6–8). But why make such a distinction at all? There is no apparent reason in the context, as was seen to be the case in the use of "purple" in Mark 15:17, 20. Likely it is simply a question of the way the author conceives the grass. In 6:39 Mark conceives it as "living" or "green" and describes it that way. In 4:28, however, although it is clear that Mark conceives it as "green," it is not described in that way. The inclusion of the modifier in one case and its omission in the other is simply due to the inadvertence of the author.

---

[55] R. Moyer, *History of Purple as a Status Symbol in Antiquity* (Collection Latomus 116; Bruxelles: Latomus Revue d 'Etudes, 1970) 37–61.

3. White

The use of the color "white" (16:5) is also not as clear as the use of purple in 15:17, 20. One might be tempted to read 16:5 "a young man . . . dressed in a white robe" (στολήν . . . λευκήν) in the light of the transfiguration story (9:2–8) and, like Matthew (Matt 28:2–3), take the designation "white" as Mark's way of describing the young man as an angel.[56] But Mark knows the difference between angels and young men (1:13; 8:38; 12:25; 13:27, 32). It is hard to imagine that Mark would not specifically have identified the young man at the tomb as an angel, if indeed he was. Mark has no hesitation in describing angels serving Jesus in the wilderness (1:13), to declare Jesus as the beloved son (of God) by heavenly voices at his baptism (1:11) and the transfiguration (9:7), and to surround Jesus on that occasion with the great, deceased Hebrews, Elijah and Moses. Why would Mark have hesitated to have Jesus' resurrection announced by an angel (unequivocally so identified) at the empty tomb and instead hint at it in an oblique way? There was no longer a secret to be kept, for Jesus had already claimed to be Messiah, the son of the blessed (14:62) before the high priest, and had been recognized as Son of God by the centurion (15:39). Quite probably the reason Mark does not specifically identify him as an angel is because he is simply a young man, and those who find him to be an angel are reading Mark in the light of Matthew and Luke.[57]

---

[56] So Adela Yarbro Collins, *The Beginning of the Gospel. Probings of Mark in Context* (Minneapolis: Fortress, 1992) 135–36, and also U. Wilckens, "στολή," *TDNT* 7 (1971) 687–91, esp. 691.

[57] See M. W. Meyer, "The Youth in Secret Mark and the Beloved Disciple in John," *Gospel Origins and Christian Beginnings* (J. E. Goehring et al., eds.; Forum Fascicles 1; Sonoma, CA: Polebridge, 1990) 94–105, esp. 97–98, and id. "The Youth in the Secret Gospel of Mark," *Semeia* 49 (1990) 139–49. Meyer argues that there is a sub-plot in Mark (with the Secret Gospel of Mark [SGM]) consisting of the following: Mark 10:17–22, SGM section 1, SGM section 2, Mark 14:51–52, Mark 16:1–8. He concludes that the νεανίσκος (in Mark 16:5) is the young man of 14:51–52. B. Standaert (*L'Evangile selon Marc. Commentaire* [Paris: Les Editions du Cerf, 1983] 112) links the young man at the tomb with John the Baptist as one of two "messengers" of the good news of Jesus (Mark 1:2). Actually there are more than two "messengers" in the gospel of Mark that bear witness to Jesus: the narrator, 1:1; John the Baptist, 1:2; a voice from heaven, 1:11; demons, 1:24, 3:11; a demoniac, 5:7; Peter, 8:29; a voice from the crowd, 9:7; 11:9–10; the centurion, 15:39; the young man at the tomb, 16:5–7. The "sudden" appearance of the young man at the tomb is no more sudden, unexpected, or incongruous than other characters that Mark introduces into the narrative. Virtually all of these characters appear suddenly: the man with the withered hand, 3:11; the demonized man at the tombs, 5:2; the Syrophoenician woman, 7:25; the rich youth, 10:17; and the woman who anointed Jesus's feet in the house of Simon the leper, 14:3.

The young man "dressed in a white robe" at the tomb may be intended to evoke the young man in 14:51–52, whom the reader last saw running away naked, but who is now dressed in a "white" robe as opposed to the finer quality σινδών (linen cloth) that he lost in the garden. But if so, why specify it as being white? The simple designation robe (στολή) would have been sufficient to contrast his present attire with his former dress, had that been the case.

It is more likely that the use of the color is a redundancy, a simple inadvertent "slip" on the part of the author. Of course the στολή is white, for that is the way males usually dressed (in undyed garments; hence white or off white; see the discussion above). The color "white" in this instance is not an arcane symbolic code that has to be explained. It is just the way Mark conceives and describes the garment, including its color for no particular arcane reason.

Mark can also describe robes (12:38) and tunics (χιτών, 6:9) without using a color code, although white is likely the way the garments were conceptualized by both author and reader, absent statements to the contrary. White generally and for formal occasions, as noted above, was the usual custom for gentlemen in the Roman world,[58] unless one were royalty, or a victorious general, or wealthy.[59] Dingy, or grey, togas were associated with a reversal of political fortunes or mourning.[60] And white garments for formal occasions seem to be the case in the Septuagint and elsewhere in the New Testament as well.[61]

The explanation for the young man at the tomb is that he just got there earlier than the two Marys.

[58] Johnston, *The Private Life of the Romans*, 159, section 237; 161, section 240; 164–65, section 244, and see the discussion above.

[59] Johnston, *The Private Life of the Romans*, 166, section 246.

[60] Johnston, *The Private Life of the Romans*, 166, 246.

[61] It is true that the state of the blessed is symbolized by the wearing of white (Rev 3:4–5; 3:18; 4:4; 6:11; 7:9.13–14; 2 Esdr 2:38–40) and that God (Dan 7:9) and angels (Matt 28:2–3, cf. 2 Macc 11:6–8) are also so portrayed. But this application of white to the state of the blessed derives initially from the high social status of white garments in the ancient world. In the LXX, for example, the robes of priests and the preferred garment for official functions is described as στολή (*TDNT* 7.688–90). For Koheleth the ideal state was that robes should always be white (Eccl 9:8). In other words, not every reference to white robes in the New Testament period inevitably evokes a divine image: it could as easily evoke the image of property, wealth, high social status, decorum, and custom. The selection of white robes to symbolize an ideal state has as much to do with the social status of white garments in the Roman periods as with the classic contrast between light and darkness and good and evil. Wilckens (*TDNT* 7. 690, note 27) reports that white was the national dress of later Jewish kings.

5. Conceptual Imprecision in the Gospel of Mark

Mark's use of "white" in 16:5 is similar to the way "spirit" is used. Mark almost always qualifies the spirit that possesses some poor misfortunate as an "unclean" spirit (1:23, 26, 27; 3:11, 30; 5:2, 8, 13; 6:7; 7:25), "dumb" spirit (9:17), "dumb and deaf" spirit (9:25), or demon (3:15, 22; 5:15, 18; 6:13; 7:26–30). In other uses of spirit Mark is always careful to specify what kind of spirit: Holy Spirit (1:8; 3:29; 12:36; 13:11) or "his" (meaning human) spirit (2:8; 8:12). In only four instances does Mark deviate from the careful distinguishing of spirit. With one exception in these four instances, it is clear that Mark *conceives* the Spirit as either "unclean" (9:20) or "holy" (1:10, 12), although it is not so specified. The exception (14:38) seems to be the "human" spirit, as used in 2:18 and 8:12.

There are two other situations in Mark where one can see the author conceptualizing in a particular way but failing to specify it that way. In the use of θάλασσα only twice does Mark describe which "sea" is being conceptualized; it is the "sea of Galilee" (1:16; 7:31). Yet it is quite clear in virtually every other instance[62] where θάλασσα is used in the text (ten instances), that Mark is speaking of the "sea of Galilee" (1:16; 2:13; 3:7; 4:1, 39; 5:1, 13, 21; 6:47–49), although Mark does not specify which sea in those cases.

Mark's use of the word "disciple" (μαθητής) provides another example of Mark conceptualizing without specifying. Mark specifies a special group of Jesus's followers as "the Twelve" (δώδεκα, 3:14, 16; 4:10; 6:7; 9:35; 10:32; 11:11; 14:10, 17, 20, 43).[63] Mark specifically names the members of this small group of twelve members at 3:14–19. Mark had, however, already named five "followers" before this selection of "twelve" (1:17, 18, 20; 2:14): Simon, Andrew, James, and John (1:16–20), and Levi, the son of Alphaeus (2:14; he is never mentioned again), whom one must assume that Mark already conceived as "disciples" even before the call narrative, though that is not specified (2:15). Mark implies at other places that there were many "followers" in addition to the "Twelve." For example, he describes "those about him with the Twelve" (4:10); "those whom he desired" out of whom "he appointed Twelve" (2:15); the women "who followed him and ministered to him" (15:40–41).

Throughout the gospel, Mark is seldom careful to specify the content of the term "disciple." It is generally used absolutely with no clarification

---

[62] The two instances where it is unclear are 9:42 and 11:23. Mark 4:41 seems to be a generic use of sea, i.e., "every sea."

[63] Mark's use of ἀπόστολοι in 6:30 is an anachronistic slip.

as to who constituted this group (2:16, 18, 23; 3:7, 9; 4:34; 5:31; 6:1, 35, 41; 7:2, 5, 17; 8:1, 4, 6, 27, 33, 34; 9:14, 18, 28; 10:10, 13, 23, 24, 46; 11:1, 14; 12:43; 13:1; 14:32). On the basis of Mark 2:15, however, one would assume that all "followers" were also disciples and hence were included in the designation "disciple."[64]

There are several places in the text, however, where Mark seems to *conceive* of "disciples" as limited to the Twelve only. For example, the number of disciples that usually went with Jesus in the boat were more likely "conceived" by Mark as the Twelve, rather than the many that Mark implies follow Jesus (cf. 4:34–41; 6:45–51; 8:10). Boats after all had a limited capacity.[65] In the third passion prediction (10:32–34), Jesus takes "the Twelve again" (10:32) and explains that the Son of man must suffer. The use of δώδεκα in this instance forces the reader to understand that the general word "disciples" in the first two passion predictions (8:31–34; 9:30–32) was conceived by Mark as the Twelve only, although Mark does not make that specific in those passages.

At the last meal of Jesus with his disciples (14:17–26), it is clearly only the Twelve that are conceived as being present (14:17, 20). That being the case, one must assume that the "disciples" with whom Jesus will eat the Passover in Mark 14:14 are also conceived as the "Twelve" only, although Mark does not make that clear in 14:12–16.[66] But, on the other hand, the word "disciples" in Mark 14:13 is probably conceived as a larger group of disciples, from whom Jesus sent two on ahead to prepare the Passover meal (14:16) that Jesus and the Twelve would eat together.

Finally, the "disciples" (i.e., "them" αὐτούς, αὐτοῖς in 10:42) that are represented as receiving the instructions in 10:43–45 are conceived as the

---

[64] Assuming that it is describing the nearest antecedent "disciples," and not the more distant "toll collectors and sinners."

[65] Shelley Wachsmann, "The Galilee Boat," *BAR* 14 (1988) 19–33, esp. 32–33 where Wachsmann concludes that fifteen persons five feet five inches tall averaging 140 pounds each could be accommodated in the Galilee boat.

[66] Adela Yarbro Collins has argued that Mark 14:12–16 and 14:17–21 were originally traditional narratives that Mark appropriated and combined. Part of her argument is based on tensions she finds between the two narratives. One of those tensions is "the unclarity about whether only the twelve or a wider group shared the meal with Jesus. Verses 12–16 imply a larger group, but vv 17–21 imply that only the twelve were present" (*Beginning of the Gospel*, 104–5). If Jesus sends two disciples ahead to prepare the Passover meal (14:13) and then subsequently "came with the Twelve" (14:17), then the "disciples" mentioned in 14:14 must have been conceived as the Twelve only, since that is all who appear to be present in 14:17–21. This is true even though 14:12–16 clearly affirms a larger group of disciples.

"Twelve" only. James and John ask for special consideration (10:35–40). When the other "ten" learn of it (10:41), they were indignant.

One final remark on Mark's use of the term "disciple" must be made. In 16:7 Mark appears to contrast Peter and the disciples in such a way that one might suspect that Peter is no longer conceived by Mark to be a "disciple," since he had denied Jesus (14:66–72). But clearly Mark is not excluding Peter, since the message is meant for all (i.e., the "disciples," including Peter and the women). Mark simply "conceives" of the group of disciples in a fluid way.

6. *Instances of Inadvertence in the Gospel of Mark*

An inadvertence is anything in the text that the author introduces without due deliberation, or anything the author likely would have modified or perhaps removed had it been noticed. All writers are subject to such "slips" of the mind in composition, and even in material that has been extensively proofed to eliminate such infelicities one can still find them. In a sense they are the debris of the creative process. Every writer knows how easy it is to omit an essential concept, word, or sentence; or carelessly to express oneself with imprecision; or even to include unnecessary expressions.[67] Mark as a writer is not immune to this common malady of all writers. What follows is a list of some of the inadvertences that can be found in Mark.

(a) Mark 1:44: It is unclear who Mark wishes to designate with αὐτοῖς.[68]

(b) Mark 1:45: The antecedent of ἤρξατο and αὐτὸν δύνασθαι is ambiguous. Either Jesus or the healed leper makes reasonable sense in the context.

(c) Mark 5:8: This verse tries to correct the fact that Mark had inadvertently failed to explain why the demoniac had come rushing up to Jesus. Mark 5:8 explains in a parenthetical statement that it was because Jesus had earlier told the demon to come out of the man. But that creates another problem; precisely when was this supposed to have happened. Jesus had never been to this area before and it could not have been in

---

[67] Two of the best known inadvertencies in the New Testament are 1 Cor 1:14–16 and Gal 1:6–7. However, the redundancies, or careless expressions, are important in that they constitute the signature of narrator/author.

[68] See Vincent Taylor, *The Gospel According to St. Mark. The Greek Text with Introduction, Notes, and Indexes* (London: Macmillan, 1959) 190 for the literature.

this encounter, since the man came running from afar (5:6), as soon as Jesus got off the boat (5:2).

(d) Mark 5:17: In 5:17 it is initially unclear who is being requested to leave the neighborhood. Mark 5:18 makes it clear that it is Jesus being requested to leave, but 5:18 does not appear to be a deliberate clarification of 5:17. In a sense Mark "inadvertently" clears up the problem that was created in 5:17.

(e) Mark 5:21–24, 35–43: Was the little girl dead or merely "sleeping"? If one believes the actors in the story she was dead (5:35, 38, 40), but if one believes Jesus, she was only asleep (5:39). Mark never clarifies the situation.[69]

(f) Mark 5:34: Mark reports that the woman was healed in 5:29, but then inadvertently has Jesus pronounce the healing words in 5:34.

(g) Mark 9:35: Mark apparently overlooks the fact that a crowd had already been introduced at 9:15. The second crowd is really unnecessary. But perhaps it is another instance of Mark's "more and bigger" emphasis.

(h) Mark 9:35: On his way to Jerusalem Jesus is instructing the Twelve (cf. 10:32–34) about his forthcoming death (9:30–32). Jesus and the Twelve enter a house and they are talking together (9:33–34). Apparently overlooking this fact, Mark has Jesus summon the Twelve—who were represented as already being present with him in the house (9:35).

(i) Mark 10:13–14: Mark never identifies who it was that brought the children to him. Because of the context (Mark 10:1), one might assume it to be the crowds, but it is unclear in Mark.

(j) Mark 10:35, 41: Mark neglects to mention the change of setting between 10:34 and 35. James and John come to him with a question (10:35), but they were already with him (10:32) and did not need to "come to him." Also in the present arrangement of the text the other ten were present to hear the exchange between Jesus and James and John. They would not have needed to be "called to Jesus" (10:42).

(k) Mark 14:44: This verse is a parenthetical statement providing information that should logically have preceded 14:43.

(l) Mark 16:4: Mark has neglected to tell the reader who removed the stone (15:46) from the tomb, even though the women going to the tomb expected to find it closed (16:3). One might assume that it was the young man who had preceded them to the tomb and who was there when they arrived (16:5), but Mark leaves it unclear.

---

[69] See C. W. Hedrick, "Miracle Stories as Literary Compositions: The Case of Jairus's Daughter," *PerRelSt* 20 (1993) 217–33.

7. Some Possible Redundancies in the Gospel of Mark

There are several instances in Mark where the author appears to have used redundant language. A "redundancy" in narration is a superfluous use of words, a repetition unnecessary to communicate the idea being expressed. It is a common feature of narrative. No writer is in absolute control of the material.

(a) Mark 4:34: In the expression τοῖς ἰδίοις μαθηταῖς the use of ἰδίοις is really unnecessary to identify whose disciples were being addressed. That is clear from the pronominal use of the article.

(b) Mark 4:39: διεγερθείς (having awakened) is redundant since the disciples had already awakened Jesus (ἐγείρουσιν) in 4:38.

(c) Mark 6:33: πεζῇ (on foot) is redundant since one would expect people to "run together" (συνέδραμον) precisely on their feet. The word is not necessary to complete the thought of the verb (cf. Acts 3:11).

(d) Mark 12:25 and 13:32: The expression angels "in heaven" is certainly not necessary to qualify which angels, as the lack of the modifying expression in 1:13, 8:38, and 13:27 shows.

(e) Mark 13:20: "Whom he chose" (οὕς ἐξελέξατο) is redundant, since such a concept is already expressed in "the elect."

(f) Finally the fact that Mark can use the word πνεῦμα without the modifier ἅγιος (holy) at Mark 1:10, 12, although that is clearly what Mark conceives in those two instances, suggests that the designation "holy" in other instances may be superfluous or gratuitous.

III. Conclusion

The graphic use of color in Mark has been explained in various ways: as an original historical allusion,[70] as a novelistic feature,[71] and as a symbol.[72] The first cannot be entertained as a plausible option. Mark does

---

[70] See, for example, A. Plummer, *The Gospel According to St. Mark* (Grand Rapids: Baker, 1982) 173 (on 6:39); C. E. B. Cranfield, *The Gospel According to Saint Mark* (Cambridge: Cambridge University Press, 1959) 218 (on 6:39); R. G. Bratcher and E. A. Nida, *A Translator's Handbook on the Gospel of Mark* (Leiden: E. J. Brill for the United Bible Societies, 1961) 206 (on 6:39).

[71] See, for example, E. P. Gould, *A Critical and Exegetical Commentary on the Gospel According to St. Mark* (New York: Scribners, 1922) 118 (on 6:39).

[72] V. Taylor, *The Gospel According to St. Mark* (New York: St. Martins, 1959) 606 (on 16:5); W. L. Lane, *The Gospel According to Mark. The English Text with Introduction, Exposition and Notes* (Grand Rapids: Eerdmans, 1974) 586–87 (on 16:5); D. E. Nineham, *Saint Mark* (Philadelphia: Westminster, 1963) 444 (on 16:5); C. F. D.

not write with the authority of an eyewitness, nor does Mark reflect the sensitivities of a historian or show any interest in chronological sequence in chapters 1–13.[73] In any case the description of the robe as white in 16:5 is not a historical allusion that goes back to an original setting in the life of Jesus.

As to the second, Mark has no real interest in enhancing the sensual visual appreciation for the reader of the text. Mark has simply missed too many opportunities in the narration to enhance the reader's visual appreciation. For example, Jesus' experience in the wilderness (1:12–13) could easily have been enhanced so as to enable the reader to experience this rather dramatic event—an "eyeball to eyeball confrontation" between Jesus and Satan! The story of Jairus's daughter (6:22–24, 35–43) could have been enhanced by showing the parents' personal suffering or describing more graphically the scene that Jesus found at the home (6:38). Particularly the narrative about the beheading of John the Baptist (6:14–29) could easily have been visually enhanced by describing the elaborate trappings of the banquet (6:21), the "seductive" dance of Herodias' daughter (6:22), or the glee of Herodias at getting John where she wanted him (6:24), or even the death of John (6:27). There are just too many missed opportunities throughout the text seriously to assume that Mark deliberately visually enhances the narrative for novelistic reasons at 6:39 and 16:5 by describing the color of the grass as green and the robe of the young man at the tomb as white.

The third option (symbolic) has been addressed earlier in the paper and absent some specific guidance from the author symbolic interpretations may only be creative readings that derive from the imagination of the reader.

This paper has attempted to establish the plausibility of the author's "conceptualization" and inadvertent narration as another way of explaining phenomena in the text.

Moule, *The Gospel According to Mark* (Cambridge: Cambridge University Press, 1965) 131 (on 16:5).

[73] C. W. Hedrick, "What is a Gospel? Geography, Time, Narrative Structure," *PerRelSt* 10 (1983) 255–68, esp. 260–61.

Divine Birth and Apparent Parents:
The Plot of the Fourth Gospel

Jo-Ann A. Brant
Goshen College

The abandonment of a child by a father, tension between the adoptive parents' desires for and authority over the foster child, confusion regarding the child's true identity given telltale signs of noble descent, the play between the hoped-for wedding and the ever present danger of death—these are ingredients of the ancient Greek novel. These are also elements of the Gospel of John. This synopsis does not resemble the scholarly plot summaries that describe the story of Jesus, the Word incarnate, who descends, fulfills God's will as the obedient son, and returns to his father.[1] The characterization of Jesus as the perfect child mistakes the message of the gospel for its plot and neglects the complication at the narrative level of Jesus having a second set of parents. With his mother, he is cold and aloof and grudgingly does as she asks. He is estranged from his brothers: they mock him and he is less than frank with them. The existence of this other family causes Jesus problems. His claim to heavenly descent is met with the counterclaim that he is the son of Joseph.[2] The tension between family loyalty and the call of God is inherent in the Christian message, but Paul and the Synoptics remedy the offensiveness of the call to convert and to alienate oneself from one's kin

---

[1] Typically, analyses of John's plot have focused upon the cosmological tale, the descent and reascent of the Word. This is perhaps epitomized by R. Alan Culpepper, "The Plot of John's Story of Jesus, *Int* 49 (1995) 347–58, esp. 356. Cf. also Raymond E. Brown, *The Gospel According to John* (2 vols., AB 29–29A; New York: Doubleday, 1966) 1.19; Godfrey C. Nicholson, *Death as Departure: The Johannine Descent and Ascent Schema* (SBLDS 63; Chico, CA: Scholars Press, 1983) 21; Robert Kysar, *John's Story of Jesus* (Philadelphia: Fortress, 1984) 18, and Dorothy A. Lee who, like many Johannine scholars, examines the elements of plot in terms of symbolic narrative pointing to the descent-ascent story, excludes the wedding at Cana and the passion from this category (*The Symbolic Narrative of the Fourth Gospel: The Interplay of Form and Meaning* [JSNTSup 95; Sheffield: Sheffield Academic Press, 1994]).

[2] John 1:45 and 6:42; cf. 7:27, 41.

by emphasizing that conversion marks the entrance into the eschatological family of God.[3] While this language is not completely absent in the Fourth Gospel, in its high Christology, God is Jesus' actual father, while Jesus assumes the role of parent calling the disciples his "little children" (13:33) who are temporarily "orphaned" at his death (14:18). In the Fourth Gospel, death for a friend's sake rather than for family is held up as the greatest expression of love (John 15:13). Familial tension is an integral part of the plot of the Gospel, just as it is in the Greek novel, and the Gospel writer deals with its offensiveness through narrative strategies and conventions also found in these novels.

Beginning with the Church Fathers, exegetes have been predisposed to deal with the role of Jesus' family at a symbolic level.[4] Mary represents either Jewish Christianity,[5] the new Eve, or the Church.[6] Jesus' brothers stand in for the Synoptics' Satan and function as temptors.[7] Recently, attention has turned from symbolic readings to readings that expose the complexity of the narrative thereby rendering the equation of particular characters with particular referents unnecessary and even undesirable.[8]

---

[3] Adriana Destro and Mauro Pesce state that the opposition between kinship and discipleship is absent in John because discipleship rather than kinship is the structural criterion for group identity. While they are correct in stating that oppositional language is absent, their own analysis points to the dramatization of the tension ("Kinship, Discipleship and Movement: An Anthropological Study of John's Gospel," *BI* 3 [1995] 266–84, esp. 266). John Painter claims that the tension between Jesus and his mother is resolved because the text "implies that the the [*sic*] eschatological family of believers has displaced the biological family" so that when Jesus hands Mary off to the beloved disciple he is constituting that eschatological family, but this conclusion rests upon a canonical reading (*The Quest for the Messiah* [Nashville: Abingdon, 1993] 198). Cf. Wayne Meeks (*The Moral World of the Early Christians* [Philadelphia: Westminster, 1986] 129) for a brief description of the pagan world's reaction to Christianity's lack of family loyalty.

[4] For a recent treatment of the symbolic structure see Craig R. Koester's *Symbolism in the Fourth Gospel: Meaning, Mystery, Community* (Minneapolis: Fortress, 1995) 81, 215.

[5] Rudolf Bultmann, *The Gospel of John: A Commentary* (G. R. Beasley-Murray, trans.; Philadelphia: Westminster, 1971) 673.

[6] Justin *Trypho* c 5; PG 6:712; Irenaeus *Adv. Haer.* 3.22:4; PG 7:959; Brown, *John*, 1.109; 2.926; Max Thurian, *Mary, Mother of All Christians* (New York: Herder and Herder, 1964) 144–66; Joseph A. Grassi, "The Wedding at Cana (John II 1–11): A Pentecostal Meditation?" *NovT* 14 (1972) 131–36, esp. 133.

[7] Brown, *John*, 1.208; Mark Stibbe argues that the brothers stand in parallel with Israel; both Jesus' spiritual and natural family reject him (*John as Story Teller: Narrative Criticism and the Fourth Gospel* [SNTSMS 73; Cambridge: Cambridge University Press, 1992] 159).

[8] Cf. Jeffrey Lloyd Staley, "Subversive Narration/Victimized Reader," *JSNT* 51 (1993) 79–98, esp. 90.

The narrative of the Fourth Gospel is a synthesis of two distinct stories—the cosmological tale and the life and death of Jesus of Nazareth—into one coherent narrative.[9] Yury M. Lotman describes two strategies that novelists use to carry two storylines. The first is a narrative frame that provides a key for interpreting the encoded rhetoric in the primary narrative that signifies the second story. In the case of the Fourth Gospel, the prologue serves as a frame that guides the reader in seeing how the story of Jesus of Nazareth is actually an episode in the story of the cosmic narrative. The prologue, therefore, legitimizes symbolic readings and inspires the scholarly plot summaries. The Fourth Gospel also uses Lotman's second strategy: the two stories are told as an uninterrupted account in which the second narrative is "introduced in fragments, such as citations, references, epigraphs, and the like."[10] In the case of the Fourth Gospel, the reader is able to understand Jesus' speech and the irony on the lips of secondary characters as symbolic reference to the cosmic narrative. Simultaneously, Jesus' words and the ironic conclusions of his audience provoke action within the historical narrative. The semiotic elements that point to the cosmic narrative function as the encoded rhetoric that generates the historical plot.

Although the ancient novels are composed for the most part later than the Fourth Gospel, both Gospel and novel emerge as examples of an anticanonical genre that continually push against the constraints of literary conventions, some of which they share, while drawing from a literary ferment, parts of which they share.[11] As a result comparable narrative structures are not coincidental. The following comparison of the Fourth Gospel to ancient Greek novels serves to draw attention to the narrative function of material commonly treated symbolically in scholarship.

---

[9] Cf. Adele Reinhartz (*The Word in the World: The Cosmological Tale in the Fourth Gospel* [SBLMS 45; Atlanta: Scholars Press, 1992]) for the distinction between cosmological and historical narratives.

[10] Yury M. Lotman, "The Text within the Text," *PMLA* 109 (1994) 377–84, esp. 382–83.

[11] Michael Holquist, "Introduction" to M. M. Bakhtin, *The Dialogic Imagination: Four Essays by M. M. Bakhtin* (C. Emerson and M. Holquist, trans.; Austin: University of Texas Press, 1981) i–xxxiv, esp. xxxi. Walter L. Reed argues persuasively for the application of Bakhtin's theories of the carnivalesque and dialogic to the Gospels (*Dialogues of the Word: The Bible as Literature according to Bakhtin* [New York: Oxford University Press, 1993]).

The Abandoned Child

Jesus finds himself in his predicament because God has left him to be raised by two people without status; he is abandoned to the physical forces of this world leaving him vulnerable to death. The typical reader refrains from making the impious charge that God has exposed his child and from having the equally impious thought that Jesus' status is not altogether legitimate.[12] The Gospel writer is careful to set God in opposition to the parents of antiquity who commonly abandoned their children.[13] God stands beyond the charge of committing an "unholy crime against his child" that Clytemnestra brings against Agamemnon when he proposes to sacrifice his daughter Iphigenia for the sake of the Argives.[14] Jesus does not question his loyalty to his divine father unlike Heracles who, abandoned by Zeus to be raised by Amphitryon, acknowledges his adoptive parent as his true father and says of his birth:

> When a house is built on poor foundations, then its descendants are the heirs of grief. Then Zeus—whoever Zeus may be—begot me for Hera's hatred.[15]

By asserting that God is compelled by the irresistible force of love rather than from a desire to see his son dead, the Gospel writer, in the language of René Girard, poetically minimizes the divine crime.[16] Several of the

---

[12] John Boswell observes that the story of Jesus' birth in the Gospel tradition is "redolent, in a starkly ironic way, of the abandonments that gave rise to the great houses of the Ionians and Romans . . ." (*The Kindness of Strangers: The Abandonment of Children in Western Europe From Late Antiquity to the Renaissance* [New York: Pantheon, 1988] 154. Cf. Daniel Ogden for a discussion of the notion of legitimacy in antiquity (*Greek Bastardy in the Classical and Hellenistic Periods* [Oxford: Clarendon, 1996]).

[13] Boswell provides the following list of heroes abandoned by their divine parents: Livy's version of the Romulus and Remus story, Oedipus, Ion, Cyrus, Paris, Telephus, Jupiter, Poseidon, Aesculapius, Hephaistos, Attis and Cybele (*The Kindness of Strangers*, 76–77). Proof that later Christians drew comparisons can be found in Johannes Burmeister, *Sacri Mater Virgo*, 1621, who adapted Plautus' *Amphitryo* into the story of Mary and Joseph. Cited in Marie Maclean, "The Heirs of Amphitryon: Social Fathers and Natural Fathers," *New Literary History* 26 (1995) 787–807, esp. 795.

[14] Euripides, *Iphigenia in Aulis* 1104–5 in *The Complete Greek Tragedies* (9 vols.; D. Greene and R. Lattimore, trans.; Chicago: University of Chicago Press, 1958) 4.353.

[15] Euripides, *Heracles* 1261–65 in *Complete Greek Tragedies*, 3.331. Maclean describes the romance of parenting the adulterine child and draws a parallel between the honoring of Joseph in the Synoptics and the honoring of Amphitryon. Joseph gets no such recognition in the Fourth Gospel ("The Heirs of Amphitryon: Social Fathers and Natural Fathers," 787–807).

[16] Cf. René Girard, *The Scapegoat* (Y. Freccero, trans.; Baltimore: Johns Hopkins University Press, 1986) 76–94. Brown recognizes a parallel between God's commitment of Jesus to death and the Aqedah and suggests that "Abraham's

Greek novelists use comparable strategies in order to sustain claims upon children for obedience to multiple sets of parents. In Longus' *Daphnis and Chloe*, Dionysophanes, Daphnis' biological father, apologizes, "Daphnis, don't hold it as a grudge against me that I exposed you; it was from no desire of mine that I formed this plan."[17] Chloe's father blames the expense of civic life for his attempt at infanticide. The excuses seem lame; after all, Longus is drawing a contrast between the natural pastoral life and the artificial city life. Animals teach humans how to be parents in this novel. A clearer parallel can be drawn between God and Persinna, the mother in *An Ethiopian Tale*, who can claim that she abandons Charikleia in order to save herself and the child; she acts on the strongest of instincts, survival and maternal love.[18] Love motivates the choice of the parent to abandon the child to death thereby rendering later claims upon the child socially and morally warranted.

Like the exposed children of the novels, Jesus has signs that point to his parentage. This is familiar territory that has been mapped by the history-of-religions school in an attempt to locate the Johannine Jesus within the construct of the Hellenistic *theios anēr.*[19] Nevertheless, the narrative function of the signs remains to be explored. Among their many roles, the signs facilitate poetic minimization by pointing to the fact that God intends to restore his son to his side (6:27, 40). Moreover, they serve to exonerate God from the charge that he has caused his son's death. Girard cites numerous cases in classical literature in which the guilt of a god is attributed to a violent community which misunderstands divine communication.[20] In the Fourth Gospel, the object of forgiveness shifts from God to Caiaphas and the Jewish leaders; the villains of the story

---

generosity in sacrificing his only son was to be beneficial to all the nations of the world" (*John,* 1.147). Nils A. Dahl (*Jesus the Christ* [Minneapolis: Fortress, 1991] 138–40) and Robert Daly ("The Soteriological Significance of the Sacrifice of Isaac," *CBQ* 39 [1977] 45–75, esp. 67–68) also see the Aqedah as preparation to see God's actions as only good. But the ancient reader was not comfortable with the idea that God commanded that Isaac, whom Abraham loved, should die (cf. *Jub.* 18:16; 4Q225; Philo, *Abr.* 170). Robin M. Jensen notes the absence of overt declarations in New Testament writings that Christ's sacrifice is prefigured by Isaac's offering ("The Offering of Isaac in Jewish and Christian Tradition," *BI* 2 [1994] 85–110, esp. 98).

[17] Longus, *Daphnis and Chloe* 4.24, in *Collected Ancient Greek Novels* (B. P. Reardon, ed.; Berkeley: University of California Press, 1989) 342–3.

[18] Heliodorus, *An Ethiopian Story* 4.8, in *Collected Ancient Greek Novels,* 432–34.

[19] Cf. W. Nicol for a succinct presentation of this theory (*The Semeia in the Fourth Gospel: Tradition and Redaction* [Leiden: E. J. Brill, 1972] 48–55).

[20] Girard, *Scapegoat,* 83.

become the ones who do not interpret the signs properly rather than the father who abandons his child to death. Similarly, the villains of the ancient Greek novels tend to be the suitors and abductors rather than the parents. When Habrocomes and Anthia, in *An Ephesian Tale*, become the objects of their pirate captors' lust, they invoke rather than curse their parents who have foolishly sent them on their journey.[21] In *The Story of Apollonius King of Tyre*, Apollonius' offence in relinquishing his natural responsibility for his child is mitigated when the adoptive parents criminally abrogate their contractual obligation. Tarsia's finery, left by Apollonius as tokens of her status, provokes jealousy and motivates her foster mother to have her murdered.[22] It is the world into which these children are sent by their parents that bears the guilt of any harm that comes to them.[23]

Finally, the Gospel writer avoids any tension between God's interest and Jesus' interest by portraying Jesus as one without doubt of his own lineage. In this respect, Jesus is unlike the exposed child of the novel. While knowledge of his lineage serves to reconcile Jesus to God's intentions and eliminate conflict at the level of the cosmic narrative, it provides the basis for conflict and, consequently plot development, at the level of the historical narrative. The fact that Jesus can claim that the Son does only what his Father does and wishes (John 5:19–29) sets him at odds with his human family whom he treats as adoptive.

Parent-Child Conflict

Comparison with the ancient Greek novels, in which the conflict between the child and his or her parents and its resolution provides plot development, illuminates the centrality of the conflict between Jesus and his human family in the plot of the Fourth Gospel. Mikhail Bakhtin argues that the narrative of the romantic novels is "an extratemporal haitus between two moments of biographical time" that "changes nothing in the life of the heroes."[24] He overlooks the consistent pattern within the novels in which a breach of filial obligation by a child is acknowledged and then repaired through the course of the narrative.[25] (For a list of

---

21 Xenophon of Ephesus, *An Ephesian Tale*, 2.1, in *Collected Ancient Greek Novels*, 139.

22 *The Story of Apollonius King of Tyre*, 31, in *Collected Ancient Greek Novels*, 756.

23 Cf. John 1:10; 14:17; 15:18–19; 17:25.

24 Bakhtin, *The Dialogic Imagination*, 89–90.

25 Cf. Kate Cooper's discussion of the ancient Greek novel's reconciliation of the civic necessity of marriage with the insistence on individual desire (*The Virgin and the*

these plot summaries see the appended chart.) Achilles Tatius furnishes a lucid example of the role of conflict between parent and child. In *Leucippe and Clitophon*, the two children first seek to violate their chastity and then flee from their parents to elope. From the ensuing peril, they learn modesty and that they must wait to satisfy their desires until they marry with parental approval. Both make atonement by seeking parental forgiveness, and Leucippe submits to a test of chastity before she can address her father without embarrassment.[26]

In the Fourth Gospel, the movement from Jesus' life in anonymity to his public career marks a shift from a life in Capernaum where he resides with his mother and brothers to a life of wandering with his disciples. The sequence of the Wedding at Cana narrative highlights the tension between Jesus' goals and those of his human family. The Gospel writer first introduces the setting, a wedding, then the fact that the mother of Jesus is there (2:1), and thirdly that Jesus is there, not with his mother, but with his disciples (2:3), the group for which he will lay down his life (15:13). The tension in the scene revolves around the same issue that is central in the novels: the matrimonial expectations of the parents and the child's own hopes. Jesus' mother seeks to facilitate the wedding by having Jesus supply wine. Given that the steward credits the provision of wine to the bridegroom, one can conclude that she places Jesus in that role. Normally, her social role as parent would be to arrange his marriage, and the fact that she is identified as his mother rather than by her proper name suggests that she acts in this capacity.

Jesus' rebuttal, "What is that to me or to you, woman?" (τί ἐμοὶ καὶ σοί, γύναι) (2:4a), dissociates him from his mother as one to whom he owes filial obedience. The implicit refusal is certainly a violation of decorum and the address "woman" may be no less an infraction. The amount of apologetic in the secondary literature for Jesus' calling his mother "woman" suggests that it is indeed problematic. Some commentators turn to the symbolic reading of her character; others claim that this is a polite address.[27] Adriane Destro and Mauro Pesce, using an anthropological

---

Bride: Idealized Womanhood in Late Antiquity [Cambridge: Harvard University Press, 1996] 20–44).

[26] Achilles Tatius, *Leucippe and Clitophon*, 2.19, 30; 8.5, 13–15, in *Collected Ancient Greek Novels*, 202–3, 271, 280–81.

[27] Brown suggests both but leans toward the symbolic reading (*John*, 1.99). Bultmann acknowledges that the address creates distance but sees no disrespect in it. He cites the example of Odysseus in disguise addressing Penelope as γύναι, *Od.* 19.221, but this means only that it is not an impolite address for strangers (*Gospel of*

methodology, suggest that Jesus' address marks his social independence from his mother's kinship status.[28] Jesus' rebuke also dissociates her objective—either to facilitate a human wedding or to cast Jesus in the role of groom— both from his own purpose and from what hers should be.[29] Tension is underscored by the fact that despite Jesus' protestations, his mother instructs the servants to "Do whatever he tells you to do" (2:5). She thereby indicates that she is aware of Jesus' inheritance of divine power, but nevertheless sees him as one who is duty bound to be obedient to her. Jesus must then break with his mother to avoid behaving as though his parentage were ambiguous. His assertion, "my hour has not yet come" (2:4b), implies that he objects to the occasion—a wedding that is not his own—and the source of the request. His hour of obedience comes on the cross (John 7:30; 8:20; 12:27; 19:30) when his blood serves as wine. The scene sets up the tension between the path to marriage that a mother would expect and the road to death on which the revelation of Jesus' true parentage will take him.

Once this clash of goals becomes apparent, Jesus leaves the protection of the company of his family in Capernaum (2:12). In the peripatetic wandering, like the journeys of the novels, death shadows Jesus' movement: his enemies repeatedly threaten to kill or to seize him before the appointed hour (5:18; 7:32; 8:59; 10:33). As in the novels, the signs function as sources of both protection and danger. Just as Callirhoe's beauty is treated as a sign of her noble birth that leads her captors to consider both sparing and killing her,[30] Jesus' signs provoke a divided response among his opponents; some rush to judgment while others remain cautious (7:25–31; 40–44; 10:19–21).

John, 116). Koester finds no precedent for this address (*Symbolism in the Fourth Gospel*, 78 n. 7).

[28] Destro and Pesce, "Kinship, Discipleship, and Movement," 270. It is more prevalent for a stranger to call a woman "mother" as a form of polite adddress than a child to call his mother "woman." Job 17:14 seems to use mother for a near relative and Judg 5:7 uses mother as an honorary title for Deborah. A. Geyser argues that the Fourth Gospel minimizes the significance of the physical relationship between Mary and Jesus as part of the anti-baptist polemic" ("The Semeion at Cana of the Galilee," *Studies in John Presented to Professor J. N. Sevenster on the Occasion of his Seventieth Birthday* [NovTSup 34; Leiden: E. J. Brill, 1970] 12–21, esp. 15–18).

[29] Destro and Pesce argue that "Jesus' sentence radicalizes the difference between him and his mother and thus clarifies the autonomous nature of his mission" ("Kinship, Discipleship, and Movement," 270).

[30] Chariton, *Chaereas and Callirhoe*, 1.10–11, cf. 2.1. in *Collected Ancient Greek Novels*, 32–33, cf. 38.

Jesus public career begins with the so-called "cleansing of the temple" at which he proclaims that God is his father (2:16). During his second appearance in Jerusalem, he asserts that he does his Father's work (5:17). At first, the crowd take Jesus' words metaphorically, as in the coronation psalm, "You are my son; today I have begotten you" (Psalm 2:7), and consequently try to make him king (6:15). When Jesus resists their interpretation, the crowd asks, "Is not this Jesus, whose father and mother we know?" (6:42), and some of his disciples reject him (6:66).

Jesus' claim to divine parentage also estranges him from his family. This is highlighted by the apparent enmity of his brothers who goad him into going to Jerusalem so that Jesus' disciples, from whom they have dissociated themselves, may see these works, that is, the signs of his heavenly descent (7:3). These works give enough legitimacy to Jesus' claim to raise the passions commonly directed toward adulterine children by their so-called brothers, namely enmity.[31]

As Jesus continues to assert his divine parentage, the crowd begins to question his human parentage. The accusation that Jesus is a Samaritan (8:48) possibly reflects a cultural bias, preserved in the Mishnaic tradition, that Samaritans universally are unable to be certain of who their fathers might be.[32] Inflamed by Jesus' seemingly blasphemous assertion, they pick up stones to hurl at him on several occasions (8:58; 10:31), but Jesus' appeal to contradictory evidence, his good works (10:37–38), warrants a trial, and so they attempt to arrest him. When the raising of Lazarus further substantiates Jesus' claim, the authorities resolve to have him legally executed (11:47–48). Their charge—which they change to sedition only after Pilate scoffs at them—is that he has claimed to be the Son of God (19:7). At this point, Jesus can withdraw from public life (11:54); he has attained his goal.

Jesus' willingness to subject himself to death is the ultimate confirmation that he is the obedient son of God who will not deny his father to save his own life (12:27–28). *An Ethiopian Story* also ends in a trial and a test of obedience. Hydaspes is resolved to sacrifice his virgin daughter Charikleia for the sake of his people (10.16). Those people—in contrast to the crowd in the Fourth Gospel who cry "Crucify him! Crucify him!"(19.6) and recognize Caesar as king—yell "let the girl live . . . we

---

[31] Maclean notes how pervasive this sentiment is in "both tragic and comic depictions of cuckoldry, adulterine children" ("Heirs of Amphitryon," 793).

[32] *m. Qidd. 4.3.*

recognize you as our king" (10.17).[33] In order to save and to marry her beloved, Charikleia must convince her father that she is married and thus qualified to act as priestess, that Theagenes is her husband and thus not qualified to be the victim, and that she is yet a virgin who waits for her father's consent. What is central to this discussion is the way both the Gospel and the novel balance compliance to the father's wishes and the realization of the hero's own desires.

Jesus' demonstration of filial piety toward his heavenly father in dying on the cross does not completely fulfill that obligation. Just as conflict between Jesus and his human family is necessary for plot development, resolution of the conflict is imperative. The command to honor one's mother and father follows directly after the commandments that pertain to God and holiness. The household codes point to the continued recognition of the centrality of this commandment in Christian life. In classical Greek literature, the parent-child bond is treated as sacred. Euripides, in particular, is preoccupied with this theme in his plays.[34] In *The Suppliant Women*, he writes:

> A wretched child
> Is he who does not return his parents' care.
> Noblest of gifts! By granting it, he earns
> Back from his children what he gives his parents.
> (361–64).[35]

Similarly, in the Greek novels, the resolution of the child-parent conflict is necessary for a felicitous conclusion. When the hero or heroine, or both, has more than one set of parents, the end leaves all parents receiving their due. In *An Ethiopian Story*, Charikleia has three fathers to satisfy. Kalasiris' reconciliation with his own sons and his subsequent death leaves her disencumbered of one superfluous parent. Although Charikles is not her biological father, she begs that he punish her for the crime of parricide (10.38)—given that Charikles has acted the part of

---

[33] Heliodorus, *An Ethiopian Story,* in *Collected Ancient Greek Novels,* 572. This close parallel to the language of Jesus' trial in the Fourth Gospel may substantiate ancient claims that Heliodorus was a Christian.

[34] Emily A. McDermott, *Euripides' Medea: The Incarnation of Disorder* (University Park: Pennsylvania State University Press, 1989) 81–82.

[35] In *Complete Greek Tragedies,* 4.151. The proper father-child relationship is perhaps best encapsulated by this exchange between Agamemnon and Iphigenia in *Iphigenia in Aulis:* "You said, "surely one day I shall see you / Happy in your husband's home." . . . I answered, "Father, you, / Old and reverent then, with love I shall / Receive into my home, and so repay you / For the years of trouble and your fostering / Care of me" (1223–30).

father, he deserves the rights of a father—and to her biological father, Hydaspes, she offers her chastity and the concomitant power to offer her as a bride.

Once the Gospel writer sets Jesus on a course of estrangement from his nurturing family, he must provide for that family lest Jesus' death smack of impiety. The death of Jesus marks the restoration of the Word to his proper status, but it is also the untimely death of a child. In order for this ending to be perceived as a successful resolution for the ancient reader, Jesus, who has essentially denied his human parents their social right of being cared for in their old age by dying, makes amends by entrusting his mother to the care of a friend with the words, γύναι, ἴδε ὁ υἱός σου . . . ἴδε ἡ μήτηρ σου (John 19:26–27). Destro and Pesce confirm this interpretation of the narrative at the level of social analysis:

> [T]he familial terminology has no metaphorical aim: becoming the son of Jesus' mother has practical consequences for the disciple. He has to take care of her in his own social setting.[36]

In providing for his mother, Jesus satisfies the reader that the resolution of the story is a synthesis of Jesus' social responsibility and personal desire. This speech-act may be fraught with symbolic implications, but it is also essential to the success of the plot.

The Matrimonial Death Metaphor

In the ancient Greek novel, the resolution of the story is the marriage. When the child dies an untimely death, that is before he or she has left the parental home or has had children, his or her demise is treated as analogous to marriage.[37] For example, Clitophon recites the following lament about Leucippe whom he presumes to be dead:

> What a resplendent wedding: your bedroom is a prisoner's cell; your mattress is the ground; your garlands and bracelets are hawsers and wrist ropes; the bride's escort is a brigand sleeping at the door! Instead of the wedding march we hear a funeral song.[38]

---

[36] Destro and Pesce, "Kinship, Discipleship, and Movement," 278.

[37] Jean-Pierre Vernant argues that marriage and sacrifice are homologous rites and notes that the term "Bride of Hades" is used in *Iphigeneia in Aulis* and becomes common in funerary practice for girls who die young (*Myth and Society in Ancient Greece* [1980] 138, cited in Helene Foley, *Ritual Irony: Poetry and Sacrifice in Euripides* [Ithaca, NY: Cornell University Press, 1985] 84–87).

[38] Achilles Tatius, *Leucippe and Clitophon* 3.10, in *Collected Ancient Greek Novels*, 214.

Charikleia, in a frenzy of despair over Theagenes' supposed death, unties her hair and tears her dress in mourning and then describes these acts as disrobing for the consummation of her marriage. She speaks to her imagined groom:

> Come then, let us dance too, in a manner befitting the malign power that controls our destiny! Let us smash this lamp to the ground and veil our performance in the black gloom of night! So this is the nuptial chamber our guiding deity has built for us![39]

For the most part, it is the heroine who is cast in the role of "Bride of Hades," but the death of a son may also be called a consummation, that of life rather than desire.[40]

In the Fourth Gospel, Jesus is cast in the role of bridegroom, but his desire is fulfilled in his death. The Gospel writer seems to be literalizing the analogy of death and marriage. John the Baptist identifies Jesus first as the lamb of God (1:29. 36), a sacrificial animal, and then as the bridegroom (3:29). In an elaborate play of words running throughout the gospel, the wedding wine that Jesus provides to reveal his glory becomes his blood at the hour of his glory (2:10–11; 4:13–14; 6:54–56; 7:37–38; 15:1; 18:11; 19:34). Jesus reinterprets a prenuptial act—the washing of his feet by Mary of Bethany—as preparation for death.[41] The excessive amount of myrrh used for his burial may also depend upon the image of the death bed as the bridal bed for its significance (cf. Cant 1:13; 3:6; 5:1). The design of this material emerges when the Gospel's intertextuality or shared heritage with the novel is acknowledged.

Conclusion

The similarity between the narrative structures and strategies of the ancient Greek novels and the Fourth Gospel makes evident that symbolic elements of the Gospel are not simply code for reading the cosmic narrative, dictated solely by christological considerations. The wedding setting at Cana, the language of the bridegroom, the perilous journey in

---

[39] Heliodous, *An Ethiopian Story*, 6.8, in *Collected Ancient Greek Novels*, 480.

[40] Cf. Charikles' father's lament in *Leucippe and Clitophon*, 1.13. Other examples from Euripides and the ancient Greek novels include the following: *Iphigeneia at Aulis*, 1080–88 (The entire play is about a ritual sacrifice portrayed as a fictitious marriage); *Heracles*, 480–484; *Alcestis*, 746, 912–925; *An Ethiopian Tale*, 1.31; 2.29; 8.11; 10.16; *Leucippe and Clitophon*, 3.7; 5.11; *Chaereas and Callirhoe*, 1.6; 3.10; 7.6; *An Ephesian Tale*, 3.5, 7, 8; *Joseph and Aseneth*, 10.9–17; 11.3.

[41] Cf. Jo-Ann A. Brant, "Husband Hunting: Characterization and Narrative Art in the Gospel of John," *BI* 4 (1996) 205–23, esp. 217–19.

which the signs and claims of Jesus' "noble" birth lead to his death are not merely symbols imposed upon the historical narrative. They are integral to the development of the plot and to the reception by its reader. While the Gospel neither presents shipwrecks or abductions nor titillates its reader with seductions, it offers an adventure of a hero in an alien world with the restoration of a child to his true parent and the fulfillment of love rather than its tragic demise as its end.

Appendix
Parent-Child Conflicts in Ancient Novels

Relationship	Conflict	Resolution
Kalasiris - Charikleia *An Ethiopian Tale*	Charikleia describes the complexity of the parentage question and her frustration that she cannot perform the rites of burial over Kalasiris. 7.14	Charikleia is exonerated insofar as Kalasiris has been reunited with his sons: "The father . . . [w]ho had come within an ace of the misery of having his children die within the sight of the eyes that gave them birth, himself became the agent of peace." 7.10–11
Charikles - Charikleia *An Ethiopian Tale*	Charikleia flees her adoptive father's house to marry Theagenes although her father has betrothed her to his nephew. 5.1	At the resolution of the novel, Charikleia confesses to him: "Father . . . to you I owe as much reverence as to those who gave me birth. I am a wicked parricide; punish me as you please; ignore any attempts to excuse my misdeeds by ascribing them to the will of the gods, to their governance of human life." 10.38
Hippias - Clitophon *Leucippe and Clitophon*	Clitophon has run from his father (who wants him to marry Kalligone his half-sister) because he has tried to seduce Leucippe.	Clitophon asks the gods what crime he has committed to be subject to bad fortune (3.10). With the aid of Leucippe's new found modesty, he remembers that he has been warned by Aphrodite to wait until marriage rather than ravishing her (4.1). When he learns that his marriage could have been sanctioned by both parents if he had had patience, Clitophon is too ashamed of what he has done to look his father in the eye (5.11). Nor can he look Sostratos in the eye (7.14; 8.4). In an address to Aphrodite, while Sostratos listens, he claims, "We did not want to wed without a father present." (8.5) Fortunately, Kalligone is married to Kallisthenes and Clitophon is free to marry Leucippe with her father's blessing.

Sostratos and Pantheia - Leucippe *Leucippe and Clitophon*	Leucippe allows Clitophon into her bed chamber to "deflower" her then flees from her parent's supervision to marry Clitophon.	While Leucippe is crying over her plight, Artemis appears and instructs her to remain a virgin until she becomes a bride, and Leucippe learns to shy away from Clitophon's advances. (4.1). When she encounters her father again, she is ashamed to look him in the eye (8.4), but after submitting herself to a test of her chastity, she is no longer embarrassed before her father. (8.13–15)
Ariston - Chaereas Hermocrates - Callirhoe *Chaereas and Callirhoe*	Ariston and Hermocrates are political rivals whose children fall in love.	The public appeal of the assembly leads Hermocrates to abandon his private wishes for the public will. (1.1) [When one considers the result—Chaereas "murders" Callirhoe, and Callirhoe marries Dionysius to whom she gives Chaereas' son—one wonders if the parents' private wishes should have prevailed.]
Ariston - Chaereas *Chaereas and Callirhoe*	Ariston, in the grip of old age and disease, pleads with his son not to abandon him: "Wait just a few days so that I can die in your arms; then bury me and leave." His mother makes a similar plea. Torn between his parents' appeals and his need to search for Callirhoe, Chaereas tries to drown himself. 3.5	The story ends with a joyful reunion between the children and their respective parents who had thought their offspring dead. Ariston and his wife are still alive despite their expectations. 8.6
Lycomedes and Themisto - Habrocomes Megamedes and Euippe - Anthia *Ephesian Tale*	The children fall in love and waste away.	The initial conflict is resolved in marriage when the parents succumb to pressure from their children and the public and after consulting an oracle who predicts that the children will suffer misadventures before their end is a happy one. 1.6

Lycomedes and Themisto - Habrocomes Megamedes and Euippe - Anthia *Ephesian Tale*	The conflict is between the parents' responsibility to keep their children safe and respect for Apollo's oracle. The parents try to palliate fate by sending their children on a dangerous sea voyage. 1.10	Without their parents' protection, the children are reduced to slavery and suffer the usual misadventures. The couple returns to Ephesus and builds tombs for their now dead parents and live happily ever after. 5.6 [In this tale Habrocomes' impiety is to disdain Eros and to act as though he were a god 1.1–2, but what he learns through his ordeals is not to disdain the happiness of the parental home for love. 2.8]
Unnamed parents - Hippothous and Hyperanthes *Ephesian Tale*	Hippothous poses as a tutor and abducts his pupil Hyperthanthes whom he loves. Hyperanthes then dies in a ship-wreck as they flee his parents.	Hippothous perpetually mourns the loss of his parents and his homeland. 3.1–3
Unnamed parents - Aegialeus and Thelxinoe *Ephesian Tale*	The lovers marry in secret. When Thelxinoe's parents try to arrange a marriage, the pair flees Sparta and reside in Syracuse.	Sparta condemns them to death, so they live impoverished but happpy lives in Syracuse. To balance the appearance of a happy tale, Xenophon describes a childless marriage and after Thelxinoe's death, her embalmed corpse becomes Aegialeus' only companion. 5.1
Megacles and Rhode - Chloe *Daphnis and Chloe*	This biological father abandons his daughter.	His excuse is that he exhausted his capital paying for dramatic choruses and warships and did not want to bring her up in poverty. Moreover, he has been punished by fathering no other children. 4.35
Dionysophanes - Daphnis *Daphnis and Chloe*	This biological father abandons his son.	He makes amends by giving Daphnis equal inheritance with Astylus. 4.24

Dryas and Nape - Chloe *Daphnis and Chloe*	The biological parents expose their child to death while these foster parents imitate the sheep and rear her, but Chloe seeks marital consent from her biological parents.	The wedding is pastoral, the adoptive parents are presented to the actual parents, and Dryas receives the ten thousand drachmas dowry that would have been his if Chloe were his daughter. 4.37
Lamon and Myrtale - Daphnis *Daphnis and Chloe*	The biological parents expose their child to death while these foster parents protect him, but Daphnis returns to his biological parents' household	Lamon, Myrtale, and the goats become Daphnis' possession. In a role reversal, Daphnis becomes the protector of those who saved his life.
Nektanebos (biological father) - Alexander *Alexander Romance*	Ignorant of this relationship, Alexander kills his father, and Nektanebos tells him that he disguised himself as Ammon and had intercourse with Olympias.	Alexander tells his mother what he has learned and she gives Nektanebos a proper burial. The author points out the irony that Nektanebos, who is Egyptian, is given a Greek burial, while Alexander, who is Greek, is given an Egyptian burial. 1.14
Ammon - Alexander *Alexander Romance*	Alexander learns that Ammon is not his father and that the god is a sort of cuckold.	At Ammon's shrine, Alexander receives an oracle from the god confirming that he is Alexander's father. 1.30
Philip - Alexander *Alexander Romance*	Philip is also a cuckold and is deceived in thinking that Alexander is his son.	Pausanias attempts to kill Philip in order to marry Olympias. Alexander acts as the obedient son and hold a dagger in Philip's hand so that Philip can cut Pausanias' throat himself. Philip then dies. 1.25

Darius - Alexander *Alexander Romance*	Darius leaves his family fatherless in order to do battle with Alexander. 2.13	Darius adopts Alexander by requesting that Alexander bury him and by saying, "Darius and Alexander shall be one family. I entrust my mother to you as though she were your mother; pity my wife as though she were your sister. My daughter Roxana I give to you as wife . . . You yourself will perpetuate the memory of Philip and Roxana will perpetuate the memory of Darius." 2.20
Deryllis and Mantinias *Antonius Diogenes*	The pair has committed some unnamed, unintentional offence against their parents.	As a consequence they have gone to Thule where they "undergo trials to make atonement" . . . "living at night but being corpses each day." 110a. The resolution of their story comes when they free their parents from a curse and hurry home to revive and save them. 110b
Pentephres - Aseneth *Joseph and Aseneth*	Pentephres wants Aseneth to marry Joseph, but Aseneth refuses to marry him because he is the son of a shepherd. She wants to marry the son of the king of Egypt.	Aseneth, upon seeing Joseph, recognizes that he is "(a) son of God." 6.4
Pentephres - Aseneth *Joseph and Aseneth*	Aseneth thinks that if she converts to Joseph's faith in order to marry him her parents will disown her.	The revelation of a heavenly man ends Aseneth's lamentation. The story does not seem to justify her remorse. Her parents, upon witnessing her transfomation, "rejoice and give glory to God who gives life to the dead." 20.7

Mother - Seven Sons *4 Maccabees*	The seven sons are martyred without leaving her grandchildren or fulfilling the responsibility of burying her	". . . If, as being a mother, the woman had been weak in spirit, she would have wept over them and spoken perhaps as follows: 'Ah, thrice-wretched woman that I am, yes more than thrice-wretched! I have borne seven sons and am the mother of none! How vain were these seven pregnancies, how futile these seven times ten months with child . . . Alas for my sons, some unmarried, others married but to no purpose! I shall never set eyes on any children of yours nor shall I know the happiness of being called grandmother. Woe is me, who had many handsome children, but am now bereft and all alone with my many sorrows! Nor shall I have any of my sons to bury me when I die.' . . . As though she had a mind of adamant and were this time bringing her brood of sons to birth into immortal life, she encouraged them and pled for them to die for piety's sake." 1.5–1 [Resurrection negates the need to supply the grandchildren.]

All quotations from ancient Greek novels are from *Collected Ancient Novels* (B. P. Reardon, ed.; Berkeley: University of California Press, 1989).

Joseph and Aseneth and *4 Maccabees* in *The Old Testament Pseudepigrapha,* 1 (J. H. Charlesworth, ed.; Garden City, N.Y.: Doubleday, 1983).

Divine Prognostications and the Movement of Story: An Intertextual Exploration of Xenophon's *Ephesian Tale* and the Acts of the Apostles

J. Bradley Chance
William Jewell College

Introduction

This paper seeks to explore intertextually two narratives, separated by less than 100 years[1] and each part of a canon. Acts is part of the Christian canon, while Xenophon's *Ephesian Tale* is part of that collection of narratives which constitutes the "canon" of ancient Greek romance.[2] I make no suggestion that Xenophon knew or read Acts. Thus, I do not use the word "intertextual" in an author-centered sense focusing on how Xenophon assumed, consumed, and subsumed Acts, but in a reader-centered sense, in which we "focus on texts as networks pointing to other texts, not to the intentions of the author."[3] Specifically, I wish to explore how each of the narratives makes use of a divine prophecy in the

---

[1] I assume the standard critical dating of around 80 CE for Luke-Acts and mid-second century for *Ephesian Tale*. For the dating of the latter see the discussion by Thomas Hägg, *The Novel in Antiquity* (Berkeley: University of California Press, 1983) 20. Gareth Schmeling (*Xenophon of Ephesus* [TWAS 613; Boston: Twayne, 1980] 11–20) places the date between 125 and 200 CE.

[2] For a general and brief introduction to the Greek novel see B. P. Reardon, ed., *Collected Ancient Greek Novels* (Berkeley: University of California Press, 1989) 1–16. It is the translation of this volume, prepared by Graham Anderson, which this paper follows. The Greek text employed is that edited by Antonius D. Papanikolaou, *Xenophontis Ephesii: Ephesiacorvm Libri V* (Leipzig: B. G. Teubner, 1973).

[3] Willem S. Vorster, "Intertextuality and Redaktionsgeschichte," in *Intertextuality in Biblical Writings: Essays in Honor of Bas van Iersel*, (S. Draisma, ed.; Kampen: Uitgeversmaatschappij J. H. Kok, 1989) 15–26. For the New Testament scholar for whom Acts would be the focal text of consideration Xenophon adds one more text to our "repertoire of intertexts" by which "the reader will assign meaning to the text or fragments of texts." Similarly, for the critic of the ancient novel, exploration of Acts might expand her or his "repertoire of intertexts" which provide the matrix for interpreting Xenophon.

beginning of the story to contribute to the movement and development of plot.[4]

Xenophon's Ephesian Tale

Introduction. Our tale begins in Ephesus where we meet Habrocomes, an arrogant and handsome young man who has angered the god Eros by failing to show the appropriate honor (1.1). Eros strikes Habrocomes with love-sickness at the sight of the young and beautiful Anthia, who is also smitten with the love bug (1.2–3). Though Habrocomes recognizes his folly and prays for forgiveness, Eros is in no mood to forgive him (1.5). In desperation, the parents of each child seek counsel from the oracle of Apollo.[5] It reads as follows (I have numbered the lines for ease of reference):

1. Why do you long to learn the end of a malady, and its beginning?
2. One disease has both in its grasp, and from that the remedy must be accomplished.
3. But for them I see terrible sufferings and toils that are endless;
4. Both will flee over the sea pursued by madness;
5. They will suffer chains at the hands of men who mingle with the waters;
6. And a tomb shall be the burial chamber for both, and fire the destroyer;
7. And beside the waters of the river Nile, to Holy Isis
8. The savior you will afterwards offer rich gifts;
9. But still after their sufferings a better fate is in store (1.6).

Interpretation of the oracle by characters and the movement of plot. Immediately, interpretation of the oracle by the characters begins. The characters then act upon their interpretations of the divine communications which get the action going.[6] The fathers are not sure what the oracle means, but they focus in on five features of it: illness (lines 1–2), flight (line 3), chains (line 5), the tomb (line 6), and help from the

---

[4] The selected focus of this paper does not allow for an examination of other "divine prognostications" in Xenophon or Acts—specifically, a number of dreams and visions which dot Xenophon and saturate the works of Luke.

[5] Parents, concerned for their children's welfare, often turned to oracles in the mythology of the time. See Schmeling, *Xenophon of Ephesus*, 26.

[6] This puts Xenophon's tale in touch with two other sophistic novels, those of Achilles Tatius and Heliodorus, both of which have been carefully analyzed by Shadi Bartsch. Interpretation of dreams and oracles play pivotal roles as interpretation leads to action which starts or keeps the story moving. This is precisely what happens in Xenophon, though he is not as sophisticated in his use of this plot device as his successors. See *Decoding the Ancient Novel: The Reader and the Role of Description in Heliodorus and Achilles Tatius* (Princeton: Princeton University Press, 1989) esp. chap. 3.

goddess (lines 7–9).[7] The fathers conclude that they should marry the children, since they interpret the prophecy to imply this to be the proper course of action (1.7.2). Readers would likely concur, for if love is the illness, marriage seems the remedy.[8] This interpretation of the oracle gets the story going, for once Habrocomes and Anthia are married the story can begin in earnest.

The fathers then focus on the statement, "[they] will flee over the sea pursued by madness" (line 4). It is curious that such words would inspire them to send the children on a voyage. Even more curious is their motive—namely to "appease" or "palliate" the oracle, two possible renderings of παραμυθεῖσθαι. Many think that Xenophon is betraying his own clumsiness, reaching for any motive to get the action going: send the lovers on sea voyage to soften the ominous prophecy about a maddening flight over the sea![9] Regardless of its clumsiness, it illustrates well how the characters' interpretation of the oracle, albeit a not terribly insightful interpretation, moves the action along.

Reflection upon and interpretation of the oracle contributes even more significantly to the plot development. Once the voyage gets underway, Habrocomes and Anthia are "fearing the oracle, and feeling uneasy about the voyage" (1.11.1). A few lines later, Habrocomes experiences a sense of dread at what lies in store for him. He says to Anthia: "If it is fated that we suffer some disaster and be separated, let us swear to one another, my dearest, that you will remain faithful to me and not submit to

---

[7] The readers find verbal connections between the oracle and the interpretation to assist them in making the explicit connections between oracle of 1.6.2 and interpretation of 1.7.1. Reference is made to νούσος and νόσος in the oracle and the fathers' thoughts, respectively. Similarly, readers find φεύξονται and φυγή; δεσμά and δεσμά; τάφος and τάφος; ποταμοῦ and ποταμός.

[8] In 1.5.9 that narrator has referred explicitly to Habrocomes' and Anthia's lovesickness as an "illness." Hence, it is quite clear to the reader that the "illness" is love. Note Greek word here, matching up with 1.6.2 and 1.7.1.

[9] This is the reading Anderson gives to the verb. See his translation in *Ancient Greek Novels,* 134 n. 6. Reardon's discussion of the verb is succinct and helpful: "The oracle (1.6) predicts that Habrocomes and Anthia will suffer misfortunes abroad—so the parents send them abroad (1.10) in order to παραμυθήσασθαι the oracle, whatever that means. It would normally mean 'console,' but has been translated as *e.g.,* 'conjure' . . . *i.e.,* 'disarm'—which explains nothing; or by K. Nickau in a[n unpublished] paper . . . as 'temper, moderate the effect of' (on the basis of a scholium to *Iliad* 5.662), or 'give a meaning other than the obvious one' (cf. Plutarch *On the Bravery of Women* 248B), *i.e.,* 'reinterpret.' Whatever the word means precisely (if it means anything precisely), the device is singularly limp." See *The Form of Greek Romance* (Princeton: Princeton University Press, 1991) 109, n. 9.

any other man and that I should never live with another woman"
(1.11.3–4). Reflection on the oracle gives rise to their oaths of fidelity. As
the plot progresses, it is their respective attempts to remain loyal to their
oaths which provide much of the tension and pathos, for the story is
fraught with challenge after challenge to the lovers' fidelity.[10] What gives
these situations special poignancy is the oath they made to each other.
And this oath is very much associated with reflection upon the oracle and
ominous prophecies it offered.

Thus, interpretation of the oracle itself contributes to the development of the story line in Xenophon. It was interpretation of the oracle
which led the fathers to marry the children and to send them on the sea
voyage which would eventually bring about the many adventures of the
couple. Further, reflection on the oracle leads the lovers to anticipate
separation and to vow fidelity. While this vow does not in itself create the
adventures to come, it infuses them with a certain tension and pathos
which would not otherwise be present.

Consciousness of the oracle and the guidance of plot. Both the narrator and
the characters are consciously aware that the action lies under the power
of the oracle. As early as 1.10, as the lovers prepare for their voyage, both
sets of parents know that what is happening is in fulfillment of the
oracle.[11] Just before the pirates attack the vessel carrying our heroes, the
narrator informs us that the prophecies were beginning to take effect
(1.12.3). In 2.1.2, Habrocomes refers explicitly back to the fulfillment of
the oracle and the revenge of Eros.[12] What we are witnessing and our

---

[10] Corymbus, the pirate captor of Habrocomes and Anthia, is in love with
Habrocomes (1.14.7). Manto, daughter of the chief pirate Apsyrtus, loves
Habrocomes (2.3–4). Habrocomes is the object of the murderous passion of Kyno,
who kills her husband Araxus because she loves Habrocomes. When her plot fails she
accuses him of the murder—leading to still more adventures for our hero (3.12).
Neither is Anthia free of temptation. While Manto is falling in love with Habrocomes,
her husband falls in love with Anthia (2.11). Anthia is rescued from one of her many
harrowing exploits by Perilaus who falls in love with her and wants to marry her
(2.13–14). She is the object of affection of a number of other would-be suitors:
Psammis (3.11), Polyidus (5.4) (whose jealous wife sends Anthia off to a brothel
where her virtue is certainly to be compromised [5.5]), and the brigand leader
Hippothous (5.9)

[11] Lycomedes and Themisto, the parents of Habrocomes, think of the more
ominous features of the oracle and "lay on the ground in despair" (1.10.7).
Megamedes and Euippe, the partents of Anthia, "were more cheerful, looking
forward to the final outcome of the oracle" (1.10.7).

[12] In 2.1.2, Habrocomes says, "The oracles are being fulfilled. Already Eros is taking
(εἰσπράττει) his revenge (τιμωρίαν) on me for my arrogance (ὑπερηφανίας)." This

heroes experiencing is the revenge of Eros playing itself out in a fated plot foreseen by the oracle. In 5.1.13, Anthia declares, "How doom-laden were the prophecies. I pray you Apollo, who gave us the harshest oracles of all, have pity on us now and bring your prophecies to their final fulfillment." Finally, when the lovers are reunited near the temple of Isis, they approach her temple and say "To you, greatest goddess, we owe thanks for our safety; it is you, the goddess we honor most of all, who have restored us" (5.13.4). No explicit mention is made here of the oracle. However, alert readers can easily recognize realization of the oracular prophecy which implied that Isis would play a role in bringing about a better fate.

These notifications inform readers that the story, though it unfolds because of human action in response to human interpretation of the oracle, is, nonetheless, guided by the divine will. Readers know it and characters know it. Our awareness that in living out the prophecies of the oracle Habrocomes is paying the price for his lack of piety, imposes on the plot the guidance of a divine hand. Anthia's desperate plea to Apollo, the couple's final prayer to Isis, and their sacrifice to Artemis convey the same impression.

How is one to take this conspiracy of the gods? Is this merely "mental furniture," and not representative of any real religious conviction, if we might draw from Reardon's discussion of religious motifs in Heliodorus?[13] More important, what does it tell us about the implied readers that Xenophon (or Heliodorus or Chariton) chose to furnish the story with so much furniture from the gallery of the gods? Perhaps we can at least conclude that when entering the fantasy world of fiction, Hellenistic readers found pleasure in a world where even bad fortune had a rhyme and reason behind it, even if they were not always sure to which god credit should be given or supplication made.[14]

---

seems an intentional echo of "Even after this prayer, Eros was still angry and intended to take (εἰσπράξασθαι) a terrible revenge (τιμωρίαν) on him for his arrogance (ὑπεροψίας, 1.4.5)." The reader already had heard of the "revenge of Eros" way back in 1.4.5, even before the oracle was given (1.6) and, thus, had perhaps already made the connection between the two. Book 1.10.2 also offered the reader the chance to see the explicit connection between oracle and the plans of the god: the lovers, lost in bliss, had already "forgotten . . . the oracle. But fate had not forgotten, nor had the god overlooked his plans." Habrocomes' comment in 2.1.2 makes the connection explicit for him and serves to remind the reader of the connection.

[13] See *Form of Greek Romance*, 148, n 32.

[14] Schmeling, *Xenophon of Ephesus*, 131–38, argues that what we have in Xenophon is "escape literature" (137). It may say something that readers find "escape" in

The oracle and the outline of the plot. Interpretation of the oracle by characters not only contributes to the development, the oracle itself helps the reader to anticipate the overall movement of the plot. Reference to "terrible sufferings and toils that are endless" (line 3) informs readers that we will encounter some frightful, yet exciting, moments. The last lines of the oracle (lines 7–9) promise a happy ending, which makes the readers feel better as they witness the lovers' trials and tribulations—a typical function of oracular foreshadowings, according to Shadi Bartsch.[15] The incidents predicted in between—flight, chains, and a tomb—also offer a rough sketch of specific trials to come: the lovers take a sea voyage which can be described as a hectic flight, they experience imprisonments, and Anthia is buried alive.

Readers discover, however, that the oracle does not offer a precise outline of events.[16] To be placed in chains at the hands of men who mingle with the sea clearly refers to the initial capture and enslavement of Habrocomes and Anthia by Corymbus and the pirates (2.12 ff.). But it would appear that the whole series of imprisonments suffered by the couple would fall under this aspect of the oracle. In fact, when Anthia is captured for a second time by pirates, she explicitly bemoans, "Once again, pirates and sea" (3.8.6). One suspects that the many additional imprisonments or captivities experienced by the lovers which do not literally involve captors who "mingle with the sea" are also presaged by this line of the oracle. Anthia's capture and recapture by Hippothous (2.11; 4.3) and her being sold to the Indian Psammis (3.11) name only

narratives which affirm that peoples' stories have a meaningful, even designed, end—a teleology of sorts. This need not necessarily imply that readers were religious or, if they were, that they literally believed that the gods worked the way they did in the narrative. One might compare in our own time such television shows as "Touched by an Angel" or, in an earlier decade, "Highway to Heaven." The recent film, "Michael," may reflect our culture's resurgent interest in things transcendant. But should some future archaeologist find these remnants of our culture in some dig, she would misread our culture to conclude that 20th century Americans thought that the things really worked in our daily worlds as these story worlds depict.

[15] *Decoding the Ancient Novel,* 83. According to Bartsch, both Heliodorus and Achilles Tatius use oracular foreknowledge as "palliatives," for if we know what to expect we can accept more easily the dangers our heroes face. Schmeling, *Xenophon of Ephesus,* 27, appears to view the oracle's outlining of events in Xenophon less as a palliative, and more as a disappointment, robbing the plot of any good surprises.

[16] Here I challenge Schmeling, *Xenophon of Ephesus,* 27, who offers a rather precise outline of the novel based on the oracle. He argues that lines 1–2 of the oracle find realization in 1.1–9; lines 3–5 in 1.10–4.2; line 6 in 3.7–4.2 (note the necessary overlap); lines 7–8 in 4.3–5.5, and line 9 in 5.6–15.

two such incidents. Likewise, Habrocomes experiences other captivities beyond his initial capture, such as being sold to an Egyptian soldier (the one with the murderous wife, Kyno) as well as his being arrested by Egyptian authorities for the Egyptian's murder (3.12). My point is that the prophecy of line 5 of the oracle refers to a series of types of events and adventures, not only a specific event when, once fulfilled, allows us to move to the next event: "And a tomb shall be the burial chamber for both, and fire the destroyer" (line 6).

Analysis of line 6 further justifies the conclusion that the oracle does not offer a precise chronological outline of events. Additionally, we also discover that some prophecies are simply not fulfilled. The first part of line 6 does find near realization in Anthia's being buried alive (3.5–8). However, the expectation raised by the oracle, that *both* would experience the tomb, is simply not realized. Both Anthia (implicitly) and Habrocomes (explicitly) anticipate being buried together. Immediately after her "rescue" from the tomb by pirates Anthia says, "My only prayer is that I may go where I shall at least see the tomb of Habrocomes" (3.8.7). Is she thinking of the oracle here and its prophecy of the tomb being the chamber for both? Should the reader? Habrocomes, upon finding Anthia's empty tomb, declares, "I, poor wretch that I am, have been deprived of your body, my only consolation. So I am absolutely determined to die. But first I will go on until I find your body, embrace it, and bury myself with you" (3.10.3). No mention is made of the oracle, but alert readers might have the expectation rekindled that the two will find themselves in a tomb together. But, it never happens.

The second part of line six regarding the fire either is not fulfilled or, if it is, reveals that the oracle does not present a series of precise chronological predictions. Where do we find realization of the prophecy that "fire [would be] the destroyer"? Is this a reference to their passion? To the various tortures and trials involving fire which are experienced by Habrocomes?[17] To the burning of the ship from which the lovers were captured by pirates (1.13–14)? None of these offers precise fulfillment, and a couple of them (the burning ship and Habrocomes' torture) are chronologically displaced if we follow the oracle.

Do we find here another example of a clumsy author—or lazy epitomizer if we assume, as fewer seem to be doing, that our current

---

[17] E.g., Apsyrtus orders Habrocomes (and only him) to be tortured with fire (2.6.2). The Egyptian authorities attempt to burn Habrocomes alongside the Nile (4.2).

Xenophon is a condensed version of a now lost fuller MS?[18] If our Xenophon is not an epitome, it would appear that we must hold our author accountable. The statements of Anthia and Habrocomes regarding each others' tombs, particularly if heard as echoes of the seemingly authoritative oracle, are likely to keep us turning the pages, anxious to see how such expectations that both will experience the tomb will find realization. But in a manner even worse than the old Saturday matinee serials, exciting expectations are not given satisfactory realization. At least in the old serials, the writers of next week's adventure had not forgotten what perilous predicament Rocket Man was left in, even if the writers were thoroughly unimaginative in getting the hero out of the mess. But Xenophon does not appear to mind raising expectations only to forget them. It might keep us turning the pages of this novel; it also might explain why there was apparently no demand for a second.

Realization of expectations raised by the last three lines of the oracle do find satisfaction, but only if the reader is willing to allow imprecision. Specifically, the reader of the oracle is likely to expect that gifts will be offered to Isis alongside the Nile by the recipients of the oracle ("*you* will afterwards offer rich gifts")—the fathers of the lovers! Regrettably, both sets of parents are dead of grief by the end of the tale and offer no such gifts. At one point, to stave of his sexual advances, Anthia tells one of her captors that her father had dedicated her to Isis (3.11.4). On two occasions, Anthia prays to Isis at Memphis (4.3.3; 5.4.6). And when finally reunited, both lovers go to the temple of Isis at Rhodes and give her full due for restoring them (5.13.4). But none of these is a precise fulfillment.

There is some exciting action which takes place near the Nile. Habrocomes is nearly crucified there for murder and then later the authorities attempt to burn him alive. In both instances he prays for deliverance, but not to Isis. The fact that Habrocomes is said to look straight at the sun, refers to the god as the Possessor of Egypt, and uses masculine pronouns indicates that Helios, not Isis, is the object of his prayer (4.2). Certainly, no offerings are actually made to Isis by the Nile. Thus, while precise realization of the details of the oracle are not

---

[18] Increasingly, critical discussions are inclined to assume that the single existing MS of Xenophon (13th century) is not an epitome. See, e.g., Schmeling, *Xenophon of Ephesus*, 21, and David Konstan, "Xenophon of Ephesus: Eros and Narrative in the Novel," in *Greek Fiction: The Greek Novel in Context* (J. R. Morgan and R. Stoneman, eds.; London: Routledge, 1994) 49–63, esp. 49.

fulfilled, there is a happy ending, for which the gods are given credit, including among them, Isis (5.13.4).

Conclusion. We can conclude this analysis of the oracle's contribution to the plot by saying that interpretation of the oracle does contribute to the plot. Second, regular allusion back to the oracle by the narrator and characters alike serves to remind the reader that the story unfolds in accordance with divine guidance, regardless of what critical readers might make of the significance of this guidance with respect to the religious character of the narrative. Third, the oracle offers a very broad outline of the story's progression, but does not offer precise chronological prediction nor accurate predictions of events to come. Readers accustomed to the enigmatic character of oracles were also accustomed to the eventual realization of the oracle and the lifting of the veil of ambiguity and enigma. Xenophon simply offers no such clear satisfaction. Only readers willing to allow for imprecision will be thoroughly satisfied with the predictive quality of the oracle.

The Acts of the Apostles[19]

Introduction. The Acts of the Apostles has near its beginning a prophecy offered by Jesus which has regularly caught readers' attentions as somehow serving to layout the narrative which follows: "But you will receive power when the Holy Spirit has come upon you; and you will be my witnesses in Jerusalem, in all Judea and Samaria, and to the ends of the earth" (Acts 1:8). This prophecy easily links up with another found in v. 5: "for John baptized with water, but you will be baptized with the Holy Spirit not many days from now." Further, verse 5 is a restatement of what we had read in Lk 24:49: "And see, I am sending upon you what my Father promised; so stay here in the city until you have been clothed with power from on high." What is more, as the intratextual complex appears to keep growing, Jesus in Lk 24:47–48 refers to his followers as "witnesses" who are to proclaim repentance and forgiveness to all nations, beginning from Jerusalem—which sounds much like the prophecy of Acts 1:8. We will refer back occasionally to this intratextual complex as it proves necessary, but will focus on Acts 1:8 itself and analyze its contribution to the plot development of Acts by focusing on the same topics which we

---

[19] I assume that most readers of this article are NT scholars. Accordingly, many foundational observations which I make regarding Acts are assumed to be "common knowledge" within the field and will not be documented as thoroughly as the preceding section on Xenophon.

used in analyzing Xenophon: 1) Do characters' interpretations of the prophecy contribute to plot development? 2) Does there appear to be a consciousness of the prophecy on the part of the characters and/or the narrator? 3) Does the prophecy outline the plot of Acts?

Interpretation of the prophecy by characters and the movement of plot. The characters of Acts lack no enthusiasm for interpreting things: scriptures, visions, dreams, and events. But do they interpret the prophecy of Acts 1:8? In Acts 2, the apostles and others with them are "filled with the Holy Spirit" and begin to speak in other languages (2:4). Peter interprets this event as the fulfillment of the prophecy of Joel 2:28–32 (Acts 2:17–21). He then goes on to tell "the Jesus story," interpreting that story as fulfillment of Ps 16:8–11 (Acts 2:25–28, 31) and, later, Ps 110:1 (Acts 2:34–35). In this sermon Peter also says, "Being therefore exalted at the right hand of God, and having received from the Father the promise of the Holy Spirit, he [Jesus] has poured out this that you both see and hear" (2:33).

This can be read as an allusion back to Acts 1:8, particularly if we hear echoing with Acts 1:8 the earlier prophecy of Jesus in Lk 24:49, "I am sending upon you what my Father promised."[20] But is Peter presenting an interpretation of the prophecy of Acts 1:8? An allusion is not an interpretation—certainly not of the explicit sort which we have encountered throughout the balance of Acts 2. Furthermore, even if we grant that an allusion still functions as an interpretation of sorts, Peter's allusive interpretation (or should we say elusive interpretation?) comes as he reflects back on the event of Pentecost, which took place quite independently of Peter's interpretation of the prophecy of Jesus. Interpretation of the prophecy does not *create* action, as it did in Xenophon. Rather, the prophecy provides a matrix for interpreting action as it unfolds or which has already taken place.

In Acts 11:15–16 Peter interprets the event of the giving of the Holy Spirit to the gentiles. As he recounts to the Judean believers the Cornelius story, Peter says of the coming of the Holy Spirit upon the gentiles: "And as I began to speak, the Holy Spirit fell upon them just as it had upon us at the beginning. And I remembered the word of the Lord, how he had said, 'John baptized with water, but you will be baptized with the Holy Spirit'" (11:15–16). In v. 16, Peter is clearly referring to Acts

---

[20] Between the two texts of Acts 1:8 and Lk 24:49 we find reference to four elements of Acts 2:33: "received" (Acts 1:8), "Father" (Lk 24:49), "promise" (Lk 24:49), and "Holy Spirit" (Acts 1:8). Acts 2:33 is an allusion back to these prophecies.

1:5—he interprets the coming of the Spirit on the gentiles (and Jews at Pentecost, for that matter) as fulfillment of Jesus' prophecy of Acts 1:5. As a result of this interpretation he did conclude that these gentiles should be baptized (11:17), an action which led his Jewish listeners to conclude that "God has given even to the Gentiles the repentance that leads to life" (11:18). Here we can say that Peter's interpretations of an event (the coming of the Spirit) and a prophecy (Acts 1:5) combine to create action which moves the plot along—the baptism of the gentiles is a key turning point in the story. Literarily, we still do have something different from what we found in Xenophon, for the interpretation comes at the end of the narration (and even re-narration) of the event. Going to Cornelius in the first place and preaching to him came not because of Peter's interpretation of the prophecy of Jesus, but because he received a very direct, unambiguous command from the Spirit to go with Cornelius' emissaries (10:20). It is only after the coming of the Spirit that Peter remembers the prophecy of Acts 1:5. Interpretation of the prophecy *after* events have occurred which can be understood as the prophecy's fulfillment does take place. But conscious and deliberate reflection on the meaning of the prophecy of the coming of the Spirit, independent of the witnessing of events which can be construed as the prophecy's fulfillment, does not occur and cannot, therefore, prompt the characters to action.

Acts 1:8 also prophesies that Jesus' followers will be witnesses in Jerusalem, Judea and Samaria, and to the end of the earth. Do we find the characters reflecting upon and interpreting this feature of the prophecy and, in response to their own interpretations, making decisions and taking steps which move the plot along? The short answer is "no." We do find Paul recounting in his first narration of his call (22:6–21) his vision of Jesus in the temple when he was told: "Hurry and get out of Jerusalem quickly, because they will not accept your testimony about me" (22:18). Paul is reflecting on his being a witness in Jerusalem, an allusion to Acts 1:8. But he is not interpreting the opening prophecy, reflecting on it, and then taking steps which move the plot along.

Similarly, Paul offers a verbal echo of Acts 1:8 when he says in 13:47, quoting Isa 49:6, "I have set you to be a light for the Gentiles, so that you may bring salvation to the ends of the earth." *Readers* know that the phrase of Acts 1:8 "to the ends of the earth" comes from Jesus' initial prophecy. Further, readers now know what the phrase "to the ends of the earth" means: to "the gentiles." But, quite unlike the parents of

Habrocomes and Anthia who reflect on the oracle and then decide to send their children on a voyage, Paul is not reflecting on the prophecy of Jesus and then deciding that he should go preach to gentiles. Specific events have merged: the gathering of "the whole city" and the jealous and blasphemous reaction of the Jews (13:44–45) lead Paul to conclude that because little fruit will be gathered among the Jews in that town, it would be profitable to go the gentiles instead. This, I think, is very different from what we find in Xenophon where interpretation of the oracle often precedes events and response to such interpretations then creates subsequent events.

Consciousness of the prophecy and the guidance of plot. We saw that in Xenophon characters' interpretions of the oracle led to certain actions which, then, contributed to the plot and its drama. In addition, both the characters and the narrator regularly made reference back to the oracle, informing and reminding the reader that events were unfolding according to the will of the gods. There is no question that the action in Acts accords with the divine will, even the divine necessity. The reader is occasionally reminded of the opening prophecy of Jesus to assist her or him in seeing this, but not very often. While the oracle in Xenophon is the primary instrument of addressing the reality of the divine will, the initial prophecy of Jesus plays only a small role in Acts.

Aside from the allusions already noted in the previous sections, the characters do not assure themselves of the reality of God's direction by reference to the opening prophecy of Jesus. They do not need to, for evidences of the God's direction of the plot abound at virtually every turn with miracles, fulfillment of scripture, visions, and dreams. This is important. The fact that Acts is saturated with on-going intrusions offering direct divine guidance does not require that the characters, or readers, be so dependent on the initial prophecy of Jesus. The explicit on-going guidance of the divine will allows both readers and characters not to have to rely almost exclusively on the initial prophecy of Jesus. As important as it is, it is only one of many reminders of divine guidance.

The narrator does on occasion remind the reader, at least implicitly, of the divine plan which guides the story by alluding to the opening prophecy for us. But Luke is far more subtle than Xenophon. We find nothing like Xenophon's statement in 1.12.3 that "the prophecies were beginning to take effect" just before the exciting action begins. Luke does tell readers, however, that after Stephen was killed persecution broke out and "all except the apostles were scattered throughout the countryside of

Judea and Samaria" (8:1). The narration takes Philip to the cities of Samaria (vv. 4–13), Azotus (Judea, v. 40), and Caesarea (Samaria, v. 40) as well as the region of Gaza (Judea, vv. 26–38). In addition, the apostles Peter and John follow up on the Samaritan mission and conclude by "proclaiming the good news to many villages of the Samaritans" (v. 25). Readers *witness* the fulfillment of the prophecy of Acts 1:8 in this chapter—but they are never *told* that it is being fulfilled. Similarly, Paul's quotation of Isa 49:6 in Acts 13:47 offers for the reader an allusion to Acts 1:8 and would allow for the quite justifiable conclusion that with Paul's turning to the gentiles this feature of the prophecy is finding realization. But we are never *told* that. The divine hand surely guides the action of Acts. But perhaps because this divine hand is seemingly everywhere, it is not necessary to offer regular reminders that the prophecy of Jesus was now finding fulfillment.

The prophecy and the outline of the plot. Here, I believe, we find the most fruitful ground for comparison. We saw above that the oracle of Xenophon offered a *general* outline of the movement of the story. Yet it did not offer a precise chronological outline. We also saw that some specific predictions contained in the oracle did not find realization. The prophecy of Acts 1:8 is similar, with the important exception that Luke is careful not to leave any prophecies of 1:8 unfulfilled. In part, Luke ensured narrative success by not burdening the prophecy with so many specific details that literal realization would have proven nearly impossible.

It has long been recognized that the general outline of Acts can be found in 1:8. The promise of the Spirit finds realization in 2:1–13. Bearing witness to Jerusalem is narrated in 2:14–8.3. The witness to Judea and Samaria is found in 8:4–25. And the last half of the gospel focuses on the mission to the ends of the earth which is understood, following the quotation of Isa 49:6 in Acts 13.47, as denoting the gentiles.

But while this broad outline is helpful, readers who attempt to squeeze the outline of Acts into rigid conformity with the outline of Acts 1:8 inevitably experience frustration. For example, is the prophecy of the coming of the Holy Spirit really to be understood as referring quite narrowly to Pentecost? Or are we not to see the consistent reports of the outpouring of the Holy Spirit in such texts as 8:15–17 (Samaritans), 9:17 (Paul in Damascus), 10:44 (gentiles of Caesarea), 13:52 (disciples of Antioch of Pisidia), and 19:6 (disciples of Ephesus) as linked to this prophecy? Are we required to conclude that the Ethiopian is not a gentile, that he is in some sense Jewish or Samaritan, since the witness to him takes place during the Judean/Samaritan mission and before the "real" gentile phase begins with the preaching to Cornelius? And where in Jesus' prophetic outline of 1:8 do we fit Paul's preaching to the Jews of Damascus in Acts 9? And what do we make of the fact that when we are now in the "ends of the earth" phase of the outline in the last part of Acts, Paul regularly preaches to Jews and even returns to Jerusalem where, we are told by a revelation of the risen Jesus, Paul has offered testimony for Jesus (Acts 23:11), supposedly long after "the Jerusalem phase" of the story should have ended?

Appeal to Apollo's oracle allows us to see that such initiatory prophecies did not have to serve as precise outlines of events. For example, just as the prediction in Apollo's oracle about "suffer[ing] chains at the hands of men who mingle with the waters" finds specific realization in the lovers' initial capture by pirates, it also serves to introduce the recurring theme of captivity. Likewise, the prophecy of the coming of the Spirit in Acts 1:8 finds specific realization in Pentecost, but it also introduces the recurring theme of the coming of the Spirit. Similarly, we recall that after the burial scene, which fulfills (almost) line 6 of the oracle ("And a tomb shall be the burial chamber for both"), Anthia is again captured by pirates, requiring her to experience again the prophecy of line 5: ("they will suffer chains at the hands of men who mingle with the waters"). Anthia seems to recognize this as she bemoans, "Once again, pirates and sea" (3.8.6). This is comparable with the "reliving" of earlier phases of the Acts 1:8 outline, such as the return to Jerusalem and Paul's witnessing there. Comparison with the oracle in Xenophon cautions against requiring too much precision of the outline of Acts 1:8.

Conclusion. Acts 1:8, like the oracle of Apollo in Xenophon 1.6, lays forth a glimpse of what is to come. Luke and Xenophon use this device more differently than similarly. In Xenophon, human interpretation of the oracle leads characters to take action—action quite necessary for the story to get going and keep going with pathos and drama. In Acts, interpretation of the prophecy of Jesus is rare, but when it occurs it does so in conjunction with a reflection on events which have taken place independently of any interpretation of the prophecy. Reflecting on the prophecy in the light of events leads characters occasionally to recall the prophecy—but they do not hazard interpretation independent of events and then move to "make things happen."

Second, Xenophon and Luke place differing emphases on the role of the opening prophecy in reminding readers (and characters) of the divine guidance which moves the story along. For Xenophon, explicit reminders of the oracle, coming both from characters and the narrator, speak to the reality of the gods' guidance of the plot. Luke, too, believes that God guides the events of his story world. However, aside from some verbal allusions, he never *explicitly* calls readers back to Acts 1:8 to remind them of this. Rather, the direct guidance and involvement of God is a regular feature of Luke's narrative with all the visions, scriptural interpretations, and prophecies. This might explain partially why Luke did not rely so heavily on the initial prophecy of Jesus.

Finally, we find in both initial prophecies a general outline of events, but we find that neither Xenophon nor Luke is bound to follow this outline with chronological precision. The biggest difference was the absence of unfulfilled predictions from Luke's initial prophecy, while Xenophon is replete with them. It may reflect simple authorial competence. There may also be something ideological or even theological. Perhaps Xenophon views his opening oracle primarily for its literary value—we have the makings here of a good story. Or perhaps Xenophon lives intellectually in a world of enigmatic oracles, none of which ever finds precise fulfillment. Perhaps it is because I have more interest in the Christian canon than the canon of ancient novels, but I sense there is something more at stake for Luke. There is more in the opening prophecy of Jesus than the makings of a good story—in fact Acts 1:8 all by itself promises to be rather boring. This is the prophecy of the Lord that directs action not only in a story world, but on the stage of salvation history—a "real history" that exists outside "the story world." Hence, Luke is not satisfied to offer readers ambiguous prophecies left unrealized or at least unexplained by the story's end.

Critics may argue that the gods and their actions are "mental furniture" in the Greek romance. Such furnishings add a desired ambiance to the story world much like a Bible on the living room coffee table, but neither requires that we assume an explicitly religious setting. If the religious aspects of Xenophon are decorative, this might explain Xenophon's willingness to allow for a somewhat imprecise oracle. Yet, even if Xenophon is more serious in what he says about divine guidance, we still must conclude that divine oracles can offer less-than-precise prognostications of forthcoming events; a conclusion borne out by the preceding study.

Only a playful and even frivolous reading of Acts could offer, with a straight face, that Luke approaches religious devotion in a less-than serious manner (though tongue-in-cheek interpretation is often chic in our post-modern times). For Luke, divine guidance cannot be reduced to a plot device, as much as it may contribute to plot. The guiding hand of God lies at the center of Luke's view of the movement of *history*, not only the movement of *story*. Thus while some specific prophecies are *not yet* fulfilled (most especially, the parousia and the restoration of all things), there is no place in Luke's narrative world, or extra-narrative world, for prophecies of divine action that may raise exciting expectations but which do not quite work themselves out. After all, "success" in the Greek romance is the happy reuniting of the lovers. Accomplishment of this goal can allow for other features (such as the precise fulfillment of a divine oracle) to be left without perfect realization. "Success" in Luke's narrative and extra-narrative worlds is the accomplishment of God's purposes which the various divine prognostications presage. Simply, this means that for Luke much is at stake: the *complete* accomplishment on the stage of both story and history of what God or Jesus predicts will happen.

"Better to Marry than to Burn": St. Paul and the Greek Novel *

Loveday Alexander
University of Sheffield, UK

In any culture, there are certain texts which act as nodal points. Such texts crystallize key moments in the process of cultural transformation; they may also (though without necessarily intending it) themselves act as catalysts in the process. The film "The Wild One," as Marlon Brando describes it, was such a text:

> None of us ever imagined that it would instigate or encourage youthful rebellion. . . . If anything, the reaction to the picture said more about the audience than it did about the film. A few nuts even claimed that *The Wild One* was part of a Hollywood campaign to loosen our morals and incite young people to rebel against their elders. Sales of leather jackets soared. . . . The public's reaction to *The Wild One* was, I believe, a product of its time and circumstances. . . . I never knew that there were sleeping desires and feelings in our society whose buttons would be hit so uncannily in that film. In hindsight, I think people responded to it because of the budding social and cultural currents that a few years later exploded volcanically on college campuses and the streets of America.[1]

In this paper I want to explore some aspects of 1 Corinthians 7, a chapter which can be seen, with hindsight, to be a similarly nodal text in an earlier process of cultural and ideological transformation. Behind it lies a familiar late-hellenistic/early imperial landscape: in front, the beginnings of "Late Antiquity" and, just around the corner, the Middle Ages. Ramsay MacMullen captures the moment acutely:

> The identification of areas where Christianity made a difference can perhaps best focus on sexual conduct. In this regard Christian ideas induced a change of law . . . . There were demonstrable changes in literature, too. Nothing similar to Heliodorus', Apuleius', or Petronius' novels could be published, nor poetry like

---

* I am grateful to friends and colleagues who have commented on various drafts of this paper (though any faults which remain are of course my own). My particular thanks are due to Sharon Gray for conducting a careful and thorough TLG search on the metaphor of "burning."

[1] In *Songs My Mother Taught Me* (Century, 1994), cited from *The Guardian,* 9 June 1994.

Catullus' or Ovid's. *There* was a difference! . . . . Here we see an absolutely remarkable impact on manners and morals that was to shape also the whole millennium to come.[2]

This particular piece of cultural transformation has attracted its fair share of attention among historians of Late Antiquity in recent years.[3] New Testament scholarship has been on the whole rather good at looking back into past traditions behind the New Testament texts, seeing them as the end of one process of development. The historians of Late Antiquity encourage us to look forward, seeing our texts as the beginning of another process. What I want to do in this paper (drawing gratefully on the insights of both) is to focus on the dynamics of change within one particular New Testament text itself, and I find that this procedure is dramatically enhanced by reading Paul alongside two Greek novels (the two early romances of Chariton of Aphrodisias and Xenophon of Ephesus) which mirror in many ways the same key moments in the process of cultural transformation.

There must indeed be an element of paradox in suggesting an association between St. Paul—surely the most unromantic of New Testeament writers—and the Greek novel. I am not indeed attempting to argue that Paul had actually read any of the Greek novels we possess—or any Greek novel at all: rather, perhaps, that the narrative world of the novels (more particularly, that of Chariton and Xenophon) has a part to play in the "imaginative economy" (to use Peter Brown's phrase) of Paul and his readers—and a significant part at that, one which may have something to do with the afterlife of some of Paul's essentially off-the-cuff remarks.

---

[2] Ramsay MacMullen, "What Difference Did Christianity Make?" *Historia* 35 (1986) 322–43, esp. 342–43. MacMullen's allusion to Heliodorus is odd, though: the *Ethiopian Story* was in fact 'published' as late as the third or possibly the fourth century, and enjoyed considerable popularity in the Christian empire, perhaps because it was rumoured that the author was a bishop. Cf. *Collected Ancient Greek Novels* (B. P. Reardon, ed.; Berkeley: University of California Press, 1989) 352. Peter Brown, *The Body and Society: Men, Women, and Sexual Renunciation in Early Christianity* (New York: Columbia University Press, 1988), chap. 1, is a valuable corrective to this view.

[3] Cf. especially Brown, *The Body and Society;* D. Halperin, J. Winkler and F. Zeitlin, eds., *Before Sexuality: the Construction of Ancient Erotic Experience* (Princeton: Princeton University Press, 1990); Simon Goldhill, *Foucault's Virginity: Ancient Erotic Fiction and the History of Sexuality* (Cambridge: Cambridge University Press, 1995); Kate Cooper, *The Virgin and the Bride: Idealized Womanhood in Late Antiquity* (Cambridge: Harvard University Press, 1996); and the literature there cited.

1. The Romantic Traveller

My observations begin with a casual piece of Pauline autobiography (rare in itself in the Epistles) in 2 Cor 11:23–27, the so-called "peristasis catalogue" where Paul lists (among other apostolic credentials) the hardships he has suffered in the course of his mission. Paul, known to us via Acts as the "traveller" par excellence of the NT, is *in propria persona* surprisingly reticent about the process of travel: the "travel notes" scattered throughout the Epistles tend to focus on destinations (churches to be visited) or on mission coverage (reckoned largely in regional terms), and pay virtually no attention to the journeys themselves. This becomes clear when we realize with some surprise that Paul never uses the verb πλεῖν (to sail) and hardly ever mentions the sea: Romans 15, for example, gives no indication as to *how* Paul was intending to make his forthcoming journeys to Jerusalem, Rome and Spain. As I have remarked elsewhere, Paul plans his journeys like a presidential candidate on the campaign trail, travelling from venue to venue without having to think about the means of travel at all, relying on his team to study the timetables and make the reservations.[4]

The exception to this pattern is 2 Corinthians 11, the only place (apart from OT quotations) where Paul mentions the sea and the only place in the Epistles where the journeying process itself is foregrounded. And what a picture he paints! Three shipwrecks to Acts' modest one, a night and a day "rocked in the cradle of the deep" (the parlour-ballad flavour is appropriate, though Paul's poetic ἐν τῷ βυθῷ appears to be echoing LXX Ps 106:24). Land-travel, too (scarcely mentioned in Acts), gets the technicolor treatment: "in journeyings often, in danger from rivers, danger from bandits, danger from my own people, danger from the Gentiles, danger in the city, danger in the desert, danger at sea." If Acts is "novelistic" in its description of Paul's voyages, Paul himself must be reckoned doubly so, at least in this passage. Not only does he include rivers and bandits, two favourite journey hazards of the novels (neither of which is mentioned in Acts), but the landscape itself, in a manner characteristic of the novelists, is divided into "city" and "desert," with no comfortable χώρα in between.

---

[4] Loveday Alexander, "'In journeyings often': Voyaging in the Acts of the Apostles and in Greek Romance," in *Luke's Literary Achievement: Collected Essays* (C. M. Tuckett, ed.; Sheffield: Sheffield Academic Press, 1995) 17–39, esp. 32–33, 36.

What are we to make of this? I am not particularly concerned to identify the origins of this material: narrative motifs of a broadly "novelistic" type can be found in more than one literary setting (e.g., the *controversiae* of the rhetorical schools), and it would be futile to argue direct dependence here on any one text or tradition. But the fact that the apostle, speaking *in propria persona,* can produce (however tongue-in-cheek) this highly-coloured snatch of autobiography may serve at least to lessen our surprise that the more extensive Pauline narratives constructed by Luke seem to have a certain number of "novelistic" features. It may also serve, paradoxically enough, to highlight the comparatively sober tone of the Lucan story.

2. The Romantic Ascetic

Armed with this hint, then, that the apostle is at least capable (when it suits him) of writing in distinctly novelistic mode, we turn to Paul's famous (or infamous) chapter on marriage, 1 Corinthians 7. At first sight, there seems little hope in this passage for presenting Paul as a romantic. It is a chapter widely regarded as containing some of the most anti-romantic statements in the NT, and is often cited as the *fons et origo* of the emergent church's obsession with sexual control and renunciation. How can the man who wrote, "It is well for a man not to touch a woman" (1 Cor 7:1), possibly be discussed in the same paper—or even the same book—as the Greek novel?

It is of course important to consider fairly the exegetical options on every verse of this complex chapter. There are good reasons for arguing (with NRSV and many commentators) that we should put quotation marks around the offending words in 7:1, so that the verse becomes a comment on what the Corinthians have proposed rather than a statement of Paul's own views. We can legitimately punctuate 7:1b as a question ("Is it good for a man not to touch a woman?"), and we may even translate, as I am tempted to do, "Is it OK (καλόν) for a man not to touch a woman?"—which rather alters the dynamics of the exchange from an aggressive assertion of ascetic principle to a hesitant questioning of the wisdom of the voluntary restraint being practised by some Corinthian couples (7:5). But it remains true, as one of my students remarked in class, that Paul is in no great hurry to distance himself from the proposal. Indeed it is clear that one of the major threads running through this chapter is Paul's own commitment to celibacy as the preferable Christian lifestyle:

I wish that all were as I myself am. But each has their own special gift from God, one of one kind and one of another. To the unmarried and widows I say that it is well for them to remain single as I do. But if they cannot exercise self-control, they should marry. For it is better to marry than to be aflame with passion [lit. "to be on fire"] (7:7–9)

I think that in view of the present distress it is well for a person to remain as he is. Are you bound to a wife? Do not seek to be free. Are you free from a wife? Do not seek marriage. . . . Those who marry will have worldly troubles, and I would spare you that. (7:26–28)

Yet even here, if we look a little more closely, it is possible to discern a distinctly romantic tinge to Paul's depiction of the married state. The problem with marriage, as Paul describes it in 7:32–35, is that it inevitably leads to divided loyalties (μεμέρισται: 7:34). But if we ask *why* this unfortunate state of affairs comes to pass, it is clear that it results solely from the couple's devotion to each other. This devotion is both mutual and (Paul implies) necessary: if people will get married, they are bound to concentrate their energies on "how to please their partner," and this is no more culpable (given the married state) in the husband than in the wife. In other words, Paul does not envisage a Miltonic relationship in which it is acceptable for the wife to devote her attention to the husband, so long as the husband keeps his mind on higher things ("He for God only, she for God in him"[5]). Marriage is a relationship involving an equal investment of "cares" (μέριμναι) on both sides.

The remarkably couple-centred focus of Paul's picture of marriage is highlighted if we read it alongside Epictetus' parallel plea for the celibate lifestyle in his evocation of the ideal Cynic:[6]

For see, he must show certain services to his father-in-law, to the rest of his wife's relatives, to his wife herself; finally, he is driven from his profession, to act as nurse in his own family and to provide for them. To make a long story short, he must get a kettle to heat water for the baby, for washing it in a bath-tub; wool for his wife when she has had a child, a cot, a cup, (the vessels get more and more numerous) . . . Doesn't he have to get little cloaks for the children? Doesn't he have to send them off to a school-teacher with their little tablets and writing-implements, and little note-books; and besides, get the little cot ready for them? For *they* can't be Cynics from the moment they leave the womb . . .

Here the distractions of marriage are far from romantic: bathing babies and placating in-laws figure prominently among the obligations which threaten the sage's philosophical calm. Much less does Paul share the sense of marriage as entailing a broader civic sphere of responsibility,

---

[5] John Milton, *Paradise Lost* IV.299.

[6] Epictetus, *Discourses* 3.22.70–71, 74, trans. W. A. Oldfather (LCL).

which undergirds the philosophical debate about marriage from Aristotle onwards. The dilemma, as Paul paints it for his readers, is reduced sharply to two options: either one devotes care and attention to τὰ τοῦ Κυρίου, that is "how to please the Lord," or one devotes care and attention to τὰ τοῦ κόσμου, glossed as "how to please one's wife/husband." This is an essentially individualistic view of marital devotion, seen as a mutual attachment equal on both sides which makes it natural (and by implication right) that each partner should be absorbed into the goal of pleasing the other. It is a view which has every right, I would suggest, to be called "romantic"; and on the map of first-century sexuality, it is hard to parallel it anywhere as well as in the novels. Both Chariton and Xenophon are at pains to stress the mutuality of affection in the core relationship between hero and heroine:[7]

> After Chaereas and Callirhoe were married, their first contact was passionate; they had an equal impulse to enjoy each other, and matching desire had made their union fruitful. (Chariton 2.8.4)

> When each of them had arrived home, they realized then what troubles had befallen them. Both felt their minds infiltrated by the image of the other; both of them were aflame with love, and the rest of the day they fuelled their desires; when they went to sleep, their misery was total, and neither could contain their love any longer. (Xenophon 1.3.3)

> Both of them felt the same emotions and were unable to say anything to each other or to look at each other's eyes but lay at ease in sheer delight, shy, afraid, panting—and on fire. . . . With this they relaxed in each other's arms and enjoyed the first fruits of Aphrodite; and there was ardent rivalry all night long, each trying to prove they loved the other more. (Xenophon 1.9.1, 9)

3. The *peri gamou* Topos in Philosophical Debate

There has been much dispute about the antecedents of Paul's fateful preference for the celibate option.[8] But whatever its ultimate origins in Paul's own psychology or religious background, it is clear that not far below the surface of this particular text (1 Corinthians 7) lies a

---

[7] Unless otherwise stated, all translations of the novel texts are taken from Reardon, *Collected Greek Novels*.

[8] Besides the commentaries on 1 Cor 7, cf. especially Brown, *The Body and Society*, 44–57; Kurt Niederwimmer, *Askese und Mysterium: Über Ehe, Ehescheidung und Eheverzicht in den Anfängen des christlichen Glaubens* (Göttingen: Vandenhoeck & Ruprecht, 1975); Will Deming, *Paul on Marriage and Celibacy: the Hellenistic Background of 1 Corinthians 7* (SNTSMS 83; Cambridge: Cambridge University Press, 1995). For the biblical and Jewish background, cf. Barnabas Lindars, "The Bible and the Call: the Biblical Roots of the Monastic Life in History and Today," *BJRL* 66 (1984) 228–45; P. R. Davies, "Who can join the 'Damascus Covenant'?" *JJS* 46 (1995) 134–42. Cf. also n. 18 below.

philosophical narrative which is thoroughly Greek, that of the ideal of the contemplative life. Its most vivid expression (and in many ways the closest parallel to Paul) is to be found in Epictetus' idealized portrait of the "Cynic" (3.22); but it has its roots in a much older tradition of anecdotal narratives exploring the philosophical ideal of the "theoretic" life, the life devoted to philosophical contemplation.[9] Almost incidentally, amongst the debates about the wise man's proper attitude to participation in civic life, the question arises "whether one should marry," εἰ γαμητέον:

> Thales is also credited with having given excellent advice on political matters. . . . Heraclides makes Thales himself say that he had always lived in solitude as a private individual [and kept aloof from State affairs]. (26) Some authorities say that he married and had a son Cybisthus; others that he remained unmarried and adopted his sister's son, and that when he was asked why he had no children, he replied "because he loved children (διὰ φιλοτεκνίαν)." The story is told that, when his mother tried to force him to marry, he replied that it was too soon, and when she pressed him again later in life, he replied that it was too late.

> (33) Hermippus in his *Lives* refers to Thales the story which is told by some of Socrates, namely, that he used to say that there were three blessings for which he was grateful to Fortune: "first, that I was born a human being and not one of the brutes; next, that I was born a man and not a woman; thirdly, a Greek and not a barbarian." (34) It is said that once, when he was taken out of doors by an old woman in order that he might observe the stars, he fell into a ditch, and his cry for help drew from the old woman the retort: "How can you expect to know all about the heavens, Thales, when you cannot even see what is just before your feet?"[10]

> Someone asked [Socrates] whether he should marry or not, and received the reply, "Whichever you do you will repent it."[11]

> Being asked what was the right time to marry, Diogenes replied, "For a young man, not yet: for an old man, never at all."[12]

> Nor again will the wise man marry and rear a family: so Epicurus says in the *Problems* and in *De Natura*. Occasionally he may marry owing to special circumstances (περίστασιν) in his life. Some too will turn aside from their purpose.[13]

---

[9] The best account of this material is in Werner Jaeger's essay 'On the Origin and Cycle of the Philosophic Ideal of Life,' printed as an Appendix (pp. 426–61) to his *Aristotle: Fundamentals of the History of his Development* (2d ed; Oxford: Clarendon, 1948).

[10] Diogenes Laertius 1.25–26, 33–34 (LCL).

[11] Diogenes Laertius 2.33 (LCL).

[12] Diogenes Laertius 6.54 (LCL).

[13] Diogenes Laertius 10.119 (LCL). A. A. Long and D. N. Sedley, *The Hellenistic Philosophers* (2 vols.; Cambridge: Cambridge University Press, 1987) §22Q.11 give a positive reading of this saying.

Much of this tradition has a distinctly misogynistic tone (as in the many stories casting Socrates' wife Xanthippe in the traditional role of the "shrew"[14]), but one of its more attractive and enduring strands is the metaphor of the philosopher as a spellbound spectator (θεωρός) at the pageant of the universe, requiring only to be left at leisure (σχολή) for the better pursuit of contemplation (θεωρία):

> Whose part is it, then, to contemplate these matters [philosophical inquiries]? The part of him who devotes himself to learning [lit: to him who has leisure], for man is a kind of animal that loves contemplation. But it is disgraceful to contemplate these things like runaway slaves; nay, sit rather free from distractions and listen, now to tragic actor and now to the citharoede, and not as these runaways do. For at the very moment when one of them is paying attention and praising the tragic actor, he takes a glance around, and then if someone mentions the word "master," they are instantly all in a flutter and upset. It is disgraceful for . . . philosophers to contemplate the works of nature in this spirit.[15]

"Free from distractions" (ἀπερισπάστως) is a key term which crops up time and again in this debate (and rarely elesewhere): both for Epictetus and for Paul, it describes the blessed state of freedom from practical concern which makes it possible for the sage to devote himself (in Paul's case herself as well) wholeheartedly to the service of God: compare 1 Cor. 7:29 & 35 with Epictetus 3.22.69:

> But in such an order of things as the present, which is like that of a battle-field, it is a question, perhaps, if the Cynic ought not to be free from distraction (ἀπερίσπαστον), wholly devoted to the service of God, free to go about among men, not tied down by the private duties of men, nor involved in relationships which he cannot violate . . .

However, the paradox is (as many commentators have recognized) that 1 Corinthians 7 is actually written in defence of the married state and against those in the church who would argue (for whatever reasons) that all sexual relationships, inside and outside marriage, should be suspended because of the present "necessity"; and it is this contrary strain in the chapter which concerns us here. Christian couples who wish to abstain from sexual intercourse in order to devote themselves to prayer are enjoined to "give what is due" to their partners, or at the most to limit their abstention to a mutually-agreed period of time (7:2–5). Christian spouses who want to separate from non-believing partners for the sake of "holiness" are told that the marriage relationship should be maintained: divorce (on these grounds) is not approved (7:10), and is not to be

---

14 E.g., Diogenes Laertius 2.34, 36–37.
15 Epictetus, *Diss* 1.29.59 (LCL).

initiated by the Christian partner (7:12–16)—though it may be accepted as a *fait accompli* if initiated by the non-believer (7:15). And engaged couples are explicitly assured that entering into a new marriage relationship is "no sin" (7:36–38)—though it would be an exaggeration to say that Paul's words actively encourage taking such a step.[16]

Where can we find the closest affinities to this more positive side of the debate? The philosophical argument about the propriety of marriage as a way of life for the wise man had by Paul's time crystallized into a recognizable *topos,* in which the "Cynic" attack on marriage was matched by a "Stoic" defence, with a repertoire of stock arguments on each side. This debate has been well documented in a number of recent studies, most fully by Will Deming.[17] It is inevitable, as Deming demonstrates, that Paul's essentially positive view of marriage should have much in common with this philosophical topos: but it is possible to overstate the similarity of the two approaches. I want to argue that Paul's position also shows significant differences from the Stoic defence of marriage, and that these place him nearer in some respects to the "romantic" ethic of the Greek novels.

There is no need to restate the full complexities of this debate here. For our purposes, it is sufficient to note that the terms in which the pro-marriage side of the debate are argued are remarkably constant, and that there are certain key features which characterize the whole tradition. Despite individual variations (and obviously the texts cited represent only a selection), the philosophical pro-marriage argument is reliant on the moral framework provided by the *polis*; focused on procreation and childrearing as primary duties; negative about passion; and entirely male-oriented.

---

[16] These verses may be addressed to the fathers of marriageable daughters (reading γαμίζειν as "to give in marriage") rather than to the engaged couples themselves: cf. A Robertson and A. Plummer, *A Critical and Exegetical Commentary on the First Epistle of St Paul to the Corinthians* (ICC; Edinburgh: T. & T. Clark, 1911) 158–60; F. F. Bruce, *1 and 2 Corinthians* (NCB; London: Oliphants, 1971) 76–77. This was a real problem in the early church (Brown, *The Body and Society,* 148–49, 191–92), and may already have been felt in St. Paul's Corinth. The alternative hypothesis that Paul's words refer to the practice of *subintroductae puellae* is rightly dismissed by Deming, *Paul on Marriage and Celibacy,* 40–47.

[17] Deming, *Paul on Marriage and Celibacy,* 50–106; D. L. Balch, *'Let Wives be Submissive': The Domestic Code in I Peter* (SBLMS 26; Atlanta: Scholars Press, 1981) 21–62; A. J. Malherbe, *Moral Exhortation, A Greco-Roman Sourcebook* (Philadelphia: Westminster, 1989); O. L. Yarborough, *'Not Like the Gentiles': Marriage Rules in the Letters of Paul* (SBLDS 80; Atlanta: Scholars Press, 1985) 31–63.

In "The Circle of Reference in Pauline Morality,"[18] Wayne Meeks observes that, "For Aristotle, the context in which character is formed and the arena in which virtue is exercised is the polis." This polis-centred frame of reference is fundamental to classical Greek moral reasoning from the fifth century onwards; its dominance in the realm of family values may be illustrated from Pericles' funeral speech, where the possibility of begetting children to replace the lost is as much civic duty as personal consolation:

> You who are of an age to beget children must bear up in the hope of having others in their stead; not only will they help you to forget those whom you have lost, but will be to the state at once a reinforcement and a security; for never can a fair or just policy be expected of a citizen who does not, like his fellows, bring to the decision the interests and apprehensions of a father.[19]

This political framework dominates the marriage debate right through the hellenistic and into the imperial period. Marriage is presented as integral to the life of the city:

> The well-born and high-minded youth, being, moreover, a product of civilization and a political being, perceiving that one's home or life cannot otherwise be complete except with a wife and children . . . having observed these things, and, being by nature political, that he must increase the fatherland, the well-born youth <will marry and have children>. For the city-states could not otherwise survive if the children best in nature, being of noble citizens, . . . should not marry in due season, leaving behind, as it were, some noble shoots as successors to the fatherland. . . . <Thus> . . . they consider joining with a woman in marriage to be among the primary and most necessary of those things which are fitting, being eager to complete every task laid upon them by nature, most especially the duty that concerns the safekeeping and growth of the fatherland, and, even more so, the honor of the Gods—for, if the race dies out, who will sacrifice to the Gods? Some wolves or a race of "bull-killing lions"?[20]

> (45) . . . that, being a member of both household and city-state, and most importantly, of the *kosmos,* he is obligated to replace each person who departs these institutions, if he does not wish to be a deserter either of the ancestral hearth of his household, or the altar of his city-state, or, indeed, the altar of God.[21]

---

[18] Wayne Meeks, "The Circle of Reference in Pauline Morality," in *Greeks, Romans and Christians: Essays in Honour of Abraham J. Malherbe* (D. L. Balch, E. Ferguson & W. A. Meeks, eds. ; Minneapolis: Fortress, 1990) 305–317, esp. 305.

[19] Thucydides 2.45 (R. Crawley, trans., *History of Thucydides* [New York: Modern Library, 1951]). Cf. further Brown, *The Body and Society,* chap. 1.

[20] From Antipater of Tarsus, *On Marriage* (SVF 3.254.23–257.10), cited from Deming, *Paul on Marriage and Celibacy,* 226–29.

[21] [Ocellus Lucanus], *On the Nature of the Universe* 45, cited from Deming, *Paul on Marriage and Celibacy,* 230–31.

Tell me, then, is it fitting for each man to act for himself alone or to act in the interest of his neighbour also, not only that there may be homes in the city but also that the city may not be deserted and the common good be served? . . . [If so] . . . it would be each man's duty to take thought for his own city, and to make of his home a rampart for its protection. But the first step towards making his home such a rampart is marriage. Thus whoever destroys human marriage destroys the home, the city, and the whole human race.[22]

There is a primary constitution (πολιτεία) in the union of a man and a woman according to law for the begetting of children and for community of life. This is called a house (οἶκος), which is the beginning [source] of a city . . . For the house is like a small city, if as is ideal, the marriage increases and children come; and if the first house is coupled with others, the other house stands as a support, and so a third and a fourth, and out of these grows a village and a city. . . . So just as the house provides for the city the seeds of its birth, so does it provide the seeds of the constitution. [23]

It follows almost inevitably from this line of argument that the marriage debate is focused on the procreation and rearing of children as primary duties:

I affirm, therefore, that marriage is also advantageous, in the first place, because it bears a truly divine fruit in the procreation of children. . . . We should keep in mind that we beget children not only for ourselves, but also for those for whose sakes we ourselves were begotten, and in the next place, for our friends and relatives . . . . Our country especially urges us to do so. For I dare say that we raise children not so much for ourselves as for our country by planning for the continuation of the state that follows us and supplying the community with our successors. . . . [24]

For many Stoic writers, in fact, this is the sole justification for sexual activity:

(44) We have sexual intercourse not for the sake of pleasure, but the procreation of children. For, in fact, the reproductive powers themselves, and the sexual organs, and the yearnings that were given to human beings by God in order to bring on sexual intercourse happen not to have been given for the sake of pleasure, but the ever-lasting continuation of the race. . . .

(45) Thus it is necessary first to comprehend this one thing: that sexual intercourse is not for the sake of pleasure. . . . For those who have intercourse not at all for the sake of having children do injustice to the most revered systems of partnership. And if, in fact, such persons as these give birth, by means of wantonness and lack of self-control, then those born will be wretched and pitiful,

---

[22] Musonius Rufus, *frag.* 14 (trans. Cora E. Lutz, "Musonius Rufus: 'A Roman Socrates,'" *YCS* 10 [1947] 92.17–20, 32–36).

[23] Areius Didymus 148,5, cited from Balch, *Let Wives,* 42.

[24] From Hierocles, *On marriage*, cited from Malherbe, *Moral Exhortation,* 101, 104.

and loathsome in the sight of Gods, and divine beings, and men, and households, and city-states.[25]

I affirm, therefore, that marriage is also advantageous, in the first place, because it bears a truly divine fruit in the procreation of children. . . .[26]

It is hardly surprising, then, to find that the philosophical moralizers tend on the whole to be negative about sexual passion: the Stoic Panaetius, to Seneca's approval, described falling in love as "a state that is disordered, uncontrolled, enslaved to another, contemptible to itself."[27] Pleasure, as we have already seen, is not a legitimate goal of sexual activity even within marriage. Even Musonius Rufus, who paints an idealized (and itself rather romantic) picture of the κοινωνία of the married couple,[28] will not allow any role for sexual activity within marriage apart from procreation:

Men who are not wanton or immoral are bound to consider sexual intercourse justified only when it occurs in marriage and is indulged in for the purpose of begetting children, since that is lawful, but unjust and unlawful when it is mere pleasure-seeking, even in marriage.[29]

And, finally, it is already clear that the terms in which the debate is framed are entirely male-oriented. This is a debate about the benefits or disadvantages of having a wife: I have seen no philosophical discussion of the benefits or otherwise of having a husband. A number of passages could be cited to illustrate this point:

Epicurus, the patron of pleasure . . . says that a wise man can seldom marry, because marriage has many drawbacks. And as riches, honors, bodily health, and other things which we call indifferent, are neither good nor bad, but stand as it were midway, and become good or bad according to the use and issue, so wives stand on the border line of good and ill. It is, moreover, a serious matter for a wise man to be in doubt whether he is going to marry a good or a bad woman.[30]

---

[25] [Ocellus Lucanus], *On the Nature of the Universe*, 44–45, cited from Deming, *Paul on Marriage and Celibacy*, 230–31. For a contrary, Cynic view, cf. Diogenes, *Epp.* 21, 47 (A. J. Malherbe, ed., *The Cynic Epistles* [SBLSBS 12; Missoula: Scholars Press, 1977] 115, 178).

[26] From Hierocles, *On marriage*, cited from Malherbe, *Moral Exhortation*, 101.

[27] Seneca, *Letters* 116.5, = Panaetius of Rhodes frg. 114: "I think that Panaetius gave a very neat answer to a certain youth who asked him whether the wise man would become a lover: 'As to the wise man, we shall see later; but you and I, who are as yet far removed from wisdom, should not trust ourselves to fall into a state that is disordered, uncontrolled, enslaved to another, contemptible to itself" (LCL).

[28] Musonius Rufus, *frag.* 14 (Lutz p.94.2–19); cf. *frag.* 13A (Lutz p.88.17–29).

[29] Musonius Rufus, *frag.* 12 (Lutz p.86.4–8); cf. *frag.* 15 (Lutz 96–100).

[30] Seneca, *De matrimonio* (ap. Jer. *Ad Iovin.* 1.48, tr. Fremantle). Cited from Deming, *Paul on Marriage and Celibacy*, 67 n. 49.

Even if he is put on the rack, the wise man is happy. . . . When on the rack, however, he will give vent to cries and groans. As regards women he will submit to the restrictions imposed by the law. . . . The Epicureans do not suffer the wise man to fall in love; nor will he trouble himself about funeral rites; according to them love does not come by divine inspiration. . . . No one was ever the better for sexual indulgence, and it is well if he be not the worse.[31]

This is reflected further in the way the defence of marriage is often presented as a direct counter to the older, misogynistic tradition which sees marriage (or rather "the wife") as a handicap to the (male) pursuit of philosophy. One of the drawbacks of marriage, on this view, is that it prevents a man from pursuing philosophical contemplation "without distraction." The pro-marriage side counters this by claiming that a wife actually facilitates the theoretic life by freeing up her husband for the σχολή necessary for philosophical pursuits. This argument, which goes at least as far back as Xenophon,[32] persists right through the Stoic side of the debate, from Antipater of Tarsus in the second century BCE to Hierocles at the beginning of the second century CE:

Whereas, in fact, if someone were able to do these and the other things which have been duly inspected by the philosophers and are recommended by them [viz., to "take command" of his wife], a wife would seem to be the lightest of all possible burdens. For it is most similar to when someone, having one hand, adds another one from somewhere, or, having one foot, gains another from somewhere else. For just as this man would indeed walk and go here and there where he would much more easily, so the man who takes a wife will more easily obtain the necessities that sustain and benefit his life. . . . Indeed, this is a perfectly settled matter for the man who loves the good and desires to direct spare time either to philosophical discourse or political matters, or both these things. For to the extent that he himself turns more and more aside from the management of his household, it is all the more necessary that he acquire this woman who will take over management, and <that he hold> himself undistracted regarding the necessities of life.[33]

And yet, living with a wife even before the birth of children is advantageous. For in the first place, when we are worn out by laboring out of doors, she solicitously entertains us by restoring and refreshing us with the greatest of care. In the next place, she makes us forget our problems. . . . I have therefore frequently marveled at those men who think that married life is burdensome. For a wife, by Zeus, is not a burden or a load, as they think, but on the contrary, she is something light and

---

[31] Diogenes Laertius 10.118 (LCL).

[32] *Oeconomicus* 7.3: "Well now, Socrates, . . . I certainly do not pass my time indoors; for, you know, my wife is quite capable of looking after the house by herself" (LCL). Cf. Deming, *Paul on Marriage and Celibacy*, 62–63.

[33] From Antipater of Tarsus, *On Marriage;* cited from Deming, *Paul on Marriage and Celibacy,* 229.

easily borne, or rather, she has the ability to relieve her husband of things that are truly annoying and burdensome.[34]

This background should be borne in mind when reading Musonius Rufus' famous argument "That women too should study philosophy."[35] The philosophically-trained wife, in Musonius' eyes, is not like those women who join the men to "practice speeches, talk like sophists, and analyze syllogisms, when they ought to be sitting at home spinning." Rather, "the teachings of philosophy exhort the woman to be content with her lot and to work with her own hands": such a woman will be "energetic, strong to endure pain, prepared to nourish her children at her own breast, and to serve her husband with her own hands, and willing to do things which some would consider no better than slaves' work. Would not such a woman be a great help to the man who married her, an ornament to her relatives, and a good example to all who know her?"[36] This happy concatenation of philosophical principle with traditional marriage patterns falls somewhat short of the intensity of mutual devotion so characteristic of the novel. Despite the community of interest which Musonius saw as the ideal foundation for marriage, the ideal philosophical couple are not expected to spend their married lives in mutual admiration or joint adventure, but to follow a more asymmetrical pattern in which the wife assumes a passive and supportive role to her philosopher husband.[37]

There are occasional glimpses of an alternative philosophical narrative which approaches rather more closely to the romantic paradigm. Musonius Rufus cites Crates (along with Socrates and Pythagoras) to prove that marriage need not be an impediment to the philosopher, even in the most extreme conditions:

> Crates, although homeless and completely without property or possessions, was nevertheless married; furthermore, not having a shelter of his own, he spent his days and nights in the public porticoes of Athens together with his wife. How, then, can we, who have a home to start with and some of us even have servants to work for us, venture to say that marriage is a handicap for philosophy?[38]

But the story of Crates and Hipparchia is a typically Cynic exemplum of a philosophical marriage which broke all the rules, and the Cynic

---

[34] From Hierocles, *On marriage;* Cited from Malherbe, *Moral Exhortation,* 101–2.

[35] Musonius Rufus 3 (Lutz, pp. 38–42); cf. also 4 (Lutz, pp. 42–48).

[36] Lutz p. 42.14–15, 28–9, 5–11.

[37] Cf. Plutarch *Mor.* 145b–146a: the husband goes out to gather philosophical honey and brings it home to his wife.

[38] Musonius Rufus, *frag.* 14 (Lutz p.92.1–6).

Hipparchia is a far cry from the meekly-spinning, home-loving "philosopher"-wife favoured by Musonius. As told by Diogenes Laertius, the story presents Hipparchia as a classic example of Cynic "shamelessness":

> Hipparchia . . . fell in love with both the doctrines and manners of Crates, and could not be diverted from her regard for him, by either the wealth, or high birth, or personal beauty, of any of her suitors, but Crates was everything to her; and she threatened her parents to make away with herself, if she were not given in marriage to him. Crates accordingly, being entreated by her parents to dissuade her from this resolution, did all he could; and at last, as he could not persuade her, he rose up, and placing all his furniture before her, he said, "This is the bridegroom whom you are choosing, and this is the whole of his property; consider these facts, for it will not be possible for you to become his partner, if you do not also apply yourself to the same studies, and conform to the same habits that he does." But the girl chose him; and assuming the same dress that he wore, went about with him as her husband, and appeared with him in public everywhere, and went to all entertainments in his company. . . . [B]ut when [Theodorus] said to her,
>
> > "Who is the woman who has left the shuttle
> >
> > So near the warp?" [Eur. *Bacch.* 1228],
>
> "I, Theodorus, am that person," she replied; "but do I appear to you to have come to a wrong decision if I devote that time to philosophy, which I otherwise should have spent at the loom?" And these and many other sayings are reported of this female philosopher.[39]

Epictetus also uses Crates as an example of a marriage which does not impede the Cynic's calling because the wife is herself a philosopher, but for Epictetus this is not the norm but the exception which proves the rule:

> Yes, but Crates married.—You are mentioning a particular instance which arose out of passionate love (ἐξ ἔρωτος), and you are assuming a wife who is herself another Crates. But our inquiry is concerned with ordinary marriage apart from special circumstances, and from this point of view we do not find that marriage, under present circumstances, is a matter of prime importance for the Cynic.[40]

W. A. Oldfather's note *ad loc.* in the Loeb edition is apposite: "That ancient marriages (which would apear to have been quite as successful as any other) were very seldom concerned with romantic passion, is well known, but seldom so explicitly stated as here." But even this out-of-the-ordinary Cynic affair is rather ambivalent as an example of romantic love. The attraction is distinctly one-sided (like Thecla, Hipparchia is determined to follow her philosopher whatever the cost; there is no sign that

---

[39] Diogenes Laertius 6.96–98, tr. C. D. Yonge (London: George Bell, 1895).

[40] Epictetus, *Diss.* 3.22.76 (LCL).

the feeling is mutual), and Crates himself is far from being an advocate of romantic marriage:

> And Eratosthenes says that he had by Hipparchia ... a son whose name was Pasicles, and that when he grew up, he took him to a brothel kept by a female slave, and told him that this was all the marriage that his father desired for him; but that marriages which resulted in adultery were themes for tragedians, and had exile and bloodshed for their prizes; and the marriages of those who lived with courtesans were the subject of the comic poets, and often produced madness as the result of debauchery and drunkenness.[41]

4. Paul and the Greek Novel

Paul's arguments for remaining in the married state in 1 Corinthians 7 form a striking contrast with the Stoic defence of marriage. Paul (in this chapter) shares none of the key characteristics outlined above. He shows no interest either in the civic framework of the Stoic marriage ethic, or in its concomitant, the duty to procreate (and, whatever may have happened in later Christian morality, there is no attempt here to restate the Stoic arguments in terms of ecclesial or cosmic responsibility). The male-centred view of marriage which we have seen to be characteristic of both "Cynic" and "Stoic" positions in the philosophical debate is strikingly absent here too:[42] many commentators have noted the remarkably even-handed perspective of this chapter, which reads, as a student once complained to me, almost as if Paul had been reading a manual on political correctness. And, far from being negative about the sexual urge, Paul goes out of his way to stress its irresistible authority (ἐξουσία), which it is "better" to give in to (unless you happen to have the even better "gift" of continence: 7:2–9, 36). In this marriage ethic, sexual fulfillment is not the shamefaced by-product of the need to perpetuate the human race which it was to become in the teaching of the mediaeval church (and which it was already in some Stoic teaching), but a "due" (ὀφειλή, 7:3)

---

[41] Diogenes Laertius 6.88–89, tr. Yonge. Deming (*Paul on Marriage and Celibacy*, 206) notes a striking parallel to the unusual word βρόχος, which Paul uses in 1 Cor 7:35, in an epigram attributed to Crates in the Greek Anthology (9.479), where the "noose" is said to be the only recourse left when hunger and time fail to quench the "flame" of love. This may be a reference to marriage, as Deming suggests (though it can also be read as a reference to suicide): but the βρόχος which Paul deprecates is not marriage but its opposite.

[42] It is not of course difficult to find parallels to the Stoic view of the husband-wife relationship in the NT (cf. e.g., Balch, *Let Wives Be Submissive*). My point is not that such views are not to be found in early Christian literature, but that they are not found in this particular text.

which is owed equally to both partners (7:3–4). In 1 Corinthians 5 and 6, sexual activity is seen as a dangerous source of pollution for the holy community. But within the context of marriage in chapter seven, not only is it "no sin" (7:28, 36), even with a non-Christian spouse (7:12–16), but it actively reverses the purity power-field and has the power to confer holiness on the unbelieving partner and children (7:14).[43]

In all these respects, Paul is surprisingly close to the imaginative world of the novelists. Both represent an idealized picture of sexual relationships which are primarily heterosexual, and legitimated by the civic ceremonies of marriage. Both admire the romantic ideal of loyalty to a partner even after death, and both envision this relationship in terms of an intense and reciprocal devotion which excludes all other interests. In the novels, as in Paul, this mutual devotion is an end in itself. The procreation of children is either not mentioned (as in Xenophon of Ephesus) or treated as incidental (as in Paul). There is a pregnancy in Chariton's *Callirhoe,* which performs a useful motive function in the plot, but the child itself is so far from being integral to the relationship with Chaereas that Callirhoe is able to leave it behind when she is reunited with her lover. In the novels, the civic framework supports the works of Eros, not the other way round. Although both marriages are blessed by the couples' respective cities, the action of the novels takes place almost entirely outside them, as if the hero and heroine need to break out of that comfortable matrix in order to discover themselves (one of the catalysts of this process is the catastrophic loss of status and identity brought about by their travels). It is a devotion as all-absorbing to the male partner as to the female: even the traditional heroic commitment to war takes second place for the romantic hero.[44] And it is a devotion which finds its proper (and frequent) expression in physical passion.

---

[43] The (unstated) paradox is that if we ask what defines the crucial difference between illegitimate sex *(porneia)* and legitimate sex (marriage), it is clear that the distinction rests on a legal status which is wholly dependent on civic—that is, secular—law: these are not "Christian" marriages but marriages already in existence within the social world of the *polis.*

[44] Cf. the reunion scene at the beginning of Chariton, Bk. 8: "The rumor spread that the admiral had found his wife. Not a soldier stayed in his tent, not a sailor on his ship, not a lodgekeeper at his door. . . . Chaereas was in the habit of sleeping on board ship, since he was busy night and day. Now, however, he handed everything over to Polycharmus, and himself went into the royal bedroom without even waiting for night to fall . . ." (8.11.13). Chaereas is no Aeneas—his military ambition is dormant throughout most of the narrative, and is only awakened when he is persuaded that *pietas* can be made to serve the interests of Love (7.1).

When Paul says that "the wife does not rule over her own body, but the husband does" (7:4), he is stating no more than a traditional view of male conjugal rights, one which would have been readily endorsed right across Greco-Roman society. But when he goes on to state that "likewise the husband does not rule over his own body, but the wife does (ibid.)," he is treading much more disputed ground. Plutarch's view of wifely modesty is much more characteristic of the moralists:

> A young Spartan woman, in answer to an inquiry as to whether she had already made advances to her husband, said, "No, but he has made them to me." This behaviour, I take it, is characteristic of the true mistress of the household, on the one hand not to avoid or feel annoyed at such actions on the part of her husband if he begins them, and on the other not to take the initiative herself; for the one course is meretricious and froward, the other disdainful and unamiable.[45]

The identification of female sexual desire as ἑταιρικόν, i.e. characteristic of courtesans and other undesirables, is common throughout ancient literature: in the novels, it is exemplified in the many rapacious women who tempt the hero to stray from the path of chastity in order to satisfy their sexual desires. Joseph's account of his pursuit by Potiphar's wife in *Testament of Joseph* provides a vivid example:

> And I struggled against a shameless woman urging me to transgress with her; but the God of Israel my father delivered me from the burning flame.[46]

This expansion of the Genesis story forms part of a cycle of hellenistic Jewish texts in which, in C. J. Bickerman's words, "the love described . . . is, as in most Alexandrian literature, only carnal. Of course, they deal only with illicit relationships; marriage was distinct from love in a society in which maidens were kept within doors until married off by their fathers."[47] But this is precisely where Paul differs from the traditional norm, and where he is best paralleled in the Greek novels. In 1 Corinthians 7, and in the novels, it is not only "bad" women who feel the heats of sexual desire. "Burning" is one of a range of metaphors (wounding, captivity, drowning) used in the novels to describe the irresistible force of passion: and it is a sensation associated as much with the legitimate loves of hero and heroine as with the unregulated passions of the various tempters who seek to assault their chastity. Paul's metaphor of sexual desire as "burning" (7:9) is commonest in the novels and in

---

[45] Plutarch, *Conj. praec.* 140c-d (LCL).

[46] T. Joseph 2.2, tr. Charles.

[47] E. J. Bickerman, *The Jews in the Greek Age* (Cambridge: Harvard University Press, 1988), chap. 22 esp. p. 208.

Greek erotic poetry.[48] Deming argues that these authors "would surely have scoffed at the suggestion that the flame of sexual passion is properly extinguished in marriage,"[49] but in fact this is precisely how the image is used: *eros*, after all, primarily means "desire," and since it is desire in its unrequited state which is most characteristically described as "fire," the fulfillment of that desire is properly seen as a way of "quenching" the flame.[50]

5. Conclusions

What are we to conclude from this very impressionistic characterization? I am not trying to construct a case for direct dependence between Paul and the novels: there are too many imponderables (including the question of date) for such a case to be plausible. Neither am I trying to place the "philosophical" and the "romantic" views in water-tight compartments: it is clear, apart from anything else, that the "romantic" view of marriage which we find in the novels was already affecting the philosophers by the first century if not before. Paul Veyne finds already in Seneca that "the existence of conjugal love is no longer a happy accident, but a norm whose realisation is assumed; for him, mutual understanding between spouses is no longer a *de facto* state of affairs which is eventually added to the marriage relationship but the very foundation of the relationship itself."[51] But this in itself, as Veyne makes clear, marks a

---

[48] E.g., Chariton 1.1.7, 8, 15; 1.3.7; 2.4.3, 5; 4.2.4; 6.3.3, 9; 6.4.5; Xen.Eph. 1.3.4; 1.5.8; 1.9.8; 1.14.7; 2.3.3; 4.5.4; Longus 1.23.1; 3.13.3; Achilles Tatius 1.5.5; 2.3.3; 2.5.2; 4.7; 5.15.5; 6.18.2; Heliodorus 1.15.4; 1.24.2; 7.9.2; 8.2.1. A TLG search (carried out for me by Sharon Gray) turns up more than 70 references in the Greek Anthology, from Callimachus onwards: cf. for example 5.57, 12.41, 48, 76, 80–85 (Meleager); 5.124, 131, 11.41 (Philodemus); 9.440 (Moschus). Brown, *The Body and Society* 55 n. 112 cites Strack-Billerbeck for the rabbinic background to this saying, but the parallels there cited are nowhere near as convincing (or as numerous) as the Greek parallels; and, as Deming points out (p. 131), the fact that Paul here uses the Attic form κρεῖττον makes a Greek background to the tag even more likely.

[49] Deming, *Paul on Marriage and Celibacy*, 131 n. 92.

[50] Cf. Achilles Tatius 5.26.2: "However angry you make me, I still burn with love for you. . . . Make a truce with me at least for now; pity me. . . . A single consummation will be enough. It is a small remedy I ask for so great an illness. Quench a little of my fire."

[51] Paul Veyne, "La famille et l'amour sous le Haut-Empire romain," *Annales (ESC)* 33 (1978) 33–63, esp. 49 (my trans.). Cf. Richard Pervo, "Aseneth and her Sisters: Women in Jewish Narrative and in the Greek Novels," in *"Women Like This": New Perspectives on Jewish Women in the Greco-Roman World* (A. J. Levine, ed.; SBLEJL 1; Atlanta: Scholars Press, 1991) 145–60, esp. 146 n. 12: "the simultaneous development

significant shift in social attitudes around the time that Paul was writing to the Corinthian church (and around the time of the emergence of the novel); and without hazarding any guesses as to whether we are talking here about influence or merely *Zeitgeist*, it is useful at least to try to identify the precise flavour of Paul's thought (in a text which was to become hugely influential in Christian circles) along the spectrum of contemporary thinking on marriage.

The picture which emerges from our analysis is that the stereotypical positions which became identified as "Stoic" and "Cynic" face each other, as it were, in mirror image at the "philosophical" end of the spectrum, and that the "romantic" view represented in the novels lies at the other. And here, as elsewhere, it seems clear that early Christian literature is closer to the "romantic" end of the spectrum than we might expect. To change the metaphor, Paul seems to be to a surprising extent on the same wavelength as the novels and their readers—and the metaphor of radio is a reminder that we are talking about communication, about broadcasting on the same emotional frequency. It may not be as odd as it appears, in other words, that the same literary form (novelistic narrative) came to be used simultaneously in the second century both for the promotion of erotic romance and for its antitype, the ideal of sexual renunciation (e.g., Paul and Thecla).

The relationship between text and world is a complex one, as Brando reminds us. One particular "button" pressed to advantage in these Christian texts may be precisely the lack of the civic framework to their moral code. To the non-citizen, the bald assumption that "there is no-one who is not part of a *polis*" must have been one of the more repellent aspects of the Stoic code: this is very much an élite morality.[52] But, as in the twentieth century, the romantic alternative, with its stress on individual commitment as the sole basis for a stable relationship, may have proved too weak a foundation for a full-blown ethic of marriage. Within the early church, at least, it could not provide a counterweight to the rival pull of asceticism with its more radical rejection of all forms of sexual relationship and all commerce with the "forms of this present world." It needed a different ethos to convince the catholic church that it

---

of romantic love as the basis for marriage . . . and the contemporaneous emergence of the typical Greek romance."

[52] Hierocles, *El. Eth.* col. 11.15–16 (cited in Malherbe, *Moral Exhortation*, 36). Cf. Brown, *The Body and Society*, 24: "The writers of the second century A.D. couched their precepts in universal terms. In reality they wrote for the privileged few."

was in its interest to support and nurture stable household structures. It is no accident that the later NT marriage ethic as seen in the *Haustafeln* is much more Stoic (as David Balch has shown) than that of I Corinthians 7, much closer to the élite polis-ideology stressing the stability of an ordered society.

Peter Brown suggests that the fateful conjunction of marriage with "Satan" in this passage may have opened the way to the later church's preoccupation with asceticism.[53] But this may not be the only reason why Paul's romantic affirmation of marriage failed in the end to capture the imagination of the Christian public. The Stoic-Cynic marriage debate is actually part of a much broader philosophical discourse on sexual options going back to Plato at least. In this wider discourse, celibacy is not the only alternative: the claims of marriage are also contested over against the advantage of homosexual love,[54] of courtesans or prostitutes, or of masturbation—the last a particular favourite with the Cynics.[55] But Paul has already eliminated most of these in chs. 5 and 6 of I Corinthians: homosexual love and the use of prostitutes, as well as irregular liaisons within the family, are ruled out for the Christian under the blanket condemnation of *porneia.*[56] This leaves the Christian with only two viable options: marriage (= "pleasing one's spouse"), or total abstinence (= "pleasing the Lord"). This stark reduction of the options to two effectively paves the way for a situation in which celibacy and romantic love become two sides of a single coin. Paul thus epitomizes a situation dramatically described by Paul Veyne, who sees the ascetic as a "dandy of morality." Philosophical asceticism, he argues, is precisely the "aesthetic variety" of the ethic of "loving obedience and conjugal sexuality" which I have called the "romantic" ethic. "This makes it easy to understand the success of this asceticism in high society of the time: asceticism is the only form of individual prowess which remains possible in a moralizing society, and, by its very nature, it is a form of elegance."[57]

---

[53] Brown, *The Body and Society,* 55.

[54] E.g., Plutarch, *Amat.* 750c: "Since [marriage] is necessary for producing children, there's no harm in legislators taking it up and singing its praises to the masses. But genuine Love has no connexion whatsoever with the women's quarters" (Loeb tr.).

[55] Cf. e.g., Diogenes, *Epp.* 42, 44: Malherbe, *Cynic Epistles,* 172–75.

[56] Auto-eroticism is not mentioned, but Paul would undoubtedly have regarded it as forbidden under the biblical injunctions against "Onanism." Cf. Philo, *Quod Deus* 16–19.

[57] Veyne, "La famille," 49–50 (my trans.).

The attraction of this form of "elegance" for Paul himself is obvious: more surprisingly, perhaps, it also has its place in the imaginative economy of the Greek novel. Passion, in the novel, is a "fire" which it is dangerous to try to suppress: to try to do so, significantly—as poor Dionysius does when first smitten with Callirhoe's beauty—is to try to "act the philosopher":

> This was good sense; but Eros, who took his restraint as an insult, set himself against Dionysius and fanned to greater heat the blaze in a heart that was trying to be rational about love (ἐπυρπόλει σφοδρότερον ψυχὴν ἐν ἔρωτι φιλοσοφοῦσαν).[58]

For the victims of Eros, as the cynical Artaxates tells the Great King, "the only remedy for love is the loved one."[59] For the fortunate couples whose mutual passion forms the pivot of the novel's action, this is no problem: they can quench the flame of desire in the legitimate pleasures of the marriage-bed:

> With this they relaxed in each other's arms and enjoyed the first fruits of Aphrodite; and there was ardent rivalry all night long, each trying to prove they loved the other more. When it was day, they got up much happier, and much more cheerful after fulfilling the desires they had had for each other for so long.[60]

But for those less fortunate victims who also suffer from a sense of honourable behaviour, like Callirhoe's suitors Dionysius and the Persian King, the alternative is framed precisely in terms of "individual prowess":

> Do not heal love's wound as other men do. Apply another remedy, one worthy of a king; wrestling with yourself (ἀνταγωνιζόμενος ἑαυτῷ)! For you—and you alone— can master even a god. [61]

The athletic imagery would appeal to the apostle—but he would also have agreed ultimately with Chariton and Xenophon that (within marriage, at least) it is "no sin" to quench the fire by surrendering.

---

[58] Chariton 2.4.5. The same phrase is used by Galen at the end of the second century to describe the admirable restraint exercized by Christians of all social classes in "cohabitation": R. Walzer, *Galen on Jews and Christians* (Oxford: Oxford University Press, 1947) 15.

[59] Chariton 6.3.7; cf. Achilles Tatius 4.7.

[60] Xenophon of Ephesus 1.9.9–10.1. cf. Chariton 1.1.6–16, 2.8.4, 8.1.13–17.

[61] Chariton 6.3.8.

Reversing Romance? *The Acts of Thecla* and the Ancient Novel[1]

Melissa Aubin
University of Florida

It was "the job of ancient romance," in the words of classicist Helen Elsom, "to teach the difference between the sexes."[2] It is exceedingly clear in our five complete examples of the ancient novel that the characters of hero and heroine exemplify an unmistakable gender difference, modeling certain definitions of gender that, not surprisingly, are thought to leave a legacy between the airbrushed paper bindings of modern romances.[3] For example, in Chariton's *Chaereas and Callirhoe*,[4] the heroine, an unparalleled beauty and a general's daughter, falls in love at first sight with the hero Chaereas, though their "happily-ever-after" is repeatedly imperiled after Chaereas, prey to a deceit similar to Othello's,

[1] I offer special thanks to Professors Ronald F. Hock (University of Southern California), Elizabeth Clark (Duke University), and Michaela Janan (Duke University) for their assistance with this project as well as the members of the SBL Ancient Fiction and Early Christian and Jewish Narrative Group. I also thank the AAR/SBL Southeastern Conference for selecting this paper for the Regional Scholar Award, and I thank the SBL Conference of Regional Secretaries for supporting the presentation of this paper at the 1996 AAR/SBL National Conference in New Orleans, LA.

[2] H. Elsom, "Callirhoe: Displaying the Phallic Woman," *Pornography and Representation in Greece and Rome* (A. Richlin, ed.; New York: Oxford University Press, 1992) 212–30, esp. 213.

[3] For a compelling exploration of parallels between ancient and contemporary romances, see Holly Montague, "Sweet and Pleasant Passion: Female and Male Fantasy in Ancient Romance Novels," *Pornography and Representation*, 231–49.

[4] For the now standard translation of this and other ancient novels, see B. P. Reardon, ed., *Collected Ancient Greek Novels* (Berkeley: University of California Press, 1989); for a Greek text and English translation of *Chaereas and Callirhoe*, see G. P. Goold, ed. and trans., *Chariton: Callirhoe* (LCL; Cambridge: Harvard University Press, 1995). For recent introductions to the ancient novel, see N. Holzberg, *The Ancient Novel, an Introduction* (London: Routledge, 1995); T. Hägg, *The Novel in Antiquity* (Oxford: Blackwell, 1983); E. L. Bowie and S. J. Harrison, "The Romance of the Novel," *JRS* 83 (1993) 159–78; and G. Schmeling, ed. *The Novel in the Ancient World* (Leiden: E. J. Brill, 1996).

mortally attacks Callirhoe in a fit of jealousy. Revived in her tomb and subsequently kidnaped by grave robbers, Callirhoe endures, among other things, sea voyages, slavery, paternity problems, and contests for her hand in marriage before she is rescued by Chaereas, who, having discovered his mistake, has pursued her through similar perils to the far reaches of Persia. As one might expect from gender stereotypes in modern romance as it has re-emerged in the centuries since the Renaissance re-discovery of Heliodorus, our heroine is always contested in order to negotiate relations between powerful men. The desire for her perfect beauty motivates her trafficking and regulates her interactions with men; she is the object of every man's desire and her beauty propels the plot as various powerful men attempt to own it.[5]

It has been claimed that precisely these affinities between the content of the ancient novel and modern romance have led to the marginalization of the romance in the academic study of classical literature. J. R. Morgan could not have expressed his dismay at this better when he described a senior scholar's response to his desire to study the ancient romances: "I was reassured, in all kindness, that I need not feel down-hearted at the prospect of spending three whole years reading silly love stories, because there were some very interesting uses of the optative to be discovered in Heliodorus."[6] But as Kate Cooper[7] and Judith Perkins[8] have admirably detailed in their recent books, *The Virgin and the Bride*, and *The Suffering Self*, the novels were not as one-dimensional as they might seem when read in the shadow of a history of scholarship that balked at their seemingly frivolous themes.

Romance and Civic Values

Cooper and Perkins argue that the ostensibly lighthearted portraits of heroines and heroes bore the weight of the Roman civic ideal, encoding marriage as a theme signifying both domestic and imperial harmony.

---

[5] For recent investigations in the roles and images of ancient romance heroines, see B. M. Egger, *Women in the Greek Novel: Constructing the Feminine* (Diss., University of California at Irvine, 1990), and S. Wiersma, "The Ancient Greek Novel and its Heroines: A Formal Paradox," *Mnemosyne* 43 (1990) 109–23.

[6] J. R. Morgan, "The Ancient Novel at the End of the Century: Scholarship since the Dartmouth Conference," *CPh* 91 (1996) 63–73; quotation from p. 63.

[7] K. Cooper, *The Virgin and the Bride: Idealized Womanhood in Late Antiquity* (Cambridge: Harvard University Press, 1996).

[8] J. Perkins, *The Suffering Self: Pain and Narrative Representation in the Early Christian Era* (London: Routledge, 1995).

Cooper cogently argues that the novels' portrayal of dangerous episodes accompanying marriage in the more elite strata of Roman society illustrated living concerns about the social consequences of imperiled marriage—dynastic strife and social instability.[9] To this end, the string of dramatic episodes that constantly call into question the possibility of a successful marriage and the resolution of this doubt in the happy union of the couple at the novels' ends represents the working out of the task of maintaining social stability at an imperial level. Perkins concurs by identifying the novels as a means for the Greek urban elite to maintain their social identity.[10] The authors' portrayal of marital *concordia* served to confirm, at a personal level, an ideal of harmony operating among all members of society. Rather than facetious love stories, then, the novels may demonstrate the necessity of marriage in the maintenance Roman civic values by complicating the task of marriage and elevating its importance in the narrative. The construction of the gender roles for the romantic hero and heroine served this end. The reader relies on a strict difference between the genders for the plot to progress, with the heroine as object of several men's affections, and the hero as agent and contender for the nuptial prize.

In addition, according to Cooper, the novel betrays an elite perspective due to the sympathetic portrayal of the curial class, concern for fertility for those who are socially compatible, and chastity between those who are not, the legitimate union of couples in marriage.[11] Such a perspective begs the question of an elite male readership. Rather than the audience of "uncultivated and frivolous-minded people" suggested by Perry,[12] Elsom has suggested that in the case of *Chaereas and Callirhoe*, the authors of romance tailored their narratives toward a male readership, in part by engineering the male gaze so that the descriptions of Callirhoe's guarded sexuality bridge the gap between the hero's and the audience's desire for the heroine.[13]

According to Cooper and Perkins, then, the novels' job of authorizing the difference between the sexes was intertwined with the job of

---

[9] Cooper, *The Virgin and the Bride*, 28–36.

[10] Perkins, *Suffering Self*, 41–76, esp. 44–45.

[11] Cooper, *The Virgin and the Bride*, 20–44.

[12] B. E. Perry, *The Ancient Romances* (Berkeley: University of California Press, 1967) 4–5.

[13] Elsom, "Callirhoe," 213ff; see also E. L. Bowie, "The Readership of Greek Novels in the Ancient World," in *The Search for the Ancient Novel* (J. Tatum, ed.; Baltimore: Johns Hopkins University Press, 1994) 435–59, who suggests an elite readership.

reinforcing the civic ideal. What, then, about the Apocryphal Acts of the Apostles, whose narratives of the apostles' exploits have led more than a few scholars to associate the works with the genre of the ancient novel? Here again, narratives are propelled by the concern for guarding the beautiful, well-born heroines from sexual penetration. Women are contended for by men and imperiled in near death situations. The string of dramatic episodes in the Apocryphal Acts leads finally to the heroine's sustained virginity and autonomy, and at times the masculinization of her appearance, rather than the reunion of lovers and marriage found *de rigeur* in the romance climax.[14]

Reversing Romance?

While we need not force the Apocryphal Acts into the genre of romance,[15] I suggest that the affinities were not accidental. Adopting certain characteristics of the novel, the Apocryphal Acts transform others in order to subvert what Cooper and Perkins isolate as the guiding ideological task of the romance—the preservation of the idea of social stability through the elevation of marriage and the praise of the curial class. Whereas the novels' authors inscribe these concerns on their heroines as brides, the Apocryphal Acts use the heroines to overturn the values drafted by the blueprint of romance. Negative portrayals of the "city" and the curial class in the Apocryphal Acts confirm this subversion. Moreover, just as Chariton enlists his readers in its ideological task by engineering the male gaze, I suggest that in the case of the *Acts of Thecla* the author uses narrative-rhetorical devices, especially situational irony, in

---

[14] R. Pervo ("Aseneth and Her Sisters: Women in Jewish Narrative and in the Greek Novels," *Women Like This: New Perspectives on Jewish Women in the Greco-Roman World* [SBLEJL 1; A. J. Levine, ed.; Atlanta: Scholars Press, 1991] 145–60) has examined portrayals of women in late antique Jewish literature and suggests that authors of Jewish fiction were familiar with Greek romance. Pervo notes that Jewish authors present their heroines in strikingly different ways than authors of Greek romance. I, too, argue that Apocryphal Acts authors intentionally depart from depictions of heroines established in the ancient novels (see below), though the rhetorical effect of this departure depends on knowledge of the ancient novels themselves.

[15] On the possibility of categorizing the Apocryphal Acts as romance, see R. Pervo, *Profit with Delight: the Literary Genre of the Acts of the Apostles* (Philadelphia: Fortress, 1987); on the canonical Acts as romance, see L. Alexander, "'In Journeyings Often': Voyaging in the Acts of the Apostles and in Greek Romance," in *Luke's Literary Achievement: Collected Essays* (JSNTSup 116; C. M. Tuckett, ed.; Sheffield: Sheffield Academic Press, 1995) 17–39.

order to enlist the reader in the subversion of the politicized plot of the romances.

Cooper has expertly illustrated this subversion in the *Acts of Andrew* and broached this issue for the *Acts of Thecla*.[16] In what follows, I shall use the narrative of the *Acts of Thecla* in order to augment discussion of this interpretation.[17] I suggest that the story is enough like the novel that the late ancient reader would have perceived the intentional differences from Greek romance and spot the resulting mischief that the author of the *Acts of Thecla* wrought with gender and the civic ideal. Most notably, the rhetorical positioning of the reader "against" the city and "for" Thecla's masculinization (at times at the expense of Paul's own masculinity) in the *Acts of Thecla* illustrates the subversion of civic values illustrated in the Greek novels.

The narrative analysis begins with a brief outline of the narrative structure of *Acts of Thecla*. The text divides into two halves, each sharing the same sequence of events. Each half contains three major episodes that provide a template for the exploits of Thecla: 1) a confrontation with and rejection of a high status male, 2) arrest and trial of Thecla as a result of this confrontation, and 3) an attempt to execute Thecla once she is condemned.[18] At the end of each succession of episodes there occurs a confrontation between Paul and Thecla in which Thecla emerges as the more informed and powerful character. The momentum mounts during the repetition of the narrative sequence as the text simultaneously orchestrates Thecla's masculinization and Paul's relative feminization,

---

[16] Cooper, *The Virgin and the Bride*, 45–66.

[17] For an edition of the Greek text for the *Acts of Thecla*, see R. Lipsius, ed. *Acta Apostolorum Apocrypha* (Hildesheim: Georg Olms Verlagsbuchhandlung, 1959) 90–104. The translation from which this paper quotes is found in "Acts of Paul," *New Testament Apocrypha* (W. Schneemelcher, ed.; R. McL. Wilson, trans.; 2 vols.; Louisville, KY: Westminster/John Knox, 1991–1993) 2.221–70. The *Acts of Thecla* may have once circulated independently from the *Acts of Paul*, in which the former is now embedded (but see Schneemelcher, *New Testament Apocrypha*, 1.222); this paper assumes that the *Acts of Thecla* has a narrative cohesion in its own right and integrity as a story apart from the surrounding *Acts of Paul*. Recent secondary literature on the *Acts of Thecla* includes most notably D. R. MacDonald, *The Legend and the Apostle: The Battle for Paul in Story and Canon* (Philadelphia: Westminster, 1983); other works that examine the text in light of its social setting include V. Burrus, *Chastity as Autonomy: Women in the Stories of the Apocryphal Acts* (Queenston, Ontario: Edwin Mellen, 1987) and S. L. Davies, *The Revolt of the Widows: The Social World of the Apocryphal Acts* (New York: Seabury, 1980).

[18] For an alternative breakdown of the narrative content of the *Acts of Thecla*, see Burrus, *Chastity as Autonomy*, 61.

and engineers sympathy between the reader and Thecla's character, and antipathy against the city and its leaders in the narrative.

This rhetorical effect results most notably from instances of situational irony. The narrator's orchestration of situational irony is apparent once one notes distinctions between narrative levels within the *Acts of Thecla*. Like any other narrative, the *Acts of Thecla* is comprised by a system of "tellers" located on various levels of discourse which can be visualized as boxes within boxes. The levels are determined by who is telling the story and to whom the story is being told. At the broadest level, the historical author tells the story to the historical ("authorial") audience. Within this level are contained stories that the characters within the *Acts of Thecla* narrative tell each other ("second degree narration")—this level is crucial for the execution of situational irony in the text. While the omniscient narrator and authorial audience hear and know all events in the narrative, the characters in the story hear only what is given in second-degree narration. Thus the knowledge of the characters can be strikingly limited.

Situational irony is the product of such differences in "knowledge" at various narrative levels, since the device depends on a character's naiveté, perceived due to the authorial audience's superior knowledge of events in the narrative and the characters' own private thoughts. Situational irony takes on rhetorical effect because the unequal allocation of knowledge by the narrator results in community-building between the reader and those the narrator portrays in a positive light (here, Thecla and her supporters), while leading the audience to alienate those who are portrayed in a negative light (Thecla's detractors). Stated differently, the narrator and reader enjoy the camaraderie of private jokes that parties in second-degree narration can not "get"—such characters often serve as the butt of these jokes due to their relative ignorance.[19] In the following section, narrrative examples of situational irony become apparent, along with a series of examples that demonstrate the "reversal" of elements common in ancient romances, most notably the gender roles of hero and heroine and the positive stance toward marriage and thus the civic ideal.

---

[19] The analysis that follows is based methodologically on the rhetorical criticism of S. Lanser (*Narrative Action and Point of View in Prose Fiction* [Princeton: Princeton University Press, 1981]).

Narrative-Rhetorical Analysis

The institution of marriage so sought after and imperiled in the novel is also an occasion for conflict in the *Acts of Thecla*, but only because it is rejected so fiercely by those Christians who would remain celibate. The *Acts of Thecla* author leaves no room for dispute about this conflict, as it already appears at the beginning of the narrative. Here, Paul, a newcomer to Iconium, issues his most elaborate religious manifesto of the text, a list of beatitudes that overwhelmingly emphasize the "blessedness" of those who abstain from sex and renounce socio-sexual values praised in the romance, even more often than the "blessedness" of those who adhere to the teachings of Jesus. Paul repeatedly blesses "those who have kept flesh pure," "the continent," and "those who have wives as if they had them not," and he reserves his final and most elaborate blessing for virgins:

> Blessed are the bodies of virgins, for they shall be well pleasing to God, and shall not lose the reward of their purity. For the word of the Father shall be for them a work of salvation in the day of his Son, and they shall have rest for ever and ever (3:18–19).

Those familiar with the text know that Paul's initial declaration of the favor which God shows to virgins functions as an important "narrative premonition" because here the author, through the voice of Paul, "gives away" the ultimate victory of Thecla over all of the dangers she will encounter in the narrative, by virtue of her "blessed" choice to remain a virgin. Furthermore, we will find that the contrapositive of Paul's statement "blessed are the virgins" will also ring true. That is, the non-virgins and detractors of the celibate lifestyle will be cursed.

In her initial appearance in the narrative, Thecla is at a window, listening to Paul's good news of the virginal life (3:7). Many elements of this scenario highlight Thecla's passivity in the final moments of her tenure in a role as a "maiden of such modesty" (3:8). In her described situation at the window, for example, Thecla is visually framed for the reader. She is described within the text as an object acted upon, "gripped" and "taken captive" by Paul's compelling message (3:7–8). Moreover, the author highlights her passivity during her parents' alarm with a simile that reduces her presence to a mere speck: "she sticks to the window like a spider" (3:9). Nonetheless, while at the window, Thecla herself frames Paul with her gaze,[20] a possible indicator of later episodes in which Thecla's portrayal supercedes that of her mentor.

In Thecla's response to the concern of her family during her hypnotic vigil, we find that she rejects the socio-sexual values expected of her. Thecla refuses to turn to her fiancé (Thamyris) and "be ashamed" and continues her vigil (3:10). Thamyris realizes that his fiancée has rejected him, and Theocleia also realizes that her daughter has rejected the traditional vocation of wifehood. Both mourn their respective losses of wife and daughter, and the "traditional" Thecla is replaced by a more sexually and socially autonomous Thecla.

The second major episode of the first narrative cycle, consisting of the first arrest and trial of Thecla, has certain precipitating circumstances in the first cycle that are not so elaborate in the second. After Thecla's rejection of her betrothed, Thamyris incites like-minded defenders of the civic ideal against Paul, and the townspeople imprison Paul for later sentencing. Eager to hear more from Paul, Thecla visits him at the jail after nightfall, confirming the defiance begun by her tacit rejection of Thamyris (3:15).[21]

Upon arriving, Thecla steps further from her initial demeanor by bribing her entrance into the jail and relinquishing distinctively feminine possessions. In order to penetrate the prison, she first offers her bracelets to the door-keeper, and then gives a silver mirror to the jailer. Thus, Thecla's physical access to Paul involves revoking her traditional gender signifiers, and indeed, in the case of the mirror, a possible signifier of her former identity (3:18). Whereas shackles bind Paul's wrists in the prison, Thecla's rebellion involves the removal of the bracelets from her own wrists. This reversal, which uses the same image to connote Thecla's "liberation" and Paul's bondage, is our first clue to the emergence of Thecla as a figure who supercedes Paul in authority and masculine license. Indeed, from this point on, Paul repeatedly appears impotent in comparison. Thus the Apocryphal Acts author's polemic against the

---

[20] I am grateful to my colleague Andrew Jacobs for this observation.

[21] Thecla's suggested erotic attachment to Paul in this scene (3:19–20) may be another strategy in the subversion of the Greek romance, since the Greek term *storgē* used to represent her affection is often defined to mean filial rather than erotic love. Narrative hints to suggest that the relationship is erotic [she was "chained to [Paul] by affection," (3:19) and she "kissed his bonds" (3:18)] may mime the charcters of the romance, leaving the narrator to clarify the situation by describing their relationship in filial terms, simultaneously evoking and altering the template of hero/heroine relationships in the ancient novels.

novel's civic ideal comes at the expense of Paul's masculinity,[22] as Thecla, tested through more severe trials, emerges as the more radical (and more masculine) opponent of traditional values ensconced in "the city."

Betrayed by slaves of the doorkeeper, Thecla is discovered with Paul by Thamyris and Thecla's family, and they incite the crowd against them, and then report the matter to the governor (3:19). We note that "the city" and "the crowd" gain a larger role in the narrative from this point on as a collective enemy of both Paul and Thecla. Numerous subsequent examples will show that the opposition between "the city" and Thecla demonstrates the extreme alienation that results from Thecla's departure from the traditional socio-sexual values practiced in the cities she visits, the very values upheld in the Greek romances. Civil authorities are Thecla's most dangerous persecutors, and they react with violence against Thecla due to the apparent threat that her alternative societal role presents to the locus of traditional social mores, the city. Indeed, as the narrative progresses, the city appears again as an enemy of Thecla's female supporters who are, in turn, enemies of the city in Thecla's defense.

Both Paul and Thecla stand before the governor of Iconium, and the only question which the governor asks of Thecla involves the rejection of her expected societal role: "Why do you not marry Thamyris according to the law of the Iconians?" (3:20). Refusing to speak, Thecla receives the foregone death sentence while Paul is merely expelled from the city, but it is not the governor who sentences Thecla. Rather, her own mother attempts to stem any influence Thecla may have on other women: "Burn her that is no bride in the midst of the theater, that all women who have been taught by this man may be afraid!" (3:20).

Here, Theocleia may react against the possibility that Thecla's decision not to marry will complicate the issue of who will care for Theocleia in her old age. Refusing to generate a family of her own jeopardizes the chance that Thecla will have the resources to offer appropriate care for Theocleia should she be widowed. At the narrative's end, however, the author demonstrates that this breach of social *mos* is little cause for

---

[22] As V. Burrus notes, Paul's credibility with the reader is damaged, as well, such that Paul: "comes precariously close to alliance with Thecla's villainous opponents. We begin to suspect that he is not in fact Thecla's helper but is, like the other males in the story, part of her problem" ("Word and Flesh: The Bodies of Ascetic Women in Christian Antiquity," *JFSR* 10 [1994] 27–51, esp. 47).

concern in the lifestyle which Thecla chooses; Theocleia will certainly receive support provided that she too convert to Christianity.[23]

The third episode of the first narrative cycle, the attempt to execute Thecla, occurs in both cycles before a crowd at a theater. Here, virgins, like Thecla only in matters of physiology, are portrayed as agents of the city who prepare the pyre on which Thecla will burn. Thecla enters naked before the governor who "marvels at the power that was in her" (3:22) despite her ostensibly vulnerable state. Once ignited, the fire, however, is soon extinguished by a thunderstorm that kills many of the spectators from the city. The retribution which is originally initiated by the city here falls upon the city, the locus of traditional values and common enemy to both Paul and Thecla.

This first cycle of narrative events ends with an episode featuring Paul and Thecla in which Thecla emerges as the more competent and "masculine" figure. Having escaped the pyre, Thecla seeks out Paul and finds him in a funeral vault on the road to Daphne. Notably, the setting for this scene is in a safe place, at a necropolis outside the "cities" of Daphne and Iconium (3:23). Here, Paul admits his own impotence in liberating Thecla by resigning himself to mourning Thecla's presumed death, and he regrettably suggests his own insincerity by prematurely breaking the mourning fast. Paul sends a child to find bread and pay for it with Paul's own cloak. Again, note the contrast of narrative elements associated with Paul and Thecla. Whereas Paul denudes himself of a cloak in this episode signifying his weakness, Thecla ironically displayed her power to the governor once she had been denuded by another.

Thecla, now a confessor, continues her "masculinization" by stating she intends to cut her hair and follow Paul as an apostle. Paul denies her request for baptism admonishing: "The season is unfavorable and you are beautiful; may no other temptation come upon you worse than the first so that you not endure and become a coward" (3:25). Ironically, Paul, whose cowardice the narrative will very soon establish, speaks of Thecla's beauty rather than her piety.

Paul's refusal to baptize Thecla and failure to recognize her sincerity seems designed to produce frustration in the eyes of the reader, who has just observed Thecla's endurance alone in the face of death for the sake

---

[23] ". . . it is because of Theocleia's thoughtless complicity in the demands of the city—its craven, seemingly endless need to harness the bodies of youth to replenish its numbers—that she emerges as one of the story's minor villains," Cooper, *The Virgin and the Bride*, 54.

of her new-found faith. Between Paul and the authorial audience, however, only the reader is privy to the dramatic demonstration of Thecla's faith at the theater. By disenfranchising the very one who has so closely adhered to his own teaching, Paul, like those who espouse the civic ideal, becomes discredited with the reader. Moreover, Paul's own exhortations to celibacy and presumed conversion of other virgins (3:18) heighten his hypocrisy here. The author's narrative technique of allocating more information about Thecla's faith to the authorial audience than to Paul carries the rhetorical function of engineering the fall of Paul's credibility with the audience. Paul, feminized and alienated in the eyes of the reader, highlights Thecla as the more "masculine" of the two as she more strongly defies values central to the "city."

Repeating the Cycle

After this ironic episode, the narrative cycle starts all over again: now, Thecla seeks an alternative societal role independently of Paul, and the new narrative episodes in which Thecla again repeatedly shuns her traditional role are more dangerous and demanding than those of the first cycle. Upon comparison of the first episode of the second cycle with its counterpart, one finds marked differences in the way Thecla reacts in her confrontation with a "traditional elite male." Thecla encounters a man described as a "prominent citizen," not unlike her jilted fiancé; he is the Syrian Alexander, "first of the Antiochenes" (3:26). Now, however, Thecla must ward off a threatening aggressor rather than a would-be husband. Unlike the former case in which Thecla rejects her fiancé at Paul's instigation, here Thecla rejects Alexander despite Paul's failure to defend her ("I do not know the woman of whom you speak, nor is she mine" 3:26). Having denied his acquaintance with Thecla despite his recently-mentioned prayers on her behalf, Paul fails to answer Thecla's cries and vanishes from the scene (3:26).

Virginia Burrus has pointedly suggested that Alexander does not hesitate to molest Thecla in the street because her departure from private space and free movement in public indicate to Alexander that she is sexually promiscuous.[24] If so, Paul's hasty retreat suggests an attempt to preserve his own honor at the expense of Thecla's safety. Rather than Thecla, it is Paul who is concerned with being seen with the "wrong"

---

[24] Burrus, *Chastity as Autonomy*, 89.

company in public, and as a result he is further alienated from the authorial audience, which is once again left to root only for Thecla.

In the parallel episode, Thecla passively rejects Thamyris, but refuses to humble herself when Thamyris urges her to "be ashamed." Now Thecla is not only unashamed, but she succeeds expertly in inflicting shame on her attacker by thrice denuding Alexander. First, in her struggle to free herself from his grip, she rips off his chlamys, an imperial or military mantle, and she also denudes him of his crown, making him appear as "one conquered." More specifically, in an Armenian text of the *Acts of Thecla*, Thecla "tore off the golden crown of the figure of Caesar, which he had on his head and dashed it to the ground."[25] Finally, Thecla denudes Alexander of his honor by successfully rebuffing him in public, disgracing his religious and political offices in her own defense. Again, whereas Thecla's nudity signifies her power, the nudity of her adversary signifies his impotence.

Presumably because of the shame Thecla has inflicted, Alexander brings her bound before the governor. Thecla now speaks on her own behalf, confesses before the governor that she did indeed defend herself against Alexander, and for this, she is condemned to the beasts. The charge which Thecla receives only after her sentencing is "Sacrilege" (3:28),[26] presumably for disregarding the cultic importance of Alexander's crown or for her more general stance against civic values. The authorial audience, having recognized Thecla all along as a model of piety superceding even Paul, may recognize the irony in the charge of sacrilege. The non sequitur portrays Thecla's indicters as woefully ignorant of who Thecla "really" is,[27] although the authorial audience is fully informed. This disparity of knowledge among first- and second-degree narrative levels renders the cruelty toward Thecla unfounded, and the authorial audience again discredits Thecla's enemies due to their ill-informed treatment of her; this disparity in levels of awareness widens significantly as the text continues.

---

[25] See MacDonald, *The Legend and the Apostle*, 41. S. R. F. Price (*Rituals and Power: The Roman Imperial Cult in Asia Minor* [Cambridge: Cambridge University Press, 1984] 124) argues that Thecla is punished in the theater for damaging the imperial image of the priest's crown; for this reference I thank Professor Ronald F. Hock.

[26] Cf. 3:20, in which Paul is labeled a "sorcerer" by a crowd of Iconians; both charges of sacrilege and magic label Thecla and Paul as improperly religious, as rejectors of civic values.

[27] I.e., how Thecla is portrayed by the narrator.

The second, more dangerous attempt to execute Thecla is now mitigated by support from sympathetic females in attendance, rather than pyre-tending virgins as before. Because the games are subsidized by Thecla's publicly-shamed aggressor, Alexander, he has jurisdiction over precisely how cruelly her execution is orchestrated. Amid these ominous circumstances, the women's cries ("A godless judgment!" and "An impious judgment has come to pass in the city!" 3:28) sound an ironic antithesis of the charge of sacrilege which seals Thecla's fate and again demonstrates the association between "the city" and Thecla's oppressors.

In order to guard her virginity during the interim between her trial and games, Thecla petitions the governor for a custodian and receives a wealthy, politically connected woman, Tryphaena, as her caretaker (3:29). By providing Thecla with refuge as an adoptive mother, Tryphaena stands in diametric opposition to Thecla's birth-mother, Theocleia, who abandoned her daughter and condemned her to death. Although Theocleia banished Thecla so that her life will not be used as an example for other women, Tryphaena does nothing other than adopt Thecla's lifestyle, using her new daughter as an exemplar, converting to Christianity, thus subverting the civic ideal despite her relationship to the emperor.

The second narrative string culminates in the final, fantastic attempt to execute Thecla. Here again, nothing is heard from Paul, but Thecla finds allies in all the other females, human and beastly, in attendance. Even the female lioness to which Thecla is bound when she processes into the theater licks Thecla's feet with compassion (3:33). Moreover, the women of the audience again blame "the city" (3:32) for Thecla's situation and vow their own support. Fearing that she may die unbaptized, Thecla hurls herself into a pool of hungry seals in the name of Christ to consecrate herself, and at that moment, a selectively-fatal flash of lightning strikes the pit, leaving the seals floating on the surface of the water (3:34). Just as Thecla's nudity compelled the governor of Iconium to weep during his attempt to burn her alive, here again, the governor of Antioch wept as she leaped denuded into a pit of seals. As she escapes from the pit, she is miraculously clothed by a cloud of protective fire "so that neither did the animals touch her nor was she perceived as naked"; lack of clothing is again an empowering rather than punitive state for Thecla.

Alexander procures two of his own bulls and decides to tie Thecla to them and then incite the bulls to rage by burning their genitals with a heated iron.[28] The scene is especially violent: a young, naked woman with her legs potentially torn open by bulls enraged by the pain inflicted on their sexual organs. Ironically, such tortures occur only because Thecla resisted Alexander's sexual advances. Interestingly, such a visual cue suggests that Alexander's last resort in punishing Thecla for appropriating "masculine" behavior involves vengeance by means of mutilating what is uniquely male. For all its retributive potential, the attempt is ineffective. Thecla is once again delivered from harm by a beneficent fire which burns the ropes that bind her to the bulls without burning her skin. Not even this miraculous event causes Alexander to relent, however.

Apparently in her fear for Thecla's life, Tryphaena faints as she stands beside the arena, and her maids cry out, "The queen Tryphaena is dead!" (3:36). At this, the collective adversary of Thecla, "the city," becomes alarmed, and Thecla's arch-persecutor, Alexander, falls at the feet of the governor and petitions in a panic for permission to cease the games before any other disasters occur. Alexander fears for his own safety, reasoning that he and the city will perish if Caesar were to attribute Tryphaena's death to Alexander's disturbing games. Once again, the consequence of Thecla's torture falls on the city, and in this case, on Thecla's individual aggressor.

Here, the author brings the technique of situational irony to its apex in the narrative. The author creates a wide disparity of awareness between the authorial audience and the enemies of Thecla. Whereas the author has privileged the reader with the information that Tryphaena has merely fainted and will revive momentarily, the joke is on Alexander who emotionally throws himself, feminized, before the governor and begs that the games cease. The twofold rhetorical effect of situational irony is brought to its height, as well: community among those with superior knowledge, supporters of Tryphaena and Thecla, is strengthened, and those with inferior knowledge, especially Alexander, are excluded and denigrated.

Thecla, victorious, appears naked before the governor who commands that she be clothed. In this case, becoming clothed proves an event that demonstrates Thecla's self-agency. She determines how and when her body should be covered, informing the governor: "the one who clothed

---

[28] Davies (*Revolt of the Widows*, 106) presents this torture scene, with its possible tendency to be especially gruesome to women, as an indication that the *Acts of Thecla* may have been authored by a woman.

me while I was naked among the beasts shall clothe me with salvation." As Maragret Miles observed, "Thecla reinterprets her nakedness away from its traditional significance, removing it from the governor's power and aligning it with her strength as a confessor of Christ."[29]

This episode leads directly to Thecla's second extended encounter with Paul. Finding him after her release, Thecla has "girded herself and sewed her mantle into a cloak after the fashion of men" (3:40). Now rid of her feminine clothes as well as her mirror and bracelet, Thecla completely sheds her tokens of femininity. Her repeated endurance does not convince Paul, who still apprehends her as a woman subject to temptation, despite the crowd of followers who have flocked to hear her teach. Given Thecla's already ongoing missionary work and her own decision to lead a mission, Paul can only impotently commission Thecla to "Go and teach the word of God" (3:41).

Before continuing her mission, Thecla returns to Iconium and persuades her mother to convert to Christianity: "Theocleia my mother, can you believe that the Lord lives in heaven? For if you desire money, the Lord will give it to you through me" (3:43). Ironically, one might assume that some of the financial resources for Theocleia may derive from Thecla's alternative mother, Tryphaena, who, upon conversion, "sent much clothing and gold, so that she could leave some of it for the service of the poor" (3:42). Having converted Theocleia, Thecla resumes her mission in Seleucia. In dramatic contrast to her initial meek and immobile appearance in the narrative, Thecla leaves the story roaming widely in public space.

How does one interpret all these paradoxes? The pattern that I have traced may offer some clues—in a nutshell, the Apocryphal Acts narrative shows 1) Thecla's commitment to virginity but her gradual masculinization alongside Paul's relative feminization, and 2) the audience's increasing sympathy for Thecla and antipathy toward those who demand Roman civic values of her, including, to some extent, Paul. This is all achieved in the template of the Roman novel, but the Christian author's strategy capitalizes on the reversal of both the novel's gender roles and sympathy for the Roman curial class for ironic effect.

---

[29] Margaret Miles, *Carnal Knowing: Female Nakedness and Religious Meaning in the Christian West* (Boston: Beacon, 1989) 58.

Conclusion

I conclude by noting that if it was indeed the job of ancient romance to teach the difference between the sexes, it was the job of Apocryphal Acts authors to confound romance readers on this front. This teaching of difference, a product of arguments over the status of the civic ideal in either ascetic or traditional Roman contexts, belies concerns about identity illustrated with and not confined to gender in both the novel and the Apocryphal Acts. Moreover, it was the common task of both genres to inscribe the morals of the stories on the heroines who, for all their endurance through narrative contortions, may very well inform the historian more about the ideological worlds of their masculinist puppeteers[30] than the very details of their lives that appear on the page. Heroes and heroines, then, are maps traced with boundaries and dimensions of more elusive social bodies and ideological territories, each illuminating the other. Those unpersuaded by the complexities offered to the reader by these ostensibly silly love stories, however, may have more luck searching for the reportedly very interesting uses of the optative to be found in Heliodorus.

------

[30] I agree with Cooper that "the challenge by the apostle to the householder is the urgent message of these narratives, and it is essentially a conflict between men" (*The Virgin and the Bride*, 55). Thus, the *Acts of Thecla* do not appear to speak first and foremost to the "liberatory" concerns of women presumed by Burrus (*Chastity as Autonomy*). Nonetheless, I disagree with P. W. Dunn ("Women's Liberation, The *Acts of Paul*, and Other Acts of the Apostles: A Review of Some Recent Interpreters," *Apocrypha* 4 [1993] 245–61) who argues that readings of the *Acts of Thecla* are guided by twentieth century feminism and urges that the documents be researched "on their own terms, without the unwarranted imposition of contemporary ideology" (p. 258). Any reading of these texts, including Dunn's, necessarily imposes what Dunn calls "contemporary ideology;" one can only hope, at best, to be as aware as possible of the methods one brings to the text and their implications.

Stories Without Texts and Without Authors: The Problem of Fluidity in Ancient Novelistic Texts and Early Christian Literature

Christine M. Thomas
University of California at Santa Barbara

There exists a long history of comparative study between ancient "fiction," however this be defined, and early Christian literature. The Apocryphal Acts of the Apostles, literary products of second-century Greek-speaking Christians, are the one category of early Christian literature most often classified as Christian novels *tout court*.[1] This designation is substantially accurate against the background of ancient literature in general; but the description "novel" does not settle the matter of appropriate generic models either for the Apocryphal Acts or for early Christian narrative texts more generally, because it answers the

---

[1] This is the position first proposed by Ernst von Dobschütz, "Der Roman in der altchristlichen Literatur," *Deutsche Rundschau* 111 (1902) 87–106, and held by: Philip Vielhauer, *Geschichte der urchristlichen Literatur* (Berlin: de Gruyter, 1975) 715–16; Eckhard Plümacher, "Apokryphe Apostelakten," *PWSupp* 15 (1978) 11–70, esp. 63; David Aune, *The New Testament in Its Literary Environment* (Philadelphia: Westminster, 1987) 149–52; B. P. Reardon, *The Form of Greek Romance* (Princeton: Princeton University Press, 1991) 165; and Richard Pervo, who nuances the definition considerably, concluding that the Apocryphal Acts are historical novels (*Profit with Delight: The Literary Genre of the Acts of the Apostles* [Philadelphia: Fortress, 1987] 121–35). Several scholars admit that the novel offers one of the literary models, but that other elements also play a significant role in their generic definition: Rosa Söder, *Die apokryphen Apostelgeschichten und die romanhafte Literatur der Antike* (Stuttgart: Kohlhammer, 1932) 216; F. Morard, "Souffrance et Martyre dans les Actes apocryphes des apôtres," in *Les Actes apocryphes des apôtres: Christianisme et monde païen* (F. Bovon et al., eds.; Publications de la Faculté de Théologie de l'Université de Genève 4; Geneva: Labor et Fides, 1981) 95–108, esp. 107–8; Jean-Daniel Kaestli, "Les principales orientations de la recherche sur les Actes apocryphes des apôtres," in *Actes apocryphes,* 49–67, esp. 65–67; Helmut Koester, *Introduction to the New Testament* (2 vols.; Philadelphia: Fortress, 1982) 2.324; Tomas Hägg, *The Novel in Antiquity* (Berkeley: University of California Press, 1983) 160–61; Niklas Holzberg, *The Ancient Novel: An Introduction* (C. Jackson-Holzberg, trans.; London: Routledge, 1995) 22–26, who wisely presents the Christian texts as the beginning of the *reception* of the novel.

question by raising a further and more serious methodological quandary. The issue is not so much the appropriateness of the comparison between such Christian literature and the ancient novels, as the validity of the particular definition of the genre of the novel that has been common coin. The accident of preservation has skewed the general picture. The five polytheist "ancient novels" that exist in their entirety are repeatedly cited as the chief examples of the genre: Chariton's *Chaereas and Kallirhoe*, Xenophon's *Ephesiaka*, the *Daphnis and Chloe* of Longos, the *Leukippe and Kleitophon* of Achilles Tatius, and the *Ethiopika* of Heliodoros.[2] These are, without exception, tales of two young people who fall in love, are separated by a series of catastrophes such as robbery, sale into slavery, pirate attacks, and shipwreck, only to be reunited happily in matrimony at the end;[3] they are rightly called "ideal romances." The stubborn entrapment, however, of the generic designation "ancient novel" within the realm of these five ideal romances, both in the work of classicists and of historians of early Christian literature, has obscured the true relationship between early Christian and polytheist literatures during the Roman imperial period.

The evidence of the fragmentary Greek novels strongly suggests that the ideal romances, far from being the center of the novelistic genre, are rather the endpoint of its development. The style of Achilles Tatius, Xenophon, and Longos attests to their relatively late date; they are works of the Second Sophistic, a literary revival movement of the second century.[4] To some extent, the distance in rhetorical style between non-

---

[2] For an example, see Reardon, *Form*.

[3] Only Longos dispenses with the motif of travel, and the dangers faced by the enamoured pair are correspondingly more subdued. Since they cannot travel to the pirates, however, the pirates come to their island of Lesbos (chap. 1.28–31).

[4] On presophistic (or nonsophistic) versus sophistic novels, see first Ben Edwin Perry, *The Ancient Romances: A Literary-Historical Account of Their Origins* (Sather Classical Lectures 37; Berkeley: University of California Press, 1967) 108–15. Also B. P. Reardon, "The Second Sophistic and the Novel," in *Approaches to the Second Sophistic* (G. W. Bowersock, ed.; University Park, PA: APA, 1974) 23–29; generally on the historical background, Bowersock, *Greek Sophists in the Roman Empire* (Oxford: Clarendon, 1969); and on the literary context most recently Graham Anderson, *The Second Sophistic: A Cultural Phenomenon in the Roman Empire* (London: Routledge, 1993), with 156–70 on the novels and related literature. Heliodoros does not fall among the sophistic novels because it is generally dated to the fourth century, on the basis of similarities between the description of the siege of Syene described in book nine and the real-life siege of Nisibis in 350 CE; the thesis was first expressed by R. Keydell in a publication of 1966, but see J. R. Morgan, "History, Romance, and Realism in the Aithiopika of Heliodoros," *ClAnt* 1 (1982) 221–65, esp. 253 and *passim*.

sophistic and sophistic is also apparent in orthography, morphology, and syntax. Many of the earlier fragments display a clean and elegant Hellenistic Greek; although the authors generally avoid hiatus and refrain from the more jarring Hellenistic neologisms and alternate morphological formations, the Atticizing, if it can be called that, is inconsistent.[5]

These earlier works demonstrate that the three Sophistic novels have undergone a genre shift. These three works are, indeed, fascinated with the past. The dramatic setting of each is a world that resembles the classical or post-classical Greek East; mention of Roman realities is studiously avoided, with the occasional lapse.[6] The earlier ideal romances, however, evince a more tangible relationship to political history. Rather than employing the historical ambience of the general setting as in the later ideal romances, the authors create main characters who are themselves direct relations of famous generals or tyrants, and eminent cultural figures walk through the early novels as scenery-dressing. The Ninos of the homonymous fragmentary novel is the legendary Babylonian ruler, and his sweetheart cousin Semiramis an Assyrian queen. Chariton's Kallirhoe is the daughter of the Syracusan general Hermokrates, known from Thucydides's history of the Peloponnesian war. The Metiochos and Parthenope from the novel fragment of the same name are respectively the son of the Athenian general Miltiades and the daughter of the Samian tyrant Polykrates.[7] These daughters and sons of leading political

---

[5] The fragments of the Ninos romance provide a good example of this uncluttered Greek. Although there are many correct Attic forms, the style is not free of Hellenistic features. See θάρσος rather than the Attic θάρρος (col. A1, l. 11); διαίτησις for διαίτημα (col. B1, l. 30); ἤμην for ἦ(ν) in the first person singular imperfect (frag. A3, l. 38; but see the Attic form in col. A2, l. 26); the sigmatic future γαμήσεται instead of the liquid γαμεῖται (frag. A3, l. 10); ἁρμόζομαι used with an accusative object rather than a dative (frag. A3, l. 14).

[6] Xenophon is the least consistent in providing a definite sense of the past. He mentions an eirenarch of Kilikia (for example, 2.13.3), an office that is only attested after 116–17 CE (David Magie, *Roman Rule in Asia Minor to the End of the Third Century* [2 vols.; Princeton: Princeton University Press, 1950] 1.647, 2.1514–15); in the same work, Habrokomes is brought before the *praefectus Aegypti* in Alexandria (for example, 3.12.6), sign of a post-Augustan date. See E. L. Bowie, "The Novels and the Real World," in *Erotica Antiqua* (B. P. Reardon, ed.; Bangor, Wales, 1977) 91–96.

[7] Hermokrates is mentioned first in Thucydides 4.58, and at length in 6.72–80; "Parthenope" the daughter of Polykrates in Herodotos 3.124, and Metiochos at 6.39–41. On *Chaereas and Kallirhoe*, see first B. E. Perry, "Chariton and His Romance from a Literary-Historical Point of View," *AJP* 51 (1930) 93–134; on the phenomenon in other works, see Perry, *Ancient Romances*, 137–40, 164–66 (Ninos) and T. Hägg,

figures illustrate the genealogical relationship between the genres of history and novel; like the main characters themselves, these prose narratives are the descendants of political historiography.

The "shift of center" necessitated by the fragments, however, comes into yet clearer focus in the works that are unlike the ideal romances. Long ruled the assumption that only the Romans had developed comic or picaresque novels; the fragments of the *Phoinikika* by Lollianos, however, with their description of perverse sexuality, ghosts, and cannibalism, easily stand their ground against the *Satyrica*, or the *Metamorphoses* of Apuleius.[8] The Greek works *Daulis, Iolaus,* and *Tinouphis* also show similar features.[9]

Moreover, the ideal romances, among all possible novelistic products, seem ill-suited on other accounts for comparison with those early Christian works most often compared with them, the Apocryphal Acts. These latter do not share the stylistic aspirations even of the Koine novel fragments such as *Ninos*, let alone the high-flown self-referential prose of an Achilles Tatius or a Longos. Even the most elegant of the Apocryphal Acts, the Greek martyrdom of the *Acts of Peter*, casts nearly half its sentences in simple paratactic style. The optative mood is all but unknown, and the subjunctive itself not always properly employed. The best of the prose often evokes effort rather than grace: pleonastic constructions and illogical usage of participial phrases abound.[10]

"Callirhoe and Parthenope: The Beginnings of the Historical Novel," *ClAnt* 6 (1987) 184–204.

[8] See the introduction in the edition by Albert Henrichs, *Die Phoinikika des Lollianos: Fragmente eines neuen griechischen Romans* (Pap. Texte Abh. 14; Bonn: R. Habelt, 1972).

[9] For brief but well-stated remarks, see S. A. Stephens and J. J. Winkler, eds., *Ancient Greek Novels: The Fragments: Introduction, Text, Translation, and Commentary* (Princeton: Princeton University Press, 1996) 4–8. See also now N. Holzberg, "The Genre: Novels Proper and the Fringe," in *The Novel in the Ancient World* (G. Schmeling, ed.; Leiden: E. J. Brill, 1996) 11–28.

[10] For a random example, see the first sentence of chapter one of the Greek martyrdom of Peter, which has five genitive participles, in three genitive absolute constructions, with six different subjects, followed by a nominative circumstantial participle and two relative clauses, all dependent on the lowly finite verb εἶπεν, which does no more than introduce a direct quotation; in the sentence, which runs for eight lines in a printed edition, there is not a single connective to be found. On the style of the Apocryphal Acts, essential is H. Ljungvik, *Studien zur Sprache der apokryphen Apostelgeschichten* (Uppsala Universitet Aarsskrift 8; Uppsala: A.-b. Lundequistska bokhandlung, 1926). There are pertinent essays by David Warren and Evie Holmberg to be published in *Harvard Studies in the Apocryphal Acts of the Apostles* (F. Bovon, ed.; Religions of the World; Cambridge: Harvard University Press, forthcoming).

Four of the five ideal romances were unquestionably written in the second century or later; they were thus composed at nearly the same time as the Apocryphal Acts. Whereas this fact opens exciting possibilities of similar audiences for the two corpora, it does muddy the question of influence. It cannot be stated without controversy that the ideal romances provided direct models for the Christian works, especially since the Apocryphal Acts are so similar in general conception to the gospel literature of the first century. Glen Bowersock has recently turned the entire question on its head by claiming that the existence of gospel literature, along with similar polytheist works of imagination masquerading as history, provided the impetus for the development of the novel as a genre.[11] The much earlier Greek novel fragments, which antedate the earliest Christian works, make his thesis impossible to sustain on a strict level, but the later ideal romances may well have drunk from the Christian spring for some of their inspiration.

Moreover, the thematic material of the Apocryphal Acts differs considerably from the ideal romances. Although both corpora contain tales of travel and adventure, replete with entertaining episodes, the Apocryphal Acts are not tales of young couples in love—rather the opposite, given the emphasis on sexual continence. Rather than legitimate matrimony, the goal of the Apocryphal Acts would seem to be broken marriages.[12] They are not, however, mere inversions of the ideal romantic genre. Formally, each Apocryphal Acts has as its narrative backbone the career and death of a single individual. If there be a generic connection with self-conscious literary productions, it would be biography. Yet the lack of such self-conscious use of generic conventions in the Apocryphal Acts, as in related Christian literature, such as the gospels, suggests that it is necessary to look elsewhere for literary models.

None of this is to deny the value of the five ideal romances for comprehension of the Apocryphal Acts. Particularly for the complex of chastity-persecution stories which appear in one guise or other in the five earliest Acts, those of John, Peter, Paul, Thomas, and Andrew, the ideal

---

[11] *Fiction as History: Nero to Julian* (Sather Classical Lectures 58; Berkeley: University of California Press, 1994).

[12] On the contrast between these two corpora, see the first two chapters of Judith Perkins, *The Suffering Self: Pain and Narrative Representation in the Early Christian Era* (London: Routledge, 1995), entitled, "Death as a Happy Ending," and "Marriages as Happy Endings."

romances provide a similar constellation of motifs.[13] In the *Acts of Paul and Thekla*, part of the *Acts of Paul* complex, Thekla becomes infatuated with Paul in stock novelistic terms, attempts to follow him, is separated from him, and is finally happily reunited with him, not once, but twice. Instead of marriage, which Thekla has rejected at the outset in her pursuit of holiness, Thekla is confirmed into another stable social role: she is commissioned to preach the gospel as her model does. Beyond this, many of the Apocryphal Acts have other elements found in the ideal romances, such as shipwrecks, brigands, sale into slavery, unruly crowds, and travel around the empire.[14] Though motifs do not a genre make, the ideal romances and the Acts are speaking the same narrative language.

Nevertheless, several other works within the broader range of ancient fiction would raise a stronger claim for close relationship with the Apocryphal Acts. Like the Acts, these concentrate on the career of one central figure, usually of overwhelming cultural or religious significance, as the guiding principle of the entire narrative. Aside from this basic biographical constraint, the structure of these novels is episodic, and the Greek style is workaday, eschewing literary pretension. These pieces are too unaware of generic conventions to be classed as biographies in a self-conscious sense. Moreover, although they are concerned with revealing the character and ethos of the central figure, and sometimes do so with the anecdotal methods known, for example, from Plutarch, the narratives are also concerned to an equal or greater extent with a presentation of a veritable "greatest hits parade" of the hero's outstanding deeds, a focus more in line with Hellenistic historiography than with biography.[15]

---

[13] Virginia Burrus, *Chastity as Autonomy: Women in the Stories of the Apocryphal Acts* (Lewiston, NY: E. Mellen, 1987), studies these narratives from the perspective of oral traditional models.

[14] The classic treatment of these motifs is Söder, *Apostelgeschichten.* Although the stock criticism, that motifs do not constitute a genre, is an accurate response to the overall argument of this work, it still contains many valuable observations on these narratives and their relationship to novelistic literature broadly construed. For critical assessment, see Karl Kerényi, "Rosa Söder, *Die apokryphen Apostelgeschichten* ...," *Gnomon* 10 (1934) 301–9.

Jean-Daniel Kaestli, "Les principales orientations de la recherche sur les Actes apocryphes des apôtres," in Bovon, *Actes apocryphes,* 49–67.

Plümacher, "Apokryphe Apostelakten," 56–65. Karl Kerényi, "Rosa Söder, *Die apokryphen Apostelgeschichten* ...," *Gnomon* 10 (1934) 301–9; Kaestli, "Orientations," 61–67. Pervo (*Profit*) treats the relationship between the novels and the Apocryphal Acts with more perspicacity.

[15] Charles William Fornara, *The Nature of History in Ancient Greece and Rome* (Berkeley: University of California Press, 1983) 34–36.

The precise limits and the proper description of this complex of works have yet to be achieved. Within the history of the research of the Apocryphal Acts, some works matching these descriptions have been drawn into comparison alongside the ideal romances, notably in the study of Rosa Söder.[16] Martin Braun classed them as "national hero romances" in a useful study that nevertheless confuses the literary issues by ignoring the many extant works in favor of investigation of (hypothetical) complexes of folktales in popular historians such as Diodorus Siculus.[17] *Sesonchosis* and *Ninos*, for example, though related to stories of national heroes, presently exist as works much closer to the ideal romance, however valuable they may be for the understanding of the development of that genre.

Without begging the question of influence by citing examples from Christian literature, the prime extant exemplars of this type of work would be the Alexander Romance, *Apollonios King of Tyre*, the *Life of Aesop*, and the *Life of Homer*. Good reasons exist to draw into consideration some of the intertestamental Jewish works in Greek, such as Tobit, *Joseph and Aseneth*, parts of Esther, and the additions to Daniel.[18] These were products of the late Hellenistic period, and display many of the novelistic features of their polytheist counterparts. Since intertestamental Jewish literature drew upon Greek literature for the development of its other genres, one might profitably assume the same relationship in this case.

Among these works, the Alexander Romance, in particular, has come into the purview of scholars of the ancient novel, although no consistent description of its generic peculiarities has taken hold. Tomas Hägg, for example, calls it both "romanticized biography" and "historical novel" in different publications. The problem is how to place it on the continuum running from novel to history; Hägg himself demonstrates the theoretical difficulties inherent in this problematique by proffering two contradictory definitions of the historical novel, one of which suits the Alexander Romance:

> On the other hand, private individuals unburdened by historicity stand at the centre [of the five erotic novels], and therefore it may be more correct to reserve the designation 'historical' for those novels that really do follow a historical course

---

[16] Söder, *Apostelgeschichten*, 186–87.

[17] *History and Romance in Graeco-Oriental Literature* (Oxford: Blackwell, 1938).

[18] Lawrence M. Wills, "The Jewish Novellas," in *Greek Fiction: The Greek Novel in Context* (J. R. Morgan and R. Stoneman, eds.; London: Routledge, 1994) 223–38; idem, *The Jewish Novel in the Ancient World* (Ithaca, NY: Cornell University Press, 1995).

of events, in however imaginative a way. ... Not until the *Alexander Romance* do we find a complete living specimen of the genre.[19]

This complex of biographical historical novels is also characterized by another feature less obvious to view, i.e., the fluidity of their narrative structure in the manuscript tradition. These works generally exist in multiple recensions that cannot be reduced to a typical stemmatic relationship; in other words, no original text can be reconstructed. The various recensions differ from one another by including or deleting entire episodes. Many of these individual episodes are also attested in excerpts or epitomes that circulated as independent works. Last, these narratives typically appeared in early ancient translations. Although these characteristics of "fluidity" are not sufficient to define a genre, precisely this lack of an original text is significant in assessing the type of writing these works were considered to be by their ancient audience. The process of excerpting, abridging, redacting, and translating that led to their variegated manuscript tradition, usually held to be a tremendous practical impediment for the editor, is in fact not problematic at all, but meaningful in itself.

The phenomenon of fluidity is, to be sure, not limited to novelistic works, but is also prevalent in many works with a performative basis, such

---

[19] Hägg, *Novel*, 125. Hägg rejects this definition in "The Beginnings of the Historical Novel," in *The Greek Novel A. D. 1–1985* (R. Beaton, ed., London: Croom Helm, 1988) 169–81, and "Callirhoe and Parthenope: The Beginnings of the Historical Novel," *ClAnt* 6 (1987) 184–204, a longer version of the former. According to the later definition, genuine historical novels narrate the affairs of *fictitious* characters, include some truly historical figures and some historical events in the public sphere affecting the personal fortunes of the characters, are set at least one or two generations back, and evidence historical verisimilitude. Works like the Alexander Romance and the *Cyropaedia* of Xenophon would fail because the central character is not fictitious. As Hägg notes, the problem with the Alexander Romance is whether it should be called a novel at all, since, once it is admitted to this class, it must be called a historical novel ("Callirhoe," 193). He would now call it a romanticized biography, whereas I prefer to stress its affinity with other novelistic works by calling it a biographical historical novel. Hägg's two articles make matters appear simpler than they are. The main events of the novel *Chaereas and Kallirhoe* are already found in the historians, Plutarch (*Dion* 3) and Diodoros Siculus (13.96.3; 13.112.4; 14.44.5), which raises the question of whether Kallirhoe, or her story, is truly fictitious in the sense Hägg wants them to be; he brushes the issue aside ("Callirhoe," 195 n. 63). Hägg's definition of the historical novel is good for general purposes, but one wonders about the utility of such a definition for the purposes of describing ancient literature, since only one sole author in all of antiquity has managed to achieve it: Chariton (many believe him to be the author of the *Metiochos and Parthenope* fragments as well; see Albrecht Dihle, "Zur Datierung des Metiochos-Romans," *WJA* n. s. 4 [1978] 47–55 and H. Maehler, "Der Metiochos-Parthenope-Roman," *ZPE* 23 [1976] 1–20).

as epic or ritual texts.[20] For this reason, it is not sufficient as a generic indicator. Among the various types of novelistic literature in antiquity, however, it is widespread. The degree to which it is apparent varies greatly among the five ideal romances, the biographical historical novels, the Jewish novellas in Greek, and the Apocryphal Acts of the Apostles.

Recently published papyri of Achilles Tatius show a degree of fluidity that is striking for an ancient literary text. The papyri contain surprisingly numerous variants, mostly on the level of the phrasing and word-order. The fragments of text are relatively brief: P. Rob. inv. 35 and P. Colon. inv. 901, two extensive fragments of the same roll, amount to about seven and one half pages of a standard-sized printed edition when placed together. In this short scope, the papyri that overlap in the part of the text that they preserve (P[4]= P. Rob. inv. 35 and P. Colon. inv. 901; and P[5]=P. Oxy LVI 3836) frequently disagree with one another, but have the support of one of the later codices, except in four cases in which P[4] stands alone in a correct reading against the combined witness of P[5] and the codices. Only once do the two papyri agree against the vellum codices; so the flux entered the manuscript tradition early.[21]

More striking is the case of the *Ephesiaka.* Although the point is debated, cogent reasons exist for believing that the five-book novel is an epitome. The initial book, for example, is much longer than the others.

---

[20] This problem of fluidity has become an issue in the edition of several varieties of Jewish religious texts, all of them non-narrative in nature. The most striking case is that of the Hekhalot literature, post-rabbinic texts; see Peter Schäfer's remarks in his edition (*Synopse zur Hekhalot-Literatur* [Tübingen: Mohr (Siebeck), 1981]) and his more general comments on rabbinic literature in idem, "Research into Rabbinic Literature: An Attempt to Define the Status Quaestionis," *JJS* 37 (1986) 139–52. See also similar remarks in the introduction to Daniel Harrington and Anthony Saldarini, eds., *Targum Jonathan of the Former Prophets* (The Aramaic Bible 10; Wilmington, DE: M. Glazier, 1987). Recent work in rabbinic literature has been characterized by more sensitivity to the oral dimensions of the text; Elizabeth Shanks is completing a Ph.D. dissertation at Yale in which she treats the Babylonian Talmud as an oral commentary on the Mishnah that changed as the Mishnah moved from a loose configuration of oral traditions to the status of fixed scripture. Since Lord's and Parry's seminal work on Homer, the phenomenon of fluidity in Greek epic is well-documented; see Gregory Nagy's recent book, *Poetry as Performance: Homer and Beyond* (Cambridge: Cambridge University Press, 1996). These parallels are revealing for our literature, since all these types of texts demonstrably possess a strong background in oral performance. The presence of a similar state of affairs in some of the Nag Hammadi texts (particularly the *Apocryphon of John*) raises the question of their possible performative background, as well.

[21] See William H. Willis, "The Robinson-Cologne Papyrus of Achilles Tatius," *GRBS* 31 (1990) 73–102, esp. 79.

Moreover, there are slight differences in narrative style between it and the later books, and jarring transitions in the later part of the narrative. Ancient testimony also numbers the books at ten, rather than five.[22] Epitomization is not a unique occurrence among ancient prose works; what is interesting is the manner of epitomization in this case. The *Ephesiaka* nowhere announces itself as an epitome of the original work, but rather presents itself as the same work of the same author. It is precisely the non-advertizement of the editorial alteration that has lead to the controversy over whether the work was, in fact, epitomized.

These two cases illustrate a striking degree of structural fluidity for ancient literary texts. But they pale by comparison with texts such as the Alexander Romance, the Jewish novellas, and the Apocryphal Acts. With the Alexander Romance, one is no longer on the familiar terrain of fixed texts, and of manuscript traditions that can be reduced to a neat half-inch of critical apparatus on the printed page. There are a profusion of later translations, versions, and rewritings that proliferated throughout the middle ages, about eighty to date.[23] Even the edition of the Alexander Romance under the name of Kallisthenes shows such variation among the manuscripts that the work itself exists in no fewer than five Greek recensions: A, β, λ, ε, γ, all edited and printed as separate editions of the same text.[24] The first two recensions (A and β) are earlier; but the three later Byzantine recensions often offer valuable readings that witness to an earlier form of the text, so it is impossible to discount them as being "late."

---

[22] See most recently David Konstan, "Xenophon of Ephesus: Eros and Narrative in the Novel," in *Greek Fiction*, 49–63. K. Bürger, "Zu Xenophon von Ephesos," *Hermes* 27 (1892) 36–67. For the other side of the argument, Tomas Hägg, "Die Ephesiaka des Xenophon Ephesios: Original oder Epitome?" *C&M* 27 (1966) 118–61.

[23] Ken Dowden, "Pseudo-Callisthenes: The Alexander Romance," in *Collected Ancient Greek Novels* (B. P. Reardon, ed.; Berkeley: University of California Press, 1989) 650–735, esp. 650. See also Richard Stoneman, "The Metamorphoses of the *Alexander Romance*," in *Novel in the Ancient World*, 601–12.

[24] A: Wilhelm Kroll, ed., *Historia Alexandri Magni* (Berlin: Weidman, 1926); β: Leif Bergson, ed., *Der griechische Alexanderroman: Rezension β* (Stockholm: Almqvist and Wiksell, 1965); Helmut van Thiel, ed., *Leben und Taten Alexanders von Makedonien: Der griechische Alexanderroman nach der Handschrift L* (Darmstadt: Wissenschaftliche Buchgesellschaft, 1974); λ: Helmut van Thiel, ed., *Die Rezension λ des Pseudo-Kallisthenes* (Bonn: R. Habelt, 1959); ε: Jürgen Trumpf, ed., *Vita Alexandri regis Macedonum* (Stuttgart: B. G. Teubner, 1974); γ: *Der griechische Alexanderroman: Rezension γ*, vol 1: Ursula von Lauenstein, ed., *Buch I* (Meisenheim am Glan: A. Hain, 1962); vol. 2: Helmut Engelmann, ed., *Buch II* (Meisenheim am Glan: A. Hain, 1963); vol 3: Franz Parthe, ed., *Buch III* (Meisenheim am Glan: A. Hain, 1968).

The variants in the Alexander Romance are more substantial than those in other literary texts, that is, more than a matter of a word or two, or even of alternate phrasing, as in Achilles Tatius. The various recensions of Alexander include and omit entire episodes, such as would seem to be the case with the *Ephesiaka*. Recension β includes an extensive letter from Alexander to his teacher, Aristotle, in which he narrates his journey to the edge of the world (2. 23–41), including a submarine dive to the bottom of the sea; this letter does not appear at all in recension A. Recension γ, a Byzantine recension, does have the letter, and it improves on it by adding further episodes not known from recension β: encounters with giant ants, rivers of sand, and centaurs.

Evaluation of the smaller variants, those on the level of words and phrases, is impeded by a contamination among the manuscripts so severe that the most recent text critic judges it impossible to set up a stemma of manuscripts, even within each of the five recensions.[25] As in the case of New Testament text criticism, one has to speak of families of manuscripts.[26] The reason is the same: the transmission of the Alexander Romance is unusually rich, and copyists were in the habit of collating one manuscript against the other, thus introducing readings from one family of manuscripts into another.[27]

Many of the constituent episodes of the Alexander Romance circulated independently, and had their own textual tradition. The piece which closes the romance, "Alexander's Last Days," circulated in a more

---

[25] Reinhold Merkelbach and Jürgen Trumpf, "Die Überlieferung," in *Die Quellen des griechischen Alexanderromans* (R. Merkelbach and J. Trumpf, eds.; 2d ed.; Munich: C. H. Beck, 1977) 93–107, esp. 103–6. See also the comments in Richard Stoneman, "Introduction," in idem, ed., *The Greek Alexander Romance* (London: Penguin, 1991) 1–27; and idem, "The Alexander Romance: From History to Fiction," in *Greek Fiction,* 117–29.

[26] The concept was developed by B. F. Westcott and F. J. Hort; see their various editions of *The New Testament in the Original Greek* published by Macmillan. Similarly, the variants of codex D of the New Testament introduce completely new information into the text at various points. The degree of wildness is greatest in the Acts of the Apostles, the most "novelistic" text in the New Testament canon, into which entire sentences are interpolated.. See Eldon Jay Epp, *The Theological Tendency of Codex Bezae Cantabrigiensis in Acts* (Cambridge: Cambridge University Press, 1966) 1–40.

[27] Even in antiquity, ancient authors citing other sources would often collate their own manuscripts against another copy, or, failing that, against another work in which their source was cited; Strabo complains that bad copyists do not collate (ἀντιβάλλω, 13.1.54). For some introductory remarks, see L. D. Reynolds and N. G. Wilson, *Scribes and Scholars: A Guide to the Transmission of Greek and Latin Literature* (Oxford: Clarendon, 1968) 1–25.

complete, independent Latin version; a Greek fragment of this text has been found on papyrus (Pap. Vindob. 31954). The letter of Alexander to Aristotle is likewise more complete in the independently-circulating Latin translation. Alexander's conversation with the Gymnosophists (3.6) is preserved separately in a Greek papyrus (Pap. Berol. 13044).

Unlike the five late Greek romances, the Alexander Romance was translated early into Latin, and into several other languages before the beginning of the middle ages. The first extant Latin translation of the Alexander Romance was done by Julius Valerius around 300 CE; this earliest translation is actually a rather free version, so free that one often cannot tell which Greek text Valerius was using. Of the other twenty-two languages into which the Alexander Romance has been translated or adapted, the other relatively early witnesses to the original Greek text are the Syriac and Ethiopic translations.

The Jewish novellas show the same features as are present in the Alexander Romance: they are texts prone to additions, epitomization, or excerpting, they have variant readings that cannot be reduced to an original text, and were the objects of frequent translation. The text of *Joseph and Aseneth,* a first-century CE treatment of the marriage of the Jewish patriarch Joseph to an Egyptian woman, is both complicated and enriched by the existence of numerous translations: Syriac, Armenian, Latin (two versions), Serbian Slavonic, Modern Greek, Rumanian, and Ethiopic. The total manuscripts number seventy. Of these, the sixteen Greek manuscripts fall into four different recensions. In each of the first three groups, the text is fairly unified. But the fourth group, which also contains seven of the eight translations, is a grab bag: it contains the oldest witnesses (the Armenian and Syriac translations) and represents the widest geographical distribution, and yet offers little help for arriving at the *Greek* text, since the four Greek manuscripts in this group, all very recent, differ greatly in the wording of the story, and even in its length.[28] This group clearly contains the oldest and best witnesses to the original text, but it is also the most confusing.

It would be easy to multiply examples among the Jewish novellas. Daniel underwent three different stages, in Hebrew, Aramaic, and Greek, in which new materials were added to make a new work, a process of

---

[28] Christoph Burchard gives a concise overview of the textual history in *The Old Testament Pseudepigrapha* (J. H. Charlesworth, ed.; 2 vols.; Garden City, NY: Doubleday, 1983–85) 2.178–81. See also Burchard, *Gesammelte Studien zu Joseph und Aseneth* (Leiden: E. J. Brill, 1996).

gradual agglutinization; at the last stage, the Greek additions are the prayer of Azariah and the song of the three young men, the stories of Bel and the Dragon, and Susanna and the elders. Esther likewise has many versions: one in Hebrew, two in Greek, and two independent translations in Aramaic. Lawrence Wills writes that Esther is "not so much a single, unique text, as it is a snapshot of a literary tradition in progress,"[29] a fitting description for the class of Jewish novellas in general.

Among the five early Apocryphal Acts, the four that are fragmentarily preserved provide the best evidence of the fluidity that is found in these other novelistic works. Like the Alexander Romance, these texts also circulated in excerpts. In each case, the martyrdom section of the acts of any given apostle circulated separately, and enjoys the richest attestation in the manuscript tradition and in the various translation languages. Other portions were also copied off separately. The *Acts of Paul and Thekla* are the best-known example, but most of the early Acts, as they now exist, appear as a congeries of excerpts. The *Acts of Paul and Thekla,* as well as the correspondence between Paul and the Corinthians, and the martyrdom of Paul, all circulated separately and had an independent manuscript tradition. The Heidelberg papyrus (Coptic PHeid 1) first proved that they exist as components of a continuous narrative, containing these three excerpts along with other episodes from the *Acts of Paul.* The Hamburg Greek papyrus likewise contains parts of Paul's travels alongside the martyrdom.[30] In the *Acts of Peter,* the story of Peter's paralyzed daughter is likewise a small excerpt in a Coptic papyrus codex (fourth or fifth century).[31] The best witness for the *Acts of Peter,* the *Actus Vercellenses,* a third- to fourth-century Latin translation, extant in a single sixth- to seventh-century Latin manuscript, Codex Vercelli, turns out to be a truncation of an earlier text. These not only excerpt the Greek *Acts of Peter,* preserving only about two-thirds of the entire work, but add three

---

[29] Wills, *Jewish Novel,* 104–5.

[30] Carl Schmidt, *Acta Pauli aus der Heidelberger koptischen Papyrushandschrift* (Leipzig: J. C. Hinrichs, 1905); and idem, ed., ΠΡΑΞΕΙΣ ΠΑΥΛΟΥ: *Acta Pauli nach dem Papyrus der Hamburger Staats- und Universitäts-Bibliothek* (Glückstadt/Hamburg: Augustin, 1936).

[31] See Carl Schmidt, *Die alten Petrusakten im Zusammenhang der apokryphen Apostelliteratur nebst einem neuentdeckten Fragment* (TU n. s. 9.1; Leipzig: J. Hinrichs, 1903); on the dating, see 2, 13.

initial chapters concerning Paul (chaps. 1–3).[32] The central section of the
Acts of John, containing the mystic dance and the address concerning the
cross, is attested separately from the travel accounts that comprise
another significant portion of these Acts.[33]

All of these texts were also translated very early into a plethora of
ancient languages, the first of them Latin, usually in the later third or
early fourth century, at about the time that Julius Valerius was making his
translation of the Alexander Romance. Other versions, which preserve
only the martyrdoms, typically include Syriac, Armenian, Coptic,
Ethiopic, Arabic, Old Church Slavonic, and sometimes Georgian.

The work of redactors and compilers did not stop here: the *Acts of Peter*
live on in numerous later reworkings: the fourth-century version
attributed to Linus, the fifth- to sixth-century version attributed to
Marcellus, the excerpts in Pseudo-Hegesippos and Pseudo-Abdias, and
the fifth-century reworkings of the tale in the *Acts of Nereus and Achilles*.[34]
A similar case has been documented by Eric Junod and Jean-Daniel
Kaestli for the *Acts of John*.[35] Most of these later editions do not have
anything approaching verbal overlap with the earliest Greek text. And
they themselves exist in a profusion of translations. The Marcellus text of
the *Acts of Peter*, for example, exists in Latin, Greek, Armenian, Old
Church Slavonic, and Coptic.

The *Acts of Thomas* enjoy an enviably complete and non-fragmentary
attestation, but even they have not escaped the quandary of the "original
text." It is not entirely clear which version was prior, the Greek or the
Syriac, and cogent arguments have been advanced for both cases.[36] Both

---

[32] Gerard Poupon, "Les 'Actes de Pierre' et leur remaniement," *ANRW* 2.25.6
(1988) 4363–83; Christine M. Thomas, "Word and Deed: The *Acts of Peter* and Orality,"
Apocrypha 3 (1992) 125–64.

[33] See the introductory remarks in Jean-Daniel Kaestli and Eric Junod, eds., *Acta
Iohannis* (Corpus Christianorum: Series Apocrypha, 1–2; Turnhout: Brepols, 1983).

[34] Texts of Linus and Marcellus in Richard Adalbert Lipsius and Maximillian
Bonnet, eds., *Acta Apostolorum Apocrypha* (3 vols.; Leipzig: Hermann Mendelssohn,
1891) 1.1–22 and 1.118–77, 178–222. Vincent Ussani, *Hegesippi qui dicitur historiae libri
V* (CSEL 66; Vienna: Hoelder-Pichler-Tempsky; Leipzig: Akademische Verlagsgesell-
schaft, 1932) 1.183–87. Hans Achelis, *Acta SS. Nerei et Achillei: Text und Untersuchung*
(TU 11.2; Leipzig: J. C. Hinrichs, 1893).

[35] See Eric Junod and Jean-Daniel Kaestli, *L'histoire des Actes apocryphes des apôtres du
IIIe au IXe siècle: le cas des Actes de Jean* (Cahiers de la Revue de théologie et de
philosophie 7; Geneva/ Lausanne/ Neuchâtel: La Concorde, 1982).

[36] Harold W. Attridge, "The Original Language of the Acts of Thomas," in *Of Scribes
and Scrolls: Studies on the Hebrew Bible, Intertestamental Judaism and Christian Origins*
(H. W. Attridge et al., eds.; Lanham, MD: University Press of America, 1990) 241–45.

versions have undergone revision, and neither represents the pristine text. The version most likely to be the original, the Syriac, in fact represents the text most heavily edited in the direction of orthodox theological whitewashing.[37]

This survey of biographical historical novels, such as the Alexander Romance, as well as the Jewish exemplars *Joseph and Aseneth,* Daniel, and Esther, demonstrates that some of the literary peculiarities of the Apocryphal Acts are not without analogues in other literatures. Like the Acts, these other novels are written in straightforward and unadorned Koine; they are structurally fluid, admitting inclusion or deletion of entire episodes with every new manuscript; they are prone to excerpting and epitomization; and they are favorite base texts for translation. Because of their similar narrative design, a biographical backbone on which are hung the various episodes of the life of the hero, and because of the thematic concentration upon an individual of great ethnic or religious significance, these would seem to be the ancient novelistic products most similar to the Apocryphal Acts.

On the score of fluidity, these novels are much closer to the Apocryphal Acts than are the ideal romances. The papyri of Achilles Tatius and the epitomization of the *Ephesiaka* suggest that the texts of novelistic works, in general, may have been less stable than those of other literary texts in antiquity. Works such as Esther, Daniel, *Joseph and Aseneth,* the Apocryphal Acts, and the Alexander Romance, however, evidence a degree of instability that, when compared with the five ideal romances, almost constitutes a difference in kind, rather than a mere difference in degree. Each of these texts was issued in several revisions, each was translated more than once, and all except *Joseph and Aseneth* had significant portions added to them over the course of their history.[38]

All of these works, moreover, are arguably anonymous, and most do not even have fixed titles in the manuscript tradition.[39] The five ideal

---

[37] For a brief example, see Yves Tissot, "Les Actes de Thomas: exemple de recueil composite," in *Actes apocryphes,* 223–32.

[38] It is possible, however, that chaps. 22–29 of *Joseph and Aseneth* are a later addition.

[39] The Alexander Romance is sometimes attributed to Kallisthenes in the manuscript tradition, but the absence of any preface indicating authorship shows that it is anonymous. The two early Latin translations of it, however, are not. The various versions of the Apocryphal Acts, likewise, are only anonymous in the earlier part of their history; the later editions are usually attributed to an author. Not even ancient tradition preserves a name for the author or compiler of the Greek *Acts of Peter;* the Latin *Actus Vercellenses* likewise have neither author nor title; they simply follow a text

romances, on the other hand, all carry the names of their authors. Only "Xenophon" of Ephesus might be considered a pen name.⁴⁰ A direct relationship seems to hold, then, between anonymity and fluidity among ancient novelistic texts. Perhaps ancient scribes perceived less obligation to protect the exact wording of texts that were not sanctioned by the name of an author. Yet, as noted, there seems to be also a slight degree of flux even for some of the five late Greek romances, so other features of these texts may play a role: the relative lack of literary pretension in these works, as well as the narrative and imaginative nature of the texts, may have also offered the scribe greater license.⁴¹

The presence of so many translations also shows the relative lack of attention to preserving the exact wording of these texts. In the case of works such as the Alexander Romance, the Apocryphal Acts, Esther, and *Joseph and Aseneth*, the multiplicity of translations in which these appear is evidence that it was not the Greek style of the originals that was considered to be the primary literary characteristic of these works; such style as they possessed would clearly be lost in translation. It was the

---

of the Pseudo-Clementines in the Vercelli manuscript. But later versions are attributed to named figures (however falsely), e.g., to Linus or Marcellus or Josephus. The same anonymity can also be argued for the *Acts of Paul*; it is ironically the only one of the Apocryphal Acts for which an author is mentioned, but the presbyter of Asia Minor who composed it is characteristically left anonymous (Tertullian, *De baptismo* 17). The *Acts of John* are preserved in later versions attributed to Prochorus and Abdias; the *Acts of Andrew* in an anonymous *Laudatio* and *Narratio*, and in a later version attributed—this time rightly—to Gregory of Tours.

⁴⁰ There are three Xenophontes mentioned in the *Suda*, the work of each of which is titled by an ethnographic adjective, which has led some scholars to conclude that these names were pseudonyms, indicating the intention to market as a type of local history the works which bore them; Perry makes this observation (*Ancient Romances*, 167–9). Significantly, the *Ephesiaka* of Xenophon, which may thus be pseudonymous, is the only one of the five late Greek romances that may be preserved solely in a form radically divergent from the original text.

⁴¹ Even the form in which these works were published indicates less literary pretension: many of them appear on codices rather than the scrolls reserved for highbrow literary works during the earlier Roman empire. The papyrus fragments of Achilles Tatius appear in three out of six instances in codices. The Apocryphal Acts are attested on numerous codices, both papyrus and vellum: the fourth- to fifth-century Coptic fragment of the *Acts of Peter* edited by Carl Schmidt is a papyrus codex, and there is the fourth-century vellum fragment in Greek; the Acts of Paul appear in the Hamburg Greek papyrus (ca. 300 CE) and the Heidelberg Coptic papyrus (6th c. CE), both codices, as is Pap. Oxy. 1602, in vellum (4th–5th c. CE). Pap. Copt. Utrecht 1 of the *Acts of Andrew* is a papyrus codex. On papyrus codices, see Eric G. Turner, *The Typology of the Early Codex* (Philadelphia: University of Pennsylvania Press, 1977) 35–42, 89–97.

narrative content that attracted the Latin- or Syriac-speaking reader, and this could be read out of any more-or-less faithful translation, and regardless of which Greek text the translation followed. These novelistic works did not circulate as the fixed original texts of named authors. They were stories both without authors and without texts.

The predominance of such fluidity in the transmission of these "text-less" works has important ramifications for the evaluation of a whole complex of issues, one of which is the concept of authorship, as is already suggested by the anonymity or pseudonymity of many of the works. Even if we grant the existence of an "original text" written by a single author, we must reckon with a whole series of people who did not strive to preserve this original text, but felt free to go about rewriting it in their own peculiar fashion. Clearly, some of the people who had a hand in transmitting these works were compilers—or authors—rather than mere scribes. The copyist here approaches the freedom and autonomy that we generally associate with an author. And the select group of people who had a hand in shaping the text, the translators and editors, was rather large.

The impulse to create a new version of the story with each retelling of it has more affinity with oral habits of performance than with the modern print-conditioned tendency towards exact reproduction of texts. A "performance" attitude toward written texts in antiquity may have been common and widespread. The written text at times served chiefly as a resource for later retellings. The continuing use of each of the Apocryphal Acts as base texts for later versions shows that this was the case; this is in fact the way in which their earliest readers treated the text.

Given the confusing, enthusiastic, and colorful succession of re-editions of the Apocryphal Acts, and texts like them, one must question whether the concept of the "original text," and the ensuing quest to reconstruct it, is the most meaningful approach to such works. As David Konstan has noted, in his discussion of the Alexander Romance as an "open text," "the effort to retrieve an original form is not only futile but detrimental," and would result in "a work that in fact no one had ever read or written."[42] Although the narrative material presented in any edition of these works is important, since it is the fabric of the tradition, it always represents only a subset of the possible narratives that may be told

---

[42] David Konstan, "The Alexander Romance: The Cunning of the Open Text," presented to the Mediterranean Religions Study Group at Brown University, November 1995, p. 7.

about the central figure. The most valuable feature of the tradition is not any final form, but the very malleability and multiformity of the tradition, which admit adjustment for the predilections and interests of audiences varying over time.

It is not by chance that these fluid narratives treat the careers and accomplishments of figures with overwhelming ethnic or religious significance. These documents, as demonstrated by their variegated transmission, had an ongoing life in their communities. Christian gospel literature clearly forms a subset of the narrative type, the biographical historical novel, which has been the subject of this article, yet with important differences. The Apocryphal Acts have indeed been more often compared with novelistic literature than has gospel literature;[43] this is unjustified if based only on canonical prejudice, but justified to the extent that the Apocryphal Acts provide a better workshop in which to observe fluid processes of narrative formation. The canonical texts ceased to evolve much earlier, although there are nevertheless clear indexes of fluidity, excerpting, and copious translation for the gospel narratives. Moreover, the basic process of the agglomeration of the gospel narratives from varied written and oral sources is completely analogous to that of the Apocryphal Acts.[44] One should conclude that the narrative processes at work in both sets of texts were the same, but that the process of development ceased much earlier for the canonical texts, and thus has left fewer traces.

The Apocryphal Acts are not sacred scripture at the point in time that one observes their fluidity. Sacred texts, in their more canonical existence, do admit adjustment to the needs and concerns of varying audiences over time; that is how they continue to be meaningful for thousands of years. Yet when scriptures exist as fixed texts, the hermeneutical "space" for alteration and adjustment exists in the penumbra of interpretive and exegetical traditions surrounding them.

---

[43] There are important exceptions. Mary Ann Tolbert places the Gospel of Mark among novelistic works, and offers many other helpful remarks on genre and audience (*Sowing the Gospel : Mark's World in Literary-historical Perspective* [Minneapolis: Fortress, 1989] 48–79). Marius Reiser uses the Alexander Romance as a point of comparison for Mark's Greek style ("Der Alexanderroman und das Markusevangelium," in *Markus-Philologie* [H. Cancik, ed.; WUNT 33; Tübingen: Mohr (Siebeck), 1984] 131–63). See also Richard I. Pervo, "Early Christian Fiction," in *Greek Fiction*, 239–54.

[44] Christine M. Thomas, "The Prehistory of the *Acts of Peter*," in *Harvard Studies in the Apocryphal Acts,* forthcoming.

The corresponding elasticity of religious texts such as the Apocryphal Acts was found in the form itself, in its fluidity. Because of this, the story of an Alexander, Joseph, Esther, or Peter could never be the domain of a single author, however gifted, and this is perhaps the underlying reason for their anonymity. How could the story of a single author in time serve the interests of audiences for several centuries? These were stories that belonged to the world.

COMPREHENSIVE BIBLIOGRAPHY

von Albrecht, M., *The History of Roman Literature*. Rev. by G. Schmeling; 2 vols.; Leiden: E. J. Brill, 1997.

Alexander, L., "'In Journeyings Often': Voyaging in the Acts of the Apostles and in Greek Romance," in *Luke's Literary Achievement: Collected Essays*. C. M. Tuckett, ed.; JSNTSup 116; Sheffield: Sheffield Academic Press, 1995, 17–39.

———, "Narrative Maps: Reflections on the Toponymy of Acts," in *The Bible in Human Society: Essays in Honour of John Rogerson*. M. Daniel Carroll *et al.*, eds.; JSOT 20; Sheffield: University of Sheffield Press, 1995, 17–57.

d'Alviella, G., *The Mysteries of Eleusis: The Secret Rites and Rituals of the Classical Greek Mystery Tradition*. Wellingborough, UK: Aquarian, 1981.

Anderson, G., "Achilles Tatius: A New Interpretation," in *The Greek Novel A.D. 1–1985*. R. Beaton, ed.; London: Croom Helm, 1988, 190–93.

———, *Ancient Fiction: The Novel in the Graeco-Roman World*. Totowa, NJ: Barnes & Noble, 1984.

———, *Eros Sophistes: Ancient Novelists at Play*. Chico, CA: Scholars Press, 1982.

———, *The Second Sophistic: A Cultural Phenomenon in the Roman Empire*. London: Routledge, 1993.

Anderson, W. C. F., "Stola," in *A Dictionary of Greek and Roman Antiquities*. 2 vols.; 3rd ed.; W. Smith *et al.*, eds.; London: John Murray, 1901, 2.716–17.

Attridge, H. W., "The Original Language of the Acts of Thomas," in *Of Scribes and Scrolls: Studies on the Hebrew Bible, Intertestamental Judaism, and Christian Origins*. H. W. Attridge *et al.* eds.; Lanham, MD: University Press of America, 1990, 241–45.

Aune, D., *The New Testament in its Literary Environment*. Philadelphia: Westminster, 1987.

Aymard, J., "Venus et les impératrices sous les derniers Antonins," *Mélanges d'Archéologie et d'histoire* 51 (1934) 178–96.

Bakhtin, M. M., *The Dialogic Imagination*. C. Emerson and M. Holquist, trans.; Austin: University of Texas Press, 1981.

———, *Problems of Dostoeyevsky's Poetics*. C. Emerson, trans.; Minneapolis: University of Minnesota Press, 1984.

Balch, D. L., *"Let Wives Be Submissive": The Domestic Code in 1 Peter*. SBLMS 26; Atlanta: Scholars Press, 1981.

Bartsch, S., *Decoding the Ancient Novel: The Reader and the Role of Description in Heliodorus and Achilles Tatius*. Princeton: Princeton University Press, 1989.

Baslez, M.-F., "L'idée de noblesse dans les romans grecs," *DHA* 16 (1990) 115–28.

Beaton, R., ed., *The Greek Novel A.D. 1–1985*. London: Croom Helm, 1988.

Bickerman, E. J., *The Jews in the Greek Age*. Cambridge: Harvard University Press, 1988.

Bompaire, J., "Le décor sicilien dans le roman grec et dans la littérature contemporaine (IIe siècle)," *REG* 90 (1977) 55–68.

Boobyer, G. H., "Mark 2:10a and the Interpretation of the Healing of the Paralytic," *HTR* 47 (1954) 115–20.

Booth, W. C., *The Company We Keep: An Ethic of Fiction*. Berkeley: University of California Press, 1988.

Boswell, J., *The Kindness of Strangers: The Abandonment of Children in Western Europe from Late Antiquity to the Renaissance*. New York: Pantheon, 1988.

Bovon, F., ed., *Harvard Studies in the Apocryphal Acts of the Apostles*. Religions of the World; Cambridge: Harvard University Press, forthcoming.

Bowersock, G. W., *Fiction as History: Nero to Julian*. Sather Classical Lectures 58; Berkeley: University of California Press, 1994.

———, *Greek Sophists in the Roman Empire*. Oxford: Clarendon, 1969.

Bowie, E. L., "The Greek Novel," in *The Cambridge History of Classical Literature. Vol. 1: Greek Literature*. P. Easterling and B. Knox, eds.; Cambridge: Cambridge University Press, 1985, 683–99.

———, "The Novels and the Real World," in *Erotica Antiqua: Acta of the International Conference on the Ancient Novel*. B. P. Reardon, ed.; Bangor, Wales, 1977, 91- 96.

———, "The Readership of Greek Novels in the Ancient World," in *The Search for the Ancient Novel*. J. Tatum, ed.; Baltimore: Johns Hopkins University Press, 1994, 435–59.

Bowie, E. L., and S. J. Harrison, "The Romance of the Novel," *JRS* 83 (1993) 159–78.

Bradley, K. R., *Slaves and Masters in the Roman Empire*. New York: Oxford University Press, 1987.

Brant, J. A., "Husband Hunting: Characterization and Narrative Art in the Gospel of John," *BI* 4 (1996) 205–23.

Bratcher, R. G., and E. A. Nida, *A Translator's Handbook on the Gospel of Mark*. Leiden: E. J. Brill for the United Bible Societies, 1961.

Braun, M., *History and Romance in Graeco-Oriental Literature*. Oxford: Basil Blackwell, 1938.

Brilliant, R., *Roman Art from the Republic to Constantine*. London: Phaidon, 1974.

———, *Visual Narratives: Storytelling in Etruscan and Roman Art*. Ithaca, NY: Cornell University Press, 1984.

Brown, P., "Art and Society in Late Antiquity," in *Age of Spirituality: A Symposium*. K. Weitzmann, ed.; New York: Metropolitan Museum of Art, 1980, 17–27.

———, *The Body and Society: Men, Women, and Sexual Renunciation in Early Christianity*. New York: Columbia University Press, 1988.

———, *The Making of Late Antiquity*. Cambridge: Harvard University Press, 1978.

Brown, R. E., *The Gospel according to John*. 2 vols.; AB 29–29A; Garden City, NY: Doubleday, 1966–1970.

Bruce, F. F., *1 and 2 Corinthians*. NCB; London: Oliphants, 1971.

Brunt, P. A., "Aspects of the Social Thought of Dio Chrysostom and the Stoics," *PCPhS* 19 (1973) 9–34.

Bultmann, R., *The Gospel of John: A Commentary*. G. R. Beasley-Murray, trans.; Philadelphia: Westminster, 1971.

Burchard, C., *Gesammelte Studien zu Joseph und Aseneth*. Leiden: E. J. Brill, 1996.

Bürger, K., "Zu Xenophon von Ephesus," *Hermes* 27 (1892) 36–67.

———, Rev. of O. Schissel von Fleschenberg, *Die Rahmenerzählung in den Ephesischen Geschichten des Xenophon von Ephesus* (1909), in *PhW* 30 (1910) 353–57.

Burrus, V., *Chastity as Autonomy: Women in the Stories of the Apocryphal Acts.* Lewiston, NY: Edwin Mellen, 1987.

————, "Word and Flesh: The Bodies of Ascetic Women in Christian Antiquity," *JFSR* 10 (1994) 27–51.

Byre, C. S., *Ekphraseis of Works of Art and Places in the Greek Epic from Homer to Nonnus.* Diss. University of Chicago, 1976.

Cadbury, H., *The Book of Acts in History.* New York: Harper and Bros., 1955.

Carcopino, J., *Daily Life in Ancient Rome: The People and the City at the Height of the Empire.* E. O. Lorimer, trans.; New Haven: Yale University Press, 1940.

Charitonidis, S., L. Kahil, and R. Ginouvès, *Les mosaïques de la maison du Ménandre à Mytilène.* Bern: Francke, 1970.

Chew, K., "Inconsistency and Creativity in Xenophon's *Ephesiaka*," *CW* forthcoming.

Clay, J. S., *The Wrath of Athena: Gods and Men in the Odyssey.* Princeton: Princeton University Press, 1983.

Collins, A., *The Beginning of the Gospel: Probings of Mark in Context.* Minneapolis: Fortress, 1992.

Cooper, K., *The Virgin and the Bride: Idealized Womanhood in Late Antiquity.* Cambridge: Harvard University Press, 1996.

Crossan, J. D., "Parable and Example in the Teaching of Jesus," *NTS* 18 (1972) 285–96.

————, *Who Killed Jesus? Exposing the Roots of Anti-Semitism in the Gospel Story of the Death of Jesus.* New York: HarperSanFrancisco, 1995.

Culpepper, R. A., "The Plot of John's Story of Jesus, *Int* 49 (1995) 347–58.

Dahl, N. A., *Jesus the Christ.* Minneapolis: Fortress, 1991.

Dalmeyda, G., "Auteur de Xénophon d'Ephèse, *BAGB* 13 (1926) 18–28.

Daly, L. W., trans., *Aesop without Morals: The Famous Fables and a Life of Aesop.* New York: Thomas Yoseloff, 1961.

Daly, R., "The Soteriological Significance of the Sacrifice of Isaac," *CBQ* 39 (1977) 45–75.

Davies, P. R., "Who Can Join the 'Damascus Covenant'?" *JJS* 46 (1995) 134–42.

Davies, S. L., *The Revolt of the Widows: Women in the Stories of the Apocryphal Acts.* New York: Seabury, 1980.

Deming, W., *Paul on Marriage and Celibacy: The Hellenistic Background of 1 Corinthians 7.* SNTSMS 83; Cambridge: Cambridge University Press, 1995.

Destro, A., and M. Pesce, "Kinship, Discipleship and Movement: An Anthropological Study of John's Gospel," *BI* 3 (1995) 266–84.

Detienne, M., and J.-P. Vernant, *Cunning Intelligence in Greek Culture and Society.* J. Lloyd, trans.; Sussex: Harvester, 1976.

Dewey, J., "Mark as Interwoven Tapestry: Forecasts and Echoes for a Listening Audience," *CBQ* 53 (1991) 221–36.

Dihle, A., "Zur Datierung des Metiochos-Romans," *WJA* n.s. 4 (1978) 47–55.

von Dobschütz, E., "Der Roman in der altchristlichen Literatur," *Deutsche Rundschau* 111 (1902) 87–106.

Donahue, J. R., *Are You the Christ? The Trial Narrative in the Gospel of Mark.* SBLDS 10; Missoula, MT: Scholars Press, 1973.

————, *The Gospel in Parable: Metaphor, Narrative, and Theology in the Synoptic Gospels.* Philadelphia: Fortress, 1988.

Dunn, P. W., "Women's Liberation, the Acts of Paul, and other Acts of the Apostles: A Review of Some Recent Interpreters," *Apocrypha* 4 (1993) 245–61.

Edwards, D. R., *Acts of the Apostles and Chariton's Chaereas and Callirhoe: A Literary and Sociohistorical Study.* Diss. Boston University, 1987.

———, "Defining the Web of Power in Asia Minor: The Novelist Chariton and his City Aphrodisias," *JAAR* 62 (1994) 699–718.

———, *Religion and Power: Pagans, Jews, and Christians in the Greek East.* New York: Oxford University Press, 1996.

———, "Surviving the Web of Roman Power: Religion and Politics in the Acts of the Apostles, Josephus, and Chariton's *Chaereas and Callirhoe*," in *Images of Empire.* L. Alexander, ed.; Sheffield: Sheffield Academic Press, 1991, 179–201.

Edwards, J., "Markan Sandwiches: The Significance of Interpolations in Markan Narratives," *NovT* 31 (1989) 193–216.

Egger, B. M., *Women in the Greek Novel: Constructing the Feminine.* Diss. University of California at Irvine, 1990.

———, "Women and Marriage in the Greek Novels," in *The Search for the Ancient Novel.* J. Tatum, ed.; Baltimore: Johns Hopkins University Press, 1994, 260–80.

Elliott, J. K., *The Apocryphal New Testament.* Oxford: Clarendon, 1993.

Elliott, Jas. K., "The Conclusion of the Pericope of the Healing of the Leper and Mark 1:45," *JTS* n.s. 22 (1971) 153–57.

———, "The Healing of the Leper in the Synoptic Parallels," *TZ* 34 (1978) 175–76.

Elsom, H. E., "Callirhoe: Displaying the Phallic Woman," in *Pornography and Representation in Greece and Rome.* A. Richlin, ed.; New York: Oxford University Press, 1992, 212–30.

Epp, E. J., *The Theological Tendency of Codex Bezae Cantabrigiensis in Acts.* Cambridge: Cambridge University Press, 1966.

Erim, K., "Aphrodisias," *AS* 32 (1982) 9–13.

———, "Aphrodisias," in *The Princeton Encyclopedia of Classical Sites.* R. Stilwell, ed.; Princeton: Princeton University Press, 1976, 68–70.

———, "Aphrodisias in Caria," *AS* 14 (1964) 25–28.

Farnell, L., *The Cults of the Greek States.* 5 vols.; Oxford: Clarendon, 1897.

Feeney, D., "Towards an Account of the Ancient World's Concept of Fictive Belief," in *Lies and Fiction in the Ancient World.* C. Gill and T. P. Wiseman, eds.; Austin: University of Texas Press, 1993, 230–44.

Fitzmyer, J. A., *The Gospel according to Luke.* 2 vols.; AB 28–28A; Garden City, NY: Doubleday, 1985.

Fleischer, R., "Aphrodisias," *LIMC* 2.1 (1984) 2–154.

———, "Artemis und Aphrodite von Aphrodisias," in *Die orientalischen Religionen im Römerreich.* M. J. Vermaseren, ed.; Leiden: E. J. Brill, 1981, 298–311.

———, *Artemis von Ephesus und verwandte Kultstatuen aus Anatolien und Syrien.* EPRO 35; Leiden: E. J. Brill, 1973.

Foley, H., *Ritual Irony: Poetry and Sacrifice in Euripides.* Ithaca, NY: Cornell University Press, 1985.

Fornara, C. W., *The Nature of History in Ancient Greece and Rome.* Berkeley: University of California Press, 1983.

Forster, E. M., *Aspects of the Novel.* San Diego: Harcourt Brace Jovanovich, 1985.

Fowler, B. H., *The Hellenistic Aesthetic.* Madison: University of Wisconsin Press, 1989.

Fowler, R. M., *Let the Reader Understand: Reader-Response Criticism and the Gospel of Mark*. Minneapolis: Fortress, 1991.

Fowler, W. W., *Rome in Social Life at Rome in the Age of Cicero*. New York: Macmillan, 1909.

Friedländer, P., *Johannes von Gaza und Paulus Silentarius: Kunstbeschreibungen justinianischer Zeit*. Leipzig: B. G. Teubner, 1912.

Frye, N., *The Secular Scripture: A Study of the Structure of Romance*. Cambridge: Harvard University Press, 1976.

Funk, R. W., "The Good Samaritan as Metaphor," *Semeia* 2 (1974) 74–81.

———, *Honest to Jesus: Jesus for a New Millennium*. San Francisco: Harper San Francisco, 1996.

Fusillo, M., "Textual Patterns and Narrative Situations in the Greek Novel," *GCN* 1 (1988) 17–31.

Galinsky, G. K., *Aeneas, Sicily, and Rome*. Princeton: Princeton University Press, 1969.

Gärtner, H., "Xenophon von Ephesos," *RE* 9A2 (1967) 2055–89.

Genette, G., *Narrative Discourse: An Essay in Method*. J. E. Levin, trans.; Ithaca, NY: Cornell University Press, 1980.

Geyser, A., "The Semeion at Cana of the Galilee," *Studies in John presented to Professor J. N. Sevenster on the Occasion of his Seventieth Birthday*. NovTSup 34; Leiden: E. J. Brill, 1970, 12–21.

Gill, C., and T. P. Wiseman, eds., *Lies and Fiction in the Ancient World*. Exeter: University of Exeter Press, 1993.

Girard, R., *The Scapegoat*. Y. Freccero, trans.; Baltimore: Johns Hopkins University Press, 1986.

Goldhill, S., *Foucault's Virginity: Ancient Erotic Fiction and the History of Sexuality*. Cambridge: Cambridge University Press, 1995.

Goodenough, E. R., *By Light, Light: The Mystic Gospel of Hellenistic Judaism*. Amsterdam: Philo, 1969.

Gould, E. P., *A Critical and Exegetical Commentary on the Gospel according to St. Mark*. New York: Scribners, 1922.

Gould, P., and R. White, *Mental Maps*. 2nd ed.; Boston: Allen & Unwin, 1986.

Grant, M., *The Climax of Rome: The Final Achievement of the Ancient World A.D. 161–337*. Boston: Little, Brown, and Co., 1968.

Grassi, J. A., "The Wedding at Cana (John 2:1–11): A Pentecostal Meditation?," *NovT* 14 (1972) 131–36.

Griffiths, J. G., "Xenophon of Ephesus on Isis and Alexandria," in *Hommages à M. L. Vermaseren*. EPRO 68; 3 vols.; Leiden: E. J. Brill, 1978, 1.409–37.

van Groningen, B. A., "Éléments inorganiques dans la composition de l'Iliade et de Odyssée," *REH* 5 (1935) 3–24.

Gundry, R. H., *Mark: A Commentary on His Apology for the Cross*. Grand Rapids, MI: William B. Eerdmans, 1993.

Hägg, T., "The Beginnings of the Historical Novel," in *The Greek Novel A.D. 1–1985*. R. Beaton, ed.; London: Croom Helm, 1988, 169–81.

———, "Callirhoe and Parthenope: The Beginnings of the Historical Novel," *ClAnt* 6 (1987) 184–204.

———, "Die *Ephesiaka* des Xenophon Ephesios, Original oder Epitome?" *C&M* 27 (1966 [1969]) 118–61.

——, *Narrative Technique in Ancient Greek Romances: Studies in Chariton, Xenophon Ephesius, and Achilles Tatius.* Stockholm: Almqvist & Wiksells, 1971.

——, *The Novel in Antiquity.* Berkeley: University of California Press, 1983.

Haight, E., *Essays on the Greek Romances.* Port Washington, NY: Kennikat, 1943.

Halperin, D., J. Winkler, and F. Zeitlin, eds., *Before Sexuality: The Construction of Ancient Erotic Experience.* Princeton: Princeton University Press, 1990.

Hanfmann, G. M.A., "The Continuity of Classical Art: Culture, Myth, and Faith," in *Age of Spirituality: A Symposium.* K. Weitzmann, ed.; New York: Metropolitan Museum of Art, 1980, 75–99.

Harrill, A. J., *The Manumission of Slaves in Early Christianity.* HUT 32; Tübingen: J. C. B. Mohr (Siebeck), 1995.

Harrington, D., and A. Saldarini, eds., *Targum Jonathan of the Former Prophets.* The Aramaic Bible 10; Wilmington, DE: Michael Glazier, 1987.

Harris, W. V., *Ancient Literacy.* Cambridge: Harvard University Press, 1989.

Hawkins, J. C., *Horae Synopticae: Contributions to the Study of the Synoptic Problem.* 2nd rev. ed.; Oxford: Clarendon, 1968.

Hedrick, C. W., "Ancient Fiction and Early Christian and Jewish Narrative Working Group," *PSN* 24 (1994) 6–7.

——, "Miracle Stories as Literary Compositions: The Case of Jairus's Daughter," *PerRelSt* 20 (1993) 217–33.

——, *Parables as Poetic Fictions: The Creative Voice of Jesus.* Peabody, MA: Hendrickson, 1994.

——, "What is a Gospel? Geography, Time, Narrative Structure," *PerRelSt* 10 (1983) 255–68.

Helms, J., *Character Portrayal in the Romance of Chariton.* The Hague: Mouton, 1966.

Henne, H., "Le géographie de l'Egypte dans Xénophon d'Ephèse," *RHPh* 4 (1936) 97-106.

Henrichs, A., *Die Phoinikika des Lollianos: Fragmente eines neuen griechischen Romans.* Pap.Texte Abh. 14; Bonn: R. Habelt, 1972.

Heubeck, A., S. West, and J. B. Hainsworth, *A Commentary on Homer's Odyssey.* Oxford: Clarendon, 1988.

Hock, R. F., "An Extraordinary Friend in Chariton's *Callirhoe:* The Importance of Friendship in the Greek Romances," in *Greco-Roman Perspectives on Friendship.* J. T. Fitzgerald, ed.; Atlanta: Scholars Press, 1996, 145–62.

——, "The Greek Novel," in *Greco-Roman Literature and the New Testament: Selected Forms and Genres.* D. Aune, ed.; SBLSBS 21; Atlanta: Scholars Press, 1988, 127–46.

——, *The Infancy Gospels of James and Thomas.* Scholars Bible 2; Sonoma, CA: Polebridge, 1995.

——, "The Rhetoric of Romance," in *Handbook of Classical Rhetoric in the Hellenistic Period 330 B.C.– A.D. 400.* S. Porter, ed.; Leiden: E. J. Brill, 1997, 445–65.

——, "Social Experience and the Beginning of the Gospel of Mark," in *Reimagining Christian Origins: A Colloquium honoring Burton L. Mack.* E. Castelli and H. Taussig, eds.; Valley Forge, PA: Trinity Press International, 1966, 311–26.

——, "A Support for his Old Age: Paul's Plea on behalf of Onesimus," in *The Social World of the First Christians: Essays in honor of Wayne A. Meeks.* L. M. White and O. L. Yarborough, eds.; Minneapolis: Fortress, 1995, 67–81.

Hock, R. F., and E. N. O'Neil, eds. *The Chreia in Ancient Rhetoric. Vol. 1: The Progymnasmata.* SBLTT 27; Atlanta: Scholars Press, 1986.

Holquist, M., "Introduction" to M. M. Bakhtin, *The Dialogic Imagination: Four Essays by M. M. Bakhtin.* C. Emerson and M. Holquist, trans.; Austin: University of Texas Press, 1981, i-xxxiv.

Holzberg, N., "Der Åsop-Roman: Eine strukturanalytische Interpretation," in *Der Åsop-Roman: Motivgeschichte und Erzählstrucktur.* N. Holzberg, ed.; MSKP 6; Tübingen: Gunter Narr, 1992, 33–75.

————, *The Ancient Novel: An Introduction.* C. Jackson-Holzberg, trans.; London: Routledge, 1995.

————, *Die Antike Fabel: Eine Einführung.* Darmstadt: Wissenschaftliche Buchgesellschaft, 1993.

————, *Der Antike Roman: Eine Einführung.* Artemis Einführungen 25; Zurich: Artemis-Verlag, 1986.

————, "The Genre: Novels Proper and the Fringe," in *The Novel in the Ancient World.* G. Schmeling, ed.; Leiden: E. J. Brill, 1996, 11–28.

————, "A Lesser Known 'Picaresque' Novel of Greek Origin: The *Aesop Romance,*" *GCN* 5 (1993) 1–16.

Hopkins, C., *The Discovery of Dura-Europos.* New Haven: Yale University Press, 1979.

Hopkins, K., *Conquerors and Slaves.* Cambridge: Cambridge University Press, 1978.

————, "Novel Evidence for Roman Slavery," *P&P* 138 (1993) 3–27.

Hower, C., *Studies on the So-Called Accursiana Recension of the Life and Fables of Aesop.* Diss. University of Illinois at Urbana, 1936.

Humphrey, J., ed., *Literacy in the Roman World.* JRASup 3; Ann Arbor: University of Michigan Press, 1991.

Hunter, R. L., "Longus, *Daphnis and Chloe,*" in *The Novel in the Ancient World.* G. Schmeling, ed.; Leiden: E. J. Brill, 1996, 361–86.

————, *A Study of Daphnis and Chloe.* Cambridge: Cambridge University Press, 1983.

Jaeger, W., *Aristotle: Fundamentals of the History of his Development.* 2nd ed.; Oxford: Clarendon, 1948.

Jedrkiewicz, S., *Sapere e Paradosso nell' Antichità: Esopo e la Favola.* Rome: Edizioni dell'Ateneo, 1989.

Jensen, R. M., "The Offering of Isaac in Jewish and Christian Tradition," *BI* 2 (1994) 85–110.

Johnston, H. W., *The Private Life of the Romans.* Chicago: Scott/Foresman, 1903.

Jones, C. P., "Dinner Theater," in *Dining in a Classical Context.* W. J. Slater, ed.; Ann Arbor: University of Michigan Press, 1991, 185–98.

Jørgensen, O., "Das Auftreten der Götter in den Büchern ι–μ der Odyssee," *Hermes* 39 (1904) 357–82.

Juel, D., *Messiah and Temple.* SBLDS 31; Missoula, MT: Scholars Press, 1977.

Junod, E., and J.-D. Kaestli, *L'histoire des Actes apocryphes des apôtres du IIIe au IXe siècle: le cas des Actes de Jean.* Cahiers de la Revue de théologie et de philosophie 7; Geneva: La Concorde, 1982.

Kaestli, J.-D., "Les principales orientations de la recherche sur les Actes apocryphes des apôtres," in *Les Actes apocryphes des apôtres: Christianisme et monde païen.* F. Bovon, ed.; Publications de la Faculté de Théologie de l'Université de Genève 4; Geneva: Labor et Fides, 1981, 49–67.

Kearns, E., "The Return of Odysseus: A Homeric Theoxeny," *CQ* 32 (1982) 2–8.

Kelly, D., *The Art of Medieval French Romance.* Madison: University of Wisconsin Press, 1992.

Kerényi, K., *Die griechisch-orientalische Romanliteratur in religionsgeschichtlicher Beleuchtung: Ein Versuch mit Nachbetrachtungen.* Tübingen: Mohr (Siebeck), 1927.

———, "Review of Rosa Söder, *Die apokryphen Apostelgeschichten . . . ,*" *Gnomon* 10 (1934) 301–9.

Keuls, E., *Plato and Greek Painting.* Leiden: E. J. Brill, 1978.

———, "Rhetoric and Visual Arts in Greece and Rome," in *Communication Arts in the Ancient World.* E. A. Havelock and J. P. Hershbell, eds.; New York: Hastings House, 1978, 120–134.

———, *The Water Carriers in Hades: A Study of Catharsis through Toil in Classical Antiquity.* Amsterdam: A. M. Hakkert, 1974.

Kloft, H., "Imagination und Realität: Überlegungen zur Wirtschaftsstruktur des Romans *Daphnis und Chloe*," *GCN* 2 (1989) 45–61.

Koester, C. R., *Symbolism in the Fourth Gospel: Meaning, Mystery, Community.* Minneapolis: Fortress, 1995.

Koester, H., *Introduction to the New Testament.* 2 vols.; Philadelphia: Fortress, 1982.

Konstan, D., "The Alexander Romance: The Cunning of the Open Text," paper presented to the Mediterranean Religions Study Group, Brown University, November 1995.

———, "Xenophon of Ephesus: Eros and Narrative in the Novel," in *Greek Fiction: The Greek Novel in Context.* J. R. Morgan and R. Stoneman, eds.; London: Routledge, 1994, 49–63.

———, *Sexual Symmetry: Love in the Ancient Novel and Related Genres.* Princeton: Princeton University Press, 1994.

Krieger, M., *Ekphrasis: The Illusion of the Natural Sign.* Baltimore: Johns Hopkins University Press, 1992.

Kussl, R., "Ahikar, Tinuphis und Äsop," in *Der Äsop-Roman.* N. Holzberg, ed.; MSKP 6; Tübingen: Gunter Narr, 1992, 23–30.

———, *Papyrusfragmente griechischer Romane.* MSKP 2; Tübingen: Gunter Narr, 1991.

Kysar, R., *John's Story of Jesus.* Philadelphia: Fortress, 1984.

Kytzer, B., "Xenophon of Ephesus," in *The Novel in the Ancient World.* G. Schmeling, ed.; Leiden: E. J. Brill, 1996, 336–60.

Laird, A., "Fiction, Bewitchment, and Story Worlds: The Implications of Claims to Truth in Apuleius," in *Lies and Fiction in the Ancient World.* C. Gill and T. P. Wiseman, eds.; Austin: University of Texas Press, 1993, 147–74.

———, "Ut figura poesis: Writing Art and the Art of Writing in Augustan Poetry," in *Art and Text in Roman Culture.* J. Elsner, ed.; Cambridge: Cambridge University Press, 1996, 75–102.

Lamarque, P., and S. H. Olsen, *Truth, Fiction, and Literature: A Philosophical Perspective.* Oxford: Clarendon, 1994.

Laumonier, A., *Les Cultes Indigènes en Carie.* Paris: E. de Boccard, 1958.

Lane, W. L., *The Gospel according to Mark: The English Text with Introduction, Exposition, and Notes.* Grand Rapids, MI: William B. Eerdmans, 1974.

LaPlace, M., "Les Légendes troyennes dans le 'Roman' de Chariton *Chairéas et Callirhoé*," *REG* 93 (1980) 83–125.

La Penna, A., "Il Romanzo di Esopo," *Athenaeum* n.s. 40 (1962) 264–314.

Lanser, S., *Narrative Action and Point of View in Prose Fiction.* Princeton: Princeton University Press, 1981.

Lee, D. A., *The Symbolic Narratives of the Fourth Gospel: The Interplay of Form and Meaning.* JSNTSup 95; Sheffield: Sheffield Academic Press, 1994.

Levi, D., *Antioch Mosaic Pavements.* 2 vols.; Princeton: Princeton University Press, 1947.

Lewis, A., R. Harris, and F. Conybeare, "The Story of Ahikar," in *The Apocrypha and Pseudepigrapha of the Old Testament.* R. H. Charles, ed.; 2 vols.; Oxford: Clarendon, 1913, 2.715–84.

Lindars, B., "The Bible and the Call: The Biblical Roots of Monastic Life in History and Today," *BJRL* 66 (1984) 228–45.

Lindenberger, J. M., "Ahiqar," in *The Old Testament Pseudepigrapha.* J. H. Charlesworth, ed.; 2 vols.; Garden City, NY: Doubleday, 1983, 2.479–507.

Ljungvik, H., *Studien zur Sprache der apokryphen Apostelgeschichten.* Uppsala: Universitet Aarsskrift 8; Uppsala: A.-b. Lundequistska, 1926.

Long, A. A., and D. N. Sedley, eds., *The Hellenistic Philosophers.* 2 vols.; Cambridge: Cambridge University Press, 1987.

Lord, A. B., *The Singer of Tales.* Harvard Studies in Comparative Literature 24; Cambridge: Harvard University Press, 1960.

Lotman, Y. M., "The Text within the Text," *PMLA* 109 (1994) 377–84.

Love, I., "Knidos," *AJA* 82 (1978) 324.

Lützeler, P., "Fictionality in Historiography and the Novel," in *Neverending Stories: Toward a Critical Narratology.* A. Fehn, ed.; Princeton: Princeton University Press, 1992, 29–44.

MacAlister, S., *Dreams and Suicides: The Greek Novel from Antiquity to the Byzantine Empire.* London: Routledge, 1996.

MacDonald, D. J., *Greek and Roman Coins from Aphrodisias.* BritARSup 9; Oxford: British Archaeological Reports, 1976.

MacDonald, D. R., *Christianizing Homer: The Odyssey, Plato, and the Acts of Andrew.* New York: Oxford University Press, 1994.

———, *The Legend and the Apostle: The Battle for Paul in Story and Canon.* Philadelphia: Westminster, 1983.

Maclean, M., "The Heirs of Amphitryon: Social Fathers and Natural Fathers," *New Literary History* 26 (1995) 787–807.

McDermott, E. A., *Euripides' Medea: The Incarnation of Disorder.* University Park: Pennsylvania State University Press, 1989.

Mack, B. L., *A Myth of Innocence: Mark and Christian Origins.* Philadelphia: Fortress, 1988.

Mack, B. L., and V. K. Robbins, *Patterns of Persuasion in the Gospels.* Sonoma, CA: Polebridge, 1989.

MacMullen, R., "What Difference did Christianity Make?" *Historia* 35 (1986) 322–43.

Maeder, D., "Au seuil des roman grecs: Effets de réel et effets de création," *GCN* 4 (1991) 1–33.

Magie, D., *Roman Rule in Asia Minor to the End of the Third Century.* 2 vols.; Princeton: Princeton University Press, 1950.

Maehler, H., "Der Metiochos-Parthenope Roman," *ZPE* 23 (1976) 1–20.

Malherbe, A. J., *Moral Exhortation: A Greco-Roman Sourcebook.* Philadelphia: Fortress, 1989.

Malina, B. J., and J. H. Neyrey, *Portraits of Paul.* Louisville, KY: Westminster/John Knox, 1996.

Marc, P., "Die Überlieferung des Äsopromans," *BZ* 19 (1910) 383–421.

Marshall, I. H., *The Gospel of Luke: A Commentary on the Greek Text.* Grand Rapids, MI: Eerdmans, 1978.

Meeks, W. A., "The Circle of Reference in Pauline Morality," in *Greeks, Romans and Christians: Essays in Honor of Abraham J. Malherbe.* D. Balch, E. Ferguson, and W. Meeks, eds.; Minneapolis: Fortress, 1990, 305–17.

————, *The Moral World of the Early Christians.* Philadelphia: Westminster, 1986.

Merkelbach, R., *Roman und Mysterium in der Antike.* Munich: C. H. Beck, 1962.

Merkelbach, R., and J. Trumpf, "Die Überlieferung," in *Die Quellen des griechischen Alexanderromans.* 2nd ed.; Munich: C. H. Beck, 1977, 93–107.

Merkle, S., "Die Fabel von Frosch und Maus: Zur Funktion der λόγοι im Delphi-Teil des Äsop-Romans," in *Der Äsop Roman.* N. Holzberg, ed.; MSKP 6; Tübingen: Gunter Narr, 1992, 110–27.

Meyer, M. W., "The Youth in Secret Mark and the Beloved Disciple in John," in *Gospel Origins and Christian Beginnings.* J. E. Goehring *et al.*, eds.; Sonoma, CA: Polebridge, 1990, 94–105.

————, "The Youth in the Secret Gospel of Mark," *Semeia* 49 (1990) 139–49.

Mignogna, E., "Aesopus Bucolicus: Come si 'mette in scen' un miracolo (*Vita Aesopi* c. 6)," in *Der Äsop-Roman.* N. Holzberg, ed.; MSKP 6; Tübingen: Gunter Narr, 1992, 76–84.

Miles, M., *Carnal Knowing: Female Nakedness and Religious Meaning in the Christian West.* Boston: Beacon, 1989.

Mittelstadt, M. C., "Longus, *Daphnis and Chloe* and Roman Narrative Painting," *Latomus* 26 (1967) 752–61.

Montague, H., ""Sweet and Pleasant Passion: Female and Male Fantasy in Ancient Romance Novels," in *Pornography and Representation in Greece and Rome.* A. Richlin, ed.; New York: Oxford University Press, 1992, 231–49.

Morard, F., "Souffrance et Martyre dans les Actes apocryphes des apôtres," in *Les Actes apocryphes des apôtres: Christianisme et monde païen.* F. Bovon, ed.; Publications de la Faculté de Théologie de l'Université de Genève 4; Geneva: Labor et Fides, 1981, 95–108.

Morgan, J. R., "The Ancient Novel at the End of the Century: Scholarship since the Dartmouth Conference," *CPh* 91 (1996) 63–73.

————, "History, Romance, and Realism in the *Aithiopika* of Heliodoros," *ClAnt* 1 (1982) 221–65.

————, "Make-Believe and Make Believe: The Fictionality of the Greek Novels," in *Lies and Fiction in the Ancient World.* C. Gill and T. P. Wiseman, eds.; Austin: University of Texas Press, 1993, 175–229.

Morgan, J. R., and R. Stoneman, eds., *Greek Fiction: The Greek Novel in Context.* London: Routledge, 1994.

Moule, C. F. D., *The Gospel according to Mark.* Cambridge: Cambridge University Press, 1965.

Moyer, R., *History of Purple as a Status Symbol in Antiquity.* Collection Latomus 116; Bruxelles: Latomus Revue d'Etudes, 1970.

Murnaghan, S., *Disguise and Recognition in the Odyssey*. Princeton: Princeton University Press, 1987.

Mylonas, G. E., *Eleusis and the Eleusinian Mysteries*. Princeton: Princeton University Press, 1961.

Nagy, G., *The Best of the Achaeans: Concepts of the Hero in Archaic Greek Poetry*. Baltimore: Johns Hopkins University Press, 1989.

———, *Poetry as Performance: Homer and Beyond*. Cambridge: Cambridge University Press, 1996.

Nickelsburg, G. W., "The Genre and Function of the Markan Passion Narrative," *HTR* 73 (1980) 153–84.

Nicholson, G. C., *Death as Departure: The Johannine Descent-Ascent Schema*. SBLDS 63; Chico, CA: Scholars Press, 1983.

Nicol, W., *The Semeia in the Fourth Gospel: Tradition and Redaction*. Leiden: E. J. Brill, 1972.

Niederwimmer, K., *Askese und Mysterium: Über Ehe, Ehescheidung und Eheverzicht in den Anfängen des christlichen Glaubens*. Göttingen: Vandenhoeck & Ruprecht, 1975.

Nimis, S., "The Prosaics of the Ancient Novels," *Arethusa* 27 (1994) 387–411.

Nineham, D. E., *Saint Mark*. Philadelphia: Westminster, 1963.

Nock, A. D., "Greek Novels and Egyptian Religion," in *Essays on Religion and the Ancient World*. 2 vols.; Z. Stewart, ed.; Cambridge: Harvard University Press, 1972, 1.169–75.

———, "ΣΥΝΝΑΟΣ ΘΕΟΣ," in *Essays on Religion and the Ancient World*. 2 vols.; Z. Stewart, ed.; Cambridge: Harvard University Press, 1972, 1.202–36.

———, "The Question of Jewish Mysteries," in *Essays on Religion and the Ancient World*. 2 vols.; Z. Stewart, ed.; Cambridge: Harvard University Press, 1972, 1.459–68.

Noelke, P., "Zwei unbekannte Repliken der Aphrodite von Aphrodisias in Köln," *AA* 1 (1983) 107–31.

Notopoulos, J. A., "Continuity and Interconnection in Homeric Oral Composition," *TAPA* 82 (1951) 81–87.

———, "Parataxis in Homer: A New Approach to Homeric Literary Criticism," *TAPA* 80 (1949) 1–23.

Oakman, D. E., "Was Jesus a Peasant? Implications for Reading the Samaritan Story (Luke 10:30–35)," *BTB* 22 (1992) 117–25.

Oettinger, N., "Achikars Weisheitssprüche im Licht älterer Fabeldichtung," in *Der Äsop-Roman*. N. Holzberg, ed.; MSKP 6; Tübingen: Gunter Narr, 1992, 3–22.

Ogden, D., *Greek Bastardy in the Classical and Hellenistic Periods*. Oxford: Clarendon, 1996.

O'Sullivan, J. N., *Xenophon of Ephesus: His Compositional Technique and the Birth of the Novel*. New York: de Gruyter, 1995.

Overbeck, F., *Über die Anfänge der patristischen Literatur*. repr. of 1882 essay: Darmstadt: Wissenschaftliche Buchgesellschaft, 1966.

van Oyen, G., "Intercalation and Irony in the Gospel of Mark," in *The Four Gospels 1992: Festschrift Frans Neirynck*. BETL 100; 3 vols.; Leuven: Leuven University Press, 1992, 2.949–74.

Painter, J., *The Quest for the Messiah*. Nashville: Abingdon, 1993.

Parsons, M., and R. Pervo, *Rethinking the Unity of Luke and Acts*. Minneapolis: Fortress, 1993.

Pavel, T. G., *Fictional Worlds*. Cambridge: Harvard University Press, 1986.

Perkins, J., *The Suffering Self: Pain and Narrative Representation in the Early Christian Era*. London: Routledge, 1995.

Perrin, N., "The High Priest's Question and Jesus' Answer (Mark 14:61–62)," in *The Passion in Mark: Studies in Mark 14–16*. W. H. Kelber, ed.; Philadelphia: Fortress, 1976, 80–95.

Perry, B. E., *Aesopica: A Series of Texts relating to Aesop or Ascribed to Him or Closely Connected with the Literary Tradition that Bears his Name*. 2 vols.; Urbana: University of Illinois Press, 1952.

———, *The Ancient Romances: A Literary-Historical Account of their Origins*. Sather Classical Lectures 37; Berkeley: University of California Press, 1967.

———, "Chariton and his Romance from a Literary-Historical Point of View," *AJP* 51 (1930) 93–134.

———, "Some Addenda to the Life of Aesop," *BZ* 59 (1966) 285–304.

———, *Studies in the Text History of the Life and Fables of Aesop*. Haverford, PA: American Philological Association, 1936.

Petri, R., *Über den Roman des Chariton*. Beiträge zur klassischen Philologie 11; Meisenheim am Glan: A. Hain, 1963.

Pervo, R., "The Ancient Novel Becomes Christian," in *The Novel in the Ancient World*. G. Schmeling, ed.; Leiden: E. J. Brill, 1996, 685–711.

———, "Aseneth and Her Sisters: Women in Jewish Narrative and in the Greek Novels," in *Women Like This: New Perspectives on Jewish Women in the Greco-Roman World*. A. J. Levine, ed.; SBLEJL 1; Atlanta: Scholars Press, 1991, 145–60.

———, "Early Christian Fiction," *Greek Fiction: The Greek Novel in Context*. J. R. Morgan and R. Stoneman, eds.; London: Routledge, 1994, 239–54.

———, "PANTA KOINA: The Feeding Stories in the Light of Economic Data and Social Practice," in *Religious Propaganda and Missionary Competition in the New Testament World: Essays honoring Dieter Georgi*. L. Bornmann *et al.*, eds.; Leiden: E. J. Brill, 1994, 164–94.

———, *Profit with Delight: The Literary Genre of the Acts of the Apostles*. Philadelphia: Fortress, 1987.

Petersen, N. R., *Literary Criticism for New Testament Critics*. Philadelphia: Fortress, 1978.

Philippides, S., "Lover's Fate: Narrator's Providence in *Chaereas and Callirhoe*," in *The Greek Novel A.D. 1–1985*. R. Beaton, ed.; London: Croom Helm, 1988, 182–89.

Plepelits, K., "Achilles Tatius," in *The Novel in the Ancient World*. G. Schmeling, ed.; Leiden: E. J. Brill, 1996, 387–416.

———, *Chariton von Aphrodisias, Kallirhoe*. Stuttgart: A. Hiersmann, 1976.

Plümacher, E., "Apokryphe Apostelakten," *RESuppl.* 15 (1978) 11–70.

Plummer, A., *The Gospel according to St. Mark*. Grand Rapids: Baker Book House, 1982.

Poupon, G., "Les 'Actes de Pierre' et leur remaniement," *ANRW* 2.25.6 (1988) 4363–83.

Pratt, L. H., *Lying and Poetry from Homer to Pindar: Falsehood and Deception in Archaic Greek Poetics*. Ann Arbor: University of Michigan Press, 1993.

Price, S. R. F., *Rituals and Power: The Roman Imperial Cult in Asia Minor*. Cambridge: Cambridge University Press, 1984.

Räisänan, H., *The "Messianic Secret" in Mark*. C. M. Tuckett, trans.; Edinburgh: T.&T. Clark, 1990.

Reardon, B. P., "Aspects of the Greek Novel," *G&R* 23 (1976) 118–31.

———, "Chariton," in *The Novel in the Ancient World*. G. Schmeling, ed.; Leiden: E. J. Brill, 1996, 309–35.

———, *Courants littéraires grecs des IIe et IIIe siècles apres J.-C.* Annales littéraires de l'Université de Nantes 3; Paris: Les Belles Lettres, 1971.

———, "The Form of Ancient Greek Romance," in *The Greek Novel A.D. 1–1985*. R. Beaton, ed.; London: Croom Helm, 1988, 205–16.

———, *The Form of Greek Romance*. Princeton: Princeton University Press, 1991.

———, "The Greek Novel," *Phoenix* 23 (1969) 291–309.

———, "Novels and Novelties, or Mysteriouser and Mysteriouser," in *The Mediterranean World: Essays Presented to Gilbert Bangani*; Peterborough, Ont., 1975, 78–100.

———, "The Second Sophistic and the Novel," in *Approaches to the Second Sophistic*. G. W. Bowersock, ed.; University Park, PA: American Philological Association, 1974, 23–29.

Reardon, B. P., ed., *Collected Ancient Greek Novels*. Berkeley: University of California Press, 1989.

Reed, W. L., *Dialogues of the Word: The Bible as Literature according to Bakhtin*. New York: Oxford University Press, 1993.

Reinhartz, A., *The Word in the World: The Cosmological Tale in the Fourth Gospel*. SBLMS 45; Atlanta: Scholars Press, 1992.

Reiser, M., "Der Alexanderroman und das Markusevangelium," *Markus-Philologie*. H. Cancik, ed.; WUNT 33; Tübingen: Mohr (Siebeck), 1984, 131–63.

Reynolds, J., *Aphrodisias and Rome*. JRSMS 1; London: Society for the Promotion of Roman Studies, 1982.

———, "The Origins and Beginnings of Imperial Cult at Aphrodisias," *PCPhS* 206 (1980) 70–80.

Reynolds, J., M. Beard, and C. Reuché, "Survey Article: Roman Inscriptions 1976-1980," *JRS* 76 (1981) 124–46.

Reynolds, L. D., and N. G. Wilson, *Scribes and Scholars: A Guide to the Transmission of Greek and Latin Literature*. Oxford: Clarendon, 1968.

Rhoads, D., and D. Michie, *Mark as Story: An Introduction to the Narrative of a Gospel*. Philadelphia: Fortress, 1982.

Richardson, N. J., "Recognition Scenes in the Odyssey and Ancient Literary Criticism," *Papers of the Liverpool Latin Seminar* 4 (1983) 219–35.

Robbins, V. K., *Ancient Quotes and Anecdotes*. FFNT; Sonoma, CA: Polebridge, 1989.

Robertson, A., and A. Plummer, *A Critical and Exegetical Commentary on the First Epistle of St. Paul to the Corinthians*. ICC; Edinburgh: T.&T. Clark, 1911.

Rohde, E., *Der griechische Roman und seine Vorläufer*. 4th ed.; Hildesheim: Georg Olms, 1960.

Ronen, R., *Possible Worlds in Literary Theory*. Cambridge: Cambridge University Press, 1994.

Rorty, R., *Consequences of Pragmatism: Essays, 1972–1980*. Minneapolis: University of Minnesota Press, 1982.

Rösler, W., "Die Entdeckung der Fiktionalität in der Antike," *Poetica* 12 (1980) 283–319.

Ruiz-Montrero, C., "Aspects of the Vocabulary of Chariton of Aphrodisias," *CQ* 41 (1991) 484–89.

———, "Chariton von Aphrodisias: Ein Überblick," *ANRW* 2.34.2 (1994) 1006–54.

———, "Una interpretación del 'estilo kai' de Jenofonte de Ephesus," *Emerita* 50 (1982) 305–23.

———, "Una observacion para la cronologia de Cariton de Afrodisias," *EstClas* 24 (1980) 63–69.

———, "Xenophon von Ephesus: Ein Überblick," *ANRW* 2.34.2 (1994) 1088–1138.

Russell, D. A., ed., *Dio Chrysostom, Orations VII, XII, and XXXIV*. Cambridge: Cambridge University Press, 1992.

Scarcella, A. M., "The Social and Economic Structures of the Ancient Novels," in *The Novel in the Ancient World*. G. Schmeling, ed.; Leiden: E. J. Brill, 1996, 221–76.

Schäfer, P., "Research into Rabbinic Literature: An Attempt to Define the *Status Quaestionis*," *JJS* 37 (1986) 139–52.

———, *Synopse zur Hekhalot-Literatur*. Tübingen: Mohr (Siebeck), 1981.

Schauer, M., and S. Merkle, "Äsop und Sokrates," in *Der Äsop-Roman*. N. Holzberg, ed.; MSKP 6; Tübingen: Gunter Narr, 1992, 85–96.

Schefold, K., "La peinture pompéienne: Essai sur l'évolution de sa signification," *Collection Latomus* 108 (1972) 52–68.

———, *Pompejanische Malerei: Sinn und Ideengeschichte*. Basel: Benno Schwabe & Co., 1952.

———, *Vergessenes Pompeji: Unveröffentlichte Bilder römischer Wanddekorationen*. Bern: Francke, 1962.

Schmeling, G., *Chariton*. TWAS 295; Boston: Twayne, 1974.

———, ed., *The Novel in the Ancient World*. Leiden: E. J. Brill, 1996.

———, *Xenophon of Ephesus*. TWAS 613; Boston: Twayne, 1980.

Schmidt, K., *Die alten Petrusakten im Zusammenhang der apokryphen Apostelliteratur nebst einem neuentdeckten Fragment*. TU n.s. 9.1; Leipzig: J. C. Hinrichs, 1903.

Schmidt, K. L., "Die Stellung der Evangelien in der allgemeinen Literaturgeschichte," in *EUCHARISTERION: Hermann Gunkel zum 60. Geburtstag*. H. Schmidt, ed.; 2 vols.; FRLANT 36; Göttingen: Vandenhoeck & Ruprecht, 1923, 2.50–134.

Schneemelcher, W., "Acts of Paul," in *New Testament Apocrypha*. 2 vols.; W. Schneemelcher, ed.; R. McL. Wilson, trans.; Philadelphia: Westminster, 1965, 2.322–90.

Scobie, A., *Aspects of the Ancient Romance and its Heritage*. Meisenheim am Glan: A. Hain, 1969.

———, *More Essays on the Ancient Romance and its Heritage*. Meisenheim am Glan: A. Hain, 1973.

Scott, K., *The Imperial Cult under the Flavians*. Stuttgart: W. Kohlhammer, 1936.

———, "Ruler Cult and Related Problems in the Greek Romances," *CPh* 33 (1938) 380–89.

Shepherd, T., "The Narrative Function of Markan Intercalation," *NTS* 41 (1995) 522–40.

Shiner, W. T., *Follow Me: Disciples in Markan Rhetoric*. SBLDS 145; Atlanta: Scholars Press, 1995.

Showerman, G., *Rome and the Romans. A Survey and Interpretation*. New York: Macmillan, 1937.

Slater, N., "The Fabrication of Comic Illusion," in *Beyond Aristophanes: Transition and Diversity in Greek Comedy*. G. Dobrov, ed.; Atlanta: American Philological Association, 1995, 29–45.

Söder, R., *Die apokryphen Apostelgeschichten und die romanhafte Literatur der Antike*. Stuttgart: Kohlhammer, 1932.

Sokolowski, F., "Aphrodite as Guardian of Greek Magistrates," *HTR* 57 (1964) 1–8.

Solmsen, F., *Isis among the Greeks and Romans*. Cambridge: Harvard University Press, 1979.

Staley, J. L., "Subversive Narration/Victimized Reader," *JSNT* 51 (1993) 79–98.

Standaert, B., *L'Evangile selon Marc: Commentaire*. Paris: Les Editions du Cerf, 1983.

Stephens, S. A., and J. J. Winkler, eds. *Ancient Greek Novels: The Fragments: Introduction, Text, Translation, and Commentary*. Princeton: Princeton University Press, 1996.

Sterling, G., *Historiography and Self-Definition: Josephus, Luke-Acts and Apostolic Historiography*. Leiden: E. J. Brill, 1992.

Stibbe, M. W. G., *John as Story Teller: Narrative Criticism and the Fourth Gospel*. SNTSMS 73; Cambridge: Cambridge University Press, 1992.

Stoneman, R., "The Alexander Romance: From History to Fiction," in *Greek Fiction: The Greek Novel in Context*. J. R. Morgan and R. Stoneman, eds.; London: Routledge, 1994, 117–29.

———, "The Metamorphoses of the *Alexander Romance*," in *The Novel in the Ancient World*. G. Schmeling, ed.; Leiden: E. J. Brill, 1996, 601–12.

———, "Riddles in Bronze and Stone: Monuments and their Interpretation in the *Alexander-Romance*," *GCN* 6 (1995) 166–67.

Suleiman, S., *Authoritarian Fictions: The Ideological Novel as a Literary Genre*. New York: Columbia University Press, 1983.

Tannehill, R. C., *The Sword in His Mouth: Forceful and Imaginative Language in Synoptic Sayings*. SBLSS 1; Philadelphia: Fortress, and Missoula, MT: Scholars Press, 1975.

Taylor, V., *The Gospel according to St. Mark*. London: Macmillan, 1959.

Thomas, C. M., "The Prehistory of the *Acts of Peter*," in *Harvard Studies in the Apocryphal Acts of the Apostles*. F. Bovon, ed.; Religions of the World; Cambridge: Harvard University Press, forthcoming.

———, "Word and Deed: The *Acts of Peter* and Orality," *Apocrypha* 3 (1992) 125–64.

Thornton, A., *People and Themes in Homer's Odyssey*. London: Methuen, 1970.

Thurian, M., *Mary, Mother of All Christians*. New York: Herder and Herder, 1964.

Tissot, Y., "Les Actes de Thomas: exemple de recueil composite," in *Les Actes apocryphes des apôtres: Christianisme et monde païen*. F. Bovon et al., eds.; Publications de la Faculté de Théologie de l'Université de Genève 4; Geneva: Labor et Fides, 1981, 223–32.

Tolbert, M. A., *Sowing the Gospel: Mark's World in Literary-Historical Perspective*. Minneapolis: Fortress, 1989.

Turner, E. G., *The Typology of the Early Codex*. Philadelphia: University of Pennsylvania Press, 1977.

van Unnik, W. C., "Les chéveux défaits des femmes baptisées," *VC* 1 (1947) 77–100.

Vermeule, C. C., *Roman Art: Early Republic to Late Empire*. Boston: Museum of Fine Arts, 1978.

————, *Roman Imperial Art in Greece and Asia Minor.* Cambridge: Harvard University Press, 1968.

Veyne, P., *Did the Greeks Believe Their Myths?* P. Wissing, trans.; Chicago: University of Chicago Press, 1988.

————, "La familie et l'amour sous le Haut-Empire romain," *Annales (ESC)* 33 (1978) 35–63.

————, ed., *A History of Private Life. Vol. 1: From Pagan Rome to Byzantium.* A. Goldhammer, trans.; Cambridge, MA: Belknap, 1987.

Via, D. O., Jr., *The Parables: Their Literary and Existential Dimension.* Philadelphia: Fortress, 1967.

Vielhauer, P., *Geschichte der urchristlichen Literatur.* Berlin: de Gruyter, 1975.

Vorster, W. S., "Intertextuality and Redaktionsgeschichte," in *Intertextuality in Biblical Writings: Essays in Honor of Bas van Iersel.* S. Draisma, ed.; Kampen: Uitgeversmaatschappij J. H. Kok, 1989, 15–26.

Wachsmann, S., "The Galilee Boat," *BAR* 14 (1988) 19–33.

Walbank, F. W., "History and Tragedy," *Historia* 9 (1960) 216–34.

Walden, J. W. H., "Stage-terms in Heliodorus's Aethiopica," *HSCP* 5 (1894) 1–43.

Walsh, P., *The Roman Novel.* Cambridge: Cambridge University Press, 1970.

Walzer, R., *Galen on Jews and Christians.* Oxford: Oxford University Press, 1947.

Weeden, T. J., Sr., *Mark–Traditions in Conflict.* Philadelphia: Fortress, 1971.

Weitzmann, K., *Illustrations in Roll and Codex: A Study of the Origin and Method of Text Illustration.* Princeton: Princeton University Press, 1947.

Weitzmann, K., and H. L. Kessler, *The Frescoes of the Dura Synagogue and Christian Art.* DOS 28; Washington, DC: Dumbarton Oaks, 1990.

Welles, C. B., ed., *The Excavations at Dura-Europos: Final Report VII, Part II.* New Haven: Dura Europos Publications, 1967.

Wharton, A. J., "Good and Bad Images from the Synagogue of Dura Europos: Contexts, Subtexts, Intertexts," *Art History* 17 (1994) 1–25.

Wheeldon, M. J., "'True Stories': The Reception of Historiography in Antiquity," in *History as Text: The Writing of Ancient History.* A. Cameron, ed.; Chapel Hill: University of North Carolina Press, 1989, 33–63.

White, H., "The Historical Text as Literary Artifact," in *The Writing of History: Literary Form and Historical Understanding.* R. Canary, ed.; Madison: University of Wisconsin Press, 1978, 41–62.

Wiersma, S., "The Ancient Greek Novel and its Heroines: A Formal Paradox," *Mnemosyne* 43 (1990) 109–23.

Wilckens, U., "στολή," *TDNT* 7 (1971) 687–91.

Willis, W. H., "The Robinson-Cologne Papyrus of Achilles Tatius," *GRBS* 31 (1990) 73-102.

Wills, L. M., *The Jewish Novels in the Ancient World.* Ithaca, NY: Cornell University Press, 1995.

————, "The Jewish Novellas," in *Greek Fiction: The Greek Novel in Context.* J. R. Morgan and R. Stoneman, eds.; London: Routledge, 1994, 223–38.

Wilson, L. M., *The Clothing of the Ancient Romans.* Johns Hopkins University Studies in Archaeology 24; Baltimore: Johns Hopkins University Press, 1938.

Wimsatt, W. K., Jr. and M. C. Beardsley, "The Intentional Fallacy," *Swanee Review* 54 (1946) 466–88.

————, *The Verbal Icon: Studies in the Meaning of Poetry.* Lexington: University of Kentucky Press, 1954.

Winkler, J. J., *Auctor & Actor: A Narratological Reading of Apuleius' Golden Ass.* Berkeley: University of California Press, 1985.

Witt, R. E., "Isis-Hellas," *PCPhS* 12 (1966) 48–69.

Wiseman, T. P., "Practice and Theory in Ancient Historiography," *History* 66 (1981) 375- 93.

Wrede, W., *The Messianic Secret.* J. C. G. Greig, trans.; Greenwood, SC: Attic, 1971.

Yadin, Yigal. *The Finds from the Bar Kokhba Period in the Cave of Letters.* Jerusalem: Israel Exploration Society, 1963.

Yarborough, O. L., *"Not Like the Gentiles": Marriage Rules in the Letters of Paul.* SBLDS 80; Atlanta: Scholars Press, 1985.

INDEX